KW-363-273

The Helm Information CRITICAL ASSESSMENTS of WRITERS IN ENGLISH

General Editor

Graham Clarke

Already published:

T.S. Eliot
Thomas Hardy
Edgar Allan Poe
Mark Twain
Henry James
Virginia Woolf
F. Scott Fitzgerald
Walt Whitman
Joseph Conrad
Charles Dickens
D.H. Lawrence
George Eliot
The Brontë Sisters

Forthcoming:

Jane Austen
James Joyce
John Steinbeck
Ernest Hemingway
Herman Melville
William Faulkner
Emily Dickinson
Willa Cather
Daniel Defoe

E.M. FORSTER
Critical Assessments

E.M. Forster by Roger Fry, 1913.

E.M. FORSTER

Critical Assessments

Edited by

J.H. Stape

VOLUME I

Memories and Impressions;
Reviews: *Where Angels Fear to Tread*
to *The Life to Come and Other Stories*

HELM INFORMATION

Selection and editorial matter
© Helm Information Ltd
Helm Information Ltd
The Banks,
Mountfield,
near Robertsbridge,
East Sussex TN32 5JY

ISBN 1-873403-37-2

A CIP catalogue record for this book is available from the British Library.

All rights reserved: No reproduction, copy or transmission of this publication may be made without written permission.

No paragraph of this publication may be reproduced, copied or transmitted save with written permission or in accordance with the provisions of the Copyright Act 1956 (as amended), or under the terms of any licence permitting limited copying issued by the Copyright Licensing Agency, 7 Ridgmount Street, London WC1E 7AE.

Any person who does any unauthorised act in relation to this publication may be liable to criminal prosecution and civil claims for damages.

Frontispiece: E.M. Forster by Roger Fry, 1913.

Typeset by Solidus (Bristol) Limited
Printed and bound in Great Britain by
MPG Books Ltd, Bodmin, Cornwall

Contents

VOLUME I:

Memories and Impressions; Reviews: *Where Angels Fear to Tread* to *The Life to Come and Other Stories*

A Passage to India (1924)

Aspects of the Novel (1927)

The Eternal Moment and Other Stories (1928)

Goldsworthy Lowes Dickinson (1934)

Maurice (1971)

The Life to Come and Other Stories (1972)

VOLUME II:

The Critical Response: Early Responses, 1907–44; The Short Fiction; Forster's Criticism; Miscellaneous Writings

Early Responses, 1907–44

The Short Fiction

Early Stories

Posthumously Published Stories

Forster's Criticism

Miscellaneous Writings

VOLUME III:

The Modern Critical Response: *Where Angels Fear to Tread* to *Maurice*

Where Angels Fear to Tread (1905)

The Longest Journey (1907)

A Room with a View (1908)

Howards End (1910)

A Passage to India (1924)

Maurice (1971)

VOLUME IV:

Relations and Aspects; The Modern Critical Response, 1945–90

Relations and Aspects

Forster and Walter Pater

Forster and Edward Carpenter

Forster and D.H. Lawrence

Forster and Other Writers

Forster Filmed

The Modern Critical Response, 1945–90

General Editor's Preface

Since the first set of *Critical Assessments* appeared on the writing of T. S. Eliot, the series has continued to expand in relation to a number of central writers within the English-speaking literary tradition. The aim of the *Critical Assessments* series is two-fold: first, to offer students and researchers authoritative overviews of the often discouraging mass of critical material on significant writers; second, to make that material, often difficult to locate and out-of-print, easily accessible within the limits of its substantive and comprehensive four-volume format. Thus each set follows a common pattern: an introduction, bibliographies, a chronology, and a chronological overview of the criticism, followed by as wide a range of critical material in relation to both the author's entire writing and to the critical developments which have followed the continuing response to the writing itself. It thus has a double advantage: offering at once contemporary responses and documentation (reviews, essays, etc.) to the most recent critical writing and a range of critical viewpoints and judgements. Students may thus gauge their own sense of a text against a 'graph' of response, often finding significantly different judgements on similar texts. The historical range included equally makes it possible to trace the changing pattern of interpretation and of viewing how the sense of a text, or the value of an author is re-assessed according to critical developments (political, psychological, semiotic, structuralist etc.) which bring to any established sense of the work invariably exciting and challenging new readings. Whilst each *Critical Assessments* thus offers a set body of critical writing, it is in no way offered as merely a reference text or collection of viewpoints of interest to the antiquarian or literary historian. I would hope that, like the emblem of each volume, each set carries with it the distinct and unique *signature* of the author—an especial and very particular critical map at once alive to and reflecting a continuing sense of debate and re-interpretation which is inevitably a part of the critical and reading process. Individually, therefore, each set of volumes offers an unparalleled opportunity to review the criticism on a specific writer. Collectively, as a series *Critical Assessments* continues to grow into an unparalleled research source on a range of writers and, inevitably, of periods and movements.

Graham Clarke
Reader in Literary and Image Studies
University of Kent

Introduction

E.M. Forster's reputation since the publication of his first novel *Where Angels Fear to Tread* in 1905 might be seen as a trajectory that appeared to have a gradual but on the whole continuously upward movement, reaching its highest point by the late 1940s and more or less remaining there until his death in 1970. In the couple of years following that, the posthumous publication of *Maurice* and a brace of minor short stories not written for public circulation occasioned a downward slide. This happens on the death of many writers, but in Forster's case it was precipitous and rapid, and lasted for something more than a decade. Part of its acuteness may be traced to his singular, even peculiar, situation as an author. Notoriously small in output, his fictions, aside from *A Passage to India*, were published during the Edwardian period while he lived on to 1970, dying during the era of the American War in Vietnam and the counterculture, a heady iconoclastic period in England and the United States that witnessed the ritual execution of no small number of sacred cows.

The assaults on Forster's reputation after his death, from various quarters, were to a certain degree predictable and were, in some sense, an exaggerated if delayed attempt to counterbalance the equally lopsided positioning of him as a secular saint and sage, a standing he had attained during the interwar years and the Second World War. Thus, by the mid-1970s at a time when new orthodoxies were beginning to be established and the academy was undergoing overt politicization in the wake of external pressures, Forster's humanism—and humanism in general—was judged to be suspect, grounded on shaky soil in the first place and riven by fundamentally irreconcilable pieties and antagonisms. Texts that were once viewed as voicing enlightened opinions, very much in the avant-garde of their time, came to be seen as potbound at best and, at their worst, politically inadequate or even regressive. Forster's portrayal of women was by some judged to be not only inept but misogynistic, and his depiction of non-middle-class and non-English characters as class-bound, snobbish, or outrightly racist. Still others, covertly or openly, took the occasion of the posthumous publication of Forster's homosexual fictions to air pent-up prejudices, using attacks on 'Forster' to advance personal agendas, while from the other side he was sometimes disparaged as a 'collaborator' who, in refusing to make public this aspect of his personal life, helped to maintain socially repressive attitudes.

While Forster's fictional output and essayistic writings were for a time under fairly intense attack, his work continued to be taught in universities, and there could be little doubt that, however he might be viewed, he was still being dealt with by critics. It now appears that the demolition crews had arrived somewhat prematurely, and that they have, for the most part, made but a small dent in the overall assessment of Forster's achievements as a novelist. As the annual outpouring of articles amply attests, his writings have continued to elicit sophisticated and nuanced critical attention from a highly diverse range of perspectives, running the gamut from the revisionist to the more traditionally inclined with its interest in aesthetic questions and technique. Moreover, in the mid-1980s and early 1990s, the appearance of widely distributed (and varyingly successful) film versions of all Forster's novels except *The Longest Journey* brought his fiction to the attention of large audiences that had not previously encountered it and that then went on to read the books for themselves. From the vantage point of the mid-1990s, with the reassessments occasioned by his death already dating back a generation—and a number of critical generations—it appears that his shares in the literary stockmarket, to invoke T. S. Eliot's famous metaphor about writers' reputations, are doing quite well indeed.

While Forster's position has reflected, been the victim of, and been boosted by the cross-currents of critical fashion, scholarly and biographical work has continued its pursuit of its traditional interests in identifying, collecting, and preserving documents related to the life and work. Like the critical activity, the quality of these endeavours has varied, but they have none the less served to keep Forster in the public eye and to put into place a frame for future work. The dawning awareness of a need for textual scholarship with the establishment of the Abinger Edition in the early 1970s, the publication of P. N. Furbank's authorized biography *E. M. Forster, A Life* (1977–8), Michael Halls's cataloguing of Forster's manuscripts in the Forster Archives at King's College, Cambridge, and the appearance of a revised version of B. J. Kirkpatrick's monumental *A Bibliography of E.M. Forster* (1985) have constituted major events in the history of Forster scholarship.

The Forster critical tradition, however, is older by far, the early treatments by critics as diverse as Virginia Woolf, I. A. Richards, Peter Burra, and E. K. Brown having laid down important lines for subsequent critical assessment. This evaluation was urged on in England by F. R. Leavis's influential apppreciation in *Scrutiny* (1938) occasioned by the first full-length book on Forster, an appreciative but not particularly subtle account by the novelist Rose Macaulay. It began in earnest in America with Lionel Trilling's brief but suggestive early study *E.M. Forster* (1943), the book that, as Forster good-humouredly quipped, made him famous. This flurry of interest, which consolidated his reputation as a major writer both in England and America, roughly coincided with the decline of the impressionistic essay and the rise of academic criticism and was additionally prompted by Forster's championship of humane values when their extinction was threatened during the 1930s and early 1940s by the rise of Fascism and the Second World War.

While the concern with the liberal tradition and with values has not abated in the criticism and evaluations of more recent decades, Forster's fiction, since the late 1940s, has been the object of intense investigation from a number of perspectives by a far-flung community of critic-scholars. And at this point in time, when his status as a 'classic' writer appears secure, even some of his minor writings have been extensively, possibly exhaustively, analyzed. A second wave of intense critical attention set in with the serious study of the Bloomsbury Group in the 1970s, set off in part by the publication of Quentin Bell's biography of Virginia Woolf in 1972, and, contradictorily, coincident with the revaluation of Forster already then underway. With the onset of the 1980s a widespread interest in gender, ethnicity, and post-colonial issues stimulated further investigations and reappraisals of Forster's writing at a time when its canonicity had also become a focus of intense debate in England and elsewhere.

The present collection aims to make available, in chronological order, an array of responses to Forster's life and work, beginning with a selection of personal recollections and obituaries some of which usefully attempt to evaluate Forster's achievement while a few focus on aspects of the private individual behind the fiction. *Volume One* then goes on to offer contemporary reviews of Forster's fiction, biographies, and essay collections, beginning with *Where Angels Fear to Tread* in 1905 and ending in 1972 with *The Life to Come and Other Stories.* While much of this response puts on record the reactions of the informed working journalist to a novelist committed to intricate fictional techniques, the views of Forster's fellow-writers—the insider's perspectives, as it were—are also presented, and, in addition, then, to including influential critics of the day such as Percy Lubbock, Edward Garnett, and R. A. Scott-James, the volume contains reviews by Virginia Woolf, Rose Macaulay, David Garnett, and Christopher Isherwood.

Volume Two concentrates first on general assessments of Forster's work as a whole, ranging from the belletristic appreciation popular into the 1930s to the increasingly sophisticated critical analyses of mid-century. The views include high praise as well as censure, the general aim being to present Forster in the round, as viewed by his contemporaries as an artist making his way and then, as his reputation solidified and his public fictional career ended, from the advantage of hindsight. It then shifts to academic criticism of the early short stories, the posthumously published short fiction, and the miscellaneous writings, the latter including studies of Forster's Commonplace Book, letters, the libretto he co-wrote for Benjamin Britten's opera *Billy Budd*, and the biography of his Cambridge friend and mentor Goldsworthy Lowes Dickinson.

Volume Three presents academic criticism of Forster's six novels, from *Where Angels Fear to Tread* to *Maurice*. The volume aims to present carefully argued analyses and explications of aspects of individual works, and these articles necessarily embrace a variety of approaches, offering a compendium of critical responses, including, among others, that of close reading, literary history, psychoanalysis, narratology, and gender studies. As appropriate, the lion's share of space has been given over to *A Passage to India*, which has now firmly moved into the place once accorded *Howards End* as Forster's most significant novelistic achievement. Its widespread appearance in university courses on English literary Modernism further justifies the more generous allotment of space to this novel, and, moreover, reflects the amount of critical interest that its aesthetic challenges and politics has elicited from critics. The chronological arrangement of the essays in the volume permits the reader to follow the evolution of the assessments of a given novel over time as well as the emergence of critical trends.

Volume Four ranges widely, beginning with reactions to Forster as a critic interested both in technical matters and the more philosophical aspects of literary production and then proceeding to discussions of his fiction, aesthetics, and thought in relation to other writers, in particular, Walter Pater, Edward Carpenter, and D. H. Lawrence, but also including Rudyard Kipling, Howard Sturgis, T. E. Lawrence, and George Meredith. (While Forster has had a considerable impact on English writing in India, interest in this body of work remains a mainly specialist activity.) Reactions to the film versions of the novels maintain the focus on Forster's work as intertextual influence and as commodified and reinterpreted by artists working in another medium. The volume's final section attempts a kaleidoscopic survey of critical responses from 1945 to 1990, offering discussions of Forster's works through approaches that have emerged, peaked, and faded in the wake of the Second World War and concentrating on the larger philosophical, ideological, and social and literary issues raised by Forster's achievement as whole rather than on individual writings.

A very large number of articles and notes, chapters in books, and books of varying quality have been devoted to Forster's work, and the present selection from this body of writing, generous as it is, can make no claim to be exhaustive. (Some articles that would in an ideal world have been included are not found here because reprint fees requested were very much beyond budget, while in other cases permission was denied.) The emphasis here falls on key essays dealing with Forster's achievement or with selected aspects of it. Extracts from tightly argued full-length studies have thus in the main been avoided in preference to critical explication and analysis that stands on its own. The collection does, however, aim to represent critical trends and to contextualize the development of Forster's reputation since the publication of his first novel in 1905. While criticism of Forster goes on in a number of countries and in various languages, the collection is also limited in reprinting work published in English. This apparent drawback has not, however, disallowed reprinting writing that was first published in Belgium, France, India, and Japan. The bibliographies noted in this volume provide further and comprehensive guidance to the large body of available criticism, and the notes to individual articles reliably point to critical studies of particular relevance to the work they consider or to the broader topics in their purview.

Chronology of Forster's Life

1879	January: Edward Morgan Forster born in London, only child of Edward ('Eddy') Morgan Llewellyn Forster and Alice Clara ('Lily'), *née* Whichelo.
1880	Edward Forster dies of tuberculosis in Bournemouth.
1883	Lily Forster and her son move to Rooks Nest, Stevenage, Hertfordshire, prototype for 'Howards End'.
1887	Privately tutored by local school master Augustus Hervey. Inherits £8,000 from great-aunt, Marianne Thornton.
1890–3	Attends Kent House School, Eastbourne, Sussex. Sexual experience initiated by a middle-age man in 1891.
1893	The Forsters move to Tonbridge, Kent. Attends Tonbridge School as a day-boy reading Classics.
1895	First trip abroad, touring northern Normandy with his mother.
1897	First publication: Latin verse and English essay in Tonbridge School magazine. Goes up to King's College, Cambridge, to read Classics. Awarded college exhibition.
1898	Wins college prizes for Latin Composition and Declamations. Meets Goldsworthy Lowes Dickinson, Fellow at King's College, an important and influential friend.
1899	Participates in Walpole Debating and Classical societies. Wins college prizes for Latin Composition and an essay on 18th and 19th century English novelists.
1900	Publishes essays in *Cambridge Review* and King's magazine, *Basileona*. Awarded second class in the Classical Tripos. B. A. conferred. Decides to continue studies for another year, reading history with Oscar Browning. Possibly begins first novel, *Nottingham Lace* (fragment posthumously published).
1901	Election to Apostles, exclusive Cambridge discussion society, bringing friendships with Lytton Strachey, Leonard Woolf, and John Maynard Keynes, the nucleus of the later Bloomsbury Group. Awarded second class in the Historical Tripos.

1901–2 Sojourns in Italy and the (then Austrian) Tyrol with his mother, a trip considerably influencing his early writing. Works on but eventually abandons *Nottingham Lace.* Writes his first short story, 'The Story of a Panic'. Returns to England via Germany. Applies to give Cambridge University extension lectures.

1903 Again sojourns in Italy with his mother and goes to Greece and Turkey on a tour of classical sites. Summers in the Tyrol. First published story: 'Albergo Empedocle' in *Temple Bar.* Begins *A Room with a View.* First piece in *Independent Review,* newly founded liberal journal, edited by Cambridge friends including Dickinson.

1904 First stint as a university extension lecturer (a regular activity through 1911), giving a course on the Republic of Florence. Works on stories and begins *The Longest Journey,* laying aside *A Room with a View* for *Where Angels Fear to Tread.* The Forsters move to Harnham, Weybridge, Surrey, their home until 1925.

1905 Spends spring and summer in Germany (now Poland) as tutor to Countess von Arnim-Schlagentin's children. *Where Angels Fear to Tread* published.

1906 Gives university extension lectures in Cornwall in February and March. Virgil's *Aeneid* with Forster's introduction and notes published. Tours France with his mother. Meets Syed Ross Masood, a partial model for Aziz in *A Passage to India.*

1907 *The Longest Journey* published. Completes *A Room with a View.* Writes play on the Deceased Wife's Sister Bill, *The Deceased Wife's Husband* (unpublished).

1908 Meets Henry James. *A Room with a View* published. Begins *Howards End.* Offers a collection of short stories to his publisher. Travels in Italy.

1909 Works on *Howards End.* Story collection rejected. Gives university extension lectures on the Renaissance at Rome. Travels to Paris with Masood.

1910 Visits the Italian Lakes and Paris. *Howards End* published. M. A. conferred. Delivers papers on Matthew Arnold and Rudyard Kipling.

1911 *'The Celestial Omnibus' and Other Stories* published. Works on 'The Heart of Bosnia' (unpublished play). Begins writing stories on homoerotic themes and a new novel, *Arctic Summer,* later abandoned. Travels in Italy with Masood. Increasingly in the Bloomsbury Group through his friendship with Leonard Woolf.

1912 Meets the Irish novelist Forrest Reid in Belfast. Travels extensively in India accompanied, at times, by Goldsworthy Lowes Dickinson and Cambridge friend R. C. Trevelyan.

1913	Begins *A Passage to India* on return. Abandons *Arctic Summer* and begins *Maurice*, the result of meeting social theorist and apologist for homoerotic love, Edward Carpenter.
1914	Writes numerous articles on India. Works as a part-time cataloguer at the National Gallery. Finishes *Maurice* (posthumously published) and works at a book on Samuel Butler (abandoned 1915).
1915	Meets and clashes with D.H. Lawrence. Continues working at the National Gallery until leaving for Alexandria as a searcher in Red Cross's Wounded and Missing Bureau.
1916	Meets C.P. Cavafy. Contributes articles to *The Egyptian Mail*.
1917–18	Relationship with Mohamed el Adl, a tram conductor. Writes articles for *The Egyptian Mail* and begins *Alexandria: A History and a Guide*.
1919	Returns to England after three years in Egypt. Friendship with Leonard and Virginia Woolf strengthens. Writes numerous reviews. Meets Thomas Hardy and Siegfried Sassoon. Briefly drama critic for *Athenaeum*.
1920	Interim literary editor of *The Daily Herald*. Writes pamphlet on the government of Egypt.
1921	In India as private secretary to Maharajah of Dewas State Senior, a sojourn urging on and contributing to *A Passage to India*.
1922	Returns to England via Egypt, visiting with el Adl, now seriously ill and soon to die. Begins *A Passage to India* again (laid aside in 1913). *Alexandria: A History and a Guide* published.
1923	*Pharos and Pharillon* published. Plans for Uniform Edition are afoot.
1924	Meets T.E. Lawrence ('Lawrence of Arabia') and journalist and autobiographer J.R. Ackerley. *A Passage to India*, finished early in the year, published. Arnold issues a Uniform Edition of Forster's novels.
1925	The Forsters move to West Hackhurst, Abinger Hammer, Surrey, their home until 1945. Meets Charles Mauron, his French translator, in France. *A Passage to India* awarded Femina-Vie Heureuse and James Tait Black prizes.
1926	Travels in Spain, France, and Scandinavia between bouts of literary journalism and reviewing.
1927	Delivers Clark Lectures at Trinity College, Cambridge, published as *Aspects of the Novel*. Elected Supernumerary Fellow of King's College (until 1933). Assembles a collection of stories.
1928	'*The Eternal Moment' and Other Stories* published. English Association lecture tour on Ibsen's plays. Engaged in controversy about Radclyffe Hall's lesbian novel *The Well of Loneliness*. Travels in Germany.

1929 Travels in South Africa, South Rhodesia, Kenya, Uganda, and Egypt, returning via France. Begins friendship with the South African writer William Plomer.

1930 Meets Constable Bob Buckingham, the beginning of his most important love relationship.

1931 Delivers 'Creator as Critic' lectures for Cambridge English Faculty. Meets novelist James Hanley.

1932 Visits Hungary, Rumania, and Poland. Goldsworthy Lowes Dickinson dies. Begins work on Dickinson's biography. Meets Christopher Isherwood. First regular connexion with the BBC.

1933 Joins committee of the London Library.

1934 Becomes president of the National Council for Civil Liberties. *Goldsworthy Lowes Dickinson* published. 'Pageant of Abinger', with music by Ralph Vaughan Williams, performed. Plans a collection of essays. Involved in protests against the Sedition Bill.

1935 Works on a comic guide to Bloomsbury and an edition of T.E. Lawrence's letters, both eventually abandoned. Addresses the International Writers' Congress in Paris. Visits Isherwood in The Netherlands.

1936 *Abinger Harvest* published. Libel suit ensues, causing its withdrawal and altered reissue.

1937 Meets Benjamin Britten. Loses *Abinger Harvest* libel suit. In Paris for the League of Nations Institute for Intellectual Co-operation. Masood and the Maharajah of Dewas State Senior die.

1938 *England's Pleasant Land*, with music by Ralph Vaughan Williams, performed and published.

1939 Becomes English PEN Centre vice-president and serves on the Lord Chancellor's Committee on Defamatory Libel.

1941 Involved in a protest about freedom of opinion and the BBC. Delivers a Warburg lecture on Indian novelists writing in English. Shortly after Virginia Woolf's suicide, delivers the Rede Lecture on her at Cambridge.

1944 Chairs PEN Areopagitica Conference in London. Delivers the W.P. Ker Memorial Lecture at the University of Glasgow.

1945 Lily Forster dies. Attends the All-India Writers' Conference at Jaipur and travels in India, returning via Egypt. Lease to West Hackhurst cancelled.

1946 Elected Honorary Fellow of King's College, Cambridge, taking up residence nearby (moving into college rooms in 1953).

1947 First trip to United States for the Harvard Symposium on Music Criticism. Visits New York and New England and then goes to the West. *The Collected Tales of E.M. Forster* published.

1948 Participates in the first Aldeburgh Festival.

1949 With Eric Crozier, writes the libretto for Britten's opera *Billy*

Budd. Second trip to United States to lecture to the American Academy and National Institute of Arts and Letters. Declines a knighthood. Prepares a new collection of essays.

1951 *Billy Budd* premieres. *Two Cheers for Democracy* published.

1953 Invested as Companion of Honour. *The Hill of Devi* published.

1956 *Marianne Thornton* published.

1960 Pens 'Terminal Note' to *Maurice.* Santha Rama Rau's dramatization of *A Passage to India* plays in Oxford and London. Defence witness in obscenity trial of Lawrence's *Lady Chatterley's Lover.*

1961 Inducted into the Royal Society of Literature as Companion of Literature. Writes 'Little Imber', last story, and publishes last review.

1969 Awarded Order of Merit.

1970 7 June: Dies at the Buckinghams' Coventry home and is cremated.

1971 *Maurice* and '*Albergo Empedocle' and Other Writings* published.

1972 '*The Life to Come' and Other Stories* published.

1978 *Commonplace Book* published.

1980 *Arctic Summer and Other Fiction* published.

Bibliography: Forster's Major Works

Novels

Where Angels Fear to Tread, London: Blackwood, 1905; New York: Knopf, 1920.
The Longest Journey, London: Blackwood, 1907; New York: Knopf, 1922.
A Room with a View, London: Arnold, 1908; New York: Putnam's, 1911.
Howards End, London: Arnold; New York: Putnam's, 1910.
A Passage to India, London: Arnold; New York: Harcourt, Brace, 1924.
Maurice, A Novel, London: Arnold; New York: Norton, 1971.

Short Fiction

The Celestial Omnibus and Other Stories, London: Sidgwick & Jackson, 1911; New York: Knopf, 1923.
The Eternal Moment and Other Stories, London: Sidgwick & Jackson; New York: Knopf, 1928.
The Collected Tales of E.M. Forster, New York: Knopf, 1947; London: Arnold, 1947 (as *The Collected Stories of E.M. Forster*).
'The Life to Come' and Other Stories, ed. Oliver Stallybrass, London: Arnold; New York: Norton, 1972.
Arctic Summer and Other Fiction, ed. Elizabeth Heine, London: Arnold, 1980; New York: Holmes and Meier, 1981.

Biographies

Goldsworthy Lowes Dickinson, London: Arnold; New York: Harcourt, Brace, 1934.
Marianne Thornton 1797–1887: A Domestic Biography, London: Arnold; New York: Harcourt, Brace, 1956.

Essays

Pharos and Pharillon, London: Hogarth Press; New York: Knopf, 1923.
Aspects of the Novel, London: Arnold; New York: Harcourt, Brace, 1927.
Abinger Harvest, London: Arnold; New York: Harcourt, Brace, 1936.
Two Cheeers for Democracy, London: Arnold; New York: Harcourt, Brace, 1951.
'Albergo Empedocle' and Other Writings, ed. George H. Thomson, New York: Liveright, 1971.

Travel Writing

Alexandria: A History and a Guide, Alexandria: Whitehead Morris, 1922.
The Hill of Devi, being Letters from Dewas State Senior, London: Arnold; New York: Harcourt, Brace, 1953.

Plays

Pageant of Abinger, London: Athenaeum Press, 1934.
England's Pleasant Land, London: Hogarth Press, 1940.

Miscellanea

Commonplace Book, London: Scolar Press, 1978.
Commonplace Book, ed. Philip Gardner, Stanford, CA: Stanford University Press, 1985.

Critical Bibliography

Biographical Studies, Memoirs, and Letters

Ackerley, J.R., *E.M. Forster: A Portrait*, London: Ian McKelvie, 1971.
Ashby, Margaret, *Forster Country*, Stevenage: Flaunden Press, 1991.
Barger, Everett, 'Memories of Morgan', *The New York Times Book Review*, 16 August 1970, pp. 2, 32–5
Beauman, Nicola, *Morgan: A Biography of E.M. Forster*, London: Hodder and Stoughton; New York: Knopf, 1993.
Belshaw, Patrick, *A Kind of Private Magic*, London: André Deutsch, 1994.
Campbell, Sandy, 'Mr Forster of King's', *Mademoiselle*, June 1964, pp. 80–1, 120–4.
Crozier, Eric, 'The Writing of *Billy Budd*', *Opera Quarterly*, 4.3, 1986, pp. 11–27.
Fagan, B.W., 'Forster and his Publishers', *Bookseller*, 28 December 1968, pp. 2070–2.
Ferguson, Howard, 'E.M. Forster at the National Gallery Concerts', *London Magazine*, 22.9–10, December 1982/January 1983, pp. 63–70.
Forster, E.M., 'Letters to George Valassopoulo', *PN Review*, 10.1, 1983, pp. 19–24.
Furbank, P.N., *E.M. Forster: A Life*, 2 vols, London: Secker & Warburg, 1977–8; New York: Harcourt, Brace, Jovanovich, 1978.
——— 'The Personality of E.M. Forster', *Encounter*, November 1961, pp. 61–2, 64–8.
——— and F.J.H. Haskell, 'E.M. Forster: The Art of Fiction: I', *Paris Review*, 1.1, Spring 1953, pp. 28–41.
Garnett, David, 'Edward Morgan Forster', *Great Friends: Portraits of Seventeen Writers*, London: Macmillan, 1979; New York: Athenaeum, 1980, pp. 96, 98–102.
Gransden, K.W., 'E.M. Forster and "Morgan": Notes and Memories', *Encounter*, May 1971, pp. 59–62.
Hanquart, Evelyne, '"My Dearest Joe": Une lecture des lettres de E.M. Forster à J.R. Ackerley (1922–1966)', *Cahiers d'études et de recherches*

victoriennes et édouardiennes, Montpellier, 4–5, 1977, pp. 97–112.

Hauser, Frank, 'A Late Début: E.M. Forster on Stage', *Grand Street*, Autumn 1984, pp. 145–8.

Hussain, Syed Hamid, ed., *Only Connect: Letters to Indian Friends*, New Delhi: Arnold-Heinemann, 1979.

King, Francis, *E.M. Forster and his World*, London: Thames & Hudson; New York: Scribner's, 1978.

Kirkup, James, 'In Memoriam E.M. Forster: Love, the Beloved Republic—A Memoir of Morgan Forster', *Eigo Seinen* Tokyo, September 1970, pp. 510–15.

Lago, Mary, *E.M. Forster: A Literary Life*, London: Macmillan, 1995.

——— and P. N. Furbank, eds, *Selected Letters of E. M. Forster*, 2 vols, London: Collins; Cambridge, MA: Harvard University Press, 1983–1985.

Lewis, Robin Jared, *E. M. Forster's Passages to India*, New York: Columbia University Press, 1979.

Mitchison, Naomi, 'Morgan Comes to Tea', *You May Well Ask: A Memoir 1920–1940*, London: Gollancz, 1979, pp. 101–6.

Natwar-Singh, K., ed., *E. M. Forster: A Tribute with Selections from his Writing on India*, New York: Harcourt, Brace, & World, 1964.

Noble, R.W., '"Dearest Forster"—"Dearest Masood": An East-West Friendship', *Encounter*, 56, June 1981, pp. 61–2, 64–72.

Panter-Downes, Mollie, 'Kingsman', *New Yorker*, 19 September 1959, pp. 51–2, 54, 57, 60, 62, 64, 66, 68, 70, 72, 75, 77–80.

Plomer, William, 'The Shield of Achilles', *At Home: Memoirs*, London: Cape, 1958, pp. 107–111.

Rau, Santha Rama, 'Remembering E. M. Forster', *Grand Street*, Summer 1986, pp. 99–119.

Raven, Simon, 'The Strangeness of E. M. Forster', *Spectator*, 5, September 1970, p. 237.

Savidis, George, 'Cavafy and Forster', *Times Literary Supplement*, 14 November 1975, p. 1356.

Stallybrass, Oliver, ed., *Aspects of E. M. Forster: Essays and Recollections written for his Ninetieth Birthday, 1st January 1969*, London: Arnold; New York: Harcourt, Brace, & World, 1969.

Stape, J.H., *An E. M. Forster Chronology*, London: Macmillan, 1993.

——— ed., *E. M. Forster: Interviews and Recollections*, London: Macmillan; New York: St Martin's Press, 1993.

Stone, Wilfred, 'The Future of Forster Biography', *Biography*, 3, 1980, pp. 253–61.

Trevelyan, Julian, 'Some Memories of E. M. Forster', *Literary Half-Yearly*, Mysore, 20, 1979, pp. 131–3.

Wescott, Glenway, 'A Dinner, a Talk, a Walk with Forster', *The New York Times Book Review*, 10 October 1971, pp. 2, 18, 20, 22.

Windham, Donald, ed., *E. M. Forster's Letters to Donald Windham*, Verona: Stamperia Valdonega, 1975.

Bibliographies, Surveys of Criticism, and Works of Reference

Beebe, Maurice, and Joseph Brogunier, comps, 'Criticism of E. M. Forster: A Selected Checklist', *Modern Fiction Studies*, 7, Autumn 1961, pp. 284–92.

Borello, Alfred, comp., *E. M. Forster: An Annotated Bibliography of Secondary Materials*, Metuchen, NJ: Scarecrow Press, 1973.

Borello, Alfred, comp., *An E. M. Forster Dictionary*, Metuchen, NJ: Scarecrow Press, 1971.

Borello, Alfred, comp., *An E. M. Forster Glossary*, Metuchen, NJ: Scarecrow Press, 1972.

Gardner, Philip, 'Introduction', *E. M. Forster: The Critical Heritage*, ed. Philip Gardner, London: Routledge & Kegan Paul, 1973, pp. 1–39.

Gerber, Helmut, comp., 'E. M. Forster: An Annotated Checklist of Writings about Him', *English Fiction in Transition*, 2.1, 1959, pp. 4–27.

Halls, Michael, 'The Forster Collection at King's: A Survey', *Twentieth Century Literature*, 31.2–3, Summer/Fall 1985, pp. 147–60.

Kirkpatrick, B.J., comp., *A Bibliography of E. M. Forster*, 2nd edition, Oxford: Clarendon, 1985.

Lago, Mary, comp., *Calendar of the Letters of E. M. Forster*, London: Mansell, 1985.

McDowell, F.P.W., comp., *E. M. Forster: An Annotated Bibliography of Writings about Him*, DeKalb: Northern Illinois University Press, 1977.

——— comp., 'E. M. Forster: An Annotated Secondary Bibliography', *English Literature in Transition*, 13.2, 1970, pp. 93–173.

——— 'Forster Scholarship and Criticism for the Desert Islander', *E. M. Forster: A Human Exploration—Centenary Essays*, eds G. K. Das and J. B. Beer, London: Macmillan; New York: New York University Press, 1979, pp. 269–82.

——— '"Fresh Woods and Pastures New": Forster Criticism and Scholarship since 1975', *E. M. Forster: Centenary Revaluations*, eds Judith Scherer Herz and Robert K. Martin, Toronto: University of Toronto Press; London: Macmillan, 1982, pp. 311–29.

Schuleter, Paul and June, comps, 'E. M. Forster', *The English Novel: Twentieth Century Criticism*, 2 vols, Athens: Ohio University Press, 1982, Vol. 2, pp. 81–97.

Stape, J.H., 'Additions to the Bibliographies of Clive Bell, E. M. Forster, and Virginia Woolf', *Notes and Queries*, 39.2, June 1992, pp. 194–6.

——— 'Further Additions to the Bibliographies of E. M. Forster and Virginia Woolf', *Notes and Queries*, 41.3, September 1994, p. 393.

Summers, Claude J., comp., *E. M. Forster: A Guide to Research,* Detroit: Garland, 1991.

Wilde, Alan, 'Introduction', *Critical Essays on E. M. Forster,* ed. Alan Wilde, Boston: G. K. Hall, 1985, pp. 1–20.

Critical Books on Forster

Advani, Rukum, *E. M. Forster as Critic,* London: Croom Helm, 1984.

Beer, J.B., *The Achievement of E. M. Forster,* London: Chatto & Windus; New York: Barnes & Noble, 1962.

Brander, Laurence, *E. M. Forster: A Critical Study,* London: Hart-Davis, 1968; Lewisburg, PA: Bucknell University Press, 1970.

Buhariwala, Shernavaz, *Arcades to a Dome: Humanism in the Novels of E. M. Forster,* Atlantic Highlands, NJ: Humanities Press, 1983.

Cavaliero, Glen, *A Reading of E. M. Forster,* London: Macmillan; Totowa, NJ: Rowman & Littlefield, 1979.

Colmer, John, *E. M. Forster: 'A Passage to India',* London: Arnold, 1967.

——— *E. M. Forster: The Personal Voice,* London: Routledge & Kegan Paul, 1975.

Crews, Frederick C., *E. M. Forster: The Perils of Humanism,* Princeton, NJ: Princeton University Press; London: Oxford University Press, 1962.

Das, G.K., *E. M. Forster's India,* London: Macmillan, 1977.

Duckworth, Alistair M., *'Howards End': E. M. Forster's House of Fiction,* New York: Twayne, 1992.

Ebbatson, Roger, and Catherine Neale, *E. M. Forster: 'A Passage to India',* Harmondsworth: Penguin, 1986.

Finkelstein, Bonnie Blumenthal, *Forster's Women: Eternal Differences,* New York: Columbia University Press, 1975.

Ganguly, Adwaita P., *India: Mystic, Complex and Real—A Detailed Study of E. M. Forster's 'A Passage to India',* Delhi: Motilal Banarsidass, 1990.

Gillie, Christopher, *A Preface to Forster,* London: Longman, 1983.

Godfrey, Denis, *E. M. Forster's Other Kingdom,* Edinburgh: Oliver & Boyd, 1968.

Gransden, K.W., *E. M. Forster,* Edinburgh: Oliver & Boyd; New York: Grove Press, 1962; revised edition 1970.

Hanquart, Evelyne, *Un Humaniste dans la cité moderne: E. M. Forster,* 2 vols, Paris: Didier, 1986.

Herz, Judith Scherer, *'A Passage to India': Nation and Narration,* New York: Twayne, 1993.

Herz, Judith Scherer, *The Short Narratives of E. M. Forster,* London: Macmillan; New York: St Martin's Press, 1988.

Joseph, David I., *The Art of Rearrangement: E. M. Forster's 'Abinger Harvest',* New Haven: Yale University Press, 1964.

Kelvin, Norman, *E. M. Forster*, Carbondale: Southern Illinois University Press; London: Feffer & Simons, 1967.

Land, Stephen K., *Challenge and Conventionality in the Fiction of E. M. Forster*, New York: AMS Press, 1990.

Lavin, Audrey A.P., *Aspects of the Novelist: E. M. Forster's Pattern and Rhythm*, Lang, 1995.

Levine, June Perry, *Creation and Criticism: 'A Passage to India'*, Lincoln: University of Nebraska Press; London: Chatto & Windus, 1972.

Macaulay, Rose, *The Writings of E. M. Forster*, London: Hogarth Press; New York: Harcourt, Brace, 1938.

McConkey, James, *The Novels of E. M. Forster*, Ithaca, NY: Cornell University Press, 1957; London: Oxford University Press, 1958.

McDowell, Frederick P.W., *E. M. Forster*, New York: Twayne, 1969; revised edition 1982.

Martial, Rose, *E. M. Forster*, London: Evans, 1970.

Martin, John Sayre, *E. M. Forster: The Endless Journey*, Cambridge: Cambridge University Press, 1976.

Martin, Richard, *The Love that Failed: Ideal and Reality in the Writings of E. M. Forster*, The Hague: Mouton, 1974.

Mason, W.H., *'A Passage to India' E. M. Forster*, New York: Barnes & Noble; Oxford: Blackwell, 1965.

Messenger, Nigel, *How to Study an E. M. Forster Novel*, London: Macmillan, 1991.

Moody, Phillipa, *A Critical Commentary on 'A Passage to India'*, London: Macmillan; New York: St Martin's Press, 1968.

Moore, Harry T., *E. M. Forster*, New York: Columbia University Press, 1974.

Morris, John, *E. M. Forster*, London: Longmans, Green, 1960.

Mukherjee, Sujit, *Forster and Further: The Tradition of Anglo-Indian Fiction*, Bombay: Orient Longman, 1993.

Oliver, H.J., *The Art of E. M. Forster*, London: Cambridge University Press; Parville: Melbourne University Press, 1960.

Page, Malcolm, *'Howards End': An Introduction to the Variety of Criticism*, London: Macmillan, 1993.

Page, Norman, *E. M. Forster*, New York: St Martin's Press, 1988.

——— *E. M. Forster's Posthumous Fiction*, Victoria, BC: University of Victoria Press, 1977.

Rapport, Nigel, *The Prose and the Passion: Anthropology, Literature, and the Writing of E. M. Forster*, Manchester: Manchester University Press, 1994.

Rosencrance, Barbara, *Forster's Narrative Vision*, Ithaca, NY: Cornell University Press, 1982.

Schusterman, David, *The Quest for Certitude in the Fiction of E. M. Forster*, Bloomington: Indiana University Press, 1965.

Scott, P.J.M., *E. M. Forster: Our Permanent Contemporary*, London: Vision Press; New York: Barnes & Noble, 1984.

Shahane, Vasant A., *E. M. Forster: A Reassessment,* New Delhi: Kitab Mahal, 1962; London: Probsthain, 1964.

——— *E. M. Forster: A Study in Double Vision,* New Delhi: Arnold-Heinemann, 1975.

Stone, Wilfred, *The Cave and the Mountain: A Study of E. M. Forster,* Stanford: Stanford University Press, 1966.

Summers, Claude J., *E. M. Forster: Literature and Life,* New York: Frederick Ungar, 1983.

Thomson, George H., *The Fiction of E. M. Forster,* Detroit: Wayne State University Press, 1967.

Trilling, Lionel, *E. M. Forster,* Norfolk, CT: New Directions, 1943.

Wakefield, G.P., *'Howards End',* Oxford: Blackwell, 1968.

Warner, Rex, *E. M. Forster,* London: Longmans, Green, 1950.

Widdowson, Peter, *E. M. Forster's 'Howards End': Fiction as History,* London: Chatto & Windus for Sussex University Press, 1977.

Wilde, Alan, *Art and Order: A Study of E. M. Forster,* New York: New York University Press, 1964.

Collections of Articles on Forster

Beer, J.B., ed., *'A Passage to India': Essays in Interpretation,* London: Macmillan, 1985; Totowa, NJ: Barnes & Noble, 1986.

Bloom, Harold, ed., *E. M. Forster: Modern Critical Interpretations,* New York: Chelsea House, 1987.

——— ed., *E. M. Forster's 'A Passage to India': Modern Critical Interpretations,* New York: Chelsea House, 1987.

Bradbury, Malcolm, ed., *E. M. Forster: A Collection of Critical Essays,* Englewood Cliffs, NJ: Prentice-Hall, 1966.

——— ed., *E. M. Forster: 'A Passage to India'—A Casebook,* London: Macmillan, 1970.

Das, G.K., and J. B. Beer, eds, *E. M. Forster: A Human Exploration—Centenary Essays,* London: Macmillan; New York: New York University Press, 1979.

Daumas, Phillipe, ed., E. M. Forster Special Double Issue, *Cahiers d'études et de recherches victoriennes et edouardiennes,* Montpellier, 4–5, 1977.

Davies, Tony, and Nigel Wood, eds, *'A Passage to India',* Theory in Practice Series, Buckingham: Open University Press, 1994.

Duckworth, Alistair M., ed., *E. M. Forster: 'Howards End—A Case Study in Contemporary Criticism,* New York: St Martin's Press, 1995.

Gowda, H.H. Anniah, ed., *A Garland for E. M. Forster,* Mysore: Literary Half-Yearly, 1969.

Herz, Judith Scherer, and Robert K. Martin, eds, *E. M. Forster: Centenary Revaluations,* Toronto: University of Toronto Press; London: Macmillan, 1982.

Lago, Mary, ed., E. M. Forster Special Issue, *Twentieth Century Literature*, 31, 1985.

Rutherford, Andrew, ed., *Twentieth Century Interpretations of 'A Passage to India': A Collection of Critical Essays*, Englewood Cliffs, NJ: Prentice-Hall, 1970.

Shahane, Vasant A., ed., *Approaches to E. M. Forster: A Centenary Volume*, New Delhi: Arnold-Heinemann; Atlantic Highlands, NJ: Humanities Press, 1981.

——— ed., *Focus on Forster's 'A Passage to India': Indian Essays in Criticism*, Madras: Orient Longman, 1975.

——— ed., *Perspectives on E. M. Forster's 'A Passage to India': A Collection of Critical Essays*, New York: Barnes & Noble, 1968.

Tambling, Jeremy, ed., *New Casebooks: E. M. Forster*, New York: St Martin's Press, 1995.

Wilde, Alan, ed., *Critical Essays on E. M. Forster*, Boston: G.K. Hall, 1985.

Chronological List of Criticism Included

Date	Author	Title	Reference	Vol. No.
Oct. 1905	Anonymous	Review, *Where Angels Fear to Tread*	*Bookman*, pp. 40–1	1.13
8 Nov. 1905	C.F.G. Masterman	Review, *Where Angels Fear to Tread*	*The Daily News*, p. 4	1.14
23 Dec. 1905	Anonymous	Review, *Where Angels Fear to Tread*	*Spectator*, pp. 1089–90	1.15
22 Apr. 1907	Anonymous	Review, *Where Angels Fear to Tread*	*The Tribune*, p. 2	1.19
26 Apr. 1907	Virginia Woolf	Unsigned Review, *The Longest Journey*	*Times Literary Supplement*, p. 134	1.16
27 Apr. 1907	Edward Garnett	Unsigned Review, *The Longest Journey*	*Nation*, pp. 357–8	1.17
3 May 1907	C.F.G. Masterman	'The Soul in Suburbia'	*The Daily News*, p. 4	1.18
6 May 1907	Anonymous	Review, *The Longest Journey*	*The Morning Post*, p. 2	1.19
15 May 1907	Anonymous	Review, *The Longest Journey*	*The Manchester Guardian*, p. 5	1.19
16 May 1907	Anonymous	Review, *The Longest Journey*	*Cambridge Review*, p. 408	1.19
June 1907	Anonymous	'Mr. E. M. Forster'	*Bookman*, 32, pp. 81–2	2.80
6 July 1907	Anonymous	Review, *The Longest Journey*	*Spectator*, pp. 24–5.	1.19
20 Oct. 1908	R. A. Scott-James	Review, *A Room with a View*	*The Daily News*, p. 4	1.20
22 Oct. 1908	Virginia Woolf	Unsigned Review, *A Room with a View*	*Times Literary Supplement*, p. 362	1.21
4 Nov. 1908	Anonymous	Review, *A Room with a View*	*The Manchester Guardian*, p. 5	1.23
23 Nov. 1908	Anonymous	Review, *A Room with a View*	*The Morning Post*, p. 2	1.23
28 Nov. 1908	C.F.G. Masterman	Unsigned Review, *A Room with a View*	*Nation*, pp. 352–4	1.22
2 Jan. 1909	Anonymous	Review, *A Room with a View*	*Spectator*, pp. 23–4	1.23
27 Oct. 1910	Percy Lubbock	Unsigned Review, *Howards End*	*Times Literary Supplement*, p. 412	1.24

28 Oct. 1910	Anonymous	Review, *Howards End*	*The Standard*, p. 5	1.28
2 Nov. 1910	Anonymous	Review, *Howards End*	*The Daily Telegraph*, p. 14	1.28
5 Nov. 1910	Anonymous	Review, *Howards End*	*Spectator*, p. 757	1.28
7 Nov. 1910	R. A. Scott-James	Review, *Howards End*	*The Daily News*, p. 4	1.25
12 Nov. 1910	Edward Garnett	Unsigned Review, *Howards End*	*Nation*, pp. 282–4	1.26
19 Nov. 1910	Anonymous	Review, *Howards End*	*Westminster Gazette*, p. 16	1.28
3 Dec. 1910	Clive Bell	Unsigned Review, *Howards End*	*Athenaeum*, p. 151	1.27
17 May 1911	Anonymous	Review, *The Celestial Omnibus*	*The Daily Telegraph*, p. 4	1.29
10 June 1911	Anonymous	Review, *The Celestial Omnibus*	*Nation*, p. 410	1.30
22 June 1911	Anonymous	Review, *The Celestial Omnibus*	*Times Literary Supplement*, p. 238	1.31
13 Aug. 1920	Katherine Mansfield	'Throw them Overboard!'	*Athenaeum*, pp. 209–10	2.81
1921	S.P.B. Mais	'E.M. Forster'	*Why We Should Read*, London, Grant Richards, pp. 152–6	2.82
17 June 1922	Anonymous	'E.M. Forster'	*The Times*, p.14	2.83
16 June 1923	R.M.,	'Things that have Interested Mr Forster'	*New Statesman*, pp. 303–04	1.34
8 Aug. 1923	John Middleton Murry	'The Magic of E.M. Forster'	*New Republic*, pp. 293–4	1.35
2 Sept. 1923	Anonymous	'Forster's Alexandria: A Pageant of History from Menelaus to Allenby'	*The New York Times Book Review*, p. 15	1.32
4 June 1924	Rose Macaulay	'Women in the East'	*The Daily News*, p. 8	1.36
14 June 1924	Leonard Woolf	'Arch beyond Arch'	*Nation and Athenaeum*, p. 354	1.37
20 June 1924	Sylvia Lynd	'A Great Novel at Last'	*Time and Tide*, pp. 592–3	1.38
28 June 1924	L.P. Hartley	Review, *A Passage to India*	*Spectator*, pp. 1048–50	1.39
July 1924	John Middleton Murry	'Bo-oum or Ou-Boum?'	*Adelphi*, pp. 150–3	1.40
July 1924	J.B. Priestley	Review, *A Passage to India*	*London Mercury*, pp. 319–20	1.41
16 Aug. 1924	Rebecca West	'Interpreters of Their Age'	*Saturday Review, of Literature* (New York), p. 42	1.42
July 1927	Edward Shanks	'Mr E.M. Forster'	*London Mercury*, 16, 1.7, pp. 265–74	2.84
Nov. 1927	Virginia Woolf	'The Novels of E.M. Forster'	*Atlantic Monthly*, pp. 642–8	2.85
12 Nov. 1927	Virginia Woolf	'The Art of Fiction'	*Nation and Athenaeum*, pp. 247–8	1.43
1927	I.A. Richards	'E.M. Forster'	*The Forum*, 78.6, pp. 914–20	2.86
22 Feb. 1928	Edmund Wilson	Extract from 'Three English Critics'	*New Republic*, pp. 21–2	1.44

Date	Author	Title	Reference	Vol. No.
Mar. 1928	I.A. Richards	'Forster and the Novel'	*Cambridge Review*, pp. 304–5	1.45
5 Apr. 1928	Anonymous	Review, *The Eternal Moment and Other Stories*	*Times Literary Supplement*, p. 256	1.47
20 Apr. 1928	C.M.	Review, *The Eternal Moment and Other Stories*	*The Manchester Guardian*, p. 7	1.48
12 May 1928	Thomas Beer	'In Six Fantasias, E.M. Forster Freshens Stale Conceptions and Credits his Readers with Sense'	*New York Evening Post*, p. 8	1.49
12 May 1928	Edwin Muir	Review, *The Eternal Moment and Other Stories*	*Nation and Athenaeum*, p. 184	1.50
20 June 1928	Morton Dauwen Zabel	'Border-Line Fiction'	*Commonweal*, p. 190	1.51
July 1928	Wilbur Cross	'Novelists at a Round Table'	*Yale Review*, pp. 792–4	1.46
13 Oct. 1928	Anonymous	Review, *The Eternal Moment and Other Stories*	*Saturday Review, of Literature*, p. 250	1.52
Oct. 1932	Howard N. Doughty, Jr	'The Novels of E. M. Forster'	*Bookman* (New York), pp. 542–9	2.87
1934	Peter Burra	'The Novels of E. M. Forster'	*Nineteenth Century and After*, 116, pp. 581–94	2.88
1934	E. K. Brown	'E. M. Forster and the Contemplative Novel'	*University of Toronto Quarterly*, 3.3, pp. 349–61	2.89
1934	Frank Swinnerton	'Post-Freud: Edward Morgan Forster'	*The Georgian Literary Scene: A Literary Panorama*, New York, Farrar & Rhinehart, pp. 390–401	2.90
21 Apr. 1934	David Garnett	Review, *Goldsworthy Lowes Dickinson*	*New Statesman and Nation*, p. 600	1.53
June 1934	Hugh Kingsmill	'Lowes Dickinson'	*English Review*, pp. 746–9	1.54
July 1934	Kingsley Martin	Review, *Goldsworthy Lowes Dickinson*	*Political Quarterly*, pp. 447–52	1.55
Dec. 1934	W. H. Auden	'Lowes Dickinson'	*Scrutiny*, pp. 303–06	1.56
1936	Frank Swinnerton	'Independent, Cantabrigian, and a Bachelor'	*Swinnerton: An Autobiography*, New York, pp. 292–4	1.1
20 Mar. 1936	Elizabeth Bowen	Review, *Abinger Harvest*	*Spectator*, p. 521	1.57
25 Mar. 1936	Christopher Isherwood	'Mr Forster Tidies Up'	*Listener*, p. 603	1.58

Apr. 1936	R. A. Scott-James	Review, *Abinger Harvest*	*London Mercury*, pp. 635–6	1.59
June 1936	Q. D. Leavis	Review, *Aspects of the Novel*	*Scrutiny*, pp. 100–05	1.60
26 Sept. 1936	John Crowe Ransom	'Gestures of Dissent'	*Yale Review*, pp. 181–3	1.61
Apr. 1937	D. A. Traversi	'The Novels of E. M. Forster'	*Arena*, 1, pp. 28–40	2.91
Summer 1937	Austin Warren	'The Novels of E. M. Forster'	*American Review*, 9.2, pp. 226–51	2.92
25 Mar. 1938	Forrest Reid	'E. M. Forster'	*Spectator*, pp. 532, 534	2.93
1938	F. R. Leavis	'E. M. Forster'	*Scrutiny*, 7, pp. 185–202	2.94
1940	Forrest Reid	'Meeting E. M.'	*Private Road*, London, pp. 115–17	1.2
1942	Lionel Trilling	'E. M. Forster'	*Kenyon Review*, 4, pp. 161–73	2.95
1943	J[ohn C[rowe] R[ansom]	'E. M. Forster'	*Kenyon Review*, 5, pp. 618–23	2.96
1943	Cuthbert Wright	'The Damned and the Saved,'	*Commonweal*, 38, pp. 557–61	2.97
1944	Herbert Marshall McLuhan	'Kipling and Forster'	*Sewanee Review*, 52, pp. 332–43	4.153
1944	William Plomer	'An Introduction to E. M. Forster'	*Penguin New Writing*, 20, pp. 138–41	2.98
Summer 1945	Hyatt Howe Waggoner	'Exercises in Perspective: Notes on the Uses of Coincidence in the Novels of E. M. Forster'	*Chimera*, 3.4, pp. 3–14	4.161
Jan. 1949	David Cecil	'E. M. Forster'	*Atlantic Monthly*, 183, pp. 60–5	4.162
3 Nov. 1951	V. S. Pritchett	'A Private Voice'	*New Statesman and Nation*, pp. 496, 498	1.62
9 Nov. 1951	Jocelyne Brooke	'Four Cheers for Mr Forster'	*Spectator*, p. 609	1.63
1 Dec. 1951	Joseph Wood Krutch	'In Defense of Values'	*Saturday Review, of Literature*, pp. 25–6	1.64
Apr. 1952	Michael Oakeshott	Review, *Two Cheers for Democracy*	*Cambridge Journal*, pp. 436–8	1.65
1953	Stephen Spender	'Personal Relations and Public Powers'	*The Creative Element: A Study of Vision, Despair and Orthodoxy among some Modern Writers*, London: Hamilton, pp. 77–91	4.163
17 Oct. 1953	William Plomer	Review, *The Hill of Devi*	*New Statesman and Nation*, pp. 457–8	1.66
25 Oct. 1953	Newton Arvin	'A Private Secretary for the Maharajah'	*The New York Times Book Review*, pp. 3, 49	1.67
30 Jan. 1954	V. S. Pritchett	'Genius and Saint'	*New Yorker*, pp. 85–9	1.68

Date	Author	Title	Reference	Vol. No.
Jan.–Feb. 1954	Steven Marcus	'Forster's India'	*Partisan Review*, pp. 115–19	1.69
1954	Richard Voorhees	'The Novels of E. M. Forster'	*South Atlantic Quarterly*, 53, pp. 89–99	4.164
Summer 1956	Lionel Trilling	'The Great Aunt of Mr Forster'	*Griffin*, pp. 4–12	1.71
12 May 1956	Ronald Bryden	Review, *Marianne Thornton*	*Cambridge Review*, p. 536	1.70
Nov. 1956	Rex Warner	Review, *Marianne Thornton*	*London Magazine*, pp. 79, 81	1.72
Autumn-Winter 1956	L. Compton	'Thornton's End'	*Chicago Review*, 10.3, pp. 83–6.	1.73
Summer 1957	Harold J. Oliver	'E. M. Forster: The Early Novels'	*Critique*, 1, pp. 15–33	4.165
1958	William Plomer	'Raising the Shield of Achilles'	*At Home: Memoirs*, London, Cape, pp. 107–11	1.3
1959	Frederick C. Crews	'*The Longest Journey* and the Perils of Humanism'	*English Literary History*, 26, pp. 575–96	3.121
Summer 1961	Robert Tracy	Review, *Alexandria: A History and a Guide*	*Carleton Miscellany*, pp. 113–17	1.33
1961	Frederick P. W. McDowell	'Forster's "Natural Supernaturalism": The Tales'	*Modern Fiction Studies*, 7.3, pp. 271–83	2.99
1961	Alan Wilde	'The Aesthetic View of Life: *Where Angels Fear to Tread*'	*Modern Fiction Studies*, 7.3, pp. 207–16	3.117
1963	Jeanne Delbeare-Garant	'The Call of the South: *Where Angels Fear to Tread* and *The Lost Girl*'	*Revue des langues vivantes*, 29, pp. 336–57	4.149
1964	Ellin Horowitz	'The Communal Ritual and the Dying God in E. M. Forster's *A Passage to India*'	*Criticism*, 6, pp. 70–88	3.136
1965	Frederick P. W. McDowell	'E. M. Forster's Conception of the Critic'	*Tennessee Studies in Literature*, 10, pp. 93–100	2.109
1965	John V. Hagopian	'Eternal Moments in the Short Fiction of E. M. Forster'	*College English*, 27, pp. 209–15	2.100
1966	Frederick P. W. McDowell	'E. M. Forster's Theory of Literature'	*Criticism*, 8.1, pp. 19–43	2.110

1966	John Lucas	'Wagner and Forster: *Parsifal* and *A Room with a View*'	*ELH*, 33, pp. 92–117	3.126
1966	H. A. Smith	'Forster's Humanism and the Nineteenth Century'	*Forster: A Collection of Critical Essays*, Englewood Cliffs, NJ, Prentice Hall, pp. 106–16	4.166
1968	James Hall	'Forster's Family Reunions'	*English Literary History*, 25.1, pp. 60–78	3.129
1968	George H. Thomson	'E. M. Forster and Howard Sturgis'	*Texas Studies in Literature and Language*, 10, pp. 423–33	4.154
1969	John Colmer	'*Howards End* Revisited'	*Literary Half-Yearly*, 10.2, pp. 9–22	3.130
12 June 1970	V. S. Pritchett	'E. M. Forster'	*New Statesman*, p. 846	1.10
18 June 1970	Noel Annan	'Morgan Forster Remembered'	*Listener*, p. 826	1.11
Sep. 1970	James Kirkup	'In Memoriam E. M. Forster: Love, the Beloved Republic—A Memoir of Morgan Forster'	*Eigo Seinen*, (Tokyo), pp. 510–15	1.12
Winter 1970	Francis Gillen	'*Howards End* and the Neglected Narrator'	*Novel*, 3.2, pp. 139–52	3.131
1970	Jeffrey Meyers,	'E. M. Forster and T. E. Lawrence: A Friendship'	*South Atlantic Quarterly*, 69, pp. 205–16	4.155
Spring 1971	Duke Maskell	'Mr Forster's Fine Feelings'	*Cambridge Quarterly*, 5, pp. 222–35	4.167
7 Oct. 1971	C. P. Snow	'Open Windows'	*The Financial Times*, p. 28	1.74
9 Oct. 1971	Colin Wilson	'A Man's Man'	*Spectator*, p. 512–13	1.75
10 Oct. 1971	Philip Toynbee	'Forster's Love Story'	*The Observer*, p. 32	1.76
1971	L. L. Lee	'"Oedipus at Colonus": The Modern Vulgarizations of Forster and Cicellis'	*Studies in Short Fiction*, 8.4, pp. 561–7	2.101
8 Oct. 1972	Angus Wilson	'Books versus Biceps'	*The Observer*, p. 39	1.77
21 Oct. 1972	J. I. M. Stewart	'Old and Gay'	*Spectator*, pp. 629–30	1.78
3 June 1973	Samuel Hynes	'Hazards of an Honest Life'	*The Washington Post Book World*, p. 3	1.79

Date	Author	Title	Reference	Vol. No.
1973	Heinz-Joachim Müllenbrock	'Modes of Opening in the Work of E. M. Forster: A Contribution to the Poetics of his Novels'	*Modern Philology*, 70, pp. 216–29	4.168
1973	Jo M. Turk	'The Evolution of E. M. Forster's Narrator'	*Studies in the Novel*, 5, pp. 428–40	4.169
Feb.–Mar. 1974	Jeffrey Meyers	'The Paintings in Forster's Italian Novels'	*London Magazine*, 13, pp. 46–62	3.118
Spring 1974	C. Rising	'E. M. Forster's *Maurice*': A Summing Up'	*Texas Quarterly*, 17.1, pp. 84–96	3.143
Fall 1974	Paul B. Armstrong	'E. M. Forster's *Howards End*: The Existential Crisis of the Liberal Imagination'	*Mosaic: A Journal for the Comparative Study of Literature and Ideas*, 8.1, pp. 183–99	3.132
1974	Douglas Bolling	'The Distanced Heart: Artistry in E. M. Forster's *Maurice*'	*Modern Fiction Studies*, 20, pp. 157–68	3.142
1974	James S. Malek	'Forster's "Albergo Empedocle": A Precursor of *Maurice*'	*Studies in Short Fiction*, 11.4, pp. 427–30	2.102
1974	Joyce Hotchkiss	'Romance and Reality: The Dualistic Style of E. M. Forster's *Maurice*'	*Journal of Narrative Technique*, 4, pp. 163–75	3.144
Feb.–Mar. 1975	Donald Salter	' "That is my ticket": The Homosexual Writings of E. M. Forster'	*London Magazine*, 14.6, 2–3, pp. 5–33	2.105
1976	Zohreh T. Sullivan	'Forster's Symbolism: *A Room with a View*, Fourth Chapter'	*Journal of Narrative Technique*, 6, pp. 217–23	3.127
1976	Eugene Webb	'Self and Cosmos: Religion as Strategy and Exploration in the Novels of E. M. Forster'	*Soundings*, 59, pp. 186–203	4.170
1976	Elizabeth Wood Ellem	'E. M. Forster's Greenwood',	*Journal of Modern Literature*, 5, pp. 89–98	4.171
1977	James S. Malek	'Persona, Shadow, and Society: A Reading of Forster's "The Other Boat"'	*Studies in Short Fiction*, 14.1, pp. 21–7	2.106

1977	Robert K. Martin	'Forster's Greek: From Optative to Present Indicative'	*Kansas Quarterly*, 9, pp. 69–73	2.107
1977	J. H. Stape	'Myth, Allusion, Symbol in E. M. Forster's "The Other Side of the Hedge"'	*Studies in Short Fiction*, 14.4, pp. 375–8	2.103
1977	Alina Szala	'North and South: Civilization in E. M. Forster's First Novel'	*Cahiers d'études et de recherches victoriennes et édouardiennes*, 4–5, pp. 27–41	3.119
1978	Paul Delany	'Lawrence and Forster: First Skirmish with Bloomsbury'	*D. H. Lawrence Review*, 11, pp. 63–72	4.150
1978	Penelope Gay	'E. M. Forster and John Ruskin: The Ambivalent Connection'	*Southern Review*, 11, pp. 283–94	4.156
1978	Wilfred Stone	'"Overleaping Class": Forster's Problems in Connection'	*Modern Language Quarterly*, 39, pp. 386–404	4.172
1979	Judith Scherer Herz	'The Narrator as Hermes: A Study of the Early Short Fiction'	*E. M. Forster: A Human Exploration*, London: Macmillan; New York: N.Y. Univ. Press, pp. 17–27	2.104
1979	S. P. Rosenbaum	'*The Longest Journey*: E. M. Forster's Refutation of Idealism'	*E. M. Forster: A Human Exploration*, London: Macmillan; New York: N.Y. Univ. Press, pp. 32–54	3.122
1979	May Buckingham	'Some Reminiscences of E. M. Forster'	*E. M. Forster: A Human Exploration*, London: Macmillan; New York: N.Y. Univ. Press, pp. 183–5	1.9
1979	Elizabeth Heine	'E. M. Forster's *Commonplace Book*'	*Contemporary Review*, 234, pp. 251–5	2.112
1979	Robert L. Selig	'"God si Love": On an Unpublished Forster Letter and the Ironic Use of Myth in *A Passage to India*'	*Journal of Modern Literature*, 7, pp. 471–87	3.137
1981	Donald Watt	'The Artist as Horseman: The Unity of Forster's Criticism'	*Modern Philology*, 79, pp. 45–60	2.111
1981	James S. Malek	'Salvation in Forster's "Dr Woolacott"'	*Studies in Short Fiction*, 18.3, pp. 319–20	2.108

Date	Author	Title	Reference	Vol. No.
1981–82	J. H. Stape	'Leonard's "Fatal Forgotten Umbrella": Sex and the Manuscripts of *Howards End*'	*Journal of Modern Literature*, 9.1, pp. 123–32	3.133
1982	Paul R. Rivenberg	'The Role of the Essayist-Commentator in *Howards End*'	*E. M. Forster: Centenary Revaluations*, London, pp. 167–76	3.134
1982	Robert K. Martin	'The Paterian Mode in Forster's Fiction: *The Longest Journey* to *Pharos and Pharillon*'	*E. M. Forster: Centenary Revaluations*, London, pp. 99–112	4.145
1982	James McConkey	'Encountering E. M. Forster'	'Writers' Panel', *E. M. Forster: Centenary Revaluations*, London, pp. 295–8	1.4
1982	Eudora Welty	'Meetings Which are not Precisely Personal'	'Writers' Panel', *E. M. Forster: Centenary Revaluations*, London, pp. 298–9	1.5
1982	Judith Scherer Herz	'E. M. Forster and the Biography of the Self: Redefining a Genre'	*Prose Studies*, 5, pp. 326–35	2.113
1982	Tony Brown	'E. M. Forster's *Parsifal*: A Reading of *The Longest Journey*'	*Journal of European Studies*, 12, pp. 30–54	3.123
1982	Dixie King	'The Influence of Forster's *Maurice* on *Lady Chatterley's Lover*'	*Contemporary Literature*, 23, pp. 65–82	4.151
1983	Douglass H. Thomson	'From Words to Things: Margaret's Progress in *Howards End*'	*Studies in the Novel*, 15.2, 122–34	3.135
1983	M. Y. Shaheen	'Forster's Meredith: Meditation and Change'	*Modern Fiction Studies*, 29, pp. 240–5	4.157
1983	Robert K. Martin	'Edward Carpenter and the Double Structure of *Maurice*'	*Journal of Homosexuality*, 8.3–4, pp. 35–46	4.147
1983	Daniel R. Schwarz	'The Originality of E. M. Forster'	*Modern Fiction Studies*, 29, pp. 623–41	4.173
Summer 1984	Robert James Merrett	'E. M. Forster's Modernism: Tragic Faith in *A Passage to India*'	*Mosaic: A Journal for the Comparative Study of Literature and Ideas*, 17, pp. 71–86	3.138

Spring 1985	Christopher Hitchens	'Busted Blue: [David Lean's] *A Passage to India*'	*Grand Street*, 4, pp. 215–17	4.158
Sept.–Oct. 1985	K. W. Gransden	'Perfection of the Life: E. M. Forster's Letters'	*Encounter*, 65, pp. 43–51	2.114
1985	S. P. Rosenbaum	'Towards a Literary History of Monteriano'	*Twentieth Century Literature*, 31, pp. 180–98	3.120
1985	Richard Keller Simon	'E. M. Forster's Critique of Laughter and the Comic: The First Three Novels as Dialectic'	*Twentieth Century Literature*, 31, pp. 199–220	4.174
1985	Joe K. Law	'"We have ventured to tidy up Vere": The Adapters' Dialogue in *Billy Budd*'	*Twentieth Century Literature*, 31, pp. 297–314	2.115
1985	Frederick P. W. McDowell	'"Moments of Emergence and of a New Splendour": D. H. Lawrence and E. M. Forster in their Fiction'	*D. H. Lawrence's Lady: A New Look at Lady Chatterley's Lover*, Athens: University of Georgia Press, pp. 58–90	4.152
1986	June Perry Levine	'Passage to the Odeon: Too Lean'	*Literature/Film Quarterly*, 14, pp. 139–50	4.159
1986	Tariq Rahman	'Edward Carpenter and E. M. Forster'	*Durham University Journal*, 79, pp. 59–69	4.148
1986	Eric Crozier	'The Writing of *Billy Budd*'	*Opera Quarterly*, 4.3, pp. 11–27.	1.6
Spring 1987	Rae H. Stoll	'"Aphrodite with a Janus Face": Language, Desire, and History in Forster's *The Longest Journey*'	*Novel*, 20.3, pp. 237–59	3.124
1987	Francesca Kazan	'Confabulations in *A Passage to India*'	*Criticism*, 29, 197–214	3.139
1987	Robert Giroux	'E. M. Forster'	*Yale Review*, 76.3, pp. 334–40	1.7
Fall 1988	Brenda R. Silver	'Periphrasis, Power, and Rape in *A Passage to India*'	*Novel*, 22, pp. 86–105	3.140
1988	James Kirkup	'At Joe Ackerley's'	*I, of all People: An Autobiography of Youth*, London, pp. 198–200	1.8
1988	Thomas L. Jeffers	'Forster's *The Longest Journey* and the Idea of Apprenticeship'	*Texas Studies in Literature and Language*, 30.2, pp. 179–97	3.125

Date	Author	Title	Reference	Vol. No.
1988	Jeanne E. Olson	'The Noble Peasant in E. M. Forster's Fiction'	*Studies in the Novel*, 20, pp. 389–403	4.175
Summer 1989	June Perry Levine	'Two Rooms with a View: An Inquiry into Film Adaptation'	*Mosaic: A Journal for the Comparative Study of Literature and Ideas*, 22, pp. 67–84	4.160
Winter 1990	Gail Fincham	'Arches and Echoes: Framing Devices in *A Passage to India*'	*PreTexts*, 2.1, pp. 52–67	3.141
1990	J. H. Stape	'Comparing Mythologies: Forster's *Maurice* and Pater's *Marius*'	*English Literature in Transition*, 33.2, pp. 141–53	4.146
1990	Tariq Rahman	'*Maurice* and *The Longest Journey*: A Study of E. M. Forster's Deviation from the Representation of Male Homosexuality in Literature'	*Studies in English Literature* (Tokyo), pp. 57–75	4.176
1991	Ilona McGuiness	'The Collaborative Rhetoric of E. M. Forster's *Goldsworthy Lowes Dickinson*'	*a/b: Auto/Biography Studies*, 6.2, pp. 253–71	2.116
1994	Jeffrey Heath	'Kissing and Telling: Turning Round in *A Room with a View*'	*Twentieth Century Literature*, 40.4, pp. 393–433	3.128

Acknowledgements

Whilst every effort has been made to locate owners of material in copyright, in some cases this has been unsuccessful. The editor and publisher apologise for any infringement and shall be glad to include any necessary corrections in subsequent printings.

The editor and publisher should like to thank the following for their kind permission to reprint copyright material: Frontispiece portrait of E.M. Forster by Dora Carrington, by courtesy of the National Portrait Gallery, London; the Lord Annan for his 'Morgan Forster Remembered; Mrs May Buckingham for her 'Some Reminiscences'; the editors of the *Cambridge Review* for the review of *Marianne Thornton* by Ronald Bryden and 'Forster and the Novel' by I.A. Richards; the editors of the *Cambridge Quarterly* for 'Mr Forster's Fine Feelings' by Duke Maskell; the editors of *Carleton Miscellany* for the review of *Alexandria: A History and a Guide* by Robert Tracy; Dr H.P. Cecil for 'E.M. Forster' by the late David Cecil; the editors of *College English* for 'Eternal Moments in the Short Fiction of E.M. Forster' by John V. Hagopian © the National Council of Teachers of English 1965; the editors of *Contemporary Literature* for 'The Influence of Forster's *Maurice* on *Lady Chatterley's Lover*' by Dixie King; the editors of *The Contemporary Review* for 'E.M. Forster's *Commonplace Book*' by Elizabeth Heine; the editors of *Criticism* for 'The Communal Ritual and the Dying God in E.M. Forster's *A Passage to India*' by Ellin Horowitz, 'Confabulations in *A Passage to India*' by Francesca Kazan, and 'E.M. Forster's Theory of Literature' by Frederick P.W. McDowell © Wayne State University Press 1964, 1966, 1987; the late Eric Crozier for his 'The Writing of *Billy Budd*' © 1986; Duke University Press for '"Overleaping Class": Forster's Problems in Connection' by Wilfred Stone, *Modern Language Quarterly* © University of Washington 1978; the editors of *Eigo Seinen* for 'In Memoriam E.M. Forster: Love, the Beloved Republic— A Memoir of Morgan Forster' by James Kirkup; the editors of *ELH* for '*The Longest Journey* and the Perils of Humanism' by Frederick C. Crews, 'Forster's Family Reunions' by James Hall, and 'Wagner and Forster: *Parsifal* and *A Room with a View by John Lucas*; the editors of *Encounter* for 'Perfection of Life: E.M. Forster's Letters' by K.W. Gransden; The English Literary Society of Japan for '*Maurice* and *The Longest Journey*: A Study of E.M. Forster's Deviation from the Representation of Male Homosexuality in Literature' by Tariq Rahman; *The Financial Times* for 'Open

Windows' by the late C.P. Snow; Dr Gail Fincham and the editors of *PreTexts* for 'Arches and Echoes: Framing Devices in *A Passage to India*'; Mr Tony Garrett for 'Books versus Biceps' by the late Angus Wilson; Mr Stephen Gilbert and Faber & Faber, Ltd, for the extract from *Private Road* by the late Forrest Reid; Mr Robert Giroux for his 'E.M. Forster'; Grand Street, published by Ben Sonnenberg, for 'Busted Blue: *A Passage to India*' by Christopher Hitchens; Sir Rupert Hart-Davis for the extracts from *At Home: Memoirs* 'An Introduction to E.M. Forster' from *Penguin New Writing*, and the review of *Hill of Devi* by the late William Plomer; Professor Judith Scherer Herz for her 'The Narrator as Hermes: A Study of the Early Short Fiction' from *E.M. Forster: A Human Exploration—Centenary Essays*, and Professor Herz and the editors of *Prose Studies* for her 'E.M. Forster and the Biography of the Self: Redefining a Genre'; Professors Judith Scherer Herz and Robert K. Martin for the extracts from 'Writers' Panel', 'The Role of the Essayist-Commentator in *Howards End*' by Paul R. Rivenberg, and 'The Paterian Mode in Forster's Fiction: *The Longest Journey* to *Pharos and Pharillon*' by Robert K. Martin from *E.M. Forster: Centenary Revaluations*; Professor Evelyn J. Hinz, editor of *Mosaic: A Journal for the Comparative Study of Literature and Ideas* for 'E.M. Forster's *Howards End*: The Existential Crisis of the Liberal Imagination' by Paul B. Armstrong, 'Two Rooms with a View: An Inquiry into Film Adaptation' by June Perry Levine, and 'E.M. Forster's Modernism: Tragic Faith in *A Passage to India*' by Robert James Merrett; Professor Dennis Jackson, editor of the *D.H. Lawrence Review*, for 'Lawrence and Forster: First Skirmish with Bloomsbury' by Paul Delany; the editors of the *Journal of European Studies* for 'E.M. Forster's *Parsifal*: A Reading of *The Longest Journey*; the editors of the *Journal of Narrative Technique* for 'Romance and Reality: The Dualistic Style of E.M. Forster's *Maurice*' by Joyce Hotchkiss and 'Forster's Symbolism: *A Room with a View*, Fourth Chapter' by Zohreh T. Sullivan; Professor Robert Langenfeld, editor of *English Literature in Transition, 1880-1920*, for 'Comparing Mythologies: Forster's *Maurice* and Pater's *Maurius*' by J.H. Stape; Professor Morton P. Levitt, editor of the *Journal of Modern Literature*, for 'E.M. Forster's Greenwood' by Elizabeth Wood Ellem, '"God si Love": On an Unpublished Forster Letter and the Ironic Use of Myth in *A Passage to India*' by Robert L. Selig, and 'Leonard's "Fatal Forgotten Umbrella": Sex and the Manuscripts of *Howards End*' by J.H. Stape; Professor Peter Lewis, editor of the *Durham University Journal*, for 'Edward Carpenter and E.M. Forster' by Tariq Rahman; the editors of *The Literary Half-Yearly* for '*Howards End* Revisited' by John Colmer; the editors of *Literature/Film Quarterly* for 'Passage to the Odeon: Too Lean' by June Perry Levine; the editors of *London Magazine* for 'The Paintings in Forster's Italian Novels' by Jeffrey Meyers, '"That is my ticket": The Homosexual Writings of E.M. Forster' by Donald Salter, and the review of *Marianne Thornton* by Rex Warner; Professor William McBrien, editor of *Twentieth Century Literature*, for 'Kissing and Telling: Turning Round in *A Room with a View* by Jeffrey Heath, '"We have ventured to tidy up Vere": The Adapters' Dialogue in *Billy Budd*' by Joe K. Law, 'E.M. Forster's Critique of Laughter and the Comic: The First Three Novels as Dialectic' by Richard Keller Simon, and 'Towards a Literary History of *Monteriano*' by S.P. Rosenbaum; Dr Ilona McGuiness and the editors of *a/b: Auto/Biography Studies* for 'The Collaborative Rhetoric of E.M. Forster's *Goldsworthy Lowes Dickinson*'; Professor Robert K. Martin for his 'Edward Carpenter and the Double Structure of *Maurice*', and Professor Martin and the editors of *Kansas Quarterly* for his 'Forster's Greek: From Optative to Present Indicative'; *New Statesman and Society* for 'E.M. Forster' by V.S. Pritchett; the editors of *Modern Fiction Studies* for 'The Distanced Heart: Artistry in E.M. Forster's *Maurice*' by Douglas Bolling, 'Forster's "Natural Supernaturalism": The Tales' by F.P.W. McDowell, 'The Originality of E.M. Forster' by Daniel R. Schwarz, 'Forster's Meredith: Meditation and Change' by M.Y. Shaheen, and 'The Aesthetic View of Life: *Where Angels Fear to Tread*' by Alan Wilde; the editors of *Modern Philology* for 'Modes of Opening in the Work of E.M. Forster: A Contribution to the Poetics of his Novels' by Heinz-Joachim Mullenbrock; the editors of *Novel: A Forum for Fiction* for '*Howards End* and the Neglected Narrator' by Francis Gillen, 'Periphrasis, Power, and Rape in *A Passage to India*' by Brenda R. Silver, and '"Aphrodite with a Janus Face": Language, Desire, and History in Forster's *The Longest Journey*' by Rae H. Stoll; *The Observer* for 'Forster's Love Story' by Philip Toynbee © 1971 *The Observer*; Professor Michael O'Shea, editor of *Studies in Short Fiction*, for '"Oedipus at Colonus": The Modern Vulgarizations of Forster and Cicellis' by L.L. Lee, 'Forster's "Albergo Empedocle": A Precursor of *Maurice*', 'Persona, Shadow, and Society: A Reading of Forster's "The Other Boat" and 'Salvation in Forster's "Dr Woolacott"' by James S. Malek, and 'Myth, Allusion, and Symbol in E.M. Forster's "The Other Side of the Hedge"' by J.H. Stape © Newberry College 1971, 1974, 1977, and 1981; the late Trekkie Parsons for 'Arch beyond Arch' by the late Leonard Woolf; Professor S.P. Rosenbaum for his '*The Longest Journey*: The Refutation of Idealism' from *E.M. Forster: A Human Exploration—Centenary Essays*; the editors of *South Atlantic Quarterly* for 'The Novels of E. M. Forster' by Richard Voorhees and 'E.M. Forster and T.E. Lawrence: A Friendship' by Jeffrey Meyers © 1954, 1970 Duke University Press; the editors of *Southern Review* for 'E.M. Forster and John Ruskin: The Ambivalent Connection' by Penelope Gay; the editors of *Soundings* for 'Self and Cosmos: Religion as Strategy and Exploration in the Novels of E.M. Forster' by Eugene Webb; the late Stephen Spender for his 'Personal Relations and Public Powers'; *The Spectator* for 'A Man's Man' by Colin Wilson and 'Old and Gay' by J.I.M. Stewart; the editors of *Studies in the Novel* for 'From Words to Things: Margaret's Progress in *Howards End*' by Douglass H. Thomson, 'The Noble Peasant in E.M. Forster's Fiction' by Jeanne E. Olson, and 'The Evolution of E.M. Forster's Narrator' by Jo M. Turk, © North Texas State University 1983, 1988, 1973 and reprinted by permission of the publisher; Miss O.M. Swinnerton for extracts from *Swinnerton: An Autobiography* and from *The Georgian Literary Scene: A Literary Panorama* by the late Frank Swinnerton; the editors of *Tennessee Studies in Literature* for 'E.M. Forster's Conception of the Critic' by F.P.W. McDowell; the editors of *Texas Studies in Language and Literature* for 'E.M. Forster and Howard Sturgis' by George H. Thomson and 'Forster's *The Longest Journey* and the Idea of Apprenticeship' by Thomas L. Jeffers, by permission of the authors and the University of Texas Press; the editors of *Texas Quarterly* for 'E. M. Forster's *Maurice*: A Summing Up' by C. Rising; the University of Georgia Press for '"Moments of Emergence and of a New Splendour": D.H. Lawrence and E.M. Forster in their Fiction' by F.P.W. McDowell, reprinted by permission of the publisher; *The Washington Post* for 'Hazards of an Honest Life' by Samuel Hynes; George Weidenfeld & Nicolson, Ltd, for the extract from *I, of All People: An Autobiography of Youth* by James Kirkup; Macmillan Press Ltd. for 'Encountering E.M. Forster' by James McConkey and 'Meetings Which are not Precisely Personal' by Eudora Welty; The Society of Authors as the literary representative of the estates of Virginia Woolf and John Middleton Murry; The Peters Fraser & Dunlop Group Ltd. for permission to reprint 'Review' by J.B. Priestley and 'Interpreters of Their Age' by Rebecca West; The Estate of Christopher Isherwood for 'Mr Forster Tidies Up'.

The editor is grateful to Messrs Akos Ersek and Raymond Gauthier for assistance, to Professor S.P. Rosenbaum for guidance, and to Japan Women's University, Tokyo, for travel and research funds.

Memories and Impressions

1
Independent, Cantabrigian, and a Bachelor

FRANK SWINNERTON

Forster, independent, Cantabrigian, and a bachelor, has never been discouraged by lack of means, by fear, or by the need to rattle his brains for ideas when those brains have been run dry by overtime. He has written only when and what he wanted to write; and if he has not wanted to write he has not done so. This has affected all his work, which has the grace and ease of an amateur's pleasure, as well as the lovely clarity derived from an intellect which all must admire.

It has at the same time affected his demeanour, so that he walks as if he were lost in a recalculation of change, or as if, far away, he heard the voice of Plato's Socrates twisting dogmatists into knots of self-contradiction. His head is consideringly cocked, his expression full of thoughtful melancholy, his eyes are fine, large, and full of intelligence. At a meeting he smiles faintly; his pale face is illumined; he is all the time going, although to the last, with pleasant constraint, he continues to ask questions; and if, going or coming or staying, one answers him carelessly he will ask more and more insistent questions until he is satisfied not only that he has understood but that his companion is upon the right lines. He has for this reason a nervous effect upon myself. I feel very bustling and bright, like an open-air doctor in a sickroom. And this is the more noteworthy because ordinarily I am not self-conscious, and only Sir John Squire affects me as strongly as he. In Squire's case, oddly enough, I do not feel bustling and brisk, but rather as I suppose an old lady to feel when some boisterous fellow flings open a window and she feels a draught.

SOURCE *Swinnerton: An Autobiography*, Garden City, New York: Doubleday, Doran, 1936; London: Hutchinson, 1937, pp. 292–4.

Forster detests insincerity. He is like his old friend and master, Lowes Dickinson, who once, being in London, spent the evening with a former associate. As they parted, the associate affably said: 'Well, now you've been here once you must come again.' Dickinson quietly but firmly answered: 'No. I shan't.' And he did not go again. In the same way, when Forster once had Robert Lynd to lunch at his club, another member, much attached to Lynd, in greeting the guest said: 'You ought to belong to this club'; and then, turning to Forster, added: 'Oughtn't he!' 'Why?' asked Forster.

The answer to that question, if I had made it, would have been 'Pure selfishness'; for Robert Lynd is a man so charming that most of his friends would wish him to be available at all times for conversation (there should be a provision in life by which really charming or stimulating people had not to run away to earn their bread). But in a sturdier community than ours the answer might have been a smack on the jaw.

Nobody in England, or certainly nobody in his own realm, which is that of thought, would wish to smack Forster on the jaw. His mind is too fine either to feel or to provoke resentment. The worst one would do with him would be to inflict a sentence of greater productiveness. And it would be enchanting to hear him in his own defence; for if he will only sit down, instead of edging forever to and fro, like one who does not know whether he would go or stay, his company can give extraordinary pleasure. He is never diffuse, but always slightly refrigerated; his mind, if bookish, is penetrated with light. Nor is it a crank mind, by which I mean one that begins with a bizarre fallacy and erects thereupon, in good faith, a monstrous series of exclusions; but is as cautious in fundamentals as it is in details. And if there is a curiously spinsterish quality in his sedateness, his calm malice, his determination not to be hurried past reason into a hurly burly of feeling, there is at the same time an integrity, a purity, a beauty, for which nobody with a spark of sensitiveness could fail to feel deep admiration. I admire him greatly, and I must upon no account be understood as belittling or ridiculing a man for whom I have sincere regard. But as a companion I think him wanting in reciprocative vivacity.

2
Meeting E. M.

FORREST REID

The Bracknels brought me neither fame nor fortune, but it brought me two friendships—with E. M. Forster and with Walter de la Mare—which have lasted from that day till this. E. M. I got to know shortly after the book was published. He had read it, written to me, and a little later, when he was over in Belfast, we met. The spot suggested by him, I find, was the Carlton Restaurant, and I was to recognize him by the clues of 'a lightish cloth cap, purple and white scarf, and great coat'. I think I should have recognized him without these clues, and I am quite sure that the meeting did not take place in the Carlton, but in my own house, for I have a distinct recollection that Pan and Nyx and Puss were present to welcome him, and that James joined us later. I can even remember James asking him how he thought of his plots—a perfectly natural and innocent question, yet one which no writer would ask, and which rarely elicits responsiveness. De la Mare, out of sheer good nature, would have risen to it determinedly, and the conversation would have become metaphysical. With E. M., who is not metaphysical, the conversation temporarily languished.

'*On goûte à faire des étiquettes une douceur qui se répand dans tout l'être,*' and at the time of E. M.'s visit I was mounting my prints of the Old Masters and arranging them according to schools and dates. There is some secret instinct by which collectors instantly recognize one another, and though E. M. was interested in the Old Masters, I divined at once that this interest would not be carried to the point of writing *étiquettes.* Therefore, though surrounding us, and fortunately concealed in boxes, drawers, and cupboards, there were at least half a dozen other collections, I made no allusion to them. To-day I should have no hesitation in mentioning even my collection of stamps. E. M. would not condemn it—condemnation is not in his line. All the same, when he presented me with a special copy of *A Passage to India,* it was accompanied by a note saying he was pandering to the basest

SOURCE *Private Road*, London: Faber and Faber, 1940, pp. 115–17.

of my passions, and, though not seriously, in a sense he meant it, meant that while it was quite harmless, this really was the most one could claim for it. But I had always had a foot firmly planted in the Philistine world: I enjoyed bridge, dog shows, playing in tournaments, book-hunting, print-collecting; and I had even been extremely happy at school, when, like Shelley and everybody else, I ought to have been miserable.

At the date of E. M.'s visit I must have been at work on *Following Darkness*, for when it was finished I dedicated it to him. I cannot remember anything in connection with the origin of this tale except that it was designed as a realistic study of adolescence, and though that to-day will appear a far from original idea, yet it was, I think, the first novel of its kind to be written in English.

3
Raising the Shield of Achilles

WILLIAM PLOMER

There was one visitor to Canning Place whose example and personality aroused an admiration and affection which were immediate and lasting. This was E. M. Forster. Although he had a perching-place in Brunswick Square and seemed to be on good terms with that group of friends and acquaintances whose similarities of social origin, outlook, interest, and habit, to say nothing of early influences at Cambridge, had caused them to be spoken of as 'Bloomsbury', he never seemed to me to be quite one of them. I saw him, and see him, as an independent.

During the years that followed I saw him often and got to know him better than any other writer of his generation. His liveliness, charm, insight, understanding, and unlikeness to anybody else made his friendship the rarest of treasures. In appearance he was the reverse of a dandy. Incurious fellow passengers in a train, seeing him in a cheap cloth cap and a scruffy waterproof, and carrying the sort of little bag that might have been carried in 1890 by the man who came to wind the clocks, might have thought him a dim provincial of settled habits and taken no more notice of him. When I said as much in an essay written during the Second World War for the French review *Fontaine*, published in Algiers, I sent him a copy for his approval or disapproval before it went to the printer. He showed it, or read it, to his mother, who said, 'There! You see what Mr Plomer says. How often have I told you, Morgan dear, that you really ought to brush your coat?'

Crouched in a corner of that imaginary railway compartment, he would have worn a kind of protective colouring, like an oak egger or a stick insect—or, rather, like a retired booking office clerk from a station on a branch line. It can never have been said of him, as it was said of another

SOURCE *At Home: Memoirs*, London: Cape, 1958, pp. 107–11.

literary man of my acquaintance, 'Nobody could possibly be as distinguished as X looks.' But one might have said that only an uncommonly distinguished man would have taken so little trouble to look like one. The moment he was engaged in conversation with anybody in the least congenial, or potentially congenial, he lighted up. First the vivacity of his mind became apparent, his openness to new impressions; then some comment, softly yet sharply striking exactly the right note, would seem to be striking the very note that nobody else would have touched upon at that moment; then gradually it might become guessable how his variety of experience and interests had combined with his originality of mind to form his powers of judgment. His is essentially a critical mind.

One did not think of him in terms of age. Recalling him in absence, one thought of certain quick darting movements and bird-like inclinations of the head; of the intense blue of his eye in certain lights, as if it had changed colour; of the sweetness of his smile; of the little puffs and spasms of laughter that rushed out beneath his untidy moustache; and of his real and not officious politeness, his winning considerateness to the shyest and least self-important persons in mixed gatherings. He often varied his surroundings and his company, but no man could be more tenacious of associations once cherished.

Years later, in a book about him, Lionel Trilling was to write that in a world at war E. M. Forster reminded us of a world of true order: 'he is one of those who raise the shield of Achilles, which is the moral intelligence of art, against the panic and emptiness which make their onset when the will is tired from its own excess.' Rose Macaulay, that staunch independent with an impassioned concern for the abolition of cant and for the proper use of words, listed, in her book about Forster, some of the things he believed in and disbelieved in. He believed, she said, in personal relationships, in individuality, in beauty, in affection, in liberty, and in democracy; he disbelieved in nationalism, empire, militarism, catchwords, Christianity, oligarchy, dictatorship, big business, schoolmasters, 'and a number of other things'. And Forster himself, in a pamphlet called *What I Believe*, provided his own explanations. It is a good thing that he did, because it must be said that words like 'beauty', 'liberty', and 'democracy' are elastic: they have been so abused by stretching that what they ought to describe may wrongly be assumed to have perished. The stretching process is not new. I have no note of the source of the following quotation, but it dates from 1799:

> Facts teach us, that *liberté* signifies the most horrible tyranny, silencing all law, and violating all property; that *égalité* signifies murdering sovereigns and the higher classes, and putting over the people men the most low, ignorant, and wicked, invested with power to insult, enslave, and drive them in flocks to be slaughtered, and placing them at a greater distance than there existed before between them and their superiors by birth and education. *Fraternité*, in France, signifies being a Frenchman; applied to other nations, it signifies,

> forcing on them a government, plundering their property, and taking their wives and daughters. *Philanthropie* is professing a general love to all mankind, and practising cruelty to every individual. *Philosophie* signifies the commission of every crime without remorse; the extinction of every sentiment religious or moral, of every generous and social feeling; the dissolution of every tie of kindred and affection; the annihilation of every quality which ornaments and distinguishes the gentleman, the scholar, and the man of taste; the banishment of chastity, modesty, sensibility, and decorum from the female sex.

Who, giving a moment's thought to what has been done in our own time in the name of 'democracy', could possibly support it or give it two cheers? E. M. Forster could. He found it less hateful than other contemporary forms of government; he credited it with the assumption that the individual is important, and that it takes all sorts to make a civilization; he found that it allows criticism, and some degree of liberty to the creative. But order, for him (it later appeared), was 'something evolved from within, not something imposed from without.' For him, yes, because he is an artist; but unfortunately what is called democracy tends more and more, like any other form of government, to impose what it calls order upon as many of the people as possible, as rigidly as possible, from without. It is a mark of E. M. Forster's energy and honesty that, instead of assuming an air of superiority and roosting more or less contentedly in the snug debris of liberalism, he has constantly tried to adjust himself to the phrases of the revolution through which he has lived, without deserting what he has believed to be true, and without relaxing that 'moral intelligence', without lowering that 'shield of Achilles'.

It is a commonplace that the artist, especially since the Romantic movement, has tended to be a solitary, an independent, an anarchist, or even a misanthrope. But the notion has become more and more accepted that it is now not only the artist's duty but his function to commit himself to public affairs. In the Canning Place days I should have been even less interested than I am now in theorizing on such a topic: but I do know that one of my main reasons for admiring E. M. Forster was that moral intelligence of the artist with which he had observed, felt, imagined, and embodied the relations between races in India. From the nature of my earliest life, I had been driven to observe inter-racial contacts and social incompatibilities, and, as I said in the preface to *Four Countries*, most of my own fiction reflects the age 'by isolating some crisis caused by a change of environment or by the sudden and sometimes startling confrontation of members of different races and classes'. It was, therefore, natural that I took special pleasure in being with him. Many of my closest friends have been uncomfortables, and of all my uncomfortable friends he has had, I think, the clearest, subtlest, deepest mind, the most generous understanding, and the most fruitfully revolutionary influence.

4
Encountering E. M. Forster

JAMES McCONKEY

Forster has been such an influence in my life that I really don't know where to begin. I understand that many people who visited Forster were readers of his novels who felt a closeness to him—a friendship—simply from reading the novels; they were responding to the accents of his voice as it is heard in his written work. I first felt Forster to be a friend in this way when I was a young man, and because of my affection for him I wanted to write a book about his fiction. After I did write such a book, I thought it time for me to sit down and write a book of my own, a novel that reflected my own values. I have that book at home in a desk drawer. It's a novel about a young man who's really quite nice, but who looks with detached irony on life; he's incapable of making commitments. He becomes entangled in a shoddy scheme and ultimately someone whom he loves dearly dies in a violent little episode as a consequence of his lack of commitment. Although he learns something from that death, he's still uncommitted as the novel ends. Forster wrote that novel before me—in *Where Angels Fear to Tread*—but so fully had I been under Forster's influence that I didn't even recognize my indebtedness.

There are many aspects of Forster that have influenced me, I think. I know in everything I've written there's some element of Forster. Actually my two favorite fiction writers of the past—of the immediate past—are Forster and Chekhov. I don't want to get into a discussion of what they have in common except to say that both of them judge human beings in reference to a spiritual totality that lies beyond human consciousness and can only be intuited now and then. A novel that I recently published, *The Tree House Confessions*, has its source in such an intuited moment of my own life. But

SOURCE 'Writers' Panel', *E. M. Forster: Centenary Revaluations*, eds Judith Scherer Herz and Robert K. Martin, London: Macmillan, 1982, pp. 295–8.

how do we know to what degree moments which we can loosely call mystical are the consequence of books we have read as well as events in our own lives? Augustine's great moment at Ostia and those other moments in which he felt that he was able to sense the divine light were prepared for by his reading of neo-Platonic documents; in his visions he was seeing in part that which he had learned from his very reading. The seed of my novel came from my own psyche and experiences, and yet I'm sure it was a consequence too of my reading of Forster and Chekhov—and Augustine.

I'd like to speak briefly of my one meeting with Forster. He wrote me a letter after my critical study had been published and said he had liked the book. He had some nice things to say about it, and he also pointed out some errors. I called Eleanor Lavish 'Lydia'; that's a typical enough scholarly error, isn't it? He said, in a postscript, '*Eleanor* Lavish, not Lydia, but she is too delighted to be included to mind.' In that same postscript he added he hoped we would meet some day. When I saw him at King's College he was alone for the summer. He'd had a heart attack. He'd bought a cake and made tea, using a faucet of his old-fashioned Victorian bathtub to fill the tea-kettle up. He wanted to be hospitable and kind, though I must have been a difficult guest. For when I climbed the steps and saw the faded letters of his name on the door, what immediately came to my mind was that reference in *The Longest Journey* to the 'grey ghost' of another name beyond Rickie Elliot's name on his Cambridge door. When Forster opened that door and I saw an elderly man who obviously had been quite ill, I burst into tears, which made it rather difficult for me to speak. I protested over and over again during that meeting that I had come not for any benefit that might accrue to me as a scholar or critic. I didn't care about that, I said. I had come just to tell him how much he had influenced my life—I said that so much I must have been a pest. He really wanted to talk, and, in a sense, I refused to listen. We had a long discussion during which I said some things that displeased him. Since I'd been living in Paris, he asked me if I preferred Paris to London. I knew what I was supposed to say, but I said 'yes'. He said he disliked Paris so much that on his trips to the South of France every year he took a big arc around it.

Toward the end of the discussion, he said something that embarrassed me so much that for years—before I came to understand it—I felt ashamed for him and myself. He said he'd made one major mistake as a young man. I said, 'What was it?' and he said, 'I trusted people too much', words that shocked me. The mistake I made was to think that his remark invalidated the purpose of my visit to see him, that it meant I could not develop a genuine personal relationship with him. I wouldn't meet the remark directly. Instead, to indicate that I understood its spiritual implications, I said, '*A Passage to India* reminds me of the later quarters of Beethoven.' He replied very frostily that he didn't like the later quartets of Beethoven, he liked the earlier ones.

Then he told me he was not writing any more but destroying manuscripts, and in my attempt to be impartial and not to intrude I said nothing about saving them. Toward the end of the discussion we were really far apart. I said I had to leave. He said he'd go down the steps with me. I said he didn't need to do that. (He was alone in King's College and the steps were worn and the cobblestones in the courtyard were quite difficult to get over, especially for a person who was elderly and unsteady on his feet.) Very acidly, he said, 'I owe it to you for your book.' We walked very slowly down the steps and across the courtyard and out the gate. As he stood next to the Victorian style pillar-box just beyond the gate, I said, 'I like that mail box very much.' I *did* like it, and felt a connection existed between it and Forster. He said, 'I like that pillar-box very much too', and then he smiled at me in such a warm way it seemed we might conceivably have embraced. I waved and he went back in.

5
Meetings Which are not Precisely Personal

EUDORA WELTY

In a way [my experience] is a sort of the obverse of Jim McConkey's because it is about a letter I got from E. M. Forster when I was a beginning writer. That is a meeting at a different point in life from when you met which was a real meeting. I had published a number of short stories but I wasn't known anywhere, and I received this letter one day where I lived in Jackson, Mississippi. It was written in New York City, and dated 28 April, 1947. I copied it off to bring:

> Dear Miss Welty:
> Finding myself in your country I feel I should like to give myself the pleasure of writing you a line and telling you how much I enjoy your work 'The Wide Net'. All the wild and lovely things it brings up have often been with me and delighted me. I am afraid that I am unlikely to have the good fortune of meeting you while I am over here since my itinerary keeps me to the North and to the West. Still there are meetings which are not precisely personal and I've had the advantage of one of these through you, and I would like to thank you for it.
>
> With kind regards and all good wishes.
> Yours sincerely, E. M. Forster.

Well, it was several moments before I was able to read the signature, partly it was his handwriting and partly it was my disbelief. The letter was kindness, undreamed-of kindness. It was also something that belongs to another realm, another kingdom in the sense of animal, vegetable or mineral kingdoms. It was response. It was what I knew Mr Forster meant me to receive from him. It had been received and had given pleasure. The letter carries some marks of tears and when I copied it off to bring to this conference my tears came back. This is the only time I've ever shared this

SOURCE 'Writers' Panel', *E. M. Forster: Centenary Revaluations*, eds Judith Scherer Herz and Robert K. Martin, London: Macmillan, 1982, pp. 298–9.

letter, mailed to me thirty-two years ago, because it seems appropriate that I should read it in this company, who well know the value it had for the young writer I was, and has for that writer today, and who can see it with me in its lasting and undimmed light. I thought that would fit in with what I was asked to do, to talk of what Forster had meant to me in my work.

I have tried to think of the other things he meant to me. He must surely have strengthened my recognition of place as a prime source of enlightenment in fiction. He gave me help, help not abstract, but directly useful toward identifying in place my own most trustworthy teacher. And he crystallized for me an instinctive belief that mystery in human relationships exists *per se,* that some relationships and that occasional human actions, perhaps of great import, may occur outside satisfactory explanations and still need to be taken into account. And I believe I've apprehended through Forster's novels something I would have otherwise missed about form. Out of itself a work may abide by, adhere to, a felt composition, a structure building itself or building upon itself. What mounts up is not so much the progress of events as the intensity of awareness of the events, the advance made by way of human revelation; that is the plot, an advance toward light. Indeed, in *Aspects of the Novel,* Forster suggested that the idea the novelist must cling to is not completion, not rounding off, but opening out. 'When the symphony is over we feel that the notes and tunes composing it have been liberated, they have found in the rhythm of the whole their individual freedom. Cannot the novel be like that?' Yes, I think it can. That is the real essence of what Forster has meant to me. I think he is so present to, so pervasive in, my understanding of experience that I can only be general about it, I can only say these fundamental things.

6
The Writing of *Billy Budd*

ERIC CROZIER

Through the last twenty years of his working life Herman Melville was a deputy inspector of customs on the New York waterfront—'mast-hemmed Manhattan,' he called it—checking ships' cargoes and passengers' baggage at four dollars a day. He retired at sixty-six and devoted his last years to *Billy Budd*. He began by writing a primitive ballad that is meant to be spoken by an able seaman awaiting execution, *Billy in the Darbies* (a slang term for fetters or handcuffs). This subject haunted him, not least because his cousin First Lieutenant Guert Gansevoort had been concerned in the notorious *Mackenzie* case of 1842, serving on a court-martial that, in peacetime, had condemned a popular young sailor and two shipmates to execution for suspected mutiny.

Melville added a preface to the ballad, telling how Billy had fallen victim to the insane malice of the ship's master-at-arms. He expanded this preface to a twelve thousand word story, *Baby Budd, Sailor.* Finally he rewrote the story at three times that length, *Billy Budd, Foretopman.* When he died in 1891, his desk contained 362 small sheets of yellow paper, covered with crossings out, rewritings, and insertions, some in pencil, some in ink, and with one chapter marked 'To be inserted.' There had never been time to make a fair copy—and who, anyway, would have wanted to read it?

His widow parceled the sheets up, and they lay forgotten for more than thirty years. In 1914 a magazine hailed *Moby Dick*, published so long ago as 1851, as 'the best sea-story ever written ... the one masterpiece of a tremendous genius.'[1] Melville's whaling classic was thus rescued from oblivion. Ten years later, in 1924, when a collected edition of his novels and tales appeared (this was first published, as *Moby Dick* had been, in London), *Billy Budd* was among them.

In 1927 E. M. Forster gave eight lectures at Cambridge on 'Aspects of the Novel': in these he discussed *Moby Dick* and *Billy Budd* as two 'difficult and

SOURCE *Opera Quarterly*, 4.3, 1986, pp. 11–27.

immensely important' examples of what he called 'prophecy' in fiction. (It was an article by Forster that, in 1941, aroused Britten's interest in the Suffolk poet George Crabbe, then virtually unknown, and his *The Borough*.)[2] Forster's Cambridge lectures, issued in book form,[3] directed the composer's attention to Melville—but *Billy Budd* did not become easily available until 1946, when it was first issued in England as a separate publication.[4] The editor was the poet William Plomer, a friend of Forster's, who in future years was to provide Britten with texts for four of his operas.

Melville had begun writing and rewriting this final tale when he was almost seventy. In 1948 Forster, also nearing seventy, fell into an acute depression: he felt useless and unwanted, afraid (according to his 'official' biographer, P. N. Furbank) lest 'he should lose the power to feel about people or take interest in them.'[5] About that time Britten was invited to compose an opera for the forthcoming 1951 Festival of Britain. He asked Forster to write the text. Forster thought himself insufficiently experienced in dramatic writing, so it was suggested that I might work with him. He had never collaborated with anyone; I was fortunate enough to have collaborated on most of Britten's early operas, first as stage director of *Peter Grimes* and *The Rape of Lucretia*, then as librettist for *Albert Herring* (which we dedicated to Forster) and other works.

Forster and I had one or two meetings to discuss the project. He was most enthusiastic, but hampered—as I was—by lack of a story. He wanted, he said, a *grand* opera (he was an ardent Wagnerian), not a chamber opera like those that Britten and I had, largely for economic reasons, been producing during the past three years.

One evening in mid-January 1949 my telephone rang, and Britten asked me to travel to Aldeburgh in Suffolk as quickly as I could. Forster was staying with him; they thought they had found the subject. I set off by bus and train next morning at first light and arrived when they were still at breakfast. They gave me some food and coffee, then they handed me a small black-jacketed volume—Plomer's 1946 edition of *Billy Budd*—and left me alone with it.

The moment I finished, they began to question me. They went on for the rest of the morning, through lunch, all afternoon. Clearly they wanted me to like the story as much as they did, but as a practical man of the theater I felt obliged to stress the enormous difficulties of the undertaking. 'They were too impatient to listen,' Furbank says in his biography of Forster, and 'Crozier overcame his doubts.'[6] It was not that simple: it will be seen later that I was not the only one with doubts.

During the afternoon Britten produced a writing pad, and we examined the story methodically. I still treasure three bits of paper, the sole written record of our first day's work. There are two pages in Britten's writing, one listing all the characters in the story, the second tabulating Melville's dramatic incidents. On the third piece of paper is a sketchy side view of a sailing ship, drawn by Britten, amplified by me, and annotated by Forster with place names—Main Deck, Quarter Deck, Captain's Cabin, and so on—to help us find our way around. We spent a long time that day and the next discussing the characters and their motivation, and one unexpected fact came to light. Most composers would have allotted the tenor role to the innocent young hero, Billy. Britten took it for granted that it would go to Melville's wise and thoughtful naval commander, Vere, who would be sung by Peter Pears. After that decision, it seemed a natural development that the action on board ship should be 'framed' by a prologue and epilogue of Vere as an elderly man looking back on the troubled days of his wartime command. In Melville's story he dies soon after Billy's execution, from wounds received in an encounter with a French warship. But for operatic purposes it seemed necessary for him to live on.

Forster liked this idea, and a week or so later, eager to try out his skills as a librettist, he wrote to me from Cambridge and enclosed the first draft of a possible opening speech, headed 'Scene 1. Vere as Chorus.'[7] The wording recalls his own precise and distinctive accents:

> I am an old man who has experienced much. I have been a man of action and fought for my King and Country at sea. I have also read books and studied and pondered and tried to fathom eternal truth.
>
> Much good has been shown to me and much evil. The evil has sometimes been absolute. And the good has never been perfect. There has always been some flaw in it, some defect, some imperfection in the divine image, some stammer in the divine speech, some fault in the angelic song. So that—I am an old man now—it seems to me that the Devil must have had his part in this make up of ours. God grant that it be a small part.
>
> On sea as on land that fight between good and evil continues. And my mind goes back to the summer of 1797, to the French wars, to the difficult and dangerous days after the Mutiny of the Nore, to the days when I, Edward Fairfax Vere, commanded the *Indomitable*.

At the bottom of this handwritten foolscap sheet, he has scribbled: 'N.B. In the story Vere dies soon after, but had better live on.' Britten was in Venice with Peter Pears at that time, recovering from an illness. I sent him a copy of the speech and wrote to thank Forster for his excellent beginning.

> I am naturally much pleased and relieved [he replied] to know that you think the opening monologue suitable. I am at the present more keen on the opera than anything else, and wish Ben was in England and all of us at work. Still, it is better he should be regaining his health, and I have just had a very satisfactory postcard from them both.
>
> I have been at the University Library this afternoon trying to find Barker's *Naval Sketches*. No luck. A few more illustrations like George Cruikshank's *Naval Flogging* might help us much.[8]

A week later (10 February 1949) he wrote again:

> I should have very much liked a talk with Ben before tangling myself up too

> much with the U.S.A. If he, you, and Peter were agreed to settle down to *Billy Budd* for the next three months or so, I should give up thoughts of leaving England. That opera is the most important bit of work which I see before me, and I would sacrifice much to it—certainly foreign travel.
>
> As far as I can see, it looks as if you and I will be joint librettists, but the enterprise is still nebulous, and I think we shall do well not to define yet. So far (which is not far) it has seemed to issue forth like a living being, without sponsors.

Britten's absence abroad gave us a month to investigate the background to Melville's story, collect books, and visit the National Maritime Museum at Greenwich. We also hoped to see Nelson's flagship, the *Victory*, at Portsmouth and inspect that 'fetid cockpit' in which the dying admiral 'had lingered for a few hours of anguish amid the horrors of darkness . . . while the shock of the broadsides made the whole frame of the vessel tremble.'[9]

Conditions in the British navy at the end of the eighteenth century were appalling, for during the ten years of war with France the number of seamen had multiplied more than eightfold, from 16,000 men in 1792 to 135,000 a decade later. This vast increase was obtained by impressment, by dragging men away from homes and families or seizing them from merchant ships. Nobody was safe from the armed gangs that roamed the country. When forcible recruitment proved inadequate, convicts were drafted straight from His Majesty's prisons to His Majesty's ships.

In the semidarkness and foul air of the lower decks, seamen were herded together like cattle. Fourteen inches was the space allowed for each man's hammock. In 1795 pay was increased for the army and the militia; in the navy it remained at the same rate as 150 years earlier. Shore leave was unknown: there would have been wholesale desertions. The food—salt beef, salt horse, salt pork, often years old—was monotonous and disgusting, and the lack of fresh vegetables even in harbor made scurvy a commonplace. On the *Victory* there was only one cooking stove for 850 men. The ship's surgeon of an ancient hulk at the Nore reported that 1,500 men had been crammed into a vessel built for half that number: 'I never was in a situation more replete with anxiety than the present, as Surgeon of the *Sandwich*.'[10]

Bad food, meager wages (paid six months in arrears to prevent desertions), savage discipline—these were endured. But the tyranny of the officers and the indifference of the admiralty to petitions or complaints finally became intolerable. 'It is almost impossible for us to put it down as cruel as it really is, with flogging and abusing above humanity,' one crew declared. 'Our usage is more like Turks than British seamen,' wrote another.[11] As the navy grew larger, and its crews came to include many landsmen, with a leaven of educated men, discontent became more general and more articulate. Grievances had gone unanswered year after year. Now it was time to act.

The crisis point came in 1779. Lord Bridport ordered the Channel Fleet to put to sea. Sixteen line-of-battle ships at Spithead and the Nore refused to obey. Their crews manned the shrouds and gave three cheers as the signal for mutiny. The revolt spread to Plymouth, the south of Ireland, the Cape of Good Hope. Soon all England was trembling to think that, in the midst of war with France, their navy was in open rebellion.

'To the Empire,' Melville wrote, 'the Mutiny was what a strike in the fire-brigade would be to London threatened by general arson.'[12] His account of naval life in 1797, though sometimes bookish, is vivid and exact: he based it on William James's *Naval History of Great Britain* and Robert Southey's *Life of Nelson* and the reminiscences of several Trafalgar veterans he had come across during his early days at sea. *Billy Budd* (Melville's only novel with a historical setting) takes place a month or two after the uprisings at Spithead and the Nore, when the *Indomitable*, a ship of seventy-four guns, is cruising down the English Channel with orders to join the Mediterranean Fleet.

On 2 March 1949 Forster and I met at Liverpool Street Station. We were excited, because at last we were on our way to Aldeburgh to begin work in earnest. Our visit coincided with a period of high tides that menaced the town with serious flooding. 'In the case of a high tide, resulting from a sudden shift of the wind to the North West after blowing for some days from the South, it is not unusual for the sea to beat over the greater part of the crag path,' a local surgeon had once recorded[13]—and Britten's house on the crag path at 4 Crabbe Street, directly facing the sea, was undoubtedly at risk. A detailed record of our busy Aldeburgh days exists in the form of letters that I wrote to Nancy Evans. None of these had been published before.[14] They begin the day after our arrival.

> 3 March 1949
>
> A fast and comfortable journey from London with Morgan [Forster], but once we arrived everything was in a state of confusion from the flood, and Ben was tired, depressed and strained from the worry of it and from having been up all the night before, in company with the whole of Aldeburgh, waiting for the sea to break through. Quite a lot of damage done, and more is threatened should there be another bad tide. Even 4 Crabbe Street may suddenly disappear.
>
> Next, to add to the confusion, Morgan is champing keen to work on *Billy*. We began this morning at 10.00, and it seems that all our days will be spent on the opera, which worries me because of other jobs and responsibilities that are on my mind. But I can't discourage Morgan's great enthusiasm or show myself unwilling: so there it is. . . .

Each morning during the next two weeks, as soon as breakfast was over, Britten went upstairs to his study to continue work on the *Spring Symphony*, which he was composing for first performance at Amsterdam in July; Forster and I went up to another room and settled down at either side of a coal fire. During our January visit I had typed out the working synopsis of an opera in five scenes, each subdivided into brief episodes. With this to guide us, we would begin our morning's work by carefully reading the relevant passage in Melville's text. Then we talked about it: we considered the characters and their motives; we checked any points of nautical procedure and life aboard ship that we did not understand (there were many of these, and our reference works proved invaluable). When we were satisfied, we drafted our own version of the episode. Sometimes one of us did this, sometimes both. I was mostly responsible for the technical scenes and the dialogues; Forster undertook 'the big slabs of narrative.' Afterward we would read our drafts aloud, comparing and criticizing them.

Midway through the morning there was a coffee break, when Britten came along to see what we had done. At lunch we discussed the problems we were encountering. After lunch we walked and talked for an hour or so, then back we went to our studies until dinnertime. Melville's short novel consists of twenty-six chapters, some little more than a page, one (the crucial trial scene) twelve times that length. By regular and concentrated work we managed in the course of what Forster subsequently described as 'sixteen remarkable *Billy Budd* days at Aldeburgh' (by my reckoning it was thirteen, 3 through 15 March), to draft the greater part of the libretto, some forty pages of typescript, leaving blanks for scenes needing further research.[15]

> We are immersed in *Billy Budd* [I wrote] like two Trappist monks. Morgan comes to my room straight after breakfast, we pull chairs as close to the fire as possible, and there we sit until lunch, endlessly discussing, suggesting, rejecting, and scribbling, in a welter of technical terms, as we try to imagine what life can have been like on a man-of-war. After two days we have sketched out the bones of the first scene, and it will take another week to finish all scenes. After that we must look for the answers to many questions before trying to write actual words. The collaboration seems to go well. Morgan is the careful, wise mind who will write most of the text and dialogue. I am the technician and will write what is needed in the way of shanties and songs, but there will not be many of those. Once our drudgery of the next week is over, the actual writing of the text will not take terribly long, for we are making clear what will need to be said, as we go along.
>
> Cold, dark, stormy weather at Aldeburgh, with the sea looking hungry and very near the house. March 15th is the next big tide and will show us what Crabbe Street must expect. On Monday, Anni [the Swiss maid] was marooned in the house and had to be rescued by car.
>
> 5[?] March 1949
>
> ... Eleven o'clock at night. I am writing this letter on the sofa, Morgan is making notes on *Billy* in the opposite armchair, Ben and Peter have gone to bed. It is bitterly cold (a S.E. wind is beating against the windows), and we have to hug the fire or freeze.
>
> Poor Ben is in a wretched state these days. Something is worrying him, spoiling his temper, jamming his work, and throwing his tummy out of gear. I can't make out what is the cause. Perhaps domestic changes—Anni going, and a new man-servant taking over; perhaps the symphony and its greater problems; even, I begin to suspect, that he does not really want to do *Billy* as

an opera but feels he cannot withdraw now that Morgan and I are so earnestly at work. It is not pleasant to see him harassed and miserable, and the wretchedness makes him at the same time a bit ashamed of himself and also defensive. Not at all like the normal, cheerful Ben.

The whole cause may be something I know nothing about, or simply that he is not properly well yet. It is worrying, though, and the long hours that Morgan and I are spending closeted together seem almost to make him a little jealous of our energy and interest, as though he is being neglected by us.

It will pass soon, I hope. Either he will solve his musical problem with the symphony, or he will get ill again and have to go back to his semi-invalidism. His present state is the horribly uncomfortable one of swinging between those two alternatives.

Morgan has put his papers away and is warming his behind at the fire, loath to plunge into the cold air of corridors and bedrooms. His age makes him feel the cold rather much, and the Aldeburgh air has a shivery bite to it.

I have just discovered what he was so busy about, over there in the armchair. He has been writing a draft of one of our first scenes (Billy's arrival on the man-of-war) to show Ben and me tomorrow, and for us to turn into libretto-form together. As it is so late we have left the warm sitting-room and gone to our respective bedrooms, where I want to write a little more to you, because in the daytime it is hardly possible to snatch a quiet half-hour between breakfast and post-time at 4.15 P.M.... It is very late, and I must put out my light, for the room has no curtains and the glare may keep Ben awake next door.

6 March 1949

My writing is whiskery because it is cold and my arm is trembling, but it is a beautiful day and I have hardly ever seen the sea look so alive with movement and sunlight. Crawling white waves tumbling over each other before an onshore wind.

I was right in my guess about Ben's wretchedness. He was going through a period of revulsion against *Billy Budd*, from a misunderstanding about the purpose of the story, and he wanted to give the whole thing up. But now he has come through and he sees that his feeling was muddled, and with that change everything has improved—health, temper, outlook, work on the symphony, and spirits.

Morgan and I have been working for the two hours since breakfast, and now he is making a draft of the scene we have been planning, on the other side of the table, while I write to you on this side. Occasionally he interrupts for advice on special points or asks for suggestions, and Ben has just been in for ten minutes to join us at elevenses, but he has gone back to his study to get on with his last movement, which is running well after weeks of doubt and indecision.

The next letter is undated but it belongs, I think, to the end of our first week:

The work goes surprisingly well at present, with great speed and ease, and Morgan and I have reached a state of agreement in which we can guess how the other's mind is working and save time by talking shorthand. Morgan is in charge of the drama, I am in command of the ship, and we share matters out between us. It is going to be a stupendous opera. Like *Grimes*—with a much better story, a fine libretto, and a classical shape. Morgan says he has no gift for the theater, but I am so thrilled by his mastery of drama and dialogue that I shall try to persuade him to write a play.

Forster had formerly written the texts for two local pageants. He brought one of these to our very first meeting in autumn 1948 as though to convince me (and perhaps himself) of his dramatic capacities. He had also written two plays, neither of which had been performed, but he did not tell me this.

14 March 1949

Ben has nearly finished the symphony; Morgan and I are rapidly nearing the end of the second act, and the third is only a short one; my head is stuffed with details of ships and sailing. When we began ten days ago, Morgan wrote and I provided technical fodder. Now we collaborate much more closely, and sometimes I write a whole scene myself or draft a scene to provide a skeleton for him to clothe. It is a fascinating experience, and I hear from Ben that he said the other day that I could have written the libretto alone, but he couldn't possibly have written it without me. Typically generous of him—he is a most kind man.

On 16 March our first intensive stint came to an end, and Forster left for Cambridge. The previous day I had written:

15 March 1949

We have come to a point where I must type the whole libretto so far as it has gone, which will be a day's work. Morgan insists, Ben tells me, that I shall be announced as joint-author with him. Isn't that splendid!

Highest tide today, but the wind is N.W.: so we are safe, and there is no flooding.

Britten had now completed the *Spring Symphony* and was turning his attention to *The Little Sweep.*[16] I had finished the libretto for this a month earlier, and it was to be staged at the forthcoming Aldeburgh Festival. Then a cable arrived from Forster, about a dispute he had had with Britten before leaving.

[?] March 1949

Here's a do! Morgan and Ben have been in violent argument about the authorship of the opera, and Morgan insists that my name should come before his, for the simple reason that C comes before F. He apparently thought about it all one night and came down beaming to breakfast with his firm decision. This morning comes his cable: 'Must regretfully insist on Eric first. Bob [Buckingham] and William [Plomer] agree with me.' He is immovable once he has made up his mind, and I don't know how to wheedle him. Nor does Ben. Oh dear...! It is important, because *Billy* is to be announced in the Press quite soon.

A week or so later, however, Forster relented.

8 April 1949

Many thanks for your welcome letters, dear Eric. You and Ben will be glad to know that I am going to be a good boy and consent to my name standing first.

> Francis Bennett [a close friend of his at Caius College] thus counselled also. Will Ben please now make the announcement, for I have already told two American little birds, and their twitterings will spread.
>
> We must manage Portsmouth after Easter. We shall discuss the opera's difficult end. Perhaps I am being deflected by Wagnerism from essential truth, but I do feel that the abortive mutiny might be an anti-climax, whereas Billy's last phrase [this is 'Starry Vere, God bless you!'—our more singable version of Melville's 'God bless Captain Vere!'], if Ben could get it into the air as he did the last phrase in *Lucretia*, might be very fine.

On leaving Aldeburgh, Forster had told me that he wanted to give me a present. At his coming-of-age, almost fifty years earlier, his aunt had made him a life member of the London Library, and he was now writing to the library to propose me for life membership too.

He was away in America during the second Aldeburgh Festival in June, but a note came for me on his return:

> 22 June 1949
>
> I have been back a day or two, and now get your welcome letter. I also hear from Ben that you have left the English Opera Group, but assume and trust you haven't left *Billy Budd* since without you I don't know how I should get on.

I had resigned from the English Opera Group in order to seek more profitable employment for the support of my first wife, two daughters (who were away at school), and myself. My total income was five hundred pounds a year; my expenditure was almost twice that amount. Forster and I shared the commissioning fee for *Billy Budd* equally: we received about eighty-two pounds each, one-sixth of the Arts Council fee, paid in two installments in September 1950 and December 1951 for work we had begun in January 1949. Britten and Forster were rich men; I was a poor one—yet my resignation from the English Opera Group caused a near-estrangement within Britten except in respect of *Billy Budd*. For that, he (like Forster) found me indispensable until the libretto should be completed. This is how I explained the situation to Nancy:

> 7 July 1949
> Burghclere, Newbury
>
> About Ben, darling ... I think he and you are right in believing such things cannot be settled by letter-writing. Either the affection and the will to work together are still there despite temporary difficulties, or they are not. We must accept the situation as it turns out to be, and if we cannot work together any longer, at least we can be grateful for the many productive and happy years we have shared until now.

Another letter followed a week later:

> It has always been a great strength and a potential weakness for the English Opera Group to be built entirely on Ben. Strength, because he is a genius; weakness, because by temperament he is inclined to form strong aversions against close friends and be unable to tolerate them thereafter. This is not

deliberate on his part: it just happens, and must be accepted.

He has sometimes told me, jokingly, that one day I would join the ranks of his 'corpses,' and I have always recognised that any ordinary person must outlive his usefulness to such a great creative artist. When that happens, the only thing is to accept it and not to make matters worse by clinging to a relationship that is outworn. I have known since early this year that Ben was done with me and that we could not work together again—not for some years, anyway.

But there is no reason why that failure should affect you as a singer. My function has changed in the last years from being a director to being a writer. Yours has not changed; it has developed, and will go on developing for many years yet; you have very much to give the Group, just as the Group has opportunities to give you. Perhaps, during the leisure of August, there may be a chance of talking with Ben in greater freedom, and the air may clear a bit.

In August 1949 Forster and I returned to Aldeburgh, he to stay at Britten's house, I to a small holiday home I had rented for my two young daughters, Blake and Joanna, and myself. Britten had been studying the first draft of our libretto, and now he wanted us to spend several weeks considering, revising, and simplifying the text. At this stage he assumed the dominance in the partnership and led our discussions. We met at his house each morning, but the rest of our days was devoted to Aldeburgh at its summer best.

14 August 1949

The weather is fine still and only one day has been too rough for bathing. This afternoon Ben and Peter gave a picnic-party on the beach for about a dozen children and various grown-ups. First we swam, then we ate, and then some of us went out in a fishing-boat. Aldeburgh looks charming from the sea, and I was astonished to realise that I had never seen it from there before.

15 August 1949

Picture Post wants to take photos of Ben and Morgan at work, and Tom Hopkinson the editor suggests I should write the article about them and the opera.[17] Kind of him. Ben and Morgan are keenly in favour, though Ben is afraid I shall minimise my own share in the collaboration. Really, the work goes very well. I believe it will be a terrific opera when finished. I had a pleasant talk with Ben this morning, and we were more relaxed than we have been for some time past and were warm and friendly to each other. He still seems to me tense, though: not specially in relation to me, but as though he were going through a prolonged internal crisis.

During this period of revision, Britten asked us for a big new chorus scene as a climax to the first act—one of the few occasions when we added anything not directly prompted by Melville. When the opera was reduced to its final two-act form, in 1960, almost nine years after the Covent Garden premiere of our original four-act version, that scene was dropped. Another of our revisions was to replace Melville's 'cracked Afterguardsman,' who incites Billy to mutiny, by the terror-stricken Novice. Apart from such structural changes as these, we went through each scene word by word, line by line, testing, strengthening, compressing. The bulk of our libretto was in prose, so a necessary task was to find occasion for lyrical episodes that would enable the composer's music to flower.

A letter I wrote in the third week of August depicts the unusual combination of domesticity, holiday making, and artistic endeavor that characterized those glorious weeks:

> I thought I would try the experiment of macaroni cheese for lunch and cooked it immediately after breakfast. While I was frantically stirring three pots on the cooker (with ten minutes to go, the beds to make, and a song to type out for Morgan and Ben), a small girl aged five popped her head through the window and said: 'Hallo! what are you doing?'—'I'm making macaroni cheese for lunch.'—'Oh!' said she in a loud voice: 'We HATE macaroni cheese!' But Blake and Joanna ate it: so all was well.... I have no news except of the domestic routine, daily work on *Billy Budd,* and taking the children to see the firework display last night. We did not go to Thorpeness. It was too far to walk at that late hour and Joanna does not like bangs. We walked up to north of the Wentworth Hotel and sat on the shingle until the wind grew cold and Joanna was almost asleep lying against me. Then home through the darkness with our eyes full of splendid rockets and Roman candles and Electric Fountains, to put two excited children to bed.
>
> I grow more and more fascinated by *Billy Budd* as an opera and could do with all the waking hours of every day to play my full part in the collaboration. I do not think there ever was a happier association than this one between Ben, Morgan and me. We are all thrilled by the work, we like each other, we respect each other's viewpoints, and yet we are so entirely different in our experience and gifts. When we have a good morning's work, the ideas that come seem to have a life of their own and to present themselves for testing by each of us in turn, and each one may add a little contribution to the subject under discussion, and gradually a whole scene is built up from hints that have been floating in the air among us. I do hope there will be more collaborations like this, for I feel confident that *Billy* as a whole will make all Ben's operas until now look like experiments leading to the first of his great mature works. It will be a tragedy if Morgan does not live long enough to write other works for him.

Forster was to live another twenty-one years, and although *Billy* remained his only experience of working with Britten, it did (says his biographer) provide exactly the stimulus he needed at a critical time and 'was the beginning for him of ten or so very contented and productive years.'[18] My own share in the collaboration inevitably became less close once I had typed out copies of the revised libretto, which had now grown from forty to fifty-seven pages. Forster and I kept in touch, but correspondence was a poor substitute for our intensive working sessions. Early in 1950 Britten began work upon the score and he invited Forster, then recovering from a serious operation, to convalesce at Aldeburgh. This was an excellent arrangement. Forster received the care and the attention and the affection that his condition demanded, and he could feel that he was making a valuable contribution to the work in progress.

At first, all went well. Later, however, the visitor began to meddle and to criticize at the vital growing point of the composer's creative process, a form of interference that, to an artist of Britten's extreme sensitivity, was intolerable. In November 1950 Britten and I went to Cambridge for a performance of *The Little Sweep*, the children's opera we had written. I was to be Forster's guest for the night at King's College, and Britten was to stay with Francis Bennett at Caius. We did not arrive at King's until a whole hour after the performance, because there was business to discuss with the conductor and we had walked back with him to his hotel; we found Forster huddled in his overcoat over a dying fire, glacial, disgusted, enraged, and inconsolable. To me, as his college guest, he was chilly but polite. To Britten, he was outrageous: he spoke to him like some low-class servant who deserved to be whipped. Then he stalked off into the night to his lodgings, a King Lear facing the oncoming storm with no Fool to keep him company.

At the time I could not understand the reason for this untypical behavior. Not until eight years after Forster's death, when I read volume 2 of Furbank's excellent biography, did I learn that Forster had taken offense with Britten some months before, feeling himself neglected, and had 'left Aldeburgh rather earlier than he had planned.'[19] A month after the Cambridge outburst, Britten came to see me, as I told Nancy:

> 9 December 1950
>
> Ben has received from Morgan a very deflating letter, full of sharply-pointed darts about *Billy*, and he is still not certain, after long discussion with Peter and with Erwin Stein, how much the criticisms are deserved. So before replying he wants to have a long talk with me and go through some of the music.
>
> It always distresses me to see Ben seriously worried, and I wish to goodness I could pour oil on the troubled waters. Another snag . . .! Morgan wants to go and stay at Aldeburgh for a time, and in the present state of affairs between them Ben feels that will be impossible—that he cannot have to consult and seek approval for every phrase he writes.
>
> Tensions between Sadler's Wells Opera and the Edinburgh Festival and the Arts Council also confuse the situation. Ben had told me of these but deliberately did not tell Morgan, in order not to disturb him any more just at present. But Morgan has heard from another source, and thinks Ben has been hiding things from him. . . . When such a misunderstanding begins between two great men, one feverishly busy, the other not busy enough, it is most difficult to bring them to a frank exchange of views and to tolerance of each other's personal need for trust and loyalty. My sympathies are with both—perhaps a little weighted on Ben's side because I have had experience of his problems and his particular methods of working. Morgan said himself, in our radio programme in August, what remarkable harmony there had been during our collaboration. But now—? A canker seems to have worked its way to the heart of things. What a terrible pity it is!

An effort had to be made to heal this rift and to stop Forster from making a bad situation worse. He strongly disliked Britten's music for Claggart's monologue, 'O beauty, o handsomeness, goodness!' and had written to tell him so in unusually selfish and arrogant words:

> It is my most important piece of writing and I did not, at my first hearing, feel it sufficiently important musically ... I want *passion*—love constricted, perverted, poisoned, but never the less *flowing* down its agonizing channel; a sexual discharge gone evil. Not soggy depression or growling remorse. I seemed turning from one musical discomfort to another, and was dissatisfied.[20]

It fell to me to warn him that more letters of this kind, with an artist as susceptible to criticism as Britten, might be disastrous. I wrote to Cambridge and received a reply characterized by the same warm spirit of friendship that had marked our whole association.

> I am most grateful for the hint about Claggart's monologue. I certainly won't mention it to Ben, and will go carefully if he mentions it to me. He took my still stronger representations about the Dirge in Scene 1 so easily that I did not realise that I was here touching him on the raw. It would as you say be lamentable if we came to mistrust each other's judgement, but I think he knows that (except in the two items above) I go with every note he has written. Your suggestion that he should postpone reconsidering the monologue until Act 3 is done is excellent. Thank you very much again.

This, so far as I know, settled the matter, and no further consideration was given to the idea of rewriting Claggart's aria. In a letter to 'Dearest Ben' after the Covent Garden premiere (1 December 1951), Forster talks of the opera's creation as having been an outstanding event and says he is 'proud and happy to have been in it and to think of it.... This opera is my Nunc Dimittis, in that it dismisses me peacefully, and convinces me I have achieved.'[21] I wrote to Britten almost the same day, telling him, 'The impact of *Billy Budd* seems to be really tremendous. *Grimes* made enough of a stir, but this new achievement of yours has fired the imaginations of an astonishing number of people. I liked particularly the remark made by K. [Sir Kenneth, later Lord] Clark to Morgan that "it is one of the great masterpieces that change human conduct."' Then, oddly enough in retrospect, I urged Britten to consider a new venture with Forster: 'Everyone who loves opera wants you and Morgan to work together again. Since I have been privileged to collaborate with you both, I feel it will not seem like interference on my part if I implore you to forget the pains of the past eighteen months in the glory of the achievement.'

But that was not to be. Our only remaining collaboration was a meeting nearly nine years later, when I traveled from Fishguard in Wales, where I was on holiday, to Aldeburgh to spend two days with Britten and Forster condensing the opera's four acts into two.

> What a happiness [Forster wrote to me after this visit] to get your sympathetic and affectionate letter, and how happy am I, too, that we have met again after so many years, and at Aldeburgh. What a pleasure that work was for the three of us! Ben has probably sent you, as he has me, his final recension of the

libretto. I think he has recensed it—if there is such a word—very well.

Our 'recensed' two-act version had its first performance as a BBC broadcast in 1960, but it did not reach the stage until 1964, when Sir Georg Solti conducted it at Covent Garden with an entirely new cast of principals. Forster was by then in his eighty-sixth year, but he was not too old to issue a smart rebuke to the music critic of the *Times*:

> Dear Sir,
>
> I have read with interest and approval your article on *An Opera of Good and Evil* in this morning's *Times*, but wish you could have managed to squeeze in a reference to Eric Crozier and myself. We did the Libretto. We worked on it in Britten's house for several weeks. We might reasonably be credited with having helped to interpret his intentions and his conception of Melville's intentions.
>
> Yours faithfully,
> E. M. Forster[22]

That precise, slightly waspish, amused, academic tone shows one side of Forster: another side is shown by the affectionate letter he wrote me that same day, which can very well serve as his (and my) valediction.

> What a marvellous evening! I can't get over it, in the happy sense of that phrase. To be in that box with you, Ben and Peter, and Nancy not far away. The food together beforehand, and the residence with you on the stage afterwards [we had taken a curtain call]—it has been like the best of dreams. With love and remembrances of all the agreeable—and it would now seem successful!—times that we have spent together.
>
> Morgan

Notes

Note: This is a revised and expanded version of an article that I wrote for the program of the San Francisco Opera Company's revival of *Billy Budd* in the fall of 1985.

1 Archibald MacMechan, 'The Best Sea Story Ever Written,' 1914.

2 E. M. Forster, 'George Crabbe: The Poet and the Man,' *The Listener* 25 (29 May 1941): 769–70.

3 E. M. Forster, *Aspects of the Novel* (London: Edward Arnold, 1927; Pocket edition, 1949), pp. 116–36.

4 Herman Melville, *Billy Budd, Foretopman*, edited and with an introduction by William Plomer (London: John Lehmann, 1946).

5 P. N. Furbank, *E. M. Forster: A Life* (London: Secker and Warburg, 1978), 2, p. 282.

6 *Ibid.*, p. 283.

7 This manuscript is in my possession. The copyright of the final published version belongs to Boosey and Hawkes Music Publishers, London and New York. The 'three bits of paper' referred to above are on permanent loan to the Britten-Pears Library, Aldeburgh, Suffolk.

8 All letters from E. M. Forster to me are in the present ownership of the Britten-Pears Library and are copyright © 1986 The Provost and Fellows of King's College, Cambridge. They are here reproduced by courtesy of the Trustees of the Britten-Pears Library, of King's College, Cambridge, and of the Society of Authors as the literary representative of the E. M. Forster Estate.

9 *Encyclopaedia Brittanica*, 11th edition, s.v. Nelson, Horatio, Viscount.

10 G. E. Manwaring and Bonamy Dobrée, *The Floating Republic* (London, 1935).
11 *Ibid.*
12 Melville, *Billy Budd, Foretopman*, p. 29.
13 Nicholas Fenwick Hele, *Notes or Jottings about Aldeburgh, Suffolk* (Ipswich, Suffolk: S. and W. J. King, 1890), p. 2.
14 These letters are in the possession of Nancy Evans and myself.
15 My typescripts of the various drafts of the libretto are on permanent loan to the Britten-Pears Library.
16 This short opera formed part of our 'entertainment for young people,' first staged at Aldeburgh on 14 June 1949.
17 My article was subsequently published as 'An Opera Team Gets to Work' in *Picture Post* (London), 15 October 1949.
18 Furbank, *E. M. Forster*, 2, p. 283.
19 *Ibid.*, p. 285.
20 Quoted in *ibid.*, pp. 285–86.
21 *Selected Letters of E. M. Forster: Volume 2 (1921–1970)*, eds Mary Lago and P. N. Furbank (London: Collins, 1985), p. 246.
22 Forster sent me a copy of his letter to *The Times* on 12 January 1964, saying, 'The enclosed will amuse and might please you. Let me have the scrawl back some time.'

7
E. M. Forster

ROBERT GIROUX

One spring day in 1947, while I was working at my desk through lunchtime, the receptionist rang my phone. For seven years I had been an editor at Harcourt, Brace and Company—located at that time at Madison Avenue and Forty-sixth Street, opposite the old Ritz Carlton—and I had just been named editor-in-chief.

'Could you see a Mr Forster?' the receptionist wanted to know. 'He's asked for Mr Brace, who is out to lunch.'

'Forster', I repeated. 'What's his first name?'

'He says it's Edward Morgan, and he's just arrived from England.'

The author of *A Passage to India*, a novel the firm had published twenty-three years earlier, had arrived on our doorstep. Mr Brace had said nothing about an impending visit from the novelist and, obviously, was not expecting his arrival. Having read Lionel Trilling's study in the New Directions series, I knew that Forster, who was almost seventy, had never visited America. There was also a recent newspaper item about a symposium on music scheduled at Harvard in May—it was now 14 April—to which Forster had rather surprisingly been invited as a principal speaker.

I hurried out to the reception room to find an unprepossessing man, about six feet tall, with a gray mustache and wispy hair, wearing steel-rimmed glasses and a rumpled gray suit. He had a large forehead, long nose, and shy chin. He wore no hat and had a light blue knapsack slung over his shoulders. His manner was friendly and genial, and he seemed younger than his years.

'I'm sorry to have missed Mr Brace', he said. 'I arrived by plane only this morning and had no time to call for an appointment.'

I asked if he were free for lunch. Mr Brace might be back by the time we returned. 'What a nice idea!' he said. We went to the Hotel Marguery on Park Avenue. It was a sunny day and they sat us outdoors under a canopy.

SOURCE *Yale Review*, 76.3 (1987), pp. 334–40.

Forster told me he was staying with friends in New York. 'There are so many locks on the doors! Do people feel unsafe here?' I admitted most people had doors with at least two locks, as I did. He saw me eyeing his knapsack, which apparently he hadn't removed since leaving England. 'The best way to travel', he said. 'No worry on the plane about baggage. It contains everything I need—clean linen, toothbrush, and a couple of Penguins. And it's comfortable; I'd forgotten I still had it on.' At that moment a train rumbled noisily through the underground tunnels on its way into Grand Central Station. Alarmed, he looked up and almost hopefully asked, 'Earthquake?' He announced he was going west to see the Grand Canyon after his Harvard lecture. Patting his breast pocket, he said, 'I have my ticket right here, and I intend to ride down to the bottom. What do you think of the Grand Canyon?' I had to admit I'd never seen it.

Back at Mr Brace's office, he told us he was preparing a new book of essays, which would be delivered in a year or so. It was eleven years since he had last published a book, *Abinger Harvest*, in 1936. The new essays, entitled *Two Cheers for Democracy*, went to press in 1951. One essay contained the memorable words, 'I believe in personal relationships. . . . I hate the idea of causes, and if I had to choose between betraying my country and betraying my friend I hope I should have the guts to betray my country.' The book also included his lecture at Harvard, 'The Raison d'Etre of Criticism in the Arts', which touched on music only lightly. His conclusion about criticism was, as he put it, 'unfavourable . . . nor have I succeeded in finding that it has given substantial help to artists'. He reinforced this view on another occasion in conversation: 'All I want from critics is praise.'

When Mr Brace proposed a cocktail party in his honor at the Ritz Carlton, he was visibly pleased. A large crowd, including book critics, publishing people, and authors like Katherine Anne Porter, Robert Lowell, and Jean Stafford, attended. Forster had requested only one guest, Lionel Trilling. When I introduced them, Forster's greeting was warm: 'So this is Mr Trilling. At last I've met the man who made me famous.'

Having agreed to a talk under auspices that concealed, as Trilling soon discovered, a Communist Party front, Forster cancelled because, he said, he disliked deception. 'If they called themselves Communist, I would have accepted. I cannot stand this pretense.' Perhaps he was remembering his experience in Paris in 1935 at the International Congress of Writers, which was under tight Communist control. Katherine Anne Porter, a delegate, wrote that Forster on that occasion was at first almost unintelligible because he paid no attention to the microphone, until at last 'there sounded into the hall clearly but wistfully a complete sentence: "I DO believe in liberty!"' The polite applause that followed, she wrote, 'covered the antics of that part of the audience near me; a whole pantomime of malignant ridicule, meaning that Mr Forster and all his kind were already as extinct as the dodo.'

With Trilling's help, I arranged for him to speak to some students at a Long Island college, where to his delight the lecture took place on a basketball court. He talked informally, mostly about his novels, and it was well received. In the question period he was relaxed and responsive until one Marxist student gave a speech while pretending to ask a question: 'Don't you agree, Mr Forster, that under our corrupt and unjust capitalistic system . . .' and so on and on and on. Forster's head sank deeper and deeper on his chest as the speaker droned on, and at the end when he repeated 'Don't you agree?' Forster raised his head, noisily cleared his throat, and said, 'Next question?'

Afterward a rather striking and very thin woman came up and introduced herself as Martha Graham, saying she was a great admirer of his work. We offered her a lift back to Manhattan in our car, and on the drive back he enjoyed her flat Midwest accent and dry sense of humor.

A year or so after Forster's return to England, Spencer Scott, the new president of the publishing firm, came into my office looking upset. He threw a handwritten letter on my desk. I recognized at once the King's College stationery used by Forster, as well as his spidery mandarin handwriting. (This was in the days before instant reproduction and Xerox, but I remember the contents verbatim.)

> Dear Mr Scott: I do not know who you are. I have been accustomed to dealing with Mr Donald Brace over the years about my books, and more recently with Mr Robert Giroux. I must confess your suggestion that I accept a reduction in royalties on *A Passage to India* from fifteen percent to ten percent is unacceptable. My novel has been on the firm's list for twenty-five years, and surely the original cost of publication has long since been fully recouped. If the firm has kept it in print, I suspect it is owing to a demand for copies from bookstores and readers. If you are indeed proposing that I take my book elsewhere, I shall reluctantly do so. I will not, however, agree to reduced royalties at this late date. Yours faithfully, E. M. Forster.

I was stunned by Scott's affront to an old and valued author. His sheepish explanation for writing Forster was the high cost of reprinting back-list titles in limited quantities, but this in no way excused either his failure to consult the editor beforehand or the ineptness of his approach. (The late Spencer Scott was capable of shocking an editor out of his shoes, as I learned on several occasions. He had become president because of an unhappy falling-out between Alfred Harcourt and Donald Brace. Scott once seriously asked me, 'Why don't we publish best-sellers only?' When he read the galleys of George Orwell's extraordinary new book, *Nineteen Eighty-Four,* he came into my office shaking his head gloomily. 'I'm worried about this book, Bob. Love and rats don't mix.') To solve the Forster crisis, I rushed a letter off to England, apologizing for a 'misunderstanding', and Forster accepted this explanation without demurral.

In 1953 he sent me the manuscript of *The Hill of Devi,* his nonfiction book about India and his years of serving as private secretary to the tragic maharajah of Dewas Senior. He revealed that in 1921 he had brought with him to India the opening chapters of *A Passage to India*, and then found himself unable to write. The pages 'seemed to wilt and go dead and I could do nothing with them. I used to look at them of an evening in my room at Dewas, and felt only distaste and despair.' It was not until he got back to England that he was able to resume and, with the encouragement of Leonard Woolf, to finish the novel.

During Forster's second and last visit to America, I learned that he was collaborating with Benjamin Britten on an opera based on Melville's *Billy Budd*. Britten had begun composing the score, and Forster and Eric Crozier were working on the libretto. I told Forster that the very first person to read through the manuscript of *Billy Budd* was Raymond Weaver, Melville's first biographer, who had been my teacher at college. Forster was incredulous: 'But I thought Constable published the book during Melville's lifetime!' No, I explained, the author's granddaughter, Mrs Eleanor Metcalf, had shown Weaver the posthumous papers in Melville's study at 104 East Twenty-sixth Street, the very room in which the author had finished writing *Billy Budd* shortly before his death in 1891. Constable *had* published the first edition, but it came out in 1924. 'Is the house in which Melville died still standing?' he asked. I said I doubted it very much, but I wasn't absolutely sure. 'Can we take a taxi to 104 East Twenty-sixth Street and find out?' He was greatly excited at the possibility of finding Melville's house, but of course when we got there, the original site and those adjoining it had been replaced by a large building. As we walked west to Lexington Avenue, he spotted the high, curved, green copper roof of the armory across the street, and pointed to it. 'Doesn't it look very much like a whale? Melville's spirit still lives on this street!' *Billy Budd* had its successful operatic premiere at Covent Garden in 1951, and soon entered the repertory of major opera houses throughout the world.

Before I had yet visited London, I mentioned that because of my Elizabethan studies my image of the city was no doubt obsolete: it was based on primitive engravings showing old London bridge covered with houses, and the sites of the theaters in Southwark. He might have found this comical, but very seriously he replied: 'Yes, of course. Be sure, when you come to London, to visit the spot along the Thames where the wagon tracks that went onto old London bridge are still visible, cut deeply into the earth.' I found the spot not far from Saint Mary Woolnoth on my first visit, located much lower than the elevations of the modern bridges. Of all my English friends, including writers and Shakespeare scholars, Forster alone told me about this memorable vestige of a great era.

The governors of Cambridge University had made Forster an honorary fellow in residence at King's College in 1946. His room was located on the first staircase of the front court of King's. Entering the court's elegant doorway and ascending the ancient stone stairway, one found his room marked by a dirty old wooden coal bin standing outside, with the name 'Forster' painted in white letters. He occupied a spacious, high-ceilinged room with tall Victorian-gothic windows. There was a grandfather clock in one corner next to a window, an upright piano beside it, and a print of Picasso's *Boy Leading a Horse* over a doorway. The room held many bookcases, heavy and handsome Victorian ones as well as plain modern shelving, and in the center was a free-standing mahogany bookcase that had belonged to his grandfather.

Once when I called at King's during a publishing trip to London, he had a visitor staying with him, whose name I did not catch. It was nearing election time in the United States, and Forster was greatly concerned that Douglas MacArthur, whom he feared and detested, would be elected president. I assured him emphatically that the general would never be nominated, let alone elected, and he seemed convinced. Later I realized that the visitor, who had scarcely opened his mouth, was J. R. Ackerley, editor of the *Listener* and a writer whose books I admired. When I called another time, I found Forster sitting in his favorite armchair, with his leg in a cast. When I asked what had happened, he replied: 'Slipped in a belfry!' He had been visiting Benjamin Britten in Aldeburgh and while climbing up to the belfry of the parish church, he had broken his ankle. He now insisted that we take a walk across the campus. He supported his weight on the metal base of the cast, and used a cane. I held back when we got outside, because he started to cut across the carpetlike lawn around which his front court and the King's Chapel were placed but he called out, 'Come along—privilege of an honorary fellow and his guests!' Centuries of care and nurture had created a very soft carpet for the fellow-in-a-cast and his guest.

In London one day he asked me to accompany him to a memorial service for Desmond MacCarthy at St Martin's-in-the-Fields. The hymns included William Blake's beautiful lines:

And did those feet in ancient time
Walk upon England's mountains green?
And was the holy Lamb of God
On England's pleasant pastures seen?

. . . . . .

I will not cease from Mental Fight,
Nor shall my Sword sleep in my hand
Till we have built Jerusalem
In England's green & pleasant land.

Afterward Forster told me something I'd never known, that these verses served as an official anthem of the Labour Party. It is surely the most distinguished poem ever used by or for a political party.

Edward Morgan Forster died at the great age of ninety-one in 1970.

Though I knew him only in the last years of his life, I consider myself fortunate to have been associated professionally with this remarkable man. The best obituary of him was written by J. R. Ackerley, who preceded him in death by three years. It appeared in the *Observer*, where Ackerley, prior to his own death, had deposited this personal testimony:

> I would say that in so far as it is possible for any human being to be both wise and worldly wise, to be selfless in any material sense, to have no envy, jealousy, vanity, conceit, to contain no malice, no hatred (though he had anger), to be always reliable, considerate, generous, never cheap—Morgan came as close to that as can be got.

8
At Joe Ackerley's

JAMES KIRKUP

I first met William Plomer, John Morris and E. M. Forster in Ackerley's flat. I think Joe had convoked them all to give me the once-over, for in those days I was even more of a curiosity than I am now. They were all reserved at first, but Forster and Morris soon loosened up. However, William remained almost completely silent, and what I remember best is his immobility. . . .

I remember the simple kindliness and friendliness of all these people towards me—a poor, unknown, struggling poet. But there was in Forster something that transcended all this: his small, rather stout, homely figure and plain, open face glowed with gentle good-will and joy. I think I have never met anyone who gave me such an impression of deep, quiet happiness and inexhaustible patience and sympathy.

Despite the constant barkings of Queenie, Morgan and I had a long conversation about all kinds of things—about the great influences on his own work, Jane Austen, Samuel Butler and Matthew Arnold, about animals and food and drink, about modern poetry, about sport and clothes and the theatre. We also talked about our mothers—for Morgan was ever as devoted to his mother as I was to mine. This was a great common bond between us. Then we started talking about the nature of friendship, a subject on which he was an expert, because he had devoted friends of all kinds—from labourers and farmers and policemen to university students, Indian scholars and great composers like Benjamin Britten. Indeed, to the very end, Morgan's most devoted friend was an ex-policeman, Bob Buckingham. In the Prefatory Note to *Abinger Harvest*, tribute is paid to his policeman friend along with Ackerley, Plomer and Isherwood.

It was his utter lack of class-consciousness and conceit that attracted me to Morgan, and allowed him, the leading English man of letters, to talk to me as an equal. Our talk about friendship was quite un-solemn and

SOURCE *I, of all People: An Autobiography of Youth* (London: Weidenfeld and Nicolson, 1988), pp. 198–200.

unpompous. But I recall he told me that only in a true democracy could friendship between men flourish in freedom. This was an important statement. Forster, like myself, did not think very highly of democracy, which is why he called his second collection of essays *Two Cheers for Democracy*, saying: 'Two cheers are quite enough: there is no occasion to give three. Only Love the Beloved Republic deserves that.' To Morgan, 'Love the Beloved Republic', was part of the Greek ideal he had inherited from Goldsworthy Lowes Dickinson, an ideal republic of loving friends far removed from the ordinary crude popular concept of homosexual relations.

On that first meeting, he made one of those spontaneous gestures that in Morgan amounted almost to genius. He had just come back from a weekend in the country, and had brought with him half a dozen fresh farm eggs. At that time, eggs were still rationed, and each person received only about one egg a month—usually a stale egg. So fresh eggs were almost as precious as gold. As he was leaving, Morgan—who at times looked rather like a fussy little brown hen himself—started to give an amusing imitation of a hen cackling after laying an egg. Then, with a smile and a hug, he presented me with one of his precious eggs, wrapped in a page of *The New Statesman*.

I was overcome not so much by the priceless gift of a fresh egg as by the symbolism of this act of perfect grace and loving friendship. With the gift of that egg, I felt Morgan had offered me not only his friendship, but a promise of poetic fertility. I did not eat the egg, but kept it carefully packed in a special little box for many years, until, in one of my numerous removals from one dismal lodging to another, it was broken. Strangely enough, the smashed egg had no bad odour, but smelt curiously sweet and wholesome. I thought the end of the world had come when that egg broke. Years later, I reminded Morgan about his gift, and he remembered our first meeting perfectly, saying: 'I remember you were wearing white socks. When you crossed your left leg on your right knee, you revealed a few inches of suntanned shin above the top of your sock.' It was this kind of detail, seen with the constantly recording eye of the born writer, that Morgan loved to remember when talking about his friends.

9

Some Reminiscences of E. M. Forster

MAY BUCKINGHAM

I first met Morgan in his flat in Brunswick Square in 1931 and was with him when he died in our house in Coventry in 1970.

Over the years our relationship changed and developed, passing through many stormy passages to a close, loving understanding.

To him I owe a great debt of gratitude. For his widening of horizons, by meeting his friends, by travel, but mostly by his talk.

I am by nature bossy, as he claimed all women are, especially nurses. He helped me to realise this and try to be less so. I was then a 23 year-old night sister in a maternity hospital knowing almost nothing outside nursing.

I now know that he was in love with Robert and therefore critical and jealous of me and our early years were very stormy, mostly because he had not the faintest idea of the pattern of our lives and was determined that Robert should not be engulfed in domesticity.

Over the years he changed us both and he and I came to love one another, able to share the joys and sorrows that came.

Our son had the names Robert Morgan and his eldest son Clive Morgan and this meant a lot to Morgan. The Battersea Rise nursery table that he inherited and wrote about he left to Clive because he liked to think how nice it would be for his children to sit at as Marianne had. The continuity pleased him however vague it may seem to others.

We were gently guided and educated by loans and gifts of books. When his Mother died in 1945 I feel that in some ways I took her place. He always came to stay with us whenever he was unwell from then on and always spent his birthday with us. His birthday was very important to him, partly I think because it fell on January 1st. He never wanted a large party, he only wanted

SOURCE *E. M. Forster: A Human Exploration: Centenary Essays*, eds G.K. Das and J.B. Beer, London: Macmillan; New York: New York University Press, 1979, pp. 183–5.

specially loved friends. When we lived in London this always included Florence Barger and Joe Ackerley. We all signed his birthday book which had been made by the children at Abinger Hammer school, signed by each child and given him when he left West Hackhurst. Later, when we were in Coventry our grandsons before they could write made their mark in it. He also made up his diary on New Year's Eve.

Because of Robert's work we had to move to Coventry in 1952 which greatly upset both Morgan and I. He never did get to like the city but I did. It was not as convenient for him to get to. The cross-country train journey from Cambridge is uncomfortable and difficult. There still is not a concert hall and at that time the only theatre never put on plays.

He visited frequently and as time went on had to stay for quite long periods when some structural alterations were being made in King's and his rooms were in danger of collapse.

From 1955 he felt he ought not to travel abroad alone and we went with him, mostly touring in France, always going to St-Rémy in Provence to visit Charles Mauron. Twice we went to Greece with the Hellenic Society. He never missed an expedition ashore. In 1958 he insisted upon climbing to the stadium at Delphi because he had recently read an ode by Pindar about it. He always did his homework for these holidays, knew where he wanted to go and what he wanted to see. He was an excellent map-reader, keeping to minor roads and finding us simple accommodation.

After 1965 his health was failing, so we didn't go abroad again but continued to go to the Aldeburgh Festival where he could meet so many friends.

He had many young friends, and was not critical of the young; he declared that the elders had said much the same things about his generation, criticising their clothes and behaviour, and said that it is not easy to be young now, the world is too complex.

The simplest machine defeated him. It took years to persuade him to have an electric gramophone and he had the greatest difficulty with tin openers, partly because of lack of strength. We were always buying him new ones to try.

When in Coventry he insisted upon our going for a walk each day, as had been his habit all through his life. Only ice stopped him, but as we couldn't go far afield it meant going every day through the same monotonous suburban streets.

He never complained, said how lucky he had been, especially in his friends. He played the gramophone a great deal, mostly Beethoven, Bach, Brahams, Mozart and Haydn, waiting for Robert to come home. I read to him when his sight deteriorated, and wrote his letters. It must have been especially hard for him whose whole life had been reading and writing, but he insisted that he was so lucky to have us to be with and King's to go to when fit enough.

We were pleased when any friends could come to help amuse him and there were several who came frequently.

He often said that he had lived too long, was aware of failing faculties. We often discussed death, especially after the death of our son, deciding there was no reason to fear it and that under certain circumstances it was to be welcomed.

Because he was president of the Cambridge Humanist Society he didn't want any religious ceremony at all, not even a memorial service, so there was a concert in Hall at King's. He did greatly care for the chapel though; it just was that he felt he must not let the Humanists down.

On 27th May 1970 we went to Cambridge to get him for the last time. He had been unable to get up from the table in Hall and was assisted to his rooms. With help he had been able to get up and potter in his room but a day or two later he collapsed and crawled to the door for help. He never walked again but his mind was perfectly clear and he was cheerful. The young resident artist Mark Lancaster helped Robert to carry him down 'A' staircase to the car and we managed to carry him up to bed in Coventry laughing and joking. Usually when ill he had a bed downstairs but he asked to be taken up to the bedroom.

On the 30th our very dear friends Audrey and Eric Fletcher came unexpectedly and stopped to supper. It became a jolly party, we took our coffee up to his room.

That was the last time he fed himself. Next morning he was weaker and this progressed each day.

On Sunday June 7th he died at 2.40 a.m. His ashes mingle with Robert's in a rose bed at the crematorium overlooking Warwick University.

So ended a long life which has enriched mine so.

10
E. M. Forster

V. S. PRITCHETT

'May I never resemble M. de Lesseps', E. M. Forster wrote when he looked at the famous statue by the Suez Canal. 'May no achievement upon an imposing scale be mine.' For forty odd years he was silent as a novelist—and once or twice said, with his usual modesty, that he had forgotten how to write novels—but in novelising his say against Imperialism, he exhausted what he would have said against modern totalitarianism. *A Passage to India* prolongs its significance in Africa and the Deep South. The fact is that he imposed by interposing.

The strength of Forster lay in this startling power of speaking in a natural private voice in public places. The 'two cheers'; the remark, almost casual, that 'the heart signs no documents'; the belief 'in an aristocracy of the sensitive, the considerate and the plucky'; the post-war plea for 'a period of apathy, inertia and uninventiveness'; the famous 'only connect', brought contemporary rhetoric to a standstill and created an abashed silence. When the noise started up again, the old incurables said that Forster was advocating weakness and passivity. No one who knew anything about liberal agnosticism was foolish enough to pay any attention to this accusation; no one who had read his novels, his essays or, above all, had ever met him could make it. His phrases had no exhibitionism; they came from a gentle yet stern and sceptical intelligence and also from a continuous sense of curiosity as moral duty. The apologist of the heart was intellectually hard. The liberal was not proposing that we could do what we liked. No one is let off in Forster's novels. There are no tears in them, just as there are no tears in Jane Austen: failure to 'connect', he sharply pointed out, leads to emptiness, panic and the mess. He was also, almost comically, ruthless—Harold dropping his oars and dying in 'The Point of It': the sort of thing he called 'a rotten business' and which indicated that sheer incomprehensibility is a naked factor in life. The room with a view in which he worked out

SOURCE 'E. M. Forster', *New Statesman*, 12 June 1970, p. 846.

his concept of a civilisation had a window looking on to the peril outside: one might find oneself 'connected' with that, but there were still no tears. Gino, in *Where Angels Fear to Tread,* breaks out into murderousness and cruelty when his kidnapped baby dies.

The scepticism and detachment of Forster belong to the humanism of his generation, and he was conscious of its dilemma. He knew there were no 'solutions' but that one still ought to inquire, that uncertainties are for serious use, that art puts a perpetual question and that, for the novelist, the problem is one of figuration not of answer, thought one ought to have the urge to answer. Given his austerity and his sense of inner danger, comedy of a special kind was his necessary form. Not the comedy of composure, manners or sociability—his upper-middle-class characters of the period are dull and fitted only for the dullest society—not, either, the comedy of the orgiastic kind: through Forster's comedy blow the icy winds of outer space. The disrespect in them is all the more deadly for being free of satire: it is positive and spiritual. No confessor could be more devastatingly offhand; more drily indicate the number of beads to be told and to point out that, all the same, they would not be enough.

It was unfortunate for Forster as a novelist that the 1914 war pulled the carpet from under his feet and left his early drawing rooms unbelievable: 'rotten luck' as he might have said, on a novelist who was not a novelist of manners. The modern reader should make the experiment of seeing some Shaw first or reading some Kipling, to see what Forster was reacting against. What was it? Fadedness, the brutally plumped cushions of Tonbridge. His contemporaries, resting on the comforts of English nationalism, thought that our trouble was social: the strength of Forster's comedy, with its rude introduction of accident, panic or mess as the likely disruptive forces, comes from a development of our tradition: his people are in situations where they are out of their depth imaginatively or spiritually. We usually console ourselves in England with the notion that the truth is simply worrying in a social way: Forster saw that the matter went, even to an annihilating extent, far deeper. In *A Passage to India,* he saw that another ethos might exist and that it would be a chaos. A grave and didactic work, this novel was also a comedy of the perils of understanding.

Forster knew that he was lucky to have grown up in a protected position and was wise enough to know that the creative mind must expose itself. The obvious criticisms that can be made of his thought must take into account that he was reacting against conventions of moral bullying and the received ideas of the late Victorian period with its inordinate stress on a certain kind of public rhetoric. It can be said that his stress on the importance of personal relationships became, in a generation less Victorian and less austere, a licence for whimsicality and Laputaism: we are never as virtuous as our mentors who have had to re-think what virtue is. By the time we had met Forster, the heart was hopelessly involved in the documents it had innocently signed. We had inherited the sins of our fathers, whereas Forster—it seemed to us in impatient moments—had only had aunts. That, of course, might make him a new mutation. We could not guess how to attain his effortless, iron humility and yet be (as he was in anything he said) a 'cert'. How was it, for example, that he was so unshy? Was that due to King's? Was it due to the blessed, precocious maturity of a boyhood that had never met adolescence? How remarkable not to have to clamber over a fence of imposed committals. How far more remarkable to have the power to develop, to perfect oneself up to a point, to be willing to wait, and at last—and surely not by accident—to choose the right time and place, to make the right experiment and to mature, as in the Indian experience, he did. Most remarkable of all, not to write when one had nothing new to say. From the opposite though complimentary position of D. H. Lawrence, he offered one something very rare—simply because it comes from genius—an absolute and simple choice, where all other choices were no more than ingenious and without authority.

He must have lived so long because he was so young. The last time I saw him, a year ago, walking across to King's College Chapel ahead of us, he had the gait, the worn heels of an eager schoolboy. Young people were instantly at ease with him, when he came and joined them in a restaurant or offered them a few alert sentences at a street corner. He had what is now old-fashioned: lack of affectation. After he had given a television interview in his rooms at King's at the time of his 80th birthday I asked him how he had felt about it, because the experience had alarmed him. He said 'I was surprised how good I was. I was very good indeed—but', he said, 'I rather felt my furniture had let me down.' He had been asked to sit at his desk so that he could be seen writing. 'What did you write?' 'One sentence', he said, 'over and over again until they had got their picture: "James Joyce is a very bad writer." I kept on writing it.' Old men get rather excitable about their naughty jokes, but these came out as discoveries and with a note that suggested that they cleared another inch or two of the human mystery.

11
Morgan Forster Remembered

NOEL ANNAN

When I came back from the war to Cambridge as a young don, I found at King's that Morgan Forster was to make his home with us. His mother had died, the lease on the house at Abinger was not to be renewed, and he had nowhere to go. And so for twenty-five years someone whom as a boy I had admired became a friend.

A few of his younger friends used to go to his room every Sunday night after dinner to read a paper on some topic or other and to talk. Forster used to listen and pottered about. He didn't say much. If the discussion became too technical or philosophical he dematerialised and floated away. He never effused. Streams of people from abroad came to pump him but they found it hard going: it was very hard to put salt on his tail if he didn't like you. He was not much gratified about friends who came from London bearing copies of his works which they wanted him to autograph. He didn't like people cashing in. His judgment was severe about people, less so about art: he said things in a deprecating voice which trailed away, deflating, mocking pomposity. He was careful about money, spent nothing on himself, hardly ever took a taxi: he spent money on his friends, particularly on the very young, and on undergraduates who had come from a working-class background.

I say all this because everyone thinks of him as one of the great prophets of tolerance in our times. And so he was. If public schools are less philistine, and the ruling class less bloody to their 'inferiors', and British colonialism, such as it still is today, less odious, it is due in part to Forster. But he was not only gentle, he was tough. What he could not bear was insensitivity, the insensitivity of the ruler, the bureaucrat and the self-satisfied. And the

SOURCE *Listener*, 18 June 1970, p. 826.

Provost of his college, as I once was, was just as likely as anyone else to get a dry little note telling him that he was betraying something which Forster thought King's ought to stand for.

I remember one occasion when I saw how insensitivity brought him anguish. Just before going into dinner in Hall, we heard the news that Ghandi had been assassinated. Forster could hardly speak. Opposite us the most complacent, self-opinionated and oak-bottomed of all the High Table bores kept up a bright chatter about Ghandi, about politics, about the university, about golf, and there were little jokes, and telling quips, and his talk went on endlessly, like a tap dripping. Forster was deeply offended. For him a man had died, a man who was perhaps half a saint, partly a lawyer, partly a politician, utterly different in morality, religion and mode of life from himself, but wholly a man of integrity who had tried to change the world by peaceful pressures. Larger and dearer to Forster than all the twopence-coloured heroes of the Western world at that time such as the Churchills and Roosevelts.

And now *he* is dead. Will he live? Will he continue to be read and admired? Forster had a long life. I don't mean that he died at 91—I mean that he was admired by generation after generation of younger writers and intellectuals. First by the post-1918 Bloomsbury circle, then by both Auden and Isherwood in the Thirties at a time when so many writers were fiercely committed to the Left, and Forster might have appeared to them as a phoney liberal. But he didn't. And he also spoke to the young in the Forties during the war when he refused to say silly, vindictive things about Germany (to which, incidentally, he paid a marvellous tribute, expressing his love for the old German *Kultur*). In the Fifties he became a grand old man of literature and professors wrote books about him. He was able to say new things about freedom and tolerance. Have you ever tried to? It is very, very hard. But Forster could—Forster did. No one could tackle better than he in the course of a short essay or broadcast the big words or overworked themes like the Artist and Society or the Challenge of our Times—ghastly titles that remind one of school exercises. And he could do so because he both never thought of his audience and never forgot it. He never thought of his audience or worried whether they would think him foolish for saying this, or not up-to-date in saying that; he was totally unself-conscious and unaffected. He never forgot his audience because, being unaffected, he addressed each reader in a perfectly normal way, never wondering who he was or whether he would understand. He was as self-confident as he was oblivious of fashion. Many of his essays will fade. But a few—the great 'What I Believe', and his musings on places he cared for and on poets such as Cafavy or Iqbal whom he knew and revered, and his essay 'On Anonymity'—will be quoted by historians trying to reconstruct the age in which he lived.

His novels will live too, and if I have left them to the last, it's really because the critics have been at them so long and written so much about them that it's surprising they are still alive. Lionel Trilling's book, which made Forster famous in America, is still the best, and all the better for being so short. But this night when his body is now ashes, if there's one thing I would like to stress about the novels, it is not their profundity or their poetry or their knowledge of human beings or their sense of good and evil. It's the quality I loved in him. It is their humour.

Do you remember Tibby in *Howards End* doing everything he can to escape his responsibility as the male head of the family when his sister becomes obsessed by Leonard Bast and then gets pregnant? Tibby, selfish, cultured, the symbol of leisure without sympathy—yet how Forster is amused by him and how pleased he was when anyone enjoyed the spectacle of Tibby! Forster liked to laugh. In real life he was often melancholy and low-temperature. Then something would catch his fancy and his ragged hedgerow of a moustache would begin to twitch and then he would utter a little cry and begin to laugh—and that is how I remember him, laughing and shaking, and crying out 'Oh! Oh!' as he heard something scandalous, indecent, foolish, silly, but something which confirmed him in his conviction that human beings, absurd and comical as they might be, were all the better for not getting puffed up and trying to be higher than the angels.

12

In Memoriam E. M. Forster: Love, the Beloved Republic—A Memoir of Morgan Forster

JAMES KIRKUP

It was during the Second World War—around 1943, I believe—that I first read a novel by E. M. Forster. It was *A Passage to India*. Until then, in my youthful ignorance and arrogance, I had looked down upon Forster—having read only his short stories—as *passé* and unworthy to stand in the company of Joyce and Proust. This, I remember, was also the attitude of my fellow-students: it was not then fashionable to think very highly of him.

When I first read *A Passage to India*, I was far from the sheltering groves of academe. I was just another helpless victim of a disgusting war, a conscientious objector to the British war effort, and isolated in a British labour camp. Forster's novel about the British in India expressed something of my own loathing for the British upper classes, for the mindless militarism of British society and for the philistine snobbery of the British in the East.

A man whom Forster admired very much, Jawaharlal Nehru, has this to say in *An Autobiography*:

> G. Lowes Dickinson is reported by E. M. Forster, in his recent life of him, to have once said about India: 'And *why* can't the races meet? Simply because the Indians *bore* the English.'

The same might be said about the British in Malaysia, Hong Kong, Africa

SOURCE *Eigo Seinen* (Toyko), September 1970, pp. 510–15.

and Japan: they are so insular and unimaginative that they are bored by the natives of those so unBritish lands.

A few years ago, I studied *A Passage to India* with my excellent and very patient students at Japan's Women's University. My lectures were recorded, and I should very much like to hear how I handled this difficult novel, in which there is so much that is incomprehensible to the Japanese. In the course of my lectures, I remember, I was amazed to find that what Forster had written about the British in India in the Twenties was still true of the British in Japan, who are mainly businessmen and bureaucrats: they are uninterested in the Japanese, who bore them. This theme of the alien, unadaptable British in foreign parts—the egotistical British glorified by jingoistic Kipling—is a theme which, as I pointed out to my students, extends from Forster's earliest short story, 'The Eternal Moment', through the books on Alexandria and his witty essays on international expositions, right through to *The Hill of Devi.*

But there was something else in this novel about India that fascinated me: its sense of unexplained mysteries in human relationships, its sudden violence and prophetic insights, its beautiful strangeness—all expressed in a rather staid, old-maidish Cambridge English tone—the very tone that makes Arthur Waley's style in *The Tale of Genji* so unforgettable. Moreover, it was the first book, apart from *The Arabian Nights* and Beckford's *Vathek,* that I had read about the East. In dingy, dangerous wartime Britain, a desperate longing was born in me to live in the East—a longing Forster was later to encourage in me, but which was not to be realized until nearly fifteen years later.

I wrote a letter to Forster about *A Passage to India* and about all his other novels and his marvellous collection of essays, *Abinger Harvest.* Only twice before had I written to an author—to Gide and Cocteau, both of whom replied and became my friends. Forster replied to my letter, and soon we were writing to one another fairly regularly. He sent me signed copies of all his books, but unfortunately these, and his wonderful letters, were all destroyed by a German bomb. But we had become friends, and that was something no bombs could destroy.

During the war, T. S. Eliot found it necessary to contribute to the 'war effort' by invoking and cynically perverting Krishna's admonition to Arjuna in *The Dry Salvages.* As a pacifist, I was very distressed by this section of *The Four Quartets*—surely the most tedious and sententious modern poem in English. (Forster has effectively demolished Eliot's critical and dramatic pretensions in *Two Cheers for Democracy.*) Fortunately, I was able to read a much finer interpretation of Krishna's doctrine in Forster's *Hymn Before Action* at the end of *Abinger Harvest.* This remarkable little essay is not well known. It was written in 1912, but seemed to me very applicable to my own situation as a pacifist in 1943. It analyses the central doctrine of the *Bhagavad-Gita.* Krishna asks Arjuna to fight and destroy his enemies even if they are close relatives. As a fine Indian writer, K. Natwar-Singh, points out in his brilliant essay on Forster and India in *Aspects of E. M. Forster*,[1]

> Arjuna must fight because it is his duty and that duty has not been assigned to him by chance. Krishna convinces Arjuna, who drives into battle rejoicing, and wins a great victory.

Natwar-Singh goes on to show, however, that Forster was more dispassionate and critical than Eliot in his interpretation of this 'great victory', for Forster writes:

> But it is necessarily and rightly followed by disillusionment and remorse. The fall of his enemies leads to his own, for the fortunes of men are all bound up together, and it is impossible to inflict damage without receiving it.

After we had exchanged a few letters, I sent Forster a long, intimate poem about some of the emotional and sexual experiences of my early youth, entitled *The Sound of Fountains*—a poem I have still not published. He wrote back immediately to say how much he liked it, and quoted especially some lines in which I described my sexual seduction by an older man. Forster was always deeply interested in sex and took a humorous view of the functions of his own body, especially in old age. During his visit to America in 1947, Forster was one of the many prominent people who were interviewed by Dr Kinsey for *The Kinsey Report*, and when I asked him how he felt about exposing his sex life in this way, he answered: 'I thoroughly enjoyed it. Indeed, I found I could not stop talking about it, and I was quite disappointed that the interview was so short.'

Though there are no overt sexual descriptions in his novels, he was always strong in the defence of the artist's right to express himself freely in such matters, as can be seen in his campaigns for such widely different works as Radclyffe Hall's lesbian novel *The Well of Loneliness* and Lawrence's very feeble *Lady Chatterley's Lover* (which Forster referred to humorously as *Lady Loverley's Chatter*). He also had a deep concern for homosexual law reform and the 'normalization' and de-mystification of the homoerotic in literature and life. I shall return later in this essay to Forster's passionate interest in sex, which, as in the case of Yeats, was to become even stronger towards the end of his life.

*

It was not until after the war that I met Forster for the first time. I was living in the London suburb of Putney, in a little bed-sitting room in Werter Road, just off Putney High Street. I had found the room quite by accident, but soon I discovered that almost directly opposite lived one of Forster's ancient maiden aunts, whom he used to visit from time to time.

Putney was also the home of a writer who became a dear friend, J. R. Ackerley, whose book on India, *Hindoo Holiday*, is a classic among English travel books. Ackerley had long been an intimate friend of Forster—a friendship, Ackerley once told me, that was entirely platonic, affectionate without sex, as was my own relationship with Ackerley. It was through Ackerley (at that time Literary Editor of the BBC weekly magazine *The Listener*, which regularly published my poems, reviews and translations) that I first met Morgan Forster.

Joe Ackerley had often talked to me about 'Morgan,' which was Forster's middle name, and the name all his friends called him by. (He disliked his first name, Edward, which he thought sounded 'too grand—like a butler.') There is a funny story about Morgan at a literary cocktail party, where an effusive but ignorant woman overheard someone calling him 'Morgan.' The woman rushed up to Forster and cried: 'Are you Charles Morgan?' 'No, I'm Morgan Forster,' he replied. 'Oh, I'm sorry,' she answered. 'I thought you were the writer.'

One afternoon sometime in 1948 or 1949 I was invited to Ackerley's flat to meet William Plomer and John Morris and—Edward Morgan Forster. I remember the simple kindliness and friendliness of all these people towards me—a poor, unknown, struggling poet. But there was in Forster something that transcended all this: his small, rather stout, homely figure and plain, open face glowed with gentle good-will and joy. I think I have never met anyone who gave me such an impression of deep, quiet happiness and inexhaustible patience and sympathy.

Despite the constant barkings of Ackerley's Alsatian bitch, Queenie, who was always jealous of her master's visitors, Morgan and I had a long conversation about all kinds of things—about the great influences on his own work, Jane Austen, Samuel Butler and Matthew Arnold, about animals and food and drink, about modern poetry, about sport and clothes and the theatre. We also talked about our mothers—for Morgan was ever as devoted to his mother as I am to mine. This was a great common bond between us. Then we started talking about the nature of friendship, a subject on which he was an expert, because he had devoted friends of all kinds—from labourers and farmers and policemen to university students, Indian scholars and great composers like Benjamin Britten. Indeed, to the very end, Morgan's most devoted friend was an ex-policeman, Bob Buckingham. In the Prefatory Note to *Abinger Harvest*, tribute is paid to his policeman friend along with Ackerley, Plomer and Isherwood.

It was his utter lack of class-consciousness and conceit that attracted me to Morgan, and allowed him, the leading English man of letters, to talk to me as an equal. Our talk about friendship was quite un-solemn and unpompous. But I recall he told me that only in a true democracy could friendship between men flourish in freedom. This was an important statement. Forster, like myself, did not think very highly of democracy, which is why he called his second collection of essays *Two Cheers for Democracy*, saying: 'Two cheers are quite enough: there is no occasion to give three. Only Love, the Beloved Republic, deserves that.' To Morgan, 'Love, the Beloved Republic,' was part of the Greek ideal he had inherited from Goldsworthy Lowes Dickinson, an ideal republic of loving friends far removed from the ordinary crude popular concept of homosexual relations.

On that first meeting, he made one of those spontaneous gestures that in Morgan amounted almost to genius. He had just come back from a week-end in the country, and had brought with him half a dozen fresh farm eggs. At that time, eggs were still rationed, and each person received only about one egg a month—usually a stale egg. So fresh eggs were almost as precious as gold. As he was leaving, Morgan—who at times looked rather like a fussy little brown hen himself—started to give an amusing imitation of a hen cackling after laying an egg. Then, with a smile and a hug, he presented me with one of his precious eggs, wrapped in a page of *The New Statesman.*

I was overcome not so much by the priceless gift of a fresh egg as by the symbolism of this act of perfect grace and loving friendship. With the gift of that egg, I felt Morgan had offered me not only his friendship, but a promise of poetic fertility. I did not eat the egg, but kept it carefully packed in a special little box for many years, until, in one of my numerous removals from one dismal lodging to another, it was broken. Strangely enough, the smashed egg had no bad odour, but smelt curiously sweet and wholesome. I thought the end of the world had come when that egg broke. Years later, I reminded Morgan about his gift, and he remembered our first meeting perfectly, saying: 'I remember you were wearing white socks. When you crossed your left leg on your right knee, you revealed a few inches of suntanned shin above the top of your sock.' It was this kind of detail, seen with the constantly-recording eye of the born writer, that Morgan loved to remember when talking about his friends. It was on the subject of friendship that Forster made some of his most illuminating remarks, including the justly famous one in the essay *What I Believe*:

> Personal relations are despised today. They are regarded as bourgeois luxuries, as products of a time of fair weather which is now past, and we are urged to get rid of them, and to dedicate ourselves to some movement or cause instead. I hate the idea of causes, and if I had to choose between betraying my country and betraying my friend, I hope I should have the guts to betray my country. Such a choice may scandalize the modern reader, and he may stretch out his patriotic hand to the telephone at once and ring up the police. It would not have shocked Dante, though. Dante places Brutus and Cassius in the lowest circle of Hell because they had chosen to betray their friend Julius Caesar rather than their country Rome.

I felt very keenly the absence of this Republic of Loving Friends when I first came to Japan. 'The Japanese,' I wrote to Morgan after two years in Sendai, 'do not understand friendship as we do. A Japanese would rather betray his friend than his country.' He wrote back saying:

> Let them betray you. It is better to show loving friendship and be betrayed for

it, than never to show it at all, never to risk a human impulse or a passionate gesture of human love. Love once shown, and friendship once offered, even to the most unworthy and treacherous person, is never lost, however soon or however often one's trust in others is broken. Give your whole heart to the Japanese, not for your own sake, but for the sake of humanity.'

Forster was one of the people who encouraged me to come to Japan, with the words: 'Japan and the East will be to future generations of Englishmen what Italy, Greece and the Mediterranean have been to the 19th Century, and to my own generation.' I regarded Forster, with his love of Egypt and India, as a kind of cultural bridge between the past and the future, between West and East.

*

During the years after 1964, I heard from him less and less, as he became more and more feeble and suffered a succession of grave illnesses and strokes. My friend Joe Ackerley, who had stayed with me in Sendai, kept me informed of Morgan's precarious state of health, and sometimes when Morgan was unable to hold a pen he would dictate letters to me through Joe, though he always insisted on signing them himself, with a very touchingly shaky 'Morgan'.

I continued to write to Morgan, and sent him little presents from the East—a Japanese paper fan, a Filipino shirt, flowers, little notebooks of handmade paper, *saké* and those charming lace-trimmed handkerchiefs printed with photographs of my favourite Japanese pop-singers which I used to buy in Asakusa. He loved these little 'doilies', as he referred to them, and particularly admired the dazzling smile and fairy fringe of Yukio Hashi.

When I won the Japan PEN Club Prize for my poem sequence *Japan Marine*, I sent him a copy. Joe Ackerley read it to him in the garden of Bob Buckingham's house in Coventry at a time when Forster was almost completely paralyzed. Ackerley wrote to me:

> I took your prize poem with me and read it to him in the small, pretty garden, full of the most delightful blackbird song. He kept exclaiming 'My! What a wonderful vocabulary!' ('Yours, not the blackbirds.') 'What a beautiful choice of words!' and asked me specially to thank you for having given him so much pleasure.

My last letter from Morgan is written from King's College in very uncertain handwriting, and dated August 2nd (?) 1967. I quote here in full because of its interesting reference to light:

> What a pretty little fan! Rather too Western an expression of delight. Still I do enjoy it and admire it very much, and would have gone out fanning myself with it at once if the rain had stopped. But it never has stopped since March, and every one, even myself, is depressed.
>
> Joe has just been here, also depressed, and never ceasing to denounce the

English and the Human Race. Since I am involved in both these rackets I have been feeling rather shy. I have therefore withdrawn myself to the subject of Light. I want to know why Light does not go even faster than it does, and have asked this question of my Indian friend next door, who is an astronomer. He replies (I think) that if it did go still faster every thing would turn solid.

In the future I may write to you again on this question. For the moment I want to thank you again for this charming gift.

Yours
Morgan Forster

The Indian friend who lived in rooms next door to him at King's was Jayant Narlikar, a brilliant young Indian mathematician who collaborated with Professor Fred Hoyle. I wrote a reply to Morgan on the subject of light, but received no reply. By that time, he was past writing and past light. I thought it was interesting that at the end of his life he should have this obsession with light: it reminded me of Goethe's final words, which are reported to have been 'More light!'

*

Most of Forster's critics complain that his output was too small, and that he never wrote anything good after *A Passage to India.* But in fact his *oeuvre* is a large one—five novels, two biographies, two books about Alexandria, a film script and the libretto for Benjamin Britten's opera *Billy Budd.* As George H. Thomson points out in *Aspects of E. M. Forster,* there are hundreds of uncollected essays, reviews, fragments of novels, juvenilia, autobiographical sketches and so on. Miss B. J. Kirkpatrick in her *A Bibliography of E. M. Forster*[2] identifies 533 contributions to periodicals and newspapers, of which Forster reprinted only 152.

Moreover, Forster was a prolific letter-writer, and those letters are amazingly interesting, funny and beautiful. Many of the hundreds of letters to his mother will shed great light on his experiences abroad in Egypt, Italy and India. One day, these letters will be published, and will reveal to the public not just E. M. Forster the novelist, but Morgan the man and the loving friend and devoted son.

Though *A Passage to India* was his last published novel, that does not mean he was not writing another. In fact, he wrote a most remarkable novel on a homosexual theme, which has had various titles, including the name of its hero, Maurice or Morris. Presumably this will be published one day.

Moreover, during his last years, Morgan wrote for his own pleasure, and for the delectation of his friends, a stream of vividly sexual short stories, some of them very beautiful, touching and funny. It seems that many writers, as they approach death, are attracted towards 'abnormal' expressions of love. In Japan, there are the marvellous final erotic flowerings of Tanizaki and, to a lesser extent, of Kawabata. Forster gloried in pornographic writing, and often wondered why more writers did not attempt it. His only reservations were that pornography should have Style, that it should be elegantly written and aesthetically satisfying. Therefore he admired *The Memoirs of Fanny Hill.* He also insisted that pornography should really excite the reader sexually. His own late stories certainly did this. Unfortunately, in the present atmosphere of puritanical stuffiness in British culture, I doubt whether these treasures of Forster's last years could ever be published without immediate police prosecution.

For a writer whose deepest concerns were the dignity of 'Love, the Beloved Republic' and absolute freedom of the writer from any kind of governmental repression or censorship (see among others his magnificent essays on 'Liberty in England' and 'Mrs Grundy at the Parkers''), this final fate of his last works is supremely sad and ironical—and woefully British. Alas, we are entering a period of increasing repression of literature, not only in Russia and other totalitarian regimes, but also in so-called democracies like Britain, France and Japan.

Perhaps this was why Morgan was no democrat: he saw too clearly how the concept of democracy could be perverted and cheapened. In his own words, he longed for something far finer than democracy, for 'an aristocracy of the sensitive, the considerate and the plucky.'

Dear Morgan, I am glad you are not alive to see these times—times in which your kind of art and aristocracy of the sensitive could never have come to their perfect flowering. I cling to my memories of you as to the last relics of a lost civilization.

Notes

1 *Aspects of E. M. Forster*, ed. Oliver Stallybrass, (London: Edward Arnold, 1969).
2 *A Bibliography of E. M. Forster*, (London: Hart-Davis, 1968) (2nd revised impression).

Reviews:
Where Angels Fear to Tread
to
The Life to Come and Other Stories

Where Angels Fear to Tread
(1905)

13
Review

ANONYMOUS

This is a book which one begins with pleased interest and gradually finds to be astonishing. Its amusing facility becomes amusing cleverness, and then, almost without realising the development, we find that the cleverness is of a larger style than we thought, and the main issues of life are confronting us where we looked for trivialities. The author takes half-a-dozen or so apparently commonplace people, picks out their little tremors and foibles with a finger which just escapes being cruel; and then, with no greater events than a visit to Monteriano, a wrong marriage, a brown baby, and a few little happenings, he depicts greatness, and Italy, and the point where humanity touches divinity; the whole thing being done with an appearance of jocularity which is very engaging and a truthfulness which is, by contrast, almost startling. The apparently commonplace people are none of them commonplace in Mr Forster's hands. Mrs Herriton, the mother-in-law; Harriet, her solid, serious daughter; Philip, her artistic, clever, ineffective son; Lilia, her vulgar, widowed daughter-in-law who—to keep her out of mischief and to give her culture—is sent travelling with the respectable but surprising Caroline Abbot; and Gino, the impossible Italian with whom Lilia falls in love—they are all distinct, and amusing, and fillipic in effect. The story is like the characters, the characters are like the story—at first clever, attractive, and seemingly with no heart, then swept almost into tragedy while scarcely knowing it. The book stands out as unusual and convincing, with its uniqueness and its persuasion accomplished in an unexpectedly fresh manner.

SOURCE *Bookman*, October 1905, pp. 40–1.

14
Review

C. F. G. MASTERMAN

Where Angels Fear to Tread is a remarkable book. Not often has the reviewer to welcome a new writer and a new novel so directly conveying the impressions of power and an easy mastery of material. Here there are qualities of style and thought which awaken a sense of satisfaction and delight; a taste in the selection of words; a keen insight into the humour (and not merely the humours) of life; and a challenge to its accepted courses.

Sawston and San Gemignano

On the surface are the commonplace outward scenes: Sawston, with its suburban existence; the queer life of the Italian bourgeoisie encamped in the incongruous surroundings of an ancient, crumbling, walled city; and the journeys between one and the other. These scenes are peopled with apparently commonplace persons, a suburban family, the child of an Italian dentist. The conversations are carried on in the departure of the train from Victoria or the railway carriage crawling up the St Gothard out of Italy. Yet from such material Mr Forster can weave a vision of life which is at once an approval and a criticism; with the clash of diverse racial characteristics, and the sudden upheaval, both in Italian and English natures, of forces scarcely noticed in the world of every day.

> When the spring came, (says one of the characters,) I wanted to fight against the things I hated, mediocrity and dulness, and spitefulness and society. I didn't see that all these things are invincible, and that if we go against them they will break us to pieces.

This triumph of the ordered conventional world over the revolt of incongruous, queer, and passionate desires is one of the motifs of the tale.

SOURCE *The Daily News*, 8 November 1905, p. 4.

The story, as far as outward scenes are concerned, is of the simplest possible description. Lilia, a girl of humble origin, is persuaded to wander in Italy by the family of her first husband, of secure wealth and respectability. She falls in love in her widowhood with Gino, the little son, scarcely of age, of an Italian dentist. She marries him, and settles down within the crumbling walls of Monteriano, under which title Mr Forster describes the astonishing little city, San Gemignano. The mother dies on the birth of a child; and the English family at Sawston plan the rescue of the infant from the unspeakable husband and all the corrupt influences of the South. Direct bribery and persuasion having failed, an attempt is made to kidnap the child, who perishes in a scene which mingles a kind of wild laughter and tears. The father, after one outburst of insane ferocity, settles down into acquiescence, and the story ends with the return of the expedition, which had failed so woefully, from the magic of the South into the rational air of England.

'A Country Behind Him'

Into such a simple narrative Mr Forster has crowded not only pieces of sharp description which give to the whole affair a convincing air of reality, but also those challenges of ultimate things which are rarely faced in the even flow of an orderly world. Sawston is challenged by Monteriano. The routine of the suburban life appears intolerable to one half of the mind, longing with a kind of physical hunger for the sun and enchantment of Italy. But in the midst of the ruins and unaccountable courses the other half turns to the security of the recognised ways—'to Sawston after the summer holidays, bicycle gymkhanas, and the annual bazaar in the garden for the C.M.S. It seemed impossible that such a happy life could exist.' Gino at first appears unspeakable; unclean, vulgarly dressed, coarsely eating his food, brutal with animals, idle, unfaithful to his wife. But there is the other side also; boundless good temper and good fellowship; the fierce and passionate devotion of the father for his child, which is utterly incomprehensible to the colder Northern nature; and something mysterious and terrible, congruous with the hot night and magic of the hills and valleys, and all the enchantment of a land where the intellect is paralysed by the emotions. 'He has got a country behind him,' is the verdict, 'that's upset people from the beginning of the world.' The country itself, with its vast slopes of olives and vineyards and little towns outlined against the cloudless sky, has 'scarcely a touch of wildness in it.' 'But it was terrible and mysterious all the same.' The collegiate church of Santa Deodata, with the frescoes of its child saints, confronts with a kind of dumb challenge all the respectabilities and good works of the English suburb.

The Challenge of Italy

The struggle between Gino and Lilia is national. 'Generations of ancestors, good, bad, or indifferent, forbade the Latin man to be chivalrous to the Northern woman; the Northern woman to forgive the Latin man.' The poverty-haunted people of the little forgotten town assemble with great joy in the theatre to applaud Donizetti's 'Lucia di Lammermoor.' Outside the window of the hotel is evidence of the fighting of 1338. 'It reaches up to Heaven,' is the summary of it all, 'and down to the other place.' The idiot who, in another country, would have been shut up is here accepted as an institution and part of Nature's scheme. 'He understands everything, but can explain nothing,' is the verdict of the landlady. 'And he has visions of the saints,' is the corroboration of 'the man who drove the cab.'

Mr Forster makes here none of the conventional attacks against conventional evils. He gives the picture of the one and the other: Italy and suburban England, worldly success against complete worldly failure, idleness in the sunlight against a beaver-like industry under grey skies, material comfort contrasted with indifference to life's minor luxuries, life lived for the future contrasted with life living on the past. He stands aside, with the detachment of the artist, presenting no verdict of judgment, preaching no obvious gospel; as dispassionate in his vision of those who are driven by ennui into good works in the middle classes of England who are successful as in those who enjoy their lives and disappear like the midge in the middle classes of Italy who have failed. He knows the indignation of the tourist as he (or she) drifts through the heat and dust, blinking wearily at historical monuments, and continually exasperated by the futile good temper of the aborigines. He knows also that this acquiescence amongst dead things means an abandonment of material advance and progress. The conquering Briton has gained the whole world; perhaps the Italian, amongst the ruins of populous cities, has preserved his own soul.

'Life was greater than he had supposed,' is the verdict rescued from it all. 'But it was even less complete. He had seen the need for strenuous work and for righteousness, and now he saw what a very little way these things would go.' Always such conceptions can be disturbed by that magic accent of the South; the laughter in the theatre; the silvery stars in the purple sky; the violets of a departing spring. Outwardly, after this plunge into another universe, life will continue in its courses. Sawston will maintain its activities in the 'service of the corpulent poor,' the book club, the debating society, progressive whist, the bazaars. Far away on its southern hillside the people of Monteriano will collect in the sunshine, discourse in the cafés, drift on in their destined and quiet ways. But in the momentary clash between the two something unaccountable, almost elfish and fantastic, has been revealed of the queer, irrational material of the soul of woman and of man;

and the world is the richer for such a revelation.

Such is the theme of this brilliant novel. It is told with a deftness, a lightness, a grace of touch, and a radiant atmosphere of humour, which mark a strength and capacity giving large promise for the future.

15
Review

ANONYMOUS

Mr Forster, who is, to the best of our belief, a newcomer in the field of fiction, has at once revealed himself as a writer to be reckoned with in his exceedingly clever but decidedly painful story. When, however, we say 'painful,' the epithet needs reserves and explanations. *Where Angels Fear to Tread* is not a story written with the deliberate aim of challenging attention by giving offence, nor is it disfigured by the wanton intrusion of disagreeable or repulsive details. On the contrary, in handling a difficult theme the author has shown in the main remarkable tact and reticence, while the chief practical lessons of the story—the dangers of international marriages, the need of domestic tolerance, and the futility of ill-considered rebellion against convention—are unimpeachable in their strong if indirect confirmation of orthodox views. All this we cordially admit; but though Mr Forster is neither cruel nor anarchical in his attitude, he deals largely with those elements in modern society which make for domestic disintegration rather than solidarity. Above all, the story is steeped in disillusionment. Steele, giving a new lease of life to a famous Greek maxim, said in reference to a good woman that 'to love her was a liberal education.' Mr Forster, on the other hand, has shown how the love felt by a good woman, so far from exerting an educational influence, may be a relapse to a primitive and barbaric instinct, a mark of degradation rather than elevation.

The personages concerned in Mr Forster's story are in no case of a truly or consistently heroic cast,—indeed, there is only one who is in any way capable of rising to the occasion, and in her case the disillusionment excited in the reader is in some ways the keenest. As for the plot, it centres in the unfortunate remarriage of Lilia Herriton, a young widow, a good-natured, impulsive, but second-rate woman, who has lived with her husband's people after his death, and has at every turn been made to feel her intellectual and social shortcomings by her mother-, brother-, and

SOURCE *Spectator*, 23 December 1905, pp. 1089–90.

sister-in-law. When, therefore, she thinks of having a *Wanderjahr* in Italy, they encourage the plan, and a companion is found in Caroline Abbott, an excellent young lady who is apparently devoted to good works, district visiting and the like, but in reality is just as anxious as Lilia to escape from her dull surroundings and see something of real life. They are both intoxicated by the sense of freedom and the charm of Italy, and Lilia, without protest from her companion, falls in love with a handsome young Italian, the son of a dentist, half Faun, half Satyr. The Herritons are horrified at the news, and Lilia's brother-in-law Philip—an ineffectual aesthete whose strong critical faculty and sense of humour are not backed by any force of character—is despatched in hot haste by his mother to break off the match, but arrives to find that the lovers are already secretly married, and returns in disgust with Miss Abbott, leaving Lilia to her fate. Alternately cowed and neglected by her husband, who had only married her for her money, which he squanders on dissipation, and disowned by her relatives and connections, Lilia, in spite of her vulgarity, attains to a tragic pitch of desolation and misery before she dies in giving birth to a son. The only person, indeed, who feels the slightest compunction is Caroline Abbott, who, smitten with remorse at her lack of foresight in encouraging the match and her cowardice in deserting her friend, resolves to rescue the child from its surroundings. Mrs Herriton, insensible to the call of natural affection, is at once roused from her indifference to the fate of the 'beastly Italian baby' by wounded pride, and a second rescue party is organised, in which Philip's sister, a narrow-minded religious fanatic, takes a leading and disastrous part. There is only one bright spot in the squalid tragedy of this episode, the courage and tact shown by Caroline Abbott, who saves the situation when it had become well-nigh desperate, awakens Philip to a sense of his worthlessness, and inspires him with the resolve to abandon the rôle of the cynical onlooker. But Caroline, having placed herself on a pedestal, abruptly shatters her claims to reverence by the humiliating confession that she too had been fascinated by the Faun-Satyr, though fully conscious of his cruelty and baseness, and was only prevented from declaring her feelings by the fact that he regarded her as a being on a wholly higher plane.

A rough outline such as the foregoing, while it gives what we hope is not an inaccurate sketch of the contents of the book, must inevitably fail to convey any impression of the persuasive skill with which Mr Forster has contrived to lend an engrossing interest to a disconcerting, and even distressing, study of contemporary civilisation. As we have said at the outset, one can read half-a-dozen excellent orthodox morals into the story, but the dominant impression left on the mind of the present writer is that under the stress of opportunity primitive instincts reassert themselves in the most carefully educated and studiously repressed natures. The cruelty and callousness of old Mrs Herriton is even more sinister, because more unexpected, than the frank inhumanity, tempered with graceful animalism, of the young Italian. Mr Forster has succeeded, with a cleverness that is almost uncanny, in illustrating the tragic possibilities that reside in insignificant and unimportant characters when they seek to emancipate themselves from the bondage of convention, or to control those who are dominated by a wholly different set of traditions. He has done this in a manner which is void of offence, but is none the less painful and disquieting. Let us hope that so original and searching a talent may yet give us a story in which the fallibility of goodness and the callousness of respectability are less uncompromisingly insisted upon.

The Longest Journey
(1907)

16
Unsigned Review

[VIRGINIA WOOLF]

Readers who remember *Where Angels Fear to Tread* remember some hours of lively entertainment, and the question at the end, 'What will the next book be?' Now that the next book, *The Longest Journey*, is before us the question seems only transferred once more, and to the credit of Mr Forster's power of entertainment we ask it as curiously as ever. For *The Longest Journey*, although it is entirely free from shyness, has still much of the character of a young book; it is so very clever and so very well pleased with its own ingenuity. Mr Forster fastens himself again, like some sharp wholesome insect, upon the life of the suburbs and the ideals of those who dwell in red brick villas and in the form rooms of public schools. And in the art of stinging these good people to exhibit their antics in a natural manner he is undoubtedly an expert; Sawston is certainly alive. His hero, Rickie Elliot, is born under the influence; 'he had opened his eyes to filmy heavens and taken his first walk on asphalt. He had seen civilisation as a row of semi-detached villas and society as a state in which men do not know the men who live next door'. But, inconveniently enough, he manages to preserve the power of seeing something beyond, and cannot acquiesce. At Cambridge, of course, he meets people who have nothing to do with the suburbs and can sit discussing the existence of objects and drawing circles within squares. 'Are they real?' 'The inside one is—the one in the middle of everything, that there's never room enough to draw'. But certain visions obscured Rickie's view of the true circle, and he is married by a suburban lady, Miss Agnes Pembroke, the sister of a master at Sawston school. Then he must give up his dell, somewhere near Cambridge, where fauns live and a fair woman pursued by suburban love can turn into a tree. But to follow the theory of Rickie's life, so skilfully developed and illustrated in its various stages—Cambridge, Sawston, Wiltshire—is hardly within our scope. It is certainly a very skilful arrangement, and yet it does not afford us so much

SOURCE *Times Literary Supplement*, 22 October 1908, p. 362.

satisfaction as the dexterity of the writer seems to intend. It is a serious matter, and yet if we are to feel it so the comedy should be a little less shrill. But the jingle which the idols make as they fall, adroitly knocked on the head by a tap of Mr Forster's pen, destroys the deeper note; there is a sound like the striking of hollow brass. But then, and we return to our 'but', how vivacious and neat-handed it all is! Mr Forster has mastered his method, and manipulates his facts, his theories, and finally his men and women with a facility that leaves the reader, as may be he is intended to be left, gasping and groping for support. Where are the connexions? Sometimes the short cut succeeds and sometimes it fails; Miss Pembroke is a success, and Mrs Failing, though pierced again and again, is almost completely missed. The method is clearly dangerous. And yet we have a sense of some larger background, where there are Greeks, if they are only there as a contradiction to Sawston; just as Rickie's vision is always shot by a pellet of suburban mud. But it is interesting and living and amusing, and we still ask, 'What will be the next?'

17
Unsigned Review

[EDWARD GARNETT]

In a passage in this elusive novel, *The Longest Journey*, Agnes, the hero's wife, says to him: 'Couldn't you make your stories more obvious? I don't see any harm in that. Uncle Willie floundered hopelessly. I had to explain, and then he was delighted.' But Rickie, the lame and weakly hero, can only reply to this, dubiously, 'You see—.' He got no further than 'you see.'

In truth it is not easy to explain the subtle quality of Mr Forster's brilliant novel to Uncle Willie and his kinsfolk. The book is one that sounds the depths of character and conduct, that discloses the finest shades of spiritual meaning, that is as elusive, as actual, as ordinary withal as a wind that sways the tree tops. It is a novel of witty surfaces, and growing surprises, with scores of fine delicate thoughts gleaming in the current of the story. The style and method of our author are as original as his outlook on life. They are as uncommon as the stuff of this fabric of life is common and everyday. All lies in the telling, and how can the art of telling, this network woven of a succession of tiny touches be brought home to Uncle Willie? The critic can only indicate the artistic quality of *The Longest Journey*, by saying that there are some faces whose character lies in the smoothness of their contours, and the almost imperceptible movements of the lips and eyes. In the first third of the book the reader may be dubious as to what it is he is gathering; in the last half he will, if he is intelligent, be visited with a baffling sense of the strangeness of life, of its commonplace complexity, of the unresting forces, of its movement and energy, of its puzzling meaninglessness, with its sudden upheavals of immense meaning. Let us, however, not exaggerate the merits of *The Longest Journey*. Let us only say that its quality is quite unusual, and that it holds within it a criticism of ordinary life which is both philosophical and witty, spiritual and full of humorous by-play.

The inner meaning of the story may be roughly defined as a shadowing

SOURCE *Nation*, 27 April 1907, pp. 357–8.

of that spiritual gulf which lies between two classes of minds, viz., of the minority who have the instinct to think for themselves, and so arrive in some degree at spiritual and mental honesty, and the majority whose valuations, dictated by stupidity, worldly prudence, social pressure and the like, are, in short, those conventional soulless valuations, which in Ibsen's *Peer Gynt*, go into the melting-pot and receive no mercy from the Button Moulder.

Rickie Elliot, the hero, whose struggle to be himself is the book's centre, is the lame and weakly son of parents who have never loved one another, and who have come to live apart. His mother, who is 'beautiful both within and without,' has married as a girl a Mr Elliot, a barrister, whose voice 'was very suave with a fine command of cynical intonation. By altering it ever so little he could make people wince, especially if they were simple or poor.' As a man, Mr Elliot 'never did or said or thought one single thing that had the slightest beauty or value.' He has means, and a set of rooms in town, and sees little of his son, whom he dubs 'Rickie,' because of his deformity, which he takes pleasure in alluding to. Both parents die when Rickie is fifteen, and the lad, who has had a solitary and unhappy childhood, passes 'cold and friendless and ignorant' through a great public school to Cambridge, which 'takes and soothes and warms and laughs at him, telling him not to be tragic.' At Cambridge we are introduced to Miss Agnes Pembroke (to whom Rickie, after a couple of years of idealising her, becomes engaged), and to her brother, Mr Pembroke, a master in the great public school at Sawston. The Pembrokes are inimitably drawn, and the sly precision of touch which defines their bright and banal insincerity of spirit, their cultured philistinism, is quite masterly.

Rickie, who is only an idealistic boy, marries the handsome and practical Agnes Pembroke, who 'warms up' for him her old feeling for her dead lover Gerald. The unhappy Rickie, by this marriage, is taken over and run henceforward by the bland and smug forces of Sawston—a provincial Philistia. The spiritual gulf between Rickie and Agnes is adroitly indicated. 'He valued emotion—not for itself, but because it is the only final path to intimacy. She, ever robust and practical, always discouraged him. She was not cold: she would willingly embrace him. But she hated being upset . . .' What an immense class of marriages, spiritual mismatings, this phrase 'she hated being upset' hits off. Rickie is boyishly weak before Mr Pembroke, and allows himself to be 'fitted into' the position of assistant master at Sawston School. 'Above all,' thought Mr Pembroke, 'it will be something regular for him to do . . . A schoolmaster has wonderful opportunities of doing good; one mustn't forget that.' So Rickie loses his independence, and Mr Pembroke gets him as his assistant master to do his dirty work for him, while Agnes fits in nicely into Dunwood House as the housekeeper. Soon Rickie perceives that he is deteriorating. He is forced to recognise that Agnes will never get nearer to him, that she is content with the daily round, the common task performed indifferently, that she regards him as a dreamer, and doesn't respect him, and that he is ceasing to love her, and that their life must be stale and stupid together. Their ideals are totally different. The Pembrokes, in fact, are the children of this world, who are wiser in their generation than the children of light:

> They live together without love. They work without conviction. They seek money without requiring it. They die, and nothing will have happened either for themselves or for others.

The crisis comes when his half-brother, the illegitimate Stephen Warham, quarrels with his aunt, Mrs Failing, and turns up at Dunwood House expecting to be helped. Agnes has intrigued against Stephen in order that Rickie shall inherit Mrs Failing's money, and she has succeeded before this, for conventional reasons, in getting Rickie not to avow his relationship, of which Stephen is then ignorant. Rickie is now guilty of the meanness of turning his back on his half-brother, while Agnes treats him as a blackmailer and interviews him cheque-book in hand. But Stephen has not come for money, he has come for sympathy. There is fine analysis of the Pembrokes' outlook when Stephen turns carelessly away from the door, spits in the gutter, and sums up the position as a 'take in.' He is hungry and penniless, and disappointed, the Elliots seem to him simply 'dirty people, not his sort.' But Rickie learns by accident a few minutes later that Stephen is not his half-brother by his detested father, but by the mother he reveres! She has loved another man, and his aunt, Mrs Failing, has kept her secret. Rickie then breaks away from the grip of the Pembrokes' gods for good.

The character studies of the bitter and malicious old woman, Mrs Failing, and of the rough, manly, and frank-hearted Stephen, whom the respectable world conspires to boycott, are admirably done. Many of the pages that describe the country life at Cadover have the rough vigour and something of the flavour of Meredith, to whose spiritual example our author is perhaps a little indebted. A quiet hatred of shams has inspired Mr Forster to one of the subtlest exposures of the modern Pharisee that we can recall in fiction. Bit by bit he gently peels off the respectable casings that enwrap his Philistines' souls.

The only criticism that we have to point against our author is that he uses the accident of sudden death too frequently in his artistic scheme. We resent Rickie's death at the close, though we cannot but admit that the squabble between Mr Pembroke and Stephen over Rickie's literary remains is too good to wish away. We may add that the vision of *The Longest Journey* is the vision of a poet doubled by a humourist, and this it is that explains the freshness and depth of this original book.

18
The Soul in Suburbia

C. F G. MASTERMAN

He 'watched his clever friend draw within the square a circle, and within the circle a square, and inside that another circle. "Are they real?" "The inside one is the one in the middle of everything, that there's never room enough to draw!"' This is human life as seen by the author of this amazingly clever book. It continues, always, at Cambridge, when men discuss metaphysics, and hope later to encounter reality; at Sawston, in the stifling miasma of the suburb, and the more stifling miasma of the English public school; at Wiltshire, challenged by the night and the wide sky. It is born by the coming of sudden death, and the incidents of change. It is confronted, sometimes perturbed, by the life of the earth. 'I say once more,' is the warning of one of the characters, 'beware of the earth.' We are conventional people, and conventions—if you will but see it—are majestic in their way, and will claim us in the end. It lives under no illusion. '"So it goes on for ever," she cried excitedly. He replied, "Not for ever. In time the fire at the centre will cool, and nothing can go on then."' But here it abides—circle within square, and square within circle, with the only one that is real, the one there is never room enough to draw. 'I see the respectable mansion,' is the confession of one. 'I see the smug fortress of culture. The doors are shut. The windows are shut. But on the roof the children go dancing for ever.'

The promise of *Where Angels Fear to Tread* is more than fulfilled in this volume. It is difficult, elusive, exasperating: with something of the cleverness of the young in it, and something of the cruelty. The influence of Meredith is there, especially of such a work as *Rhoda Fleming*, with the strong acknowledgment in both of the strange impalpable influences which the earth exercises over her children. There is little story: when Mr Forster wishes to get rid of his characters he murders them ruthlessly with sudden death on a railway crossing or in the football field. There is a cold satire upon the normal respectable life, the revolt against convention and

SOURCE *The Daily News*, 3 May 1907, p. 4

routine, and the hypocrisies which make up the world of every day, combined with a kind of quality of elusiveness and suggestion which opens the vision of far horizons even in the suburban street or the school playing-field. *The Longest Journey* is not a great novel; but it has embedded in it many of the ingredients of greatness. Its author will go far.

The Contest

'Rickie' Elliot, a cripple, clever, a teller of stories, in which the natural world is alive, and the old gods suddenly return, is passing through Cambridge, through marriage to a dreary, conventional pretty woman, to a respectable career as a house master in a suburban public school. There is one force, pulling him always into the accepted ways. The other is that of his illegitimate brother, the child of romance and passion, reared in the Wiltshire Downs: to the outward eye a rather crude rustic, with an unnatural thirst for drink, and half formed doubts concerning religion and the conventions. But he has great allies: the Downs themselves, huge and impressive under the quiet sky; all the natural impulse of the world of out-of-doors; all the interpretations which make the real life seem unreal.

The contest is undecided. The end is cut short by death; but the night before the tragedy Rickie had nearly surrendered, knowing (a disquieting revelation) that the earth is round, and 'the day is straight below, shining through other windows into other homes'; stimulated by remembrance of the lighted paper flames which they had sent sailing down the dark tunnel towards the sea.

> They played as boys who continued the nonsense of the railway carriage. The paper caught fire from the match, and spread into a rose of flame. 'Now gently with me,' said Stephen, and they laid it flower-like on the stream. Gravel and tremulous weeds leapt into sight, and then the flower sailed into deep water, and up leapt the two arches of a bridge. 'It'll strike!' they cried; 'no, it won't; it's chosen the left,' and one arch became a fairy tunnel, dropping diamonds. Then it vanished for Rickie; but Stephen, who knelt in the water, declared that it was still afloat, far through the arch, burning as if it would burn for ever.

The Ascendant Force

Rickie had been raised in the heart of it all.

> He had opened his eyes to filmy heavens, and taken his first walk on asphalt. He had seen civilization as a row of semi-detached villas, and society as a state in which men do not know the men who live next door. He had himself become part of the grey monotony that surrounds all cities.

Later his half-brother, driven by revolt into the morass of London, was to feel something of the horror of the earth-born for this quick, populous life, and is comforted by the knowledge that 'there's no such thing as a Londoner. He's only a country man on the road to devilry.'

After a few crowded hours of glorious life at Cambridge, the whole dead weight of these dead things rolls back upon him again. He is enmeshed in the net of the public school: choked in the existence of the House Master, with his little ineffectual aphorisms of dignity and honour, and effort to steer the young of the new generation into similar conventional ways. It is an atmosphere of dust and futility; with his brother-in-law, the skilled 'organizer' and type of it all; and every chink or crevice closed which might admit fresh air or a vision of the Infinite beyond.

> His technical position was that of master to a form low down on the Modern Side. But his work lay elsewhere. He organized. If no organization existed, he would create one. If one did exist, he would modify it. 'An organization,' he would say, 'is after all not an end in itself. It must contribute to a movement.' When one good custom seemed likely to corrupt the school he was ready with another; he believed that without innumerable customs there was no safety, either for boys or men. Perhaps he is right, and always will be right. Perhaps each of us would go to ruin if for one short hour we acted as we thought fit, and attempted the service of perfect freedom. The school caps, with their elaborate symbolism, were his; his the many-tinted bathing-drawers, that showed how far a boy could swim; his the hierarchy of jerseys and blazers. It was he who instituted Bounds, and Call, and the two sorts of exercise paper, and the three sorts of caning, and 'The Sawstonian,' a bi-terminal magazine. His plump finger was in every pie. The dome of his skull, mild but impressive, shone at every master's meeting. He was generally acknowledged to be the coming man.

It is all harmonised to the same chromatically spectral life: with the 'decent water colours in the drawing room' and 'Madonnas of acknowledged merit on the stairs,' and 'the strip of brown holland that led diagonally from the front door to the door of Herbert's study,' and the Master asking blandly, 'What does philosophy do? I fancy that in the long run Herbert Spencer will get no further than the rest of us;' and the woman who can never understand—who never could understand—why Rickie loved her, and why he left her, and why he would never come back to her again.

Outside on the open road is this crude, simple figure, with his absurd doubts and absurd assertions: a child of impulse, living, not comprehending; not desiring to comprehend.

> One of those sixpenny books tells Podge that he's made of hard little black things; another that he's made of brown things, large and squashy. There seems a discrepancy; but anything is better for a thoughtful youth than to be made in the Garden of Eden.

A book (it is to be feared) only for the few, but full of suggestion, of insight, of astonishing cleverness: the work of one who is determined to face the world of real things.

19
Extracts from Five Anonymous Reviews

1

One of the points in which Fiction is most at loggerheads with Fate lies in its admiration of the successful. It always devotes its keenest sympathies to those who succeed—whether in love, in honour, in ethical or material prosperity. In real life, of course, seventy-five out of every hundred people—to be on the optimistic side—are doomed, almost from their birth, to be failures—and most of them know it. Which is doubtless why they like, in Fiction, to be transported into a happier world, where success is the rule rather than the exception. And that was why, when a great man, half a century ago, wrote a novel without a hero, such was in itself a sufficiently remarkable fact to differentiate from all its fellows. That, again, is why not one out of ten novels of to-day deserves a similar sub-heading—however it may be with heroines.

Mr E. M. Forster, having already earned the right to do so by one clever novel, *Where Angels Fear to Tread*, now dares to give us a study of an amiable failure, which he might well, had he so chosen, have christened with the other half of the proverb, 'Fools Rush In.' For Rickie Elliot is a fool of the nobler type that is not far removed from genius, and he moves in a world of fools, less admirable than himself. Therein, be it said, lies the weak point of an undeniably clever book. We may live in a world of fools, but some of us, without being geniuses, are not unadmirable. And just as it is false to Art and Nature to paint all humanity as very white or very black, so is it to make the general grey too monotonous—if, chasing our several worthless baubles, we present one universal monotone of foolishness, there are at least lights and shades in other aspects of our characters. How can they talk

SOURCES 1. *The Tribune*, 22 April 1907, p. 2.
2. *The Morning Post*, 6 May 1907, p. 2.
3. *The Manchester Guardian*, 15 May 1907, p. 5.
4. *Cambridge Review*, 16 May 1907, p. 408.
5. *Spectator*, 6 July 1907, p. 24–5.

of your tapping the people neatly with your pen on the head at the end and it all crumbles away—it was something like that—I don't quite remember—never was anything deeper (?true) [...]—no irresponsible pen-tappings would send those people off into nothingness—and, what the timid *Angels* hadn't got, it has lovable people in it—Rickie is absolutely dear—and there is Ansell, and the young animal—but don't ever marry an Agnes, will you, for if you did your future is certain—there it is in your book prophetically set forth. Well, I can't tell you how truly beautiful I think it, and if I could it would only make you shrug your shoulders, for what does it matter what the foolish and the illiterate think? But I think you must be very happy—you've got very near to the 'words of eternal life'.

2

Those who like to confine their acquaintance to really nice or happy people should avoid reading *The Longest Journey*. They will thus miss more entertainment than it is perhaps kind to tell them about. A set of people from whom as neighbours or relations we should all pray to be delivered proves absorbing company with Mr Forster as merciless showman. Rickie Elliott, of unhappy childhood and inherited lameness, having 'crept cold and friendless and ignorant out of a great public school, preparing for a silent and solitary journey and praying as a highest favour that he might be let alone,' finds his prayer unanswered at Cambridge, and during a few magic years makes friends and the nearest approach to rational happiness accorded to any of the prominent characters in the book. Unfortunately he is taken in marriage at the age of twenty-three. His motive is clear and his side of the transaction admirably related. He had seen Agnes Pembroke in the arms of a previous lover—Gerald Dawes, with the figure of a Greek athlete and the face of an English one, so that 'just where he began to be beautiful the clothes started'—and she is transfigured for him by the memory of that moment and of one other when that lover lay in her arms—dying of football injuries. Her motive is perhaps less clear. She recognises the possibility of greatness in Rickie and snatches for herself a treasure which she cannot understand, and so destroys. Deserted by his Cambridge friends and giving up unconvincing short stories about Dryads for school-mastering, Rickie is soon swallowed up in the 'beneficent machine' of his brother-in-law's boarding-house at a gimcrack Eton, and acts the lies and conventionalities without which he learns that the machine would not be beneficent. From this he escapes—or rather is dragged out—for a moment, but dies, gone bankrupt once more, and admitting with his last breath the rightness of his aunt's view that 'the important things in life are little things and that people are not important at all.' Then the events of the last chapter suggest that after all he had been right and his aunt wrong. Mr

Forster pillories his characters with diabolic humour. Agnes, the mock unconventional, who got over the birth and death of her horrible child as she got over everything; Rickie's aunt, first introduced as the possibly influential lady who never pushed anyone because she found them always rebound and crush her, and exposed more fully later as a person who had laughed so much that she had forgotten what people were like; Rickie's father, who by laughing at the wrong time sent his wife off almost against her will with another man (again an extraordinarily clever and convincing episode); Mr Pembroke the organiser, phrasemaker, and bland tactician; Rickie himself, under the primal curse of 'knowledge of good-and-evil'—one after another are found wanting. One character escapes this criticism, yet it is not certain that Mr Forster has not attempted the impossible in endeavouring to make intelligible and attractive the blend of pagan god and modern hooligan which goes to make Stephen Wonham. Mr Forster, however, can be tenderly imaginative as well as mordant. He can show qualities yet more remarkable when now and again in some subtly-horrifying episode he lets the natural and animal rise to the surface through the iridescent scum of the conventional. The book as a whole is more provocative than satisfying. Formal criticism might say that it does not hang together enough, that there is a want of balance between the various ingredients, that there are too many bolts from heaven to give unity of character a chance, but too few to make a fine melodramatic thunderstorm. The sudden death-rate among the significant characters, exclusive of two children, one of whom is done to death quite wantonly on the railway, is 44 per cent. The method of Rickie's appointment as a schoolmaster is more diverting than absolutely convincing. But it would be altogether out of place to quarrel with a writer of Mr Forster's performance and promise about formal unities or small points. It is better to be thankful for what he has already given us and to await the next book—as all who read this and his first one will do—with eager anticipation.

3

Mr E. M. Forster has written a second novel which possesses all the characteristics which made his first remarkable. In *The Longest Journey* Mr Forster is as brilliant, as incoherent, as original, and as pessimistic as he was in *Where Angels Fear to Tread.* His hero, Rickie Elliott, is endowed with an abnormally sensitive temperament, aggravated by a lonely childhood and unhappy schooldays. He is intellectual but not clever, and he first really 'finds himself' in the congenial society of a small set of reading and thinking men at Cambridge. Then he proceeds to lose the self which he had found in marriage with a woman whom he only fancies that he loves, and whose 'spiritual apathy' is gradually and irrevocably revealed to him when it is too late. His marriage is only a part of the tragedy of his existence. Not less destructive to the vitality of his real self is the occupation of assistant to his brother-in-law, a schoolmaster with a genius for organising away personality and systematising life into convention. Rickie's awakening is achieved through the instrumentality of an illegitimate brother, a being conceived by Mr Forster as almost wholly animal but unmistakably real. Rickie forsakes his wife and abandons his profession, and devotes himself to writing and to taking charge of his irresponsible brother, in saving whose life he is shortly afterwards killed. The book is full of strong and vivid writing, and also of studied eccentricities and abruptnesses which subject the reader to a continuous succession of shocks. Mr Forster (like the erratic philosopher Ansell, who plays a wholly incredible part in his story) seems to be intent on preaching the gospel of reality, in opposition to the convention, organised make-believe, and etiquette which he sees as ruling nine-tenths of civilised life. He writes in a spirit of revolt, which breeds sincerity and conviction, but which perhaps leads him to identify the real to an unnecessary extent with the grotesque and the eccentric. But his studies of the unreal are exceedingly good. Best of all is Herbert Pembroke, who devotes himself to the task of converting a suburban grammar school into an imitation Eton, prepares himself to be ready to enter holy orders when the prospect of scholastic promotion renders it expedient, and proposes marriage at two days' notice when the possession of a wife seems a necessary qualification for becoming a house master. This personification of unreality is the most real character that Mr Forster has yet drawn.

4

If Mr Forster had written nothing but *Where Angels Fear to Tread* we should have thankfully admired him: and now that he has *The Longest Journey* to his credit our sentiments are only more pronounced. Mr Forster has a future; not that he will write very much better books, though even that may happen, but the public, when he has written more, will realise that it has been entertaining a genius unawares, and will behave as it does on those occasions. The scene of his new novel is laid for the most part in Cambridge. There is no 'local colour,' no description of the May Races, but the mental atmosphere of a small group of undergraduates in a certain College has been caught and unerringly put into words. We watch Rickie from his University days to his death some ten years later, gradually altering the views of life which he once held so easily: and we watch Ansell steadily holding to his own, and becoming an almost diabolical young fool who thinks that because he uttered a principle of life in his College rooms it is his duty to stand to it afterwards at the expense of his friend's happiness. Agnes, who marries Rickie, and nearly pulls him down to her level, is the ideal woman of a misogynist, banal, scheming, unprincipled without the excuse of being immoral; she has the distinction of having Mr Pembroke to her brother, and he draws forth from Mr Forster's pen a brilliant analysis of character. He is introduced to us in the first chapter as being 'not in orders, but on the verge of them'—a delightful phrase. Gerald, the boorish athlete, who was engaged to Agnes, and whose 'clothes hide him where he begins to be beautiful,' dies with a horrible suddenness, which marks all the very numerous deaths in this story. Stephen Wonham, a glorious pagan, is the most interesting character in the book after Rickie. He turns out to be his half-brother, and seems to be a kind of complement to him. The book is so admirably written, so full of brilliant things, that it is difficult to decide whether the design is as good as the workmanship. Personally, we think that the design falls short of the excellence which marks the book in other respects. Whether this is so or not, it remains a very remarkable novel. May we hope, in conclusion, that Mr Forster will collect his short stories from the *Independent Review*, and publish them as soon as may be.

5

We confess to preferring agreeable to disagreeable people in books as well as in life. A few disagreeable persons, to be sure, may serve the useful purpose of intensifying our sense of the amiability of the others, but when nearly all are disagreeable we ask the author to show some reason for offering us this glut of disagreeableness. There may be very good reasons, of course. The author may have made a faithful transcript from life, and it would be wrong, even disastrous, to shut out from art the results of industrious observation merely because they are disagreeable. But if the author does not make us feel quite sure that, like a Hebrew prophet, he is telling the truth, or that which has the value of truth, for our good, then we suspect him of perversity. We have a right to condemn his judgment in selection even before we can test the trusthworthiness of his evidence. The word 'abnormal' is used often in this story, and it might be justly applied to the behaviour of most of the characters. A few grains of geniality would have saved them nearly all their crises. This is a pity, because Mr Forster has genuine and unusual talents. He invents excellent phrases without labouring them. He is capable of humour, too, as one sees sometimes when it is not overlaid with an 'abnormal,' almost brutal, cynicism. The study of the rival factions in the prosperous school which is gradually turning itself from a commercial foundation drawing its strength from day-boys into an ordinary public-school with a majority of boarders and *esprit de corps* and everything else handsome about it is really first-rate.

Rickie Elliot, the hero of the story, is one of a clique of Cambridge undergraduates who spend their afternoons going long 'grinds' in the country instead of playing games. They talk philosophically and despise the Philistines. Mr Forster very nearly gives a new illumination to that old relation of youth,—the athlete and the 'prig,' or, to put it more in the words of the schoolboy, the bully and the 'smug.' Rickie is a congenital cripple (his agreeable father, who was also a cripple, called him Rickie because he was rickety!), and he had a miserable time at school. At Cambridge he is conscious of a rehabilitation. He is given a new chance; he finds that he need not be good at games to command some respect; he makes friends, and is extremely happy. Perhaps the pride of spirit of the philosophy-talking clique and their contempt for stupid physical robustness is somewhere near a truth which is not often expressed. At all events, an examination of the outlook on University life of a lame philosopher would be welcome to a world rather wearied by the snobbery of 'muscular Christianity.' The author, however, sheers off from this subject. The philosophers are not nearly so clever as they think they are, and we cannot help feeling that if culture necessarily led to the superfluous crises which blight so many lives in this story, the urbane Matthew Arnold would turn in his grave; and for ourselves, we should seriously consider whether a Pass degree and a severe course on the river would not be the most salubrious curriculum for our sons. While Rickie is still at Cambridge he falls in love with Agnes Pembroke, a young woman who seems quite amiable till Mr Forster's mordant cynicism gets to work on her character. She is already engaged to be married to an athletic young soldier who is a Greek god in appearance, but not exactly Hellenic in intellect. Mr Forster, who is not afraid of risking ridicule, kills off this god-like creature by an accident in a suburban football match. We are not sorry to lose him, as we cannot easily believe in his character. No British officer, we hope, would be vulgar and, as it were, unsportsmanlike enough to fume with rage at the awkward but well-meaning cripple who 'insults' him by generously offering him money so that he may be married without delay. When death has cleared the way for Rickie, he very abnormally sets up the figures of the deceased Dawes and Agnes in his mind as images made radiant and consecrated by the greatest event in Agnes's life. He rubs salt into her wounds. 'You've got to mind it,' he says, if she shows signs of letting time do its work of consolation. Even after he himself has surrendered to circumstances and become engaged to Agnes, though he had vowed that he would never tell his love, he deplores her insensibility to the past. As for his clever friends, they are rude and awkward beyond belief in the presence of Agnes. Rickie fails as an author, soon learns to despise the worldliness of his wife, and abandoning literature, accepts the offer of her pompous schoolmaster brother to become his junior house master. The best part of the book follows.

The estrangement of Rickie from his wife, and also from his friends, grows complete over the affair of his half-brother. All his life he has not suspected the nature of his relationship to Stephen Wonham—a kind of

Tony Lumpkin not without his good points in an uncouth way—and when the truth is revealed to him he is induced by his wife to conceal it. There is no more reason for doing this than there used to be for similar acts in the old-fashioned 'three-decker' novels; but we must say that the author graduates and accumulates very skilfully the prevarications, which are little more than acts of convenience at the moment, yet lead up to a wrong of real magnitude. Even then we cannot believe that the man who had been Rickie's greatest friend at Cambridge would have come, when the wrong was exposed, and denounced Rickie in a preposterous scene before a roomful of schoolboys without having made the least attempt to help him or warn him beforehand. Rickie, at all events, is left to atone for much injustice to his half-brother. How he pays for his fault is the *dénoûement* of the story, and we shall not disclose it. This novel is worth consideration, not for what it is, but for what it nearly is. It is a token of what Mr Forster may yet do,—unless, unhappily, the 'abnormality' of his invention is constitutional and ineradicable.

A Room with a View
(1908)

20
Review

R. A. SCOTT-JAMES

There is just enough that is right in Mr Forster to triumph over the mass of him that seems to us to be wrong. There is no use denying that he begins by irritating us exceedingly. He is full of views; what is worse, he is full of subtlety, a subtlety that rises up and assails you in pregnant epigram or paraded restraint. He insists on assuming—with that blind faith in unrealities which only the 'intellectual' is capable of—that Early Victorian rules of propriety are the rules of today, and he flagellates these extinct, or, at least, dying, moral mannerisms with caustic, but belated, satire.

The truths with which he is concerned are sometimes of so subtle a character that he forgets, if he has ever known, some of the elementary ones. For instance, he is so intent on showing that all that is 'British' is hypocritical and hollow that he forgets that an English young lady, travelling in Italy, is not so strictly chaperoned as an Italian young lady, and that even the prim inhabitants of an English pension do not regard it as indecent for a lady who has fainted at the sight of a murder in the streets to be escorted home by an acquaintance who has the ill-breeding to be a man. Or, again, while we may admit, with Mr Forster and the two Messrs. Emerson, that springtime and love are admirable things, and that 'we have no rights' over a cabman's soul, we still think it was reasonable for the occupants of a hired carriage to object when their driver, not content with taking his sweetheart on the box, loaded her with embraces. It was just as reasonable to object as it is unreasonable to bring in the moral problem of the 'proprieties.' If Mr Forster would be more intent on story-telling and less intent on instruction he would save the strength which he spends in tilting at windmills.

SOURCE *The Daily News*, 20 October 1908, p. 4.

In Florence

And yet this is a brilliant novel, a novel which begins by being brilliantly dull and ends by being humanly absorbing. The author gradually gets into his stride, and comes to know his own characters, and make us know them. Dull and trivial as they may seem, they learn to be natural, and the prim, the semi-suburban, the conventional is suddenly brought into contrast with the primitive earnestness of flesh and blood and feeling. Lucy has been through her Italy, and has endured the constraint of Miss Bartlett's foolish chaperonage. She has walked, Baedeker in hand, through the streets and churches of Florence; she has endured and, indeed, accepted the chatter of a pension; she has talked to the kindly parson, Mr Beebe, listened to the spiteful parson, Mr Eager, and been submerged beneath the ungoverned outpourings of Miss Lavish, the local-colour novelist. She has been forced to talk to Mr Emerson, père, and Mr George Emerson, fils, whom the pension will not tolerate; by the latter she has been rescued at the fateful moment when an Italian, bleeding from a death wound, seems to speak to her as the blood spirts from his mouth. Startled into reality by this literal 'call of the blood' she has conversed with a live man almost with freedom; and, again, she has come upon him suddenly among the 'cataracts' of violets, when without hesitation the crude man has 'stepped quickly forward and kissed her'; and she has been whisked away by the prim Miss Bartlett, and engaged to that cultured gentleman, Mr Cecil Vyse.

The Man of Culture

Then it is that the story begins to move with a more powerful irony and a more real effect of passion. Lucy is at home now at Windy Corner. Her kind, querulous, solicitous mother is in the house; so is her noisy, brainless, healthy brother, Freddy. Cecil Vyse begins to pervade the scene. From his intellectual throne in a corner of London, where he is surrounded by ideas in the shape of books and the philistinism of metropolitan culture, he ventures to descend to the unsophisticated circle of Windy Corner. He had known Lucy for years, but Italy had 'worked some marvel in her. It gave her light, and—which he held more precious—it gave her shadow. Soon he detected in her a wonderful reticence. She was like a woman of Leonardo da Vinci's, whom we love not so much for herself as for the things she will not tell us.' He looks for 'charm' in her; he would be shocked by any positive assertion of character. He likes to speak to her of books, and poetry, and pictures, and to be heard; and once, under the appropriate influence of the fields and trees, he even submits himself to the 'momentary cult of the fresh air' and the delight at her simplicity. And so he explains his newly-acquired feeling for pathways:

'I had got an idea—I daresay wrongly—that you feel more at home with me in a room.'

'A room?' she echoed, hopelessly bewildered.

'Yes. Or, at the most, in a garden, or on a road. Never in the real country like this.'

'Oh, Cecil, whatever do you mean? I have never felt anything of the sort. You talk as if I was a kind of poetess sort of person.'

'I don't know that you aren't. I connect you with a view—a certain type of view. Why shouldn't you connect me with a room?'

She reflected a moment, and then said, laughing:

'Do you know that you're right? I do. I must be a poetess after all. When I think of you it's always as in a room. How funny!'

To her surprise, he seemed annoyed.

'A drawing-room, pray? With no view?'

'Yes, with no view, I fancy. Why not?'

'I'd rather,' he said reproachfully, 'that you connected me with the open air.'

She said again, 'Oh, Cecil, whatever do you mean?'

The Man of Fact

> Views are really crowds—crowds of trees and houses and hills—and are bound to resemble each other, like human crowds—and . . . the power they have over us is something supernatural, for the same reason. . . For a crowd is more than the people who make it up. Something gets added to it—no one knows how—just as something has got added to those hills.

It is not Cecil who teaches Lucy that; it is George Emerson, the man who had kissed her when she came through the cataracts of violets, who kisses her again when she is another man's fiancée, who teaches her that Cecil is 'the type who's kept Europe back for a thousand years,' who has been 'playing tricks on people, on the most sacred form of life that he can find.'

Mr Forster breaks through the bonds of his own art; the very lessons he began laboriously to teach crumble beneath the central human facts which at the last hold his and our attention. The fine, primitive, deep things which do not deny the flesh, even if they are not 'of it,' are dear to him, so that he forgets his horrible artificialities, and becomes genuine. The book grows on the reader, and, if he reads with care, he will have cause to be grateful to Mr Forster.

21
Unsigned Review

[VIRGINIA WOOLF]

Mr E. M. Forster's title *A Room with a View* is symbolical, of course; and to explain the sense which he conveys by it will introduce our comment also. Lucy Honeychurch and her elderly cousin Charlotte go to stay at a pension in Florence; their rooms, they grumble, have no view. A gentleman promptly exclaims, 'I have a view; I have a view', and proceeds to offer them his room and the room of his son George. They are outraged, but they consent; and when cousin Charlotte has insisted that she shall occupy the young man's apartment, because he is a bachelor, she discovers, pinned over the washstand, 'an enormous note of interrogation'. 'What does it mean? she thought.... Meaningless at first, it gradually became menacing, obnoxious, portentous with evil'. But if we are not cousin Charlotte, in age or temper, if, moreover, we have read what Mr Forster has written in the past, we are amused rather than bewildered. We are more than amused, indeed, for we recognize that odd sense of freedom which books give us when they seem to represent the world as we see it. We are on the side, of course, of Mr Emerson and his son George, who say exactly what they mean. We care very much that Lucy should give up trying to feel what other people feel, and we long for the moment when, inspired by Italy and the Emersons, she shall burst out in all the splendour of her own beliefs. To be able to make one thus a partisan is so much an achievement, the senses that one sees truth from falsehood is so inspiriting, that it would be right to recommend people to read Mr Forster's book on these accounts alone. If we are honest, we must go on to say that we are not so confident by the time the book is at an end. The story runs simply enough. Lucy is kissed by George Emerson, and the ladies fly to Rome. In Rome they meet Mr Cecil Vyse, a young man who feels of his own accord what other people feel, both about art and about life. When Lucy is back again in her ugly home in Surrey she agrees to marry Mr Vyse, but happily the Emersons take the villa

SOURCE *Times Literary Supplement*, 26 April 1907, p. 134.

over the way, and Lucy is made to own that she can tell the true from the false before it is too late. To compress the motive of the book into this compass is, of course, to simplify it absurdly, for nothing is said of the cleverness, the sheer fun, and the occasional beauty of the surrounding parts. We sketch the story thus, however, because we believe that it was meant to take this line, and we are conscious of some disappointment when for one reason or another it goes a different way, and the view is smaller than we expected. The disappointment is not due to any change of scene, but to some belittlement, which seems to cramp the souls of the actors. Lucy's conversion becomes a thing of trifling moment, and the views of George and his father no longer spring from the original fountain. But should we complain when we have originality and observation, and a book as clever as the other books that Mr Forster has written already?

22

Unsigned Review: 'The Half-Hidden Life'

[C. F. G. MASTERMAN]

Mr Forster has earned the right to serious criticism. His work—limited to three novels and some shorter stories and sketches—has revealed individuality, distinction, and a power of suggestion which opens large issues. *A Room with a View*, the title of his latest book, might stand for a title of all his work. He reveals in minute and exact detail the 'room' and its contents: the patterned paper on the walls, the sofas and antimacassars, the elaborate, grotesque, or stuffy artifice of conventional construction. And beyond, he shows the 'view': outside man's handiwork, judging, sometimes condemning, always disturbing, the contented occupants of the artificial arena. Dawn flares through the blinds, the sunset casts haunting shadows on the carpets and cushions, outside is the sound of tempest or the challenging silence of the night. And the conflict amongst all his characters—set in the moment where two eternities meet, which is always a moment of supreme choice—arises just from the fact that although their natural and accepted habit approves of the orderly comfort of the 'room,' there is within all of them some wild or exultant element which responds to the high calling of the 'view'.

The 'room' may take many shapes and forms. In that fascinating and tragic farce, *Where Angels Fear to Tread*, it is found (for one nation) in the spreading securities of suburban London, for another in the crumbling dead streets of a little Tuscan city. In *The Longest Journey*, it varied from the traditional decencies of the older Universities—with their secret for the fashioning of the completed English gentleman—to the traditional decencies of the English countryside, the English gentleman, completed, pursuing his ordered and tranquil existence in that station of life to which

SOURCE *Nation*, 28 November 1908, pp. 352–4.

he has been called. In his latest novel the scene also changes; from the English pension at Florence, with its enthusiasm for the work of Karl Baedeker and John Ruskin, to the spreading suburbs of Surrey, in those regions where the new rich and the emigrant clerk are making desolate the hills which look southward to the sea. Both of these are outposts of man's civilisation: both, therefore, places of especial danger. The *pension* has high bulwarks in the atmosphere of breezy clergymen and maiden ladies, in the advantage which can be given by such outside aids in the city as joint excursions of British tourists, English afternoon tea shops, and the 'cultured English community' resident in Florence. But in the immediate background is a nation with a thousand centuries behind it: passion in the city square leading to sudden death: Phaethon and Persephone, who will drive the blithe and unsuspecting party up the hillside to Fiesole, disguised as an Italian coachman and his 'sister': with (at the summit) a field blue with violets and the vision of 'fifty miles of Italian spring.' And the little semi-urban village of the Surrey hillside, although linked firmly to the city by the South Eastern Railway, and stuffed with all the material of contemporary life—illustrated papers, and tennis courts, and clever conversation—has also below it deep pinewoods with a lake in the heart of them, and a wide southern plain leading beyond to one grey glimpse of sea. Here are things which own no allegiance to convention, fit habitation for those which still survive of all the older gods. And to Mr Forster, as to Heine and others, the older gods have not perished: they but remain, abiding in patience, until the tyranny of denial be overpast. In one of his sketches in the *Independent Review* (not yet republished), 'A Panic Fear,' in a party on picnic in a valley of Greece, Pan appears for a moment, and asserts his supremacy: in a gust or tumult, suddenly coming and going, no man knowing whether in external Nature or the mind of man. And it is Pan who here appears, in the hills above Florence first, and later in the well-trimmed garden of an English suburban residence in the neighborhood of Dorking: when George Emerson kisses Lucy Honeychurch, first in violation of all standards of conventional respectability, and later in violation of all standards of conventional honor.

It is this hidden life—secure and silent, and often, through a lifetime, undisturbed—that Mr Forster sets himself to reveal in the characters of the working world. It is a current flowing, mysterious, elusive, behind the motives and desires which make the web of conscious apprehension. The efforts to explore it are like occasional soundings swung into an unfathomed deep: adventures upon an uncharted shore. The normal activity of existence flows on, men are getting and spending, enjoying bodily exercise, discussing their surface politics, philosophies, and religions: women are 'falling in love' with conventional figures, and (for the most part) accepting with satisfaction the affection and the convention. But beyond and behind it all, are tides and oceans which may at any time surge up into the sheltered ports and harbors, and sweep the little craft which have found shelter there far out to sea. The tiny, intelligent life is outraged and defiant: it protests and it weeps, it refuses to face realities, it lies heartily and continuously to the outside world and to itself. Sometimes it triumphs in the re-establishment of order: the ship has regained the shelter again, and its occupants, wasted by the struggle, anchor more firmly in the shadows, and declare that they will never more put out to sea: sometimes the upheaval is permanent: the land drops behind the horizon, and the vessel rides buoyantly over the waste or waters, rejoicing in the challenge of its vast and incalculable tides. And all these spiritual conflicts the author can set—with a quiet and detached vision, more ironical than any deliberate interference or exposition—amid the dust and dead flowers of a tourist-haunted Italian city, or between the tennis-court and the drawing-room of an English suburban villa.

From the beginning of this story of the spiritual adventure of George Emerson and Lucy Honeychurch, the chief protagonists have some advantage denied to their contemporaries; weak places (as it were) in the wrappings of convention, which may wear thin through the influence of circumstance, and leave them exposed to naked reality. George—from start to finish a rather shadowy, indefinite figure—is the son of a father who has refused to accept the recognised standards, just because they are the standards which are recognised. His revolt, indeed, is as much on the surface as the standards themselves: it is not a revolt from the depth: and his protests of emancipation come in the end to exhibit themselves as ridiculous, and as tedious as the normal praises of imprisonment. But he has been teaching his son. 'He has the merit,' is the explanation of the clergyman, 'of saying exactly what he means. He no more thought of putting you under an obligation than he thought of being a bore. It is so difficult—at least I find it difficult—to understand people who speak the truth.' 'A type,' is the summary, 'one disagrees with rather than deplores.' Lucy finds him willing to act as guide in Santa Croce. 'I hope you have not been put to any great inconvenience,' she declares. 'My dear,' the old man answers, 'I think that you have been repeating what you have heard older people say. You are pretending to be touchy. But you are not, really. Stop being so tiresome.' His loud and incredulous comments in the Peruzzi Chapel drive forth in silent indignation a congregation and lecturer 'directing them now to worship Giotto, not by tactile valuations, but by the standards of the spirit.' 'My father has that effect on everyone,' explains George, ruefully, 'he will try to be kind.' 'I hope we all try,' said she, smiling nervously. 'Because we think it improves our characters,' he answers; 'but he is kind to people because he loves them: and they find it out, and are offended or frightened.'

And Lucy, though springing from and encompassed by convention, has radiant youth on her side, and music, with a reaction also, intensifying in bitterness, against her cousin and companion Miss Bartlett, a spinster too obviously dedicated to the worship of false gods. In her playing, 'passion was there, but it could not be easily labelled: it slipped between love and hatred and jealousy; and all the furniture of the pictorial style. And she was tragical only in the sense that she was great, for she loved to play on the side of Victory.' And she is not unmoved also by the general spirit of revolt and vague disturbance: which has come to one who 'reigned in many an Early Victorian castle, and was queen of much Early Victorian song.'

> In her heart, also, there are springing up strange desires. She, too, is enamoured by heavy winds, and vast panoramas, and green expanses of the sea. She has marked the kingdom of this world, how full it is of wealth and beauty and war—a radiant crust, built around the central fires, spinning towards the receding heavens. Men, declaring that she inspires them to it, move joyfully over the surface, having the most delightful meetings with other men; happy, not because they are masculine, but because they are alive. Before the show breaks up, she would like to drop the august title of the Eternal Woman, and go there as her transitory self.

Given these persons, the machinery of Chance or Natural Design effects the rest. The unrestful challenge of old things in Florence is stimulated by the emotional experience of a murder in the Square; then a spring expedition to the hills, and a chance encounter there, when Pan had scattered the excursionists, breaks through the recognised barriers. In a vision of the earth's exuberance, violets appearing as beauty gushing out to water the earth, he, a man, sees her, a woman; nothing else but the approving earth under a limitless sky. From that moment the thing works itself out to inevitable conclusion. There is the spirit of high comedy in it. Mr Forster can describe with sure touch the queer satisfactions and still queerer repugnances which make up the strange region of modern things. Had this element been there alone, the book would have been merely an excellent satirical judgment of manners and conventions. Had the other element stood alone—the revelation of the hidden life—it would have been mystical, intangible, illusory. By the fusion of the one with the other, he is able to present work humorous and arresting, with a curious element in it of compelling strength and emotion.

23
Extracts from Three Anonymous Reviews

1

When Lucy, the heroine of *A Room with a View*, by E. M. Forster, found herself at the Pension Bertolini in a room without a view, it was to the Emersons, father and son, that she owed the change which gave her a sight of the busy life of Florence and of Fiesole across the city's towers. And it was George Emerson who afterwards made a window in her being to let in the light.

Mr Forster is a humorist who has looked on many aspects of human life with kindly and discerning eyes. Underneath his satire and his mockery of the shows of life there lies a very real belief in the things which really count—in the joy of the sun and the free air, in sincerity of soul, and in passion. He is an optimist in spite of his irony, for there is no hint of the obstacles which chance and circumstance may throw in the way of the disciple of nature, nor can we divine how he would have had his heroine behave if George Emerson had convinced her of sin after instead of before the union with Cecil. We have left ourselves no space to pass in review the characters which fill this admirable comedy. They are not described, but display themselves in action, they are all typical and at the same time clearly individualised. Here and there, as in the ways and speech of Cecil, we catch echoes of Mr Bernard Shaw and our author has in many respects a kindred spirit to Meredith, but he owes no debt to one writer or the other. He has his own humour and his own philosophy and his own admirable style. But he should beware of farce, in which he is unlikely to excel.

SOURCES 1. *The Manchester Guardian*, 4 November 1908, p. 5.
2. *The Morning Post*, 23 November 1908, p. 2.
3. *Spectator*, 2 January 1909, pp. 23–4.

2

There is much that is strong and admirable in *A Room with a View*, and we must congratulate Mr E. M. Forster on having added considerably to his reputation. His satire is clever and biting, but his sense of humour and the occasional ridiculousness of his situations save his satire from being ill-natured. In the first part of the book the scene is laid in Florence, and is mostly taken up with discussions and dialogues and witticisms, but the characters are introduced in an original manner, which argues well for further acquaintance with them. The real human interest begins in Part II, at Windy Corner, overlooking the Sussex Weald, the bourgeois home of Lucy and Freddy and their amusing mother Mrs Honeychurch. The threads of life had combined together to weave Lucy into a fresh, natural adorable creature; but art, in the shape of a lover, with the additional aid of a chaperon had conspired to print a conventional stamped pattern on the original pure homespun. Lucy gets engaged to Cecil, a distinguished sensitive person, who despises the world and thinks this method a test of refinement. Windy Corner was not perfect, but it had a way of getting the 'grittiness out of life,' and Cecil was not altogether at home in this atmosphere. Much family merriment is expended over the announcement of the engagement, and even Anne, the maid, seemed to put down each plate at the table as 'if it were already a wedding present.' Cecil tries to improve Lucy, and, according to *Punch*, people do not want to be improved except in their worldly circumstances. Anyway, George Emerson accepted honesty as a natural birthright, and believed it 'grew heavenwards like the flowers,' also he could love passionately, and Cecil was at heart an ascetic. It is all very well told, for it requires ingenuity and originality to conceive a character like George Emerson and touch him with a magic wand so that his love episodes appear spontaneous and sincere instead of vulgar and uncontrolled, as they might have done with a less skilful pen. There is such a thing as the genius of love, and this man had it, and it is the function of such genius that it bursts all bonds and sees the naked truth by the light of its own inner force. Mr Beebe, a family friend, had said of Lucy that one day the 'water-tight compartments in her will break down, and music and life will mingle.' So these two bright, brave natures face life together, and Cecil retires, a wiser man. Truth to say, his renunciation of Lucy makes us almost like him, 'for nothing in his love became him like the leaving of it.'

3

Mr Forster's new novel is not only much the best of the three he has written, but it clearly admits him to the limited class of writers who stand above and apart from the manufacturers, conscientious or otherwise, of contemporary fiction. To note improvements first, one finds in *A Room with a View* greater sympathy with and interest in his own *dramatis personae.* In *The Longest Journey,* for example, Mr Forster's detachment at times reached the verge of callousness, and personages were suddenly killed off in a manner suggesting that he had got bored with them and wanted to make a fresh start. In the novel before us the characters are treated more patiently, sympathetically, and with greater consistency, and the author's attitude not only leads to a greater continuity, but is far more effective in securing and riveting the interest of the reader. Again, the freakish and somewhat cynical humour which disfigured his earlier work is here replaced by a kindlier tolerance. In short, Mr Forster, while retaining all the freshness and unconventionality of his outlook, has come to regard the human comedy with greater respect and sanity. When the story opens, Lucy Honeychurch, an attractive young English girl chaperoned by a middle-aged cousin, Charlotte Bartlett, has just arrived at the Pension Bertolini in Florence. The proposal of two Englishmen, father and son, to exchange their rooms with those allotted to Lucy and her cousin, clumsily offered and reluctantly accepted, forms the 'take off' of the ensuing romance. The Emersons are looked at somewhat askance on social and other grounds by the other visitors in the *pension,* including two elderly spinsters of the Mrs Nickleby type, and a strong-minded novelist; but Lucy is on her *Wanderjahr,* temporarily emancipated from the shackles of villadom, and athirst for adventure. George Emerson, the son, happens to be at hand when Lucy is the unwilling witness of a painful street tragedy, his timely support begets mutual confidence, and in a moment of expansion, though not without provocation, he so far forgets himself as to kiss her at a picnic. Lucy is really angry; she has no difficulty in persuading herself that she cares nothing for young Emerson, and Charlotte sweeps her away from the danger zone to Rome, where they join forces with their friends the Vyses. Thus when the action is resumed in Surrey Lucy has just become engaged to Cecil Vyse, a highly presentable and altogether blameless prig. But by a coincidence of which Mr Forster is so far aware that he is at pains to account for it with considerable ingenuity, the Emersons become the tenants of a neighbouring villa, and renewed propinquity forces on Lucy the need of reconsidering her position, with results that may be readily forecasted when the characters of her two suitors are taken into account. The conclusion, however, is not easily arrived at, for Lucy, with all her charm and intelligence, belongs to that not inconsiderable tribe of people who habitually misinterpret their genuine instincts. She is not a *femme incomprise* so much as a girl who cannot understand herself. Periods of rebellion alternate with periods of abject slavery. To make matters worse, she relies, at a critical period in her development, on the judgment of her cousin, who is an excruciatingly conscientious prude. The gradual emancipation of Lucy from Charlotte's influence, and that of other representatives of narrow-minded conventionality, is illustrated with great subtlety and humour, and it is much to the credit of Mr Forster that, while enlisting the sympathies of his readers on the side of Lucy in her struggles towards self-assertion, he by no means fails to render justice to those who thwart and resist her. Charlotte, though exasperating and ridiculous is not altogether contemptible; indeed, one parts from her with a certain compassion for this angular poor relation, incapable of exciting affection, and always conscious of her obligations. Excellent also is the portrait of Cecil Vyse, the blameless and cultured young man who was perfectly at his ease with books and pictures, but incapable of reading the hearts of men and women. With a touch of fantastic humour, more surprising than convincing, Mr Forster discovers in Cecil an element of nobility in the hour of his defeat; while Mr Beebe, the witty, tolerant, and conciliatory clergyman, develops a vein of inhumanity at the close for which we are not sufficiently prepared.

Mr Forster's novel lends itself readily to quotation, but we must content ourselves with only a few extracts. Thus Mrs Honeychurch's crudely practical point of view is happily illustrated by her explanation of her son's hostility to his prospective brother-in-law:—'You are jealous of Cecil because he may stop Lucy knitting you silk ties.' On the other hand, Cecil's aesthetic interest in Lucy is defined by the phrase: 'She was like a woman of Leonardo da Vinci's, whom we love not so much for herself as for the things that she will not tell us'; while his failure to rise to a great occasion suggests the comment: 'Passion should believe itself irresistible... Above all, it should never ask for leave when there is a right of way.' We get a vivid picture of Lucy's neighbours in Surrey by the reference to 'their kindly affluence, their inexplosive religion, their dislike of paper-bags, orange-peel, and broken bottles.' Mrs Vyse's pretensions to culture are well hit off in the account of her dinner-party 'consisting entirely of the grandchildren of famous people. The food was poor, but the talk had a witty weariness that impressed Lucy.' And again: 'Mrs Vyse was a nice woman, but her personality, like many another's, had been swamped by London, for it needs a strong head to live among many people. The too vast orb of her fate had crushed her; she had seen too many seasons, too many cities, too many men for her abilities, and even with Cecil she was mechanical, and behaved as if he was not one son, but, so to speak, a filial crowd.' Lastly, Charlotte's failure in life is almost explained in the exaggerated deference of her appeal: 'Dearest Lucia, may I trespass upon you for a pin?'

There are no remarkable or heroic people in the book, but Mr Forster has the happy knack of making stupid people interesting and tiresome people amusing. And he has a gift for dialogue which should stand him in excellent stead if he ever turns his attention to the stage.

Howards End
(1910)

24
Unsigned Review

[PERCY LUBBOCK]

Mr E. M. Forster has now done what critical admirers of his foregoing novels have confidently looked for—he has written a book in which his highly original talent has found full and ripe expression. Neither of its three clever, imperfect, slightly baffling predecessors was quite at unity with itself. In each case there was an uncertainty of attack and a want of harmony in the method which prevented an exceptionally fine sense of character from making its proper effect. All this is put right in *Howards End.* Here Mr Forster has finally got his method under control, and has seized his idea in a grasp that completely encircles it; so that the peculiar freshness and individuality of his gift can now be properly seen and understood. It is in the first place securely founded, this gift, upon a power of generalization which holds the tightly-handled plot compactly together. But Mr Forster works from the centre outwards, and reaches the graces and humours of the surface of his story with a mind quite clear as to the structure beneath. His generalization starts from the everlasting opposition of the two types which between them hold civilized life together, the people who are not interested in 'personal relations' but who alone make the world practically habitable for the other type, the people who are not interested in the thing done but only in the human beings who do it. The Wilcox family stand for the first, English, honest, unimaginative, exasperating, and the Schlegel family for the second, of mixed blood and restless brains and hampering imaginations, certainly not less exasperating, the Wilcoxes being those who deal in realities without understanding them, the Schlegels those who understand realities without dealing in them. The Schlegels, indeed, must do all the understanding, and the question is whether they can understand enough for both and so effect an alliance with the Wilcoxes, instead of standing aside and making fun of them. Margaret Schlegel makes the attempts and dares a compromise: 'More and more', she said, 'do I refuse to draw my

SOURCE *Times Literary Supplement*, 27 October 1910, p. 412.

income and sneer at those who guarantee it'. Helen, her sister, is *intransigeante*, and faces the disaster to which her consistency brings her. Mr Forster seizes the very essence of the contrast, and again and again pierces his material, with the sharpest needles, at the exact psychological point. It is another question whether the actual incidents of the story, apart from the perfect justice of the psychology, are well invented and disposed; and here we could make some criticisms. But we are dealing with a very remarkable and original book, and we will not linger over faults which do not touch its central virtue. Nor need more be said of the character drawing than that it has all the light shrewdness we have seen before in this writer's work, with the added clarity of practice. What gives Mr Forster's writing its quite unique flavour is something more than this. It is the odd charming vein of poetry which slips delicately in and out of his story, showing itself for a moment in the description of a place or a person, and vanishing the instant it has said enough to suggest something rare and romantic and intangible about the person or the place. It is a refinement which belongs to realism, not romance, for it is simply due justice done to an element in life too momentary and swift for most realism, so called, to overtake. But where quick-fingered lightness and deftness are demanded there Mr Forster never fails; and he has caught in this book a sensitive reflection of life on which he is very heartily to be congratulated.

25
Review

R. A. SCOTT-JAMES

'Only connect ...' is Mr Forster's motto. It is because he has taken this motto not only for his book but also for his method of work that he has achieved the most significant novel of the year. Those who seek to express a philosophic view of life in fiction generally strain their characters till they are puppets of their philosophy. Those, on the other hand, who are content to trace individual characters realistically are in danger at all times of losing the scheme and purpose of their work. It is because they do not 'connect'; because to write a novel near to nature on the one hand, and true to the larger vision on the other requires tremendous labour of thought making perception and wisdom fruitful; the fitting of the perception of little things with the perception of universal things; consistency, totality, *connection*. Mr Forster has written a *connected* novel.

Mr Forster's method is a sort of bridge between that of Mr Conrad and that of Mr Galsworthy. The former, I am told, starts the making of a story with an incident which impressed itself on his imagination, and round this primary situation the story is hinged; the latter, starting with a generalisation, selects facts which illustrate it. Both methods are legitimate, and the one by Mr Conrad, the other by Mr Galsworthy, have been successfully used. But who could say of *Howards End* that the one method or the other had been adopted? The novel rises like a piece of architecture full-grown before us. It is all bricks and timber, but it is mystery, idealism, a far-reaching symbol.

House and Home

And as it happens Howards End, from which the title is taken, is itself a house. Though the scene is only occasionally placed in this old house, with its wych-elm, its garden, and its Hertfordshire environment, Howards End

SOURCE *The Daily News*, 7 November 1910, p. 4.

is always the background of the story. It is always there as a soft refrain which comes back and back amid a hundred new situations. This house itself is a sort of symbol of everything in England, old and new, changeless, yet amid flux. It connects in itself two ideas which seem to be sundered as the Poles. First of all it is a *home.* To Mrs Wilcox, who was born there, it stands for everything personal, intimate, cherished; not merely 'bricks and mortar,' but a 'Holy of Holies into which Howards End had been transfigured.' But in the second place it is property; it is bricks and mortar simply; it is exchangeable for money; it is part of the economic order of things, and has no sacred connection save that which attaches to the 'right of property.' For Henry Wilcox, and for Charles, his son, it is no home; it is only a house. 'To them Howards End was a house: they could not know that to her it had been a spirit, for which she sought a spiritual heir.'

For Mrs Wilcox thought she had found a spiritual heir to her home in Margaret Schlegel; and she had indicated her wishes in a little pencil note which the Wilcoxes ignored.

> May they not have decided even better than they supposed? Is it credible that the possessions of the spirit can be bequeathed at all? Has the soul offspring? A wych-elm tree, a vine, a wisp of hay with dew on it—can passion for such things be transmitted where there is no bond of blood? No, the Wilcoxes are not to be blamed. The problem is too terrific, and they could not even perceive a problem.

If Margaret Schlegel stands for the refinement which has survived culture, the personal force which combined intellect, perception, and charm, her sister Helen is more truly the antithesis to the Wilcoxes, or, to be precise, the eldest son Charles Wilcox. Helen is all that which is known as 'temperament.' With what vivacity Mr Forster makes her talk, with what high spirits and impulsive generosity she always acts! She does not see so clearly as Margaret does the danger of the Schlegel life, which is all ideas, enlightenment, and fineness, the danger that it may become 'sloppy.' For a moment Helen had responded to the lure of the Wilcox energy, the pushful, practical, masterful makers of the world, the people who lived 'the outer life of "telegrams and anger."' She had responded, in her impulsive, slightly hysterical way, at the touch of a younger Wilcox, but she shrank away again to a settled hostility against it; whereas to Margaret this life—the life of 'telegrams and anger'—

> was to remain a real force. She could not despise it, as Helen and Tibby affected to do. It fostered such virtues as neatness, decision, and obedience, virtues of the second rank, no doubt, but they have formed our civilization. They form character, too; Margaret could not doubt it: they keep the soul from becoming sloppy. How dare Schlegels despise Wilcoxes, when it takes all sorts to make a world?

Poetry and the Economic Basis

For Mr Forster does not let us forget that even Helen Schlegel, with all her indifference to material things, with her recklessness, her generosity, her habit of taking no thought, has a secured income of six hundred a year. And that is the great difference between her and Mr Bast, the miserable little clerk, who yearned after the infinite, but was by pressure of poverty and social pretensions compelled to yearn even more after his lost umbrella. Helen is willing to do anything for the squalid Mr Bast, because he is unfortunate, and because he has ideals. But Margaret is more practical without suffering loss on the finer side.

> The imagination (she says) ought to play upon money and realise it vividly, for it's the—the second most important thing in the world. It is so slurred over and hushed up, there is so little clear thinking—oh, political economy, of course, but so few of us think clearly about our own private incomes, and admit that independent thoughts are in nine cases out of ten the result of independent means. Money: Give Mr Bast money, and don't bother about his ideals. He'll pick up those for himself.

Margaret, then, does not give rein to her bias. It is Helen who is the *extreme* of the spiritual life, plunging into it like a gambler, seeing the moment but not seeing whither it leads. And her antithesis is the brutal Charles, who stands equally recklessly on his right of property—on the speed of his motor-cars, the decisiveness of his actions, the effectiveness of his anger and his telegrams. He is all prose, and goes to prison; Helen is all passion, and has a bastard child. But Margaret has her feet at least firmly planted on the earth, and she is able to make a success of marriage with Henry Wilcox.

> Only connect! That was the whole of her sermon. Only connect the prose and the passion, and both will be exalted, and human love will be seen at its height. Live in fragments no longer. Only connect, and the beast and the monk, robbed of the isolation that is life to either, will die.

In thus drawing together one or two of the threads with which the story supplies us, I may seem to have emphasised too much the theoretical or philosophical side of this novel. A philosophical novel it is, but its fineness as philosophy is just that which would have delighted the late William James. At all points it is life itself, experience itself, which is the touchstone and the fabric of Mr Forster's theory. No cut-and-dried view of life, no summary of society, but a consciousness of the infinitely variable thing that is human nature, obedient to no laws but the laws of personality. If personality dwindles into a piece of mechanism in Charles Wilcox and diffuses itself into a lost aspiration in Mr Bast, it is even so the product, albeit a wrecked product, of the millions of personal forces that have made England. Each of these persons whom he shows to us is pathetically individual—pathetically, because it is hardly possible to be otherwise when you expose a limited human soul in the naked light of the whole universe; and it is for this reason that Mr Forster, vainly holding up before us an ethical ideal with hopeful intention, is often depressing to a bewildering extent. Yet the persons are too human to affect us long in this way. Charles is real enough to be hateful. Which of us has not known a Tibby, self-possessed, unbiassed in his narrow intellectual freedom, unaware of the world, and scornful of it? Mrs Munt, the fussy aunt, is an admirable intrusion of comedy. Poor, squalid Mr Bast, with his drunken 'Jacky,' his poverty, his democratic gentility, and his one romance in life, is an exquisite piece of diabolical character-drawing. And there is Evie, and Dolly, and the sweet Miss Avery; and permeating the book, like Howards End itself, is the simple, dignified, homely figure of Mrs Wilcox, whose personality haunts us even as the genius of the house seems to take wings of fancy in Mr Forster's hands, and put us among fantastic, other-worldly things. 'Couldn't you and I camp out in this house for the night?' cries Helen, inflamed with fancies which its owners, who hated her, could never have understood.

> 'Because my plans—'
>
> '—Which you change in a moment.'
>
> 'Then because my life is great, and theirs are little,' said Helen, taking fire. 'I know of things they can't know of, and so do you. We *know* that there's poetry. They can only take them on hearsay. We know this is our house, because it feels ours. Oh, they may take the title deeds and the doorkeys, but for this one night we are at home.'
>
> 'It would be lovely to have you once more alone,' said Margaret. 'It may be a chance in a thousand.'
>
> 'Yes, and we could talk.' She dropped her voice. 'It won't be a very glorious story. But under that wych-elm—'

There is life, imagination, and the very flame of action giving quality to this novel over and above the technique with which it is built up and the wisdom with which it is informed.

26
Unsigned Review

[EDWARD GARNETT]

The habit of orthodox criticism is to be stiff or condescending to a new author when he first appears with an original book, and to increase the measure of praise according to his repeated successes. Mr E. M. Forster has now given us four novels, and his last, *Howards End*, will probably receive compound interest on whatever sum of approval was bestowed on *The Longest Journey*. It is as well. *Howards End*, by its far-sighted criticism of middle-class ideas, is a book that says most effectively those very things that the intelligent minority feel, but rarely arrive at formulating.

The story is built out of the intercourse of the sisters, Margaret and Helen Schlegel, with the Wilcoxes, a typically prosperous British family. Helen and Margaret are neither 'English to the backbone' nor 'Germans of the dreadful sort.' They are children of an idealistic German father, who, after a life of variegated interests, had settled down in England and married a rich Englishwoman. The girls, who think for themselves, are 'emancipated' in their ideas, naturally live the surface life of 'culture,' Continental travel, visiting friends, attending concerts, picture galleries, &c., which in general suffices to keep the woman of independent means from showing too consciously that she wants something better. The Schlegels have made the acquaintance of the Wilcoxes in a Continental hotel, and Helen is on a visit to Howards End, Mrs Wilcox's modest, old-fashioned house in Herts, when Paul, the youngest son, kisses her on the lawn by starlight, and an absurd squabble between Helen's aunt, Mrs Munt, and Charles Wilcox, leads to the two families breaking off relations. Helen, at the outset, had been under the spell of the Wilcoxes.

> She had liked giving in to Mr Wilcox, or Evie, or Charles; she had liked being told that her notions of life were sheltered or academic, that Equality was nonsense, Votes for Women nonsense, Socialism nonsense, Art and

SOURCE *Nation*, 12 November 1910, pp. 282–4.

> Literature, except when conducive to strengthening the character, nonsense. One by one the Schlegel fetiches had been overthrown, and, though professing to defend them, she had rejoiced.

But when, the morning after the love passage, Paul comes down to breakfast looking frightened lest she should give him away,

> Helen feels for a moment that the whole Wilcox family is a fraud, just a wall of newspapers, and motor-cars, and golf-clubs, and that if it fell she should find nothing behind it but panic and emptiness.

Margaret defends the Wilcoxes. They represent to her 'the great outer life, which, though obviously horrid, often seems the real one.' But Helen knows that the Wilcoxes, once bereft of this 'outer life,' have nothing to fall back on. They 'dodge emotion.' They hold it of little importance, or if they recognise it they are afraid of it. On the other hand, it is true that the Wilcoxes have their hands on all the ropes. Their 'outer life' fosters such virtues as neatness, decision and obedience—virtues of the second rank, no doubt, but they have formed our civilisation. They form character, too; they keep the soul from becoming 'sloppy.' It seems destined that no further occasion will be given the two families of criticising one another, but fate has it otherwise. The Wilcoxes take one of the expensive new flats that shut out the light from the Schlegels' old house in Wickham Place, and soon Margaret finds herself on intimate terms with the sweet and retiring mother, Mrs Wilcox, who, from the point of view of her over-energetic family, is as much behind the times as is the honest, unpretentious old house, Howards End.

The artistic setting of the novel certainly owes much to the spiritual background, which is symbolised by the old-world atmosphere of Howards End. We require something by which we can measure Mr Wilcox, busy with his company promoting and his new fortune, made out of oil and rubber, his sound Imperialism, his motoring, his shooting, and his energy in local politics. Mrs Wilcox and Howards End both have spiritual grace, and the old house reflects the unobtrusive charm and settled standards which the pushing husband, the self-assertive son, Charles, and the athletic daughter, Evie, despise. But Mrs Wilcox, who understands her family, is stricken suddenly and dies in a nursing home, leaving a scribbled message for her husband, 'I should like Miss Schlegel (Margaret) to have Howards End.' This dying request, after being carefully debated by the Wilcoxes, is dismissed as 'unbusinesslike' and 'unlike mother,' the whim of an invalid, in fact, and the family, being destitute of imagination, are incapable of realising that Howards End, which to them is merely a saleable property of bricks and mortar and a large garden, was a spiritual sanctuary to the dead woman. Several years pass, and when the Schlegels and the Wilcoxes come together again, Mr Wilcox has grown tired of being left to his own devices by his married children, and Margaret feels solitary and old-maidish. She is thrilled by the idea of this elderly man turning to her for companionship, and when he offers her his hand and heart, she accepts gladly, despite Helen's bitter opposition.

In the working out of the fortunes of the two families, now united by marriage, Mr Forster shows to great advantage his rare gift of philosophic criticism. His characters are real enough, but their importance as individuals is less than their significance as contemporary signposts. It is the ideas behind them, the code of manners and morals, and the web of forces, material and mental, that are woven before our eyes in the life of London, that Mr Forster is deeply concerned with, and from the standpoint of the interested looker-on we can only admire the dexterity with which the disaster that overtakes the Wilcoxes is bound up with the fate of the insignificant clerk, Leonard Bast, and his disreputable wife, Jacky. Briefly, the Basts are befriended by the passionate Helen, and accidentally the disclosure is forced upon Margaret of an unsavory episode in Mr Wilcox's past life. Margaret condones the past offence; but a little later, when Helen, who has taken refuge in Germany, discloses that the child she is going to bear will be illegitimate, Mr Wilcox plays the part of the outraged moralist and the stern *père de famille*. Leonard Bast is, in fact, the father of Helen's child, and in a scuffle with him the bullying George commits what is technically manslaughter, and is sent to prison for three years. The shock of the tragedy of Leonard's death crumbles down Mr Wilcox's philistine defences, and the novel ends with a retrospective chapter, in which a humbled Helen, a calm Margaret, and a broken-spirited Mr Wilcox are shown living together peacefully in the tranquil atmosphere of the old house, Howards End. We say that one must admire the ingenuity with which the fabric of the plot is woven out of the fortuitous yarn of the meetings and the accidental relations of the three sets of characters; but in closing the book, we perceive that Mr Forster has sacrificed the inflexibility of artistic truth to the exigencies of his philosophical moral. There is too much ingenious dove-tailing of incidents, too much of accidental happenings, too much twisting and stretching and straining of human material for *Howards End* to rank high as a work of art. The individuality of each figure is made obedient to the convenience of the author's purpose, and, though great pains are taken to make the whole story and all its parts probable, at critical junctures Helen's action or Mr Wilcox's attitude are perceptibly strained to produce a dramatic situation. Not grossly strained, be it remarked, but perceptibly; but it is just this clever ingenuity that robs the work of artistic inevitability. It would, however, be doing both the author and our readers poor service to make much of a subsidiary defect in the author's accomplished method. The novel's original value, which is great, rests primarily on the acute analysis of the middle-class British code of ideas and standards, typified by the rise and progress of the Wilcoxes. Mr Forster understands the outlook of Villadom perhaps better than the fourscore of writers who speak from the 'vantage ground of its bulwarks. He is no partisan, but renders justice in a manner that may well bring those he paints to sue for mercy.

27
Unsigned Review

[CLIVE BELL]

This novel, taken with its three predecessors, assures its author a place amongst the handful of living writers who count. It is the story of a conflict between points of view. The Schlegels are clever, sensitive, refined; they have a feeling for beauty and truth, a sense of justice and or proportion; they stand for what is best in modern civilization: the Wilcoxes are vulgar, blatant, and brutal; such time as they can spare from money-making they devote to motors and bridge and suburban society; they stand for all that is worst. The two families are thrown together. The younger Miss Schlegel, Helen, is uncompromising; one cannot touch pitch without being soiled, she feels; the elder, Margaret, who refuses 'to draw my income and sneer at those who guarantee it', marries Mr Wilcox. Helen and the reader have to watch Margaret's fine edges grow blunt, till at last, by one of those *dei ex machinis* of which Mr Forster is too fond, the irreconcilables are reconciled, and some of them live happily ever after.

The effects of this novel are that the protagonists are points of view rather than characters; that the two chief events—Margaret's marriage and Helen's seduction—are unconvincing; and that, in our judgment, the moral is wrong. We do not object to didacticism; but we cannot admit that what is bad ought to be loved, or that the finer feelings are not too high a price even for enlarged sympathies. The great thing in the book is the sisters' affection for each other; personal relationships, except those between lovers, have never, we venture to say, been made more beautiful or more real. But, from beginning to end, it is full of brilliant and delicate strokes, which reveal, with surprising clearness, those subtle states of mind and elusive but significant traits that are apt to escape even the most acute observation.

SOURCE *Athenaeum*, 3 December 1910, p. 151.

28
Extracts from Four Anonymous Reviews

1

Mr Forster's work—*Howards End* is Mr Forster's fourth novel—occupies a niche entirely by itself in the house of contemporary fiction. It is not like anything else that is being done, and everything that he writes develops his original statement consistently and clearly. It is this doctrine of courage and common sense that gives Mr Forster's book so compelling a fascination, and he has never before vindicated both his message and his method so ably as in his new novel. In its broadest outline the subject of *Howards End* is the all-pervading influence of Place, and it is curious to note that this has been the subject of several recent novels. But Mr Forster develops his theme beyond its ordinary range. In his other novels—especially in *The Longest Journey*—the influence of place has been felt, but now it is the faith, the creed, the gospel of the persons of his story. Every one is tested by the walls, the chimneys, the garden of *Howards End*. Do they see, do they understand, can they connect? The Wilcox family has the house in its possession. Mrs Wilcox (the most arresting and subtle character in all Mr Forster's gallery) does understand and dies, leaving the place to the one person who shares her knowledge. But the Wilcoxes—good, honest, stubborn, blind—cling to their possession, and during the rest of the book we see the house quietly, subtly, actively, setting to work to deliver itself into the hands of its proper possessor. When the book is closed the reader glances apprehensively about him—regards his tables and chairs with alarm, invests the meanest lodging with terribly secret activity.

SOURCES 1. *The Standard*, 28 October 1910, p. 5.
2. *The Daily Telegraph*, 2 November 1910, p. 14.
3. *Spectator*, 5 November 1910, p. 757.
4. *Westminster Gazette*, 19 November 1910, p. 16.

One can fancy only too easily the way that such a theme would have been treated by other writers. There would be great slabs of scenery, the house would be drawn again and again, every actor in the comedy would have passed sniffing about the garden and exclaiming in emphatic asides that he always felt so odd in that part of the country and he really did not know what was happening to him. Mr Forster emphasises nothing; he draws the house in several sharp, startling lines, and then leaves it to his readers. He makes no statement, and he flings his characters from place to place, from incident to incident, from life to death, from death to immortality with an apparent indifference. It seems possible, as we read, that anything may happen to any one, and that there are no rules or laws at all—and then, at the end, 'Only Connect' Mr Forster whispers, and everything falls into its place and the ordinary certainty of life is revealed.

There are a great many other things in the book. The characters of Margaret and Helen, Mrs Wilcox, Mr Wilcox, and Leonard, are wonderfully rendered, and there are scenes—the coming of Margaret to Howards End, Leonard's death, Margaret's motor drive through the country—that are unforgettable. Mr Forster's humour, too, is quite unlike anyone else's humour, and it is always surprising and unforeseen. With this book he seems to us to have arrived, and, if he never writes another line, his niche should be secure.

2

There is no doubt about it whatever. Mr E. M. Forster is one of the great novelists. His stories are not about life. They are life. His plots are absorbing because his characters are real; he does not create them, but observes them. While he has not the grand manner nor the supreme wit and uncanny humour of Meredith, the humour of the man looking down from a height above the rest of his fellows, he has in an unusual degree the intelligence which probes the actions of human beings, and, above all, the spirit, as he himself would say, which connects. We are concerned here chiefly with two families—the Schlegels, two sisters, Margaret and Helen, and their brother Tibby, together with one or two relations and the Wilcoxes. The Schlegels, of Anglo-German parentage, are intellectuals, and never has an intellectual atmosphere been better transferred to paper. They are interested in all the 'movements' of the day; their outlook is independent, and their spirits are fierce and vigorous. The Wilcoxes are an ordinary English bourgeois family, with the qualities and defects of such families. The two sets are mixed up together by fate, and in the clash is the comedy. From the beginning the ideas of the girls arrest us, from the moment that Margaret says to her philosopher father,

> 'To me one of two things is very clear. Either God does not know His own

> mind about England and Germany, or else men do not know the mind of God.'

Later on she remarks,

> 'It seems silly to speak about "the Continent," but really it is all more like itself than any part of it is like England. England is unique. The Continent, for good or for evil, is interested in ideas. Its literature and art have what one might call the kink of the unseen about them. People will there discuss with humility questions that we here think ourselves too good to touch with tongs.'

Margaret is a remarkable girl, and, like such girls, singularly pure-minded and proud of thought. Henry Wilcox, the middle-aged head of his family, is quite different. He has no pride of thought, his conduct is not above reproach, but he is eminently respectable, a good and useful citizen. The other members of the two families are proper pendants to and variations of them. Margaret and Henry fall in love, and a great part of the book is the history of their courtship and marriage and its effect on them and their belongings. Howards End, the Wilcoxes' country house, furnishes the *leit-motif* throughout. And now we come to a character who plays an important part in the story, though really outside it, a character on whom the author has bestowed some of his best work, in connection with whom there are scenes which betray the veritable genius of the writer. It is Leonard Bast, the little clerk, with a longing for higher things. We venture to say, though it may be our limitation rather than the author's, that Bast, the most fascinating of all the characters, does not ring true. Would such a man have had the pluck to commence life as he did? Surely he was too nervous, too suspicious, to have formed the connection with 'Jacky' which led to marriage. And again, we submit, as they say in the law courts, that Leonard Bast's seduction of Helen Schlegel is an unlikely incident. At any rate, it strikes a false note such as is never struck, for instance, in Meredith's novels. We do not feel that it is inevitable, but that it is the author's will, and that he is doing violence to his characters in bringing it about. There are one or two other blemishes. But all will agree as to the value of the book, as to its absorbing interest, the art and power with which it is put together, and they will feel with us that it is a book quite out of the common by a writer who is one of our assets, and is likely to be one of our glories.

3

There is no novelist living on whom one can more confidently rely for unexpected developments than Mr Forster. Surprise, whether consciously or unconsciously administered, is of the essence of his method. The expert reader can usually predict the course of events after reading the first fifty pages of an average novel; but it would need clairvoyance of the highest order to forecast the ultimate issue of Helen Schlegel's visit to Howards End, and of the premature revelation of her attachment to Paul Wilcox. Mr Forster's story may be roughly described as a set of free variations on the old theme of *amantium irae*. In this case the plot is entirely concerned with the relations of two families, the Schlegels and the Wilcoxes, and the more they fall out the closer they are drawn together. Anything more radically dissimilar than the two households it would be difficult to imagine. The Schlegel girls—the brother is a negligible and contemptible youth who counts for little in the story, though his pedantic egotism has an amusing side—are orphans, the daughters of a German idealist who settled in England, but without a trace of Teutonic stolidity. They are adventurous amateurs of culture, brilliant inconsequent talkers, deeply interested in music and literature, in the poetry and romance of life. On the other hand, Mr Wilcox is a very prosperous, capable, somewhat cynical man of the world. He and his sons and daughters have all of them 'got their hands on the ropes.' They own motor-cars and country places; their houses are splendidly and solidly equipped; they appreciate comforts, taboo sentiment, and, with one exception, face emergencies without emotion or nerves. The Schlegels are partly attracted by qualities which they do not possess; but the real link is Mrs Wilcox, a graceful, kindly, distinguished, inarticulate, but sympathetic woman, who has a genuine, and even passionate, affection for the country place which gives its name to the story. The acquaintance begins with a chance meeting on the Continent. Helen Schlegel, the more attractive, impulsive, and undisciplined of the two sisters, is invited to stay with the Wilcoxes, and in an expansive mood tumbles into love with one of the sons. But Paul Wilcox is a weakling, uncertain of himself, and afraid of his father, and the attachment is abruptly and violently ended before it has reached the stage of an engagement. Helen's lack of reticence leads to a *contretemps* which provokes an unpleasant family quarrel, and relations are broken off. Relations are resumed, however, when the Wilcoxes, by one of the convenient coincidences of which Mr Forster so liberally avails himself, take a flat within a stone's-throw of the Schlegels' house in town. This time it is Margaret, the elder, plainer, but much more interesting sister, who is impressed by the Wilcoxes, and, after a false start, strikes up a close friendship with Mrs Wilcox. At this point Mr Forster resorts to a favourite device of his to develop his plot,—that of abruptly killing off one of the characters. Mrs Wilcox, who is the victim of this habit of literary homicide, dies suddenly, leaving written instructions to her husband to present Howards End—her own property—to Margaret Schlegel. These instructions he deliberately disregards as fanciful and disloyal, and his family are disposed to harbour renewed resentment against the Schlegels. But in spite of himself he is convinced that Margaret's affection for his wife was disinterested, and a fresh *rapprochement* is brought about, which proceeds by leaps and bounds until Margaret consents to become his wife. Now the Schlegels, in their forthcoming, expansive way, had taken up and encouraged a half-baked young clerk with literary aspirations whom they first met at a concert. Leonard Bast is married to an undesirable wife with a past; his manners are uncouth and his character lamentably weak. But he has a romantic side to him, and the kindly, if unjudicious, patronage of the Schlegels brings a ray of sunshine into his sordid life. This friendly interest, however, brings the Basts into contact with the Wilcoxes, and on the eve of Margaret's marriage leads to a painful disclosure of the previous relations between Mrs Bast and Mr Wilcox, and to an extraordinary act of self-sacrifice on the part of Helen Schlegel. The sequel is concerned with the unflinching way in which Margaret, belying the 'sloppiness' of her early career, uses the weapon of her knowledge to conquer her husband and rescue her sister from social outlawry. The situation is not a pleasant one; but it is impossible to deny the extreme cleverness with which Mr Forster has utilised the lapse of Henry Wilcox to balance that of his sister-in-law, though we cannot bring ourselves to regard the latter as probable. Again, the sudden elimination of the wretched Leonard Bast is grotesquely managed. The Schlegels, always on the look-out for originality, come across a pathetic, ineffective little clerk with leanings towards adventure both of the mind and body. He is married to a woman of no intelligence at all, who has entrapped him in his youth, and there is a breathless scene when Helen Schlegel rushes the pair of them down to Shropshire, where Mr Wilcox is marrying off his daughter, and the startling fact bursts upon Margaret, whose own marriage is about to take place, that Mr Wilcox during the lifetime of his first wife has had relations with the unspeakable and irresponsible 'Jacky.'

Helen also discovers the fact, and her piercing sympathy with the troubles of the poor little clerk brings about her sudden undoing. The way in which the truth, when it comes out, forms the pivot of the final struggle between Margaret's essential rightness of mind and her husband's crude and illogical want of principle is realised in a masterly way.

In the end there is happiness between the warring factions. Love and reason have triumphed. Unfortunately it is just here that Mr Forster, having elaborated his theme at great length throughout the book, hastily takes leave of us with a very slight gathering up of the threads, and we are left wondering exactly how the happiness we are assured has descended once more upon Howards End can have come about. We are not quite satisfied with his sketched-in explanation, and Mr Wilcox's conversion somehow recalls that of Mr Dombey.

But the faults of this book are as nothing compared to its merits. The way in which the characters—even those minor ones who have not been mentioned above—are made to live before us is of the essence of all great fiction. *Howards End* is essentially a novel of character, but where it differs from a good deal of clever modern work done more or less upon the same lines is that Mr Forster has gone back to the old canons of fiction and exhibited his characters in action. That is to say, he has made it his business to tell us a story about them. Things are always happening in *Howards End*, and although there is a great deal of talk, and very good talk, both from the characters themselves and also from the author, it is not all talk. That is why *Howards End* will be widely read. There will be many who will read it for the story alone, and they will be right to do so, for the best novels have always contained the best stories.

4

In *Howards End* Mr E. M. Forster has written a very remarkable book, though he has hardly achieved an altogether satisfactory novel. It is in his treatment of the 'personal relations' that he excels—those factors in human life which stood for 'the real' in the lives of Margaret and Helen Schlegel as against the mere externals of intercourse which in their strange elliptic parlance they sum up in the two symbols 'telegrams and anger.' Symbols mean far more to those two women than the actual facts of life; they are a curious complex pair, living in a world of dreams and ideals, yet with a far-sighted common-sense sometimes materialising, contradictory traits of which we see the germ both in parentage and education. Mr Forster has handled these two women with an intimacy which is little short of amazing. Perhaps Helen is not always quite convincing, especially at the supreme crisis of her life; but his analysis of the almost more complex Margaret, who can step down from the clouds to make a commonplace marriage with a middle-aged unimaginative gentleman, whom she can love well if not passionately, is quite extraordinary. He gets inside the very soul of the woman, and touches with an equally sure hand the trivial things of every day and the great moments of her development. It is almost with surprise that we realise that the author, who can show such very unusual insight into the rarefied atmosphere of the idealist's inner life, can at the same time appreciate all that goes to the making of the more conventional types. His delineation of the Wilcoxes, who stand for the contradiction of everything which the Schlegels have taught themselves to cherish, is no less admirable than his treatment of the two women and their very individual brother, one of the most lifelike and remarkable portraits in the book. To give an outline of the story would be to give no idea of the value of the book, which is dependent on the 'personal relations' of those involved, in the contrast and balance of character. Mr Forster has little sense of form; his book has no constructive harmony. But he is something of a seer, something of a mystic, though his mysticism is somewhat intangible, and he can hardly put it into shape. The strange influence of Howards End, realised by the Schlegels rather than by the Wilcoxes, to whom it belonged;

the curious personality of Miss Avery, who makes, as it were, a connecting-link between the Schlegels and Howards End, are suggested rather than insisted on. But with Mrs Wilcox, the real owner of Howards End, who recognised Margaret as her spiritual heir, and who, in leaving her Howards End, felt that she was conveying an atmosphere to one who could appreciate it, Mr Forster is more definite.

Mrs Wilcox thus represents a sort of over-soul. But for this development we had been quite unprepared, and herein lies the real weakness of Mr Forster's book. He has given us no cause to expect this evolution. He has evidently a strong impression which he wishes to produce, but he fails to produce it because of his treatment of Mrs Wilcox in the flesh. Spiritualists would doubtless tell us that manifestation on this material plane has but little relation to a higher one. Mr Forster is working in a particular medium, and he must use that medium to get his effect. He fails with Mrs Wilcox, perhaps because he takes too much for granted on the part of his reader. And his book suffers in consequence. Nevertheless it remains quite one of the most remarkable novels of the year.

The Celestial Omnibus and Other Stories (1911)

29
Review

ANONYMOUS

Mr E. M. Forster's exact intention in some of these stories is a little vague and elusive, so that from time to time one has the impression that pleasant though they are to read, they must have been even pleasanter to write. Especially is this so with *Other Kingdom*, which, we fancy, a good many readers will give up as a bad job somewhere about the middle, but then, let it be added, there are many more who will enjoy it to the end. Of the other five our favourites are the first, 'The Story of a Panic', and 'The Curate's Friend'. The former is a most poetical and delightful piece of writing, which describes how an English boy of 14, holiday-making with a party of dullish people in Italy, suffers a change, miraculously wrought, from a lethargic, peevish lad into an elfin creature, a spirit of the woods, for whom henceforth life among mortals, cribbed and confined between four walls, is impossible. We leave him escaping into the woods, while the Italian boy, the only one of the party who has understood his secret, falls dead in his effort to aid his escape. It is a fanciful tale, full of charm and power, and shows Mr Forster in a very different mood from the acute reality of his *Howards End*, which dissected real people with so much adroitness. *The Celestial Omnibus* is in the same vein, an allegory of the real and unreal, the world of imagination as against the fairyland of commonsense. As we have hinted, Mr Forster here writes a little too much for himself, and pays hardly enough attention to the readers who may clamber after him in the dark, but there is great charm in the volume, and it will be welcomed by that public which the author has gained for himself. Mr Forster is always distinguished in his work, but we hope that he will not become 'precious,' because as yet he has not shown that it is necessary for him to do so to get his full effects.

SOURCE *The Daily Telegraph*, 17 May 1911, p. 4.

30
Review

ANONYMOUS

Mr E. M. Forster's treatment of the supernatural is a proof that even the oldest pebbles from the brook can be made available by the hand of the cunning slinger who sallies forth bent on the overthrow of Goliath. It is a testimony to Mr Forster's art that he rarely takes the sword in hand himself, but divides the camp of villadom against itself, and incites the superior inmates to fall on their Philistine brethren and cut off their heads. A particularly neat example is 'The Story of a Panic', which sets forth how the great God Pan appears at a picnic in a chestnut wood at Rapallo, where the two Miss Robinsons and their nephew Eustace, and the curate Mr Sandback, and Mr Leyland, an artist, and the respectable narrator and his wife have foregathered. The party is incontinently filled with a bestial fear, and takes to mad flight—everybody, that is, except Eustace, who is found, later on, lying on his back, playing with a lizard. Nothing can be got out of him, but that evening Eustace behaves very strangely, talking familiarly to ragged old peasant women, and even throwing his arms round Gennaro, an impertinent fisher-lad, who is acting as waiter at the boarding-house. Eustace behaves still more strangely in the night, escaping from his bedroom and standing in the garden, in his nightshirt, saluting, praising, and blessing the great forces and manifestations of Nature. The boy easily eludes his English relatives and friends who give him chase, but Gennaro is seduced by the promise of a few lire to betray him into their hands. Ultimately the forces of Nature prove too strong for the powers of British respectability, and, in a vivid scene at the close, Eustace is seen leaping down the hillside, laughing and shouting in an inhuman voice, while the perfidious Gennaro breaks his neck by falling from the terrace in a dispute over the payment of the lire. Mr Forster gets his effects by making his cultured people uneasily self-conscious that these incredible events would be beautiful if read of in the classics, but are to be repressed sternly when

SOURCE *Nation*, 10 June 1911, p. 410.

they apply, spiritually, to themselves. In 'The Road from Colonus', we find an admirable burlesque of modern insincerity in the description of the facile enthusiasm of a party of English tourists, who halt at a tiny khan, or country inn, in Messenia. Old Mr Lucas drinks of the spring, gushing from a hollow tree, and straightway forgets all about his suburban vexations, and determines to remain, lotus-eating, 'in the benedictory shades of the planes.' When his family discover that he is in earnest, they take strong measures to remove him from the dangerous locality. Mr Lucas has indeed lost all sense of the suburbs by drinking the enchanted water of the spring of eternal youth. But his family is deaf to his appeals, and he is worsted and carried back to his hateful old life. Here, as in 'Other Kingdom', the things of the spirit are in league with the powers of the supernatural world, and at war with the prosaic pettiness of our daily outlook and environment. The artistic appeal is successful, because the uncanny element symbolises the unforeseen turns of the wheel that fate has in store for every man, and there is a constant appeal made from man-made law to the mysterious workings of Nature. Mr Forster's literary arrows are sharp and shining, and they wing his quarry none the less effectually because they are feathered with magic plumage.

31
Review

ANONYMOUS

There were not a few readers who used to watch the magazines carefully for Mr E. M. Forster's Short Stories, before he gathered in a wider public with his novels; and these may turn the pages of *The Celestial Omnibus* with a sense that it is peculiarly theirs, by right of having been first in the field with appreciation. The little volume contains only half-a-dozen of these earlier pieces; and without recalling and regretting certain omissions, let us say that we re-read those we are given with a confirmed admiration of their originality and grace. The difficulty about criticizing them is that they are all so lightly fitted together and airily thrown off that it seems brutal to hold them down and examine them. If we did so we might find that the slippery little allegories which run through them would not always bear sustained pressure, and we should certainly find that some of them are very loosely written. But it is more to the point to notice how neatly the two elements in the contrast which is the subject of them all are made to play in and out of each other. Heavy-handed literalness gets so daintily mocked and flouted in these anecdotes that we hardly dare try to say what the contrast is; but, vulgarly put (it is safer to be vulgar than to be solemn), it is between those who are 'in the know' on the subject of nature and poetry and the finer sentiments, and those who are not. If Mr Forster were ever capable of being heavy or solemn himself, it would be a dangerous subject. But we cannot catch him out; the people in his stories who understand, who have eyes to see Pan in a chestnut wood and fauns on the Wiltshire Downs, are too agreeable to make us ever feel inclined to side with the stupid ones against them. As for the stupid ones, we know how unerringly and with what elfish sharpness Mr Forster pins them down in their most unsuspecting moments. If the style, as we hinted, is not always equable, it must be said that in most of the stories Mr Forster deliberately adopts the difficult method of making one of the stupid people the narrator, so that the revelation of character has

SOURCE *Times Literary Supplement*, 22 June 1911, p. 238.

to be unconscious—and that, of course, means that to keep the manner consistent with itself needs a highly practised hand. But the lapses of this sort do not affect more than two or three of the stories, and anyhow they are all very entertaining. We cannot think the volume adorned by the somewhat scratchily symbolic 'end-papers'.

Alexandria: A History and a Guide (1922)

32

Forster's Alexandria: A Pageant of History from Menelaus to Allenby

ANONYMOUS

It is with an art so simple as to seem almost naïve that E. M. Forster pictures ancient and modern Alexandria in thirteen short essays. With the single exception of 'Eliza in Egypt', where he seems to be leaning a bit on Mr Lytton Strachey's mode of approach, Mr Forster's brief pictures hark back to no models. There appear to be several reasons for this unqualified success within a hundred and twenty pages. First of all, of course, is the finely poised intellect which approached Alexandria with none of the pre-romantic conceptions, none of the desire to display 'color' or to moon about 'the grandeur that was Greece and the glory that was Rome.' It was the late war that flung Mr Forster into modern Alexandria, and while he was there it is patent that he co-ordinated his mind with his eyes. He saw the city as something more than a ruin and a point of association with ancient times. His sensitive nature received it as a spiritual cockpit, as a place where two civilizations strove for supremacy, where Greece and Asia met at a high point of time, where paganism and Christianity fought one of their last duels. Something formidable and fierce crashed down to nothingness here, and it was a something even vaster than Alexander the Great. Civilized existence spun on its axis here and faced in a new direction.

All of this is implied in *Pharos and Pharillon,* without the least approach to a didacticism of any sort. Indeed, the book is permeated with an unforced but leavening humour that is never obvious but which unmistakably fills the reader's mind with a viewpoint that is as logical as it is calmly put. From the first essay, which describes the great lighthouse, the Pharos,

SOURCE *The New York Times Book Review,* 2 September 1923, p. 15.

which certainly stands in Mr Forster's mind as a symbol of the old Alexandria, to the charming concluding essay on the poetry of C. P. Cavafy, a modern Alexandrian poet, there is not a false touch in the book. This pageant of Time, which begins with the landing of Menelaus upon Ras of Tin and ends with the guttural shouts of the cotton brokers in the Bourse, is but the slow picture of the gradual destruction of an age of color and madness and pagan pomp into one of materialistic greed. Between the two extremes move numberless phantoms, Menelaus, Alexander the Great, Clement, St Athanasius, all the bewildered passions struck to being by the clashing of two worlds. From it all we gather one truth, and this seems to be one of the theses which Mr Forster would prove: it is only ideas that live. The Copts, for instance, still believe with Timothy the Cat that Christ's nature was single, but Timothy the Cat, the Pharos, the Temple of Serapis, all these visual evidences of spiritual struggle have vanished as though they had never been. The passing of the old city is beautifully expressed in one of C. P. Cavafy's poems, quoted by Mr Forster.

When at the hour of midnight
an invisible choir is suddenly heard passing
with exquisite music, with voices—
Do not lament your fortune that at last subsides,
your life's work that has failed, your schemes that have proved illusions.
But like a man prepared, like a brave man,
bid farewell to her, to Alexandria who is departing.
Above all, do not delude yourself, do not say that it is a dream, that your ear was mistaken.
Do not condescend to such empty hopes.
Like a man for long prepared like a brave man,
like the man who was worthy of such a city
go to the window firmly,
and listen with emotion,
but not with the prayers and complaints of the coward
(Ah, 'supreme rapture,')
listen to the notes, to the exquisite instruments of the mystic choir
and bid farewell to her, to Alexandria whom you are losing.

Of course, the name of Alexander the Great dominates the city, for was it not his very own? He came there with Dinocrates, the architect, and ordered him to build a Greek city between the sea and the lake. He was a Philhellene. His dream was to extend Greece over the world and it was only after he made the pilgrimage to the Oasis of Siwa and was hailed by the priest in the temple there as 'the Son of God' that his aspirations altered. From that moment he no longer regarded Greece as the centre of the world. Mr Forster sets down his summary of Alexander's life after the beginning of the African city in a prose that is as fascinating as conversation. We almost hear the author speaking.

> The building of Alexandria proceeded, and copied or magnified forms from the perishing peninsula overseas. Dinocrates planned Greek temples and market-places, and they were constructed not slavishly but with intelligence, for the Greek spirit still lived. But it lived consciously, not unconsciously as in the past. It had a mission, and no missionary should ever create. And Alexander, the heroic chaos of whose heart surged with desire for all that can and cannot be, turned away from his Hellenic town-planning and his narrow antiquarian crusade, and flung himself again, but in a new spirit, against the might of Persia. He fought her as a lover now. He wanted not to convert but to harmonize, and conceived himself as the divine and impartial ruler beneath whom harmony should proceed. That way lies madness. Persia fell. Then it was the turn of India. Then the turn of Rome would have come and then he could have sailed westward [such was his expressed intention] until he had conquered the Night and eastward until he had conquered the Day. He was never—despite the tuition of Aristotle—a balanced young man, and his old friends complained that in this latter period he sometimes killed them. But to us, who cannot have the perilous honour of his acquaintance, he grows more lovable now than before. He has caught, by the unintellectual way, a glimpse of something great. If dangerous, and that glimpse came to him first in the recesses of the Siwan Oasis. When at the age of 33 he died, when the expedition that he did not seek stole toward him in the summer-house at Babylon, did it seem to him as after all but the crown of his smaller quests? He had tried to lead mankind. He had succeeded in both. But was the universe also friendly, was it also in trouble, was it calling on him, on him, for his help and his love? The priest of Amen had addressed him as 'Son of God.' What exactly did the compliment mean? Was it explicable this side of the grave?

It is doubtful if Alexander the Great has ever been approached in this manner before. If he has ever been so sympathetically dealt with and accepted as a personality. The same method is applied by Mr Forster to those other figures who stand out in the history of ancient Alexandria, Romans, early Christians, fanatic bishops, Ptolemy Epiphanes, the reader observes them as actual personages with the endless veils of legend which have so transmogrified them into other substances than flesh candidly removed. When we turn to the second section of the book, concerned with the modern city, a section in which the sketches are groups under the name Pharillon after the lesser house which succeeded the Pharos, we find that the personalities have vanished. It is no longer a city affording background to figures which stand out in bold relief. It is rather an atmosphere with which Mr Forster has to deal here, and he does it as cleverly, as charmingly, as he treated the major names which we associate with Alexandria. The modern city is not even the empty husk of its old splendor; it is another city entirely, existing with a viewpoint that has no more to do with the ancient Alexandria than Newark, New Jersey. The direction of an old road remains. Walled into some forgotten cellar, legend has it, the body of Alexander lies lapped in gold and laid in a coffin of glass. But the Christian and the Arab have destroyed all else, excepting a few tumble-down ruins, pitiful hints of a past splendor. Alexandria is no longer a city of the soul; it is based on cotton and onions and eggs today, ill-built, ill-planned and ill-drained. It is such a scene as this that Mr Forster pictures in his last few sketches, a scene where the British Army of Occupation has broken up the Ptolemaic ruins to make roads.

It should be emphasized that Mr Forster's book is by no manner of deduction a history. The facts are quite secondary to his interpretation of them. Rather has he put together a series of spiritual attitudes, brooding over a fragment of fact until he has evolved from it a recreated atmosphere. Therefore the book is quite as much an exposition of the author as it is of Alexandria, and this must be borne in mind during the reading. It is a many-sided contemplative nature that may be observed in the paragraphs of this volume. When the occasion requires he writes with a rare sense of poetical values, setting down lovely descriptions, as in that sketch entitled 'The Solitary Place', where he describes the country stretching westward from Lake Marlout. His humor is nearly always in evidence, a subtle, quick observation that is both kind and gentle. And his spiritual unity with Alexandria is, perhaps, the most important aspect of the book. It is a miracle that one so spiritually drawn to the atmosphere which existed should have been set down here during the war. E. M. Forster found himself in Alexandria and Alexandria is to be found in E. M. Forster. The result is an unconscious, careless revelation. Nowhere can the reader discover the professional literary man who, set down in a strange place, thinks, 'Well, I may as well keep my hand in by writing about it.' What may be found is an unquestioned meeting of affinities.

33
Review

ROBERT TRACY

In the sixties of the last century, as every schoolboy knows, the Japanese were hard at work attempting to reproduce in their homeland the civilization of the distant West. It was then—according to a legend current among American naval officers before Pearl Harbor—that Queen Victoria, eager to assist, presented the Japanese Emperor with an obsolete and battered cruiser as the beginning of a modern navy. The Japanese were very pleased, and, after they had learned to sail the vessel, inquired if they could buy several more like it. Alas, there were no more to be had—any sister-ships had long since been scrapped. And so they decided to build their own cruisers. They worked hard and long, and they succeeded so well that soon the Emperor had two more cruisers in his fleet, perfect duplicates of the original down to every carefully made dent and patch on the outmoded boilers, every scrupulously splintered railing, every streak of rust at the hawse-hole.

Something of the same anxiously imitative spirit must have animated the editors of Anchor Books as they prepared this new edition of a little-known work of E. M. Forster, *Alexandria: A History and a Guide* (first edition, Alexandria, 1922; second, the same, 1938). First of all, the book is obsolete. Written during World War I, it is more than forty years out of date, and consequently useless as a guide. Nor is it of much value as a history of Alexandria, since it is full of blunders of one sort or another. And, like the Japanese who so carefully preserved each imperfection of their obsolete cruiser, the publishers of this new edition have chosen—after, one assumes, some deliberation—to preserve carefully each mistake, each flaw, even each misprint found in the first edition of the book, and to send it forth again with all its imperfections upon it. Such fidelity to error may be of some interest to the Forster specialist, but hardly to anyone else, and it is unlikely that the specialist is precisely the audience the Anchor people had in mind.

SOURCE *Carleton Miscellany*, Summer 1961, pp. 113–17.

Why then should this book appear? Is the eminence of the author, the sales value of his name, enough to justify such a sloppy piece of editing and publishing?

It seems even more unpardonable when one realizes that Forster himself acknowledged the imperfection of the book when he published a revised and corrected edition in 1938. For some reason the publishers have not chosen to reprint this version, less out of date by some fifteen years and free from at least the more obvious blunders of the first edition. For example, by 1938 Forster realized that the British army which invaded Egypt in 1801 numbered 15,000 men under Sir Ralph Abercromby, not 1500 under Sir Ralph Abercromby, and that the vivid description of the city as it was in 1610 was not written by John Sandys (otherwise unknown) but by the poet George Sandys, more famous perhaps as the first man to attempt literary work in the confines of the United States (he translated Ovid's *Metamorphoses* in Virginia, in the sixteen-twenties). He was aware that historians censured rather than censored the Ptolemies for their unconventional ways of showing fraternal affection, that there was no longer a Sultan, that the Graeco-Roman Museum had been considerably enlarged, that the Rue Rosette had been rechristened Rue Fuad I (it has since been rechristened again, and is now Avenue El-Horreya). He knew that Captain Norden, the Danish traveller, had visited Alexandria in 1737 and not 1757, that the Arab walls were built in 881 (not 811), that the British expedition of 1807 was led by General Fraser (not Frazer), that the brief account of the Battle of Alexandria (21 March, 1801) needed to be expanded and clarified, and that the sweeping assertion that Alexandria had dropped to total insignificance during the Middle Ages was ridiculously inaccurate and had to be unsaid. Forster made all of these necessary corrections before he allowed the second edition of the book to appear, but in spite of his thorough revision, the reader of this third edition finds it all undone. Here is poor Abercrombie back tramping the desert with his 1500 men, here are the historians busily censoring the Ptolemies, here is the ghostly John Sandys, and the vanished Sultan rides once more along the vanished Rue Rosette—all the errors have crept merrily back into their places. The new wings (new as of 1934) have been ruthlessly clipped from the Graeco-Roman Museum in the maps which have been carefully redrawn to show us the building as it was in 1922. Nor has the bibliography fared any better. Though Forster revised it to include important books about Alexandria published during the twenties and thirties, the reader looks in vain for them here.

By these complaints I do not wish to suggest that the 1938 text is an entirely trustworthy basis for a third edition, either. Both early versions are alike in erroneously assuming that Nicaea is on the Black Sea and that Actium is on the Adriatic. No reputable scholar now believes that Achilles Tatius was a bishop (nor did they in 1922). The Mosque of Abou el Abbas Moursi was not built but *re*-built in 1767. If there has been no Sultan in

Egypt since March 1922, there has been no King since July 1952. It was a shot from HMS *Inflexible*, not HMS *Superb*, that blew up the powder magazine at Fort Adda during the bombardment of 1882, and the shot was not fired 'in the evening' but about 1:30 p.m. The Timonium (more properly, Timoneum), Mark Antony's island hermitage where he planned to imitate Timon's misanthropy, was just off the palace, not off the island of Pharos. The present Greek Patriarch is not named Photius (d. 1925; the present incumbent is Christopher II, who has been reigning since June 1939), and he does not hold any position 'from the Sultan of Turkey direct.' Furthermore, the Patriarchate was moved to Alexandria neither sixty nor eighty years ago, but in 1847, and His Beatitude's full title is not 'Patriarch of Alexandria, Libya, Pentapolis, Ethiopia, and all Egypt,' but, much more magniloquently, 'Pope and Patriarch of the Great City of Alexandria, Libya, Pentapolis, Ethiopia and all Africa, Father of Fathers, Shepherd of Shepherds, Pontiff of Pontiffs, Thirteenth Apostle, and Oecumenical Judge.' The Ptolemies did not marry their own sisters in imitation of the god Osiris, but because their pharaonic predecessors had done so. Many of these mistakes are minor ones, but taken all together they add up to a book which has, for one reason or another, an error on every fourth or fifth page. Most of them can be blamed on the publishers, and all of them could have been avoided by someone's spending an afternoon in a well-equipped library.

So much for the disturbing flaws in this little book. What of its virtues, which have already moved some sober reviewers to near rapture? Well, there is the joy of a verbal game well-played. There is the pleasure of seeing a master of style at work, a master who is not above a certain sly parody. Forster has long since proclaimed himself an admirer of the fine, clear, faintly disdainful prose of the old Murray handbooks and of what he calls, in *Where Angels Fear to Tread*, 'the hidden charms of Baedeker.' In that novel he is speaking, to be sure, of the evocative power of almost any page of those magnificent guidebooks, their ability to summon up a whole landscape and way of life for the receptive browser. But there is an even subtler delight in the delicately bathetic prose, the brilliant descents and *volte-faces* that are the signature not of Baedeker himself but of the nameless genius who translated the books into a remarkable English. Consider, for example, the eggshell fragility of the following sentence from *Southern Italy and Sicily*: 'The popular idea of cleanliness in Southern Italy is behind the age, dirt being perhaps neutralized in the opinion of the natives by the brilliancy of their climate.' Or, from the same volume, the bland insistence that 'the traveller should adopt the Neapolitan custom of rejecting fish that are not quite fresh,' and the warning against eating oysters from Santa Lucia 'where the shellfish are kept in undesirable proximity to the mouths of the sewers.' (Once begun, it is almost impossible to stop quoting Baedeker. I will report one more and have done, the drily lyrical sentences from *Southern France* that describe the countryside near Beziers in words that recall at once Milton's Eden and the *lacrimae rerum*: 'pleasant walks to the south of the city. Guide 3fr. Adders abound.') In the guide portion of this book Forster has used this kind of writing too sparingly, but in the historical portion there are frequent examples. We learn of the heretic Arius that

> Learned and sincere, tall, simple in his dress, persuasive in his speech, he was accused by his enemies of looking like a snake, and of seducing, in the theological sense, 700 virgins.

Gnosticism 'taught that the world and mankind are the result of an unfortunate blunder.'

> In spite of his sincerity, [Plotinus] became fashionable, and the psychic powers that he had acquired not only gained him, on four occasions, the Mystic Vision which was the goal of his philosophy, but also discovered a necklace which had been stolen from a rich lady by one of her slaves.

But even here one has a reservation. These sentences and others like them are a joy to read, but they point up a disturbing flaw that is apparent whenever Forster attempts to explicate complicated modes of thought. If he is weak on history, his theology is even weaker, a serious problem in a book whose core is an account of the 'spiritual city' of Alexandria. Lytton Strachey's sardonic account of the Oxford Movement is hugely entertaining, but by turning the whole episode into rich comedy he fails to leave us the slightest opportunity of appreciating the seriousness and sincerity of the people involved. In the same way Forster's account of Gnostics and Monothelites is written with too evident a concern for the absurd. His treatment makes it almost impossible to believe that intelligent people ever took Neo-Platonism or Monophysism seriously, that they were, and perhaps to some still are, living issues. It all adds up to more than an 'arid theological Odyssey.'

There are one or two other blind spots. There is a trace of the Victorian preference for the Hellenic over the Hellenistic in the frequent use of the word *decadent* when speaking of Ptolemaic or Byzantine Egypt, a preference for a Greece of woodsy mystery and athleticism unhampered by thought—and too much thought, in one guise or another, is the villain of all Forster's works. There is a rather simplified version of Islam—even the English of Chandrapore would approve of Islam as it is presented here, as a sound, no nonsense kind of religion for soldiers impatient of the theological subtleties of subject peoples. Coupled with what seems to be a strong bias against modern Egypt, for reasons that may be justified but are not entirely clear, it is, in its attitudes, in some ways a curious book for an author who was at the same time at work on *A Passage to India.*

And in some ways not. It is one of the only two books that Forster published between *Howards End* (1910) and *A Passage to India* (1924), and it is of the greatest interest as an approach to the latter work. (The other book of this period, *Pharos and Pharillon*, 1923, is also about Alexandria. It is a series of essays describing episodes from Alexandrian history, and would have been a far better choice for republication than the guide book were it not marred here and there by a kind of jocose attitude toward Jews that is no longer considered very funny.) Inevitably some of the major concerns of *A Passage to India* are touched on here, especially what is the central problem of that novel, as it is of *Alexandria*, divinity and man's relation to divinity. In *A Passage to India* Aziz is sustained by an affirmation of Moslem orthodoxy, Fielding worships a kind of liberal humanism, the British officials are sure that their Imperial and civilizing mission is divinity manifest. Mrs Moore, who is most consciously seeking God, is at first repelled by her revelation of divinity as a hollow 'boum . . . boum,' a divinity with no message for mankind, indifferent to the human need for comfort and law. Like Professor Godbole and the other Hindus, she realizes after her visit to the Caves that God cannot be actively won, that divinity can be touched only by a total surrender of personality; the final message of the festival, where the Hindus find their god in grease and dust, is that there is no theological way to God. 'God si love.' In its espousal of their rational and its distrust of ingenuity and logic *A Passage to India* is a deliberate rejection of all the unbridled speculation that the 'spiritual city' of Alexandria represents to Forster. He derides the Alexandrian philosophers' over-subtle answers to the great problem they posed themselves, God's 'relation to the rest of the universe and particularly to man,' their 'favourite problem of linking human and divine.' They wanted God to be 'both far and close,' he remarks, and it is clear that his meditations upon these matters while writing *Alexandria*, and his recognition of the human tendency to 'magnify the human in the divine' was the theme that gave form to his scattered impressions and memories of India, and thus shaped his most important novel.

Pharos and Pharillon
(1923)

34
Things that have Interested Mr Forster

R. M.

Put an English novelist in Egypt, and the usual result will be large sales. Every circulating library counts among its subscribers many votaries of *l' Adonis noir.* Now Mr E.M. Forster, who spent several years in Egypt during the War, is one of the few important contemporary novelists. It is a wretchedly long while since he has published a novel, and one certainly hopes that he will give us one with an Oriental setting. For he is known to have seen much of the East from a point of view which is not that of the English merchants, administrators and soldiers, from among whose wives the novelists of Egypt and India have been too exclusively recruited. That he will one day write a 'novel of passion' is to be hoped—under such a heading comes most of the highest as well as of the vilest fiction—but it will certainly not be of the type inaugurated by Mr Hichens; and so far the chief public result of Mr Forster's life in Egypt has been a book entitled *Alexandria: A History and a Guide*, which appeared last year in that city. This book has not been published in England, but the present reviewer found some copies a short while ago in a Gerrard Street bookshop, and even those who know neither the city nor the author's other work, can be safely recommended to procure one: those who know either will not need the recommendation. The book, of course, includes much that is of importance only to those who visit Alexandria; so now Mr Forster offers us, through the polite medium of the Hogarth Press, a book which resumes in somewhat different form the most generally interesting parts of the larger work, in addition to much that is entirely new. It is regrettable that he has not included in *Pharos and Pharillon* chapters to correspond with the admirable sketches in the guide-book of Alexandrian poetry and science;

SOURCE *New Statesman*, 16 June 1923, pp. 303–04.

indeed, the only admissible complaint against the new book is that it contains only eight pages.

The curriculum of most English schools is carefully drawn up to exclude the Silver Ages of Greek and Latin literature, for fear, presumably, of the boys growing more interested in life or art than in syntax: and history is taught only in relation to victorious empires. So that the noble name of Alexandria wakes little response in the minds of many who would call themselves educated. Yet there is no city in the world, save Rome and perhaps Byzantium, with so long, rich and varied a history. Homer sends Menelaus to its site, but it is to Alexander the Great that it owes its foundation and its name. After his death one of his generals founded there the incestuous line of Ptolemies under which it most magnificently flowered. This dynasty ended with the asps, but the city, though now only the capital of a Province, did not fall. Greek and Jew and Christian made it for six centuries the centre of their disputes; there the Septuagint was miraculously made, there Plato developed the doctrine of the Logos, there the Neo-Platonists reasoned about the attainment of ecstasy, there Gnostic and Arian, Monophysite and Monothelite elaborated their heresies. And then the Arabs came, and for over a thousand years Alexandria owned one God and no history. Amr, the Mohammedan general, had taken a city containing '4,000 palaces, 4,000 baths, 400 theatres, 1,200 greengrocers, and 40,000 Jews.' Napoleon eleven and a half centuries later found there only a wretched Turkish town with 4,000 inhabitants. To-day it is once more a populous and prosperous city, but if it is famous, it is only for its cotton. It still has a perfect climate.

Here is part of a long quotation made by Mr Forster from *Plotinus*:

> To any vision must be brought an eye adapted to what is to be seen, and having some resemblance to it. Never did eye see the sun unless it had first become sunlike, and never can the soul have vision of the first Beauty unless itself be beautiful.

'And never,' one may add, 'can the mind perceive Alexandria unless itself become Alexandrian.' This condition has been fulfilled by Mr Forster. Refined, philosophic and inquisitive, he has some sympathy for St Clement, little or none for St Athanasius, and a passionate admiration for the young, the godlike Alexander of Macedon, but he treats all alike as real persons. When he calls Arius and Athanasius 'clergymen' and speaks of their 'taking duty,' one may think that he tames them too much, but the method is all that is commendable. He writes about everything in the unparagoned history of Alexandria which interests him, and he commands our eager admiration whether he is telling the story of Pharos the great lighthouse, of the accession to the throne of Ptolemy Epiphanes, of a Jewish deputation to Caligula, of an eighteenth-century missionary lady who visited Egypt, of the coming of Spring to the skirts of the Desert or of a fashionable street in the modern Levantine city. He uses irony, but so delicately you would hardly know it; and behind his scepticism one is just aware of an ardent and almost mystical quality of mind. It was the strength of old Alexandria, he writes somewhere in the guide-book, that

> she did cling to the idea of love; and much philosophic absurdity, much theological aridity must be pardoned to those who maintain that the best thing on earth is likely to be the best in heaven.

The last essay in *Pharos and Pharillon* is devoted to the poetry of a Greek dweller in modern Alexandria, Mr C. P. Cavafy. Here is the translation quoted by Mr Forster of a poem entitled *Alexandrian Kings.*

An Alexandrian crowd collected
to see the sons of Cleopatra,
Caesarion and his little brothers
Alexander and Ptolemy, who for the first
time were brought to the Gymnasium,
there to be crowned as Kings
amidst a splendid display of troops.

Alexander they named King
of Armenia, of Media, and of the Parthians.
Ptolemy they named King
of Cilicia, of Syria, and Phoenicia.
Caesarion stood a little in front,
clad in silk the colour of roses,
with a bunch of hyacinths at his breast.
His belt was a double line of sapphires and amethysts,
his sandals were bound with white ribbons
embroidered with rosy pearls.
Him they acclaimed more than the small ones.
Him they named 'King of Kings!'

The Alexandrians knew perfectly well
that all this was words and empty pomp.

But the day was warm and exquisite,
the sky clear and blue,
the Gymnasium of Alexandria a triumph of art,
the courtiers' apparel magnificent,
Caesarion full of grace and beauty
(son of Cleopatra, blood of the Lagidae!)
and the Alexandrians ran to see the show,
and grew enthusiastic, and applauded
in Greek, in Egyptian, and some in Hebrew,

> *bewitched with the beautiful spectacle,*
> *though they knew perfectly well how worthless,*
> *what empty words, were these King-makings.*

The intrinsic beauty of this poem is justification enough for its inclusion in a review of the book that introduces it to us. But there is more than this. It is the work, says Mr Forster, of 'an artist who is not interested in facile beauty,' and whose mind 'stands at a slight angle to the universe.' How closely these criticisms apply to the critic who makes them! And how akin to his genius is the poem in its mixture of appreciation with detachment, and in its careful impersonality. In *Pharos and Pharillon* Mr Forster has taken most beguiling themes, and made of them as distinguished a book as this year is likely to produce. An artist of exceptional sympathy, humour, intellect, and individuality, he refuses to be defined. But his classic pudor is infinitely more intriguing than the personal candours of others, and having raked unsuccessfully, though with the intensest enjoyment, his Alexandrian sketches, we await his next book with impatient and heightened curiosity.

35
The Magic of E. M. Forster

JOHN MIDDLETON MURRY

The fortune of war cast Mr Forster upon Alexandria, and Alexandria cast her spell upon him. Of all our modern writers he was the most eminently fitted to receive it. We know this, because he alone has been able to communicate it to us and to make us feel, what in our minds we know, that only this debatable ground, where Greece and Asia strove for harmony and the human sought to include the infinite, could contain the music by which the god Hercules bade farewell to Antony. Strange and elusive and impalpable things have happened in this borderland. It belongs as much to imagination as to the actual. Monks battered in the heads of monks and hanged bishops over their altars in the churches of Alexandria. But on the plains near by the veritable voice of Antony once whispered:

> Unarm, Eros, the long day's work is done,
> And we must sleep.

And many years before, in the great oasis of Siwa, Alexander had heard the summons of God. 'A scare he did get,' says Mr Forster and with subtle diffidence that is all his own, 'a fright, a psychic experience, "a turn,"' and then his mind flits softly into a wistful immensity, flutters on the extreme verge of human imagining, is tossed about by winds from other worlds, dreaming of the king who has haunted the memory of Europe for more than two thousand years.

> When at the age of thirty-three he died, when the expedition that he did not seek stole towards him in the summer-house at Babylon, did it seem to him as after all but the crown of his smaller quests? He had tried to lead Greece, then he had tried to lead mankind. He had succeeded in both. But was the universe also friendly, was it also in trouble, was it calling on him, on

SOURCE *New Republic*, 8 August 1923, pp. 293–4.

> him, for his help and his love? The priest of Ammon had addressed him as 'Son of God.' What exactly did the compliment mean? Was it explicable this side of the grave?

There, in a paragraph, is Mr Forster. He is at the centre of his subject and at the centre of himself. What more perfect correspondence could we desire? Under this sign, which he so exquisitely interprets, Alexandria was created to bear the young god's name. Round about this central mystery the contradictory history of the great city falls into order and coherence. Enigmas are enigmatic no longer when the strange key is your natural possession. The smile of Sphinx is sisterly if you know it in your heart.

So the story of Alexandria, seen (or it may be refracted) through Mr Forster's mind, becomes a manifestation of himself. Here is a world of events that he can comfortably inhabit; in this garment the very tricks of his mind can be accommodated. He was made for it and it for him; for his friend the Alexandrian poet, Cavafy, also, in whose diaphanous verses, as in Mr Forster's prose, the outward incoherence of Alexandria that is and was seems refracted into unity. Cavafy Mr Forster presents to us as 'standing at a slight angle with the universe.' At the same slight angle we see Mr Forster, who stands by him, also inclined. This to many, perhaps to most, certainly to all those who pride themselves on 'seeing straight' and on 'calling a spade a spade'—unnecessary tautology—will appear a deplorable attitude. They will be constitutionally unable to adjust themselves to the angle of vision; they will never understand how much of new and true these crooked people see.

And, of course, if they trouble to say anything at all about it, they will say, 'But how *very* personal!' they will resent the implicit impertinence. For it *is* very impertinent when a single mind grasps the history of a great city as a single thing, as living and mysterious as itself. One little man, not to be distinguished from five hundred others when he sidles down the Strand, dares to regard battles and schisms and the fates of empires as functions of himself. Even prime ministers and newspaper-owners do not go so far: they have a sense, if not of the ridiculous, of what will not be tolerated in them. Yet this little man has the audacity to snip with his scissors at the stuff of history and make himself a suit of clothes. It is terrible. It is more terrible even than this. For the first time certain people begin to notice of what wonderful stuff the suit is made. Suddenly they recognize it as the authentic asbestos, immortally enduring. And naturally they begin to feel that there is something right and true in this use of the vague and faded material; it shines so splendidly now. It must have been waiting for the little man.

The implications of this conclusion are rather awful. That is, why the majority of people avoid it. A more real reality is an alarming thing to have about; worse still is the thought that it is reserved for odd people to make contact with it, for people who, abandoning the good old practice of looking things in the face, cock their heads sideways at them and get a glimpse of what is behind. To this dubious race Mr Forster indisputably belongs. Being a dubious character, he goes off to a dubious city, to that portion of the inhabited world where there is most obviously a bend in the spiritual dimension, to a place that is now brother to that spot on the Windsor Road where Mr Barnstaple heard the sound, 'sharp like the snapping of a lute-string,' which was the music to his entry into Utopia—to a tense and exciting 'field' (as the physicists would call it) where the atmosphere is preternaturally keen and there is a lucid confusion of the categories. At this point a spinning eddy marks the convergence of two worlds, and in its vortex contradictories are reconciled. It is nothing less than a crack in the human universe. Mr Forster wanders off to put his ear to it. He finds Mr Cavafy already engaged in the enterprise. So they listen together. They hear the defunctive music which attended Mark Antony to his last triumph, the words which were whispered by the priest of Ammon to the son of God, and the Bedouin singing 'tunes to his camel that he can only sing to the camel, because in his mind the tune and the camel are the same thing.'

There is a vortex in Alexandria, and Mr Forster, being sensitive to such disturbances, was drawn into it inevitably. That is how we would explain this book and the glittering, shimmering magic that dances in and out of its pages. You may suggest, if you are interested in these inquiries, that if Mr Forster were put anywhere else on the earth's surface, he would be found behaving oddly and glancing sideways at creation. Certainly he has shown an inclination that way before. That is why we remember his former books. They were not exactly good books, sometimes they were almost childish books, but they were in parts peculiar. But *Pharos and Pharillon*—except for one essay which recalls Mr Lytton Strachey—is wholly peculiar and wholly good. Therefore we conclude that in Alexandria Mr Forster found his spiritual home; the queer fish found it easier to breathe in those suspiciously crystalline waters. Whether he knew what had befallen him the moment he arrived there, or whether it was his encounter with Mr Cavafy and his recognition in him of a fellow-exile from the world of things which simply are what they are called—no matter which of these encouraged him to expand his own idiosyncrasy in the favoring air, it is certain that Mr Forster has never yet been so convincingly himself or so manifestly different from his fellow-writers.

Yes, we must look for the cause in Alexandria. For we can detect the same magic, scent the same emanation from the antique and king-trodden earth, in the poetry of Mr Cavafy which Mr Forster quotes.

When at the hour of midnight
an invisible choir is suddenly heard passing
with exquisite music, with voices—
Do not lament your fortune that at last subsides,

your life's work that has failed, your schemes that have proved illusions.
But like a man prepared, like a brave man,
bid farewell to her, to Alexandria who is passing . . .

And we have further evidence. Does not Mr Forster himself invoke the city to explain the hopes of Clement of Alexandria that the great opposites, Greek naturalism and Christian supernaturalism, might be reconciled?

> He lived in a period of transition, and in Alexandria. And in that curious city, which had never been young and hoped never to grow old, conciliation must have seemed more possible than elsewhere, and the graciousness of Greece not quite incompatible with the grace of God.

In that same curious city, we feel, Mr Forster first gained the courage of his own vision and first dared to venture himself wholly into a 'field' that is by right his own. Let us also have courage to compare small things with great, and say that Mr Forster, like the young king he finds 'more lovable' for the vision, 'has caught by the unintellectual way a glimpse of something great, if dangerous, and that the glimpse came to him first'—if not 'in the recesses of the Siwan oasis'—in the streets of the great city north of it.

A Passage to India
(1924)

36
Women in the East

ROSE MACAULAY

Mr E. M. Forster is, to many people, the most attractive and the most exquisite of contemporary novelists (for a contemporary novelist he has, fortunately, now once more become). Further, he is probably the most truthful, both superficially and fundamentally. His delicate character presentation—too organic to be called drawing—his gentle and pervading humour, his sense and conveyal of the beauty, the ridiculousness, and the nightmare strangeness, of all life, his accurate recording of social, intellectual and spiritual shades and reactions, has fine-spun honesty of thought, his poetry and ironic wit—these qualities have made him from the first one of the rather few novelists who can be read with delight.

No one now writing understands so well as he the queer interaction of fantasy and ordinary life, the ghosts that halo common persons and things, the odd, mystic power of moments. Neither does anyone, I think, understand quite so well, or convey with such precision and charm, what ordinary people are really like, the way they actually do think and talk. His people are solid, three-dimensioned, and he sees them both from without and within.

A Passage to India is his fifth novel, and his first for fourteen years. Those who fear that his peculiar gifts may be wasted in a novel about India can be reassured; they have full scope. He can make even these brown men live; they are as alive as his Cambridge undergraduates, his London ladies, his young Italians, his seaside aunts; they are drawn with an equal and a more amazing insight and vision. And in the Anglo-Indians, male and female, he has material the most suitable ready to his hand.

The Ruling Race

Never was a more convincing, a more pathetic, or a more amusing picture drawn of the Ruling Race in India. A sympathetic picture, too, for Mr Forster is sympathetic to almost everyone. Here, for instance, is the Club,

SOURCE *The Daily News*, 4 June 1924, p. 8.

after a supposed insult offered by an Indian to an Englishwoman:

> They had started speaking of 'women and children'—that phrase that exempts the male from sanity when it has been repeated a few times. Each felt that all he loved best in the world was at stake, demanded revenge, and was filled with a not unpleasing glow.... 'But it's the women and children,' they repeated, and the Collector knew he ought to stop them intoxicating themselves, but had not the heart.

Somewhere between the two camps, the Anglo-Indians and the Indians, are the newcomers to India—an old lady and a girl, not yet hardened and harrowed into the Anglo-Indian outlook, but full of honest, interested curiosity. These two women are alive with all the imaginative actuality with which Mr Forster invests his old and his young females. He is almost alone in this, that he enters into the minds of old ladies, and attributes to them those sensitive reactions to life, those philosophic, muddled speculations as to the universe and personal relationships, which most novelists only find younger persons worthy to contain or to emit. The old lady in this book is the most clear-sighted, sensitive, civilised and intellectually truthful person in her circle. She speculates like a male or female undergraduate.

> She felt increasingly (vision or nightmare?) that, though people are important, the relations between them are not, and that in particular too much fuss has been made over marriage. Centuries of carnal embracement, yet man is no nearer to understanding man. And to-day she felt this with such force that it seemed itself a relationship, itself a person who was trying to take hold of her hand.

What other novelist would attribute such thoughts to a lady of sixty-five who has just been told of the engagement of her son?

A Civilised Girl

It is such patient, imaginative realism as this that distinguishes Mr Forster from most writers. His young woman, too, is an achievement—a queer, unattractive, civilised, logical, intellectually honest girl, who wanted to understand India and the Indians, and came up against the wall of Anglo-India between herself and them. *A Passage to India* is really a story about this Anglo-Indian wall, and the futile occasional attempts, from either side, to surmount it. I suppose it is a sad story, as most truthful stories of collective human relationships must be; it is an ironic tragedy, but also a brilliant comedy of manners, and a delightful entertainment. Its passages of humour or beauty might, quoted, fill several columns. But they cannot profitably be isolated; Mr Forster is not, in the main, a detachable epigrammist; his wit and his poetry are both organically contextual. This novel has a wider and a deeper range than any of his others.

He has quite lost the touch of preciousness, of exaggerated care for nature and the relationships of human beings, that may faintly irritate some readers of his earlier books. He used once to write at times too much as a graduate (even occasionally as an undergraduate) of King's College, Cambridge (perhaps the most civilised place in the world), who has had an amour with Italy and another with the god Pan. In *A Passage to India* (as, indeed, in *Howards End*), Pan is only implicit, the mysticism is more diffused, the imagination at once richer, less fantastic, and more restrained. It is a novel that, from most novelists, would be an amazing piece of work. Coming from Mr Forster, it is not amazing, but it is, I think, the best and most interesting book he has written.

But I should like very much to know what Anglo-Indians will think of it.

37
Arch beyond Arch

LEONARD WOOLF

A little while ago I wrote in these columns that the book of this publishing season to which I looked forward most eagerly was Mr E. M. Forster's new novel, *A Passage to India.* And now it has appeared and I have read it and— Well, there are few things more exciting than to look forward to the publication of a new book, by a living writer, to read it, and to find one's hopes realized. That, at least, has happened to me with *A Passage to India.* But it only adds to the difficulty of writing about it. It is very easy to criticize a book which you know to be bad or which you think to be good; your real difficulties begin with a book by a contemporary which seems to you to be very good. There is, for instance, that terrible question: 'How good?' A question which, in the case of Mr Forster, it is hopeless to try to answer in 1,200 words.

*

There are, first, certain obvious things which must be said about *A Passage to India.* It is superbly written. Mr Forster seems now to have reached the point at which there is nothing too simple or to subtle for his pen; he is able to find words which exactly fit, which perfectly express, every thought which comes to him, and neither the thought nor the words are those which would come to anyone else in the world except Mr Forster. If that is not one of the essential characteristics of a great writer or of great writing, then I have no knowledge or understanding of either. Let me quote:-

> She had come to the state where the horror of the universe and its smallness are both visible at the same time—the twilight of the double vision in which so many elderly people are involved. If this world is not to our taste, well, at all events there is Heaven, Hell, Annihilation—one or other of those large things, that huge scenic background of stars, fires, blue or black air. All heroic

SOURCE *Nation and Athenaeum*, 14 June 1924, p. 354.

> endeavour, and all that is known as art, assumes that there is such a background, just as all practical endeavour, when the world is to our taste, assumes that the world is all. But in the twilight of the double vision, a spiritual muddle is set up for which no high-sounding words can be found; we can neither act nor refrain from action; we can neither ignore nor respect Infinity. Mrs Moore had always inclined to resignation. As soon as she landed in India it seemed to her good, and when she saw the water flowing through the mosque-tank, or the Ganges, or the moon, caught in the shawl of the night with all the other stars, it seemed a beautiful goal and an easy one. To be one with the universe! So dignified and so simple. But there was always some little duty to be performed first, some new card to be turned up from the diminishing pack and placed, and while she was pottering about, the Marabar struck its gong.

*

In this book there are all the elements which made Mr Forster's previous novels of such promise. There is the extraordinarily subtle and individual humour, the lifelikeness of the characters, the command of dialogue, the power of opening windows upon what is both queer and beautiful. The difference between *A Passage to India* and the former novels is that now Mr Forster knows exactly how to use the elements of his genius. The promise of *Where Angels Fear to Tread* was renewed, but not fulfilled, in *Howards End.* None of these former books 'came off,' and there were in them disconcerting lapses into 'silliness,' if I dare say so—the silliness, not of a stupid, but of a clever man. But there is no silliness, no lapse, no wobbling in *A Passage to India*; it marches firmly, triumphantly, even grimly and sadly—the adverbs can only be explained by reading the book—through the real life and politics of India, the intricacy of personal relations, the story itself, the muddle and the mystery of life.

*

I have left my last paragraph for what I shall find most difficult to say. I ought, I know, to have said something about the plot, the story, the novel. They are extraordinarily interesting, but they are the superficies of the book. Even what I have been writing about in the previous paragraphs is on, or only just below, the surface. Nearly all great books, certainly nearly all great novels, have deep beneath their surface a theme or themes which are what give to the whole book its form, real meaning, greatness. Most writers are content with a single informing idea of this sort as the basis of their book, but what makes Mr Forster's novel so remarkable is that he has a large number of such 'themes,' which, interwoven with great imaginative subtlety, weave a strange and beautiful texture for the book itself. The old lady, Mrs Moore, a superb character in the book, felt that 'outside the arch there seemed always an arch, beyond the remotest echo a silence.' I feel the same about the book, when I look back on it, if one adds, perhaps, that beyond the remotest silence there is again an echo. There is the story itself with the two ladies who wanted to see India, the Anglo-Indian society of Chandrapore, and Aziz the only living Indian whom I have ever met in a book, and his friendship—which failed to be a friendship—with the Englishman Fielding. Behind that is an arch of politics, the politics of Anglo-India, and the nationalist India. And beyond that is another arch, half mystery, half muddle, which permeates India and personal relations and life itself—

> and all the time, [as Mrs Moore says,] this to do and that to do and this to do in your way and that to do in her way, and everything sympathy and confusion and bearing one another's burdens. Why can't this be done and that be done in my way and they be done and I at peace? Why has anything to be done, I cannot see.

And beyond that the terrible arch of 'personal relations'—do 'we exist not in ourselves, but in terms of each other's minds'?—and 'the friendliness, as of dwarfs shaking hands.' And beyond that the still more terrible arch of disillusionment—'the shadow of the shadow of a dream.' So the book builds itself up, arch beyond arch, into something of great strength, beauty, and also of sadness. The themes are woven and interwoven into a most intricate pattern, against which, or in which, the men and women are shown to us pathetically, rather ridiculously, entangled. That is how the book presents itself to me immediately after having read it, and perhaps my description may be hardly intelligible to anyone who has not read it. If so, all I can do is to advise him to rush out to the nearest bookseller, buy a copy of the book, and read it for himself.

38
A Great Novel at Last

SYLVIA LYND

Reader, lo here, at last, a great book. There have been brilliant books in recent years, witty books, original books, books written in limpid and exquisite English; but not until now has there been a book that was all these things, and at the same time a book of large plan and sustained achievement, a book of new knowledge as well as of wisdom and imagination, a book that illumines a social and political problem and leaves it so revealed that the old revelations of it fade into trumpery insignificance. All this and more may be said of *A Passage to India.* When elderly persons, asking less for the sake of information than in order to bring home to the present generation that it is a generation of vipers, ask 'Where are our great books nowadays?' they can henceforth confidently be answered with: *A Passage to India.*

It is to Jane Austen that one must turn for a parallel in English fiction to the work of Mr Forster. Like her he has the supreme gift of making things happen 'naturally,' he has her ear for the exact turn of speech that contains character and humour perfectly sharpened but without the faintest exaggeration of caricature, he has her gift for making a procession of ordinary events as exciting as such processions are in reality, and like her he sees both young and old with equally interested and detecting eyes. The impartiality, the humour, the irreverence, and the candour, not imprisoned in lady-hood, of Jane Austen—imagine all these applied to an examination of the relationships of east and west in India at the present day, of India seen not only from the English club but also from the native bungalow and the native palace, and you have some idea of the richness, the variety and the astonishingness of *A Passage to India.* To call it a beautiful book, beautiful as is its style and beautiful as is the poise of its author's spirit, would be misleading. Neither Western civilisation nor Eastern civilisation is beautiful nor are they beautiful in impact. *A Passage*

SOURCE *Time and Tide,* 20 June 1924, pp. 592–3.

to India is a delicious and terrible book. It is at once comical and agonising.

Mr Forster takes a group of some dozen characters, English, Moslem and Hindu, and measures to each his share of sympathy, understanding and derision. The Indians in this book are not, as in all other Anglo-Indian novels, deplorable but unavoidable pieces of the scenery. They are not cast for the roles of simple villains or clowns. They are men with different conventions from Englishmen—how different has never been revealed before. And they are not of one pattern. Professor Godbole, the Brahman, is as different from Dr Aziz, the Mohammedan with the English medical degree, as both are from Cyril Fielding the liberal Englishman, eccentric in India, and as he is from Mr Turton of the Residency, and as Mr Turton, the fine austere Anglo-Indian is from the brutal Major Callendar.

To visit Ronny Heslop the young magistrate, in Chandrapore, come his mother Mrs Moore, the best type of intelligent Englishwoman, and Miss Quested, a plain, conscientious English girl to whom he is half-engaged. Miss Quested is anxious to see 'the real India.' This can only be done by becoming personally friendly with Indians, a state of affairs that English rule does not encourage. Attempts to bridge the gulf always end disastrously, declare the English residents of Chandrapore. They prefer to act 'Cousin Kate' and play bridge. Mrs Moore and Miss Quested are not deterred, however, Mrs Moore because her naturalness and free mind put her at once into sincere relations with everyone, Miss Quested because she feels that to try to 'understand' India is the right thing to do. By touch after touch of delicate comedy and delicate revealing detail, Mr Forster conveys the exquisite discomfort of the attempt to bridge the gulf.

Dr Aziz, out of mixed motives of vanity and friendliness, organises an expedition for Mrs Moore and Miss Quested to some famous caves in the neighbourhood of Chandrapore. He expends vast sums on the entertainment. He borrows an elephant. He sleeps overnight at the railway station for fear of being late. The whole thing worries him desperately. Mrs Moore and Miss Quested are not at all anxious to go; but out of politeness they do not like to refuse. And so the party sets off for a disaster as complete as the wildest prophets among the *memsahibs* could desire. Mrs Moore gets a touch of sun and becomes a crabbed, dying woman, instead of a figure of health and wisdom. Miss Quested for some reason less comprehensively explained, flees from the caves believing herself the victim of attempted outrage. It is a horrid picnic. Race prejudice bursts in upon it like an infuriated bull. Mr Forster now hovers above a world not only filled with absurdities and misconceptions, but churned to frenzy with hatred and the desire of vengeance. Each of his characters shows himself as he is at a crisis as clearly as he did among every-day occurrences. The description of the trial of Dr Aziz is one of the most overwhelmingly exciting things in English literature. It is like the gliding of the pilgrim ship at the beginning of *Lord Jim*, or the chase between that other Jim and Israel Hands in *Treasure Island*.

It is the pinnacle of the miserable comedy. It does not cease to be grotesquely funny because it is also sternly serious.

Mr Forster seizes his opportunity with the finest precision whether he is twisting the emotions of his characters into the knot of conflict or disentangling them into the innumerable strands of triumph and humiliation and dismay that follow it. Fielding, whose sense of justice is stronger than his racial feeling has taken the side of Dr Aziz in the struggle. Fielding is garlanded with flowers, but he finds himself irresistibly impelled in the end to call Dr Aziz 'little rotter,' though he knows it to be less than half the truth. East and West are left by Mr Forster as completely separate as in the most stirring melodrama of the Mutiny, or in the plainest tale from the hills.

This may not be the moral of Mr Forster's novel for everyone, however. *A Passage to India* is one of those books so rich in implication as well as in statement, that each reader may draw his own conclusion from it, just as each of us draws a different conclusion from what he experiences of life. One thing is certain, friendship whether between nations or individuals can only be based on knowledge, and it is an enlargement of knowledge, not only of India, but of human motives, that Mr Forster has made so superb a contribution. I should like to quote passage after passage to illustrate Mr Forster's beautiful fairness, perceptiveness and sense of the mystery of life, but where the excellence is so consistent every page demands quotation and I must direct my readers straight to the book itself.

39
Review

L. P. HARTLEY

Of all the novels that have appeared in England this year, Mr Forster's is probably the most considerable. If it had merely been up to his standard, its pre-eminence would scarcely have been challenged; and in its scope and its effect it surpasses his previous books. In them, delightful as they were, evidences of partiality, imperfect sympathy, eccentricity of outlook so pronounced as sometimes to seem an obsession, spoiled the exquisite flavour and distinction of his work. Perhaps spoiled is too strong a word; but they gave it a partisan air, almost an air of propaganda; as though it were Mr Forster's mission to show that all the evil in the world came out of philistinism, suburbanism and the Public Schools. One trembled for the stupid well-meaning person who blundered into Mr Forster's pages, disturbed his fawns at their play, and recommended corporal punishment for them. Such a one did not get off lightly.

Some such distinction between types Mr Forster preserves in his last, and as we think his best, book. The Anglo-Indians stand for much that Mr Forster dislikes: insensitiveness, officialdom, stupidity, repressiveness, rudeness. The Indians are the children of Nature, affectionate, courteous, eager, irresponsible, wayward. Mr Forster's heart lies with them, but his sympathy does not blind him to the defects of their qualities; their impracticability, their double-dealing, conscious and unconscious, the crust of shallow intrigue which makes action, when they take it, of none effect. Nor does he fail to do justice to the redeeming qualities of their rulers. They are, of course, the qualities that make themselves felt in a crisis; and a crisis is foreign to the spirit of the East, which does not so much rise as sink to an emergency.

A Passage to India is much more than a study of racial contrasts and disabilities. It is intensely personal and (if the phrase may be pardoned) intensely cosmic. The problem of the English in India lies midway between

SOURCE *Spectator*, 28 June 1924, pp. 1048–50.

these two greater considerations, linking them up and illuminating them. To the question, can the English as a foreign ruling caste arrive at a working arrangement with the Indians? Mr Forster answers perfunctorily, No. And to the question (more interesting to the novelist) can an individual Englishman with the best will in the world reach terms of intimacy with an Indian similarly disposed? Mr Forster again seems to say, with infinite hesitation and regret, that he cannot:

> 'Why can't we be friends now?' said (Fielding) holding him (Aziz) affectionately. 'It's what I want. It's what you want.'
>
> But the horses didn't want it—they swerved apart; the earth didn't want it, sending up rocks through which riders must pass single file; the temples, the tank, the jail, the palace, the birds, the carrion, the Guest House that came into view as they issued from the gap and saw Mau beneath: they didn't want it, they said in their hundred voices, 'No, not yet,' and the sky said 'No, not there.'

All the characters except perhaps Fielding, the unconventional Anglo-Indian schoolmaster whom the ladies of the station in their spiteful way called 'not quite pukka,' are at the mercy of their moods and nerves. Most novelists take it as a postulate that personality is capable of little variation, that it is within narrow margins determinable and accountable, and on this assumption work out problems of relationship to a logical conclusion. Mr Forster sees human beings very differently. They have little sure hold over themselves; they are subject to skiey influences and 'dangers from the East'; they reach out for a prevailing mood and find it gone. They are infinitely receptive and 'suggestible.' Hence their failure to come into touch with each other. They desire the most intimate spiritual contacts, but they have no assurance of success because they do not know, from one moment to another, where the weight of their desires will lie: gravity pulls their personalities this way and that, they cannot count on themselves. The 'incident' of the Marabar Caves would have been a strain on the most tough-minded person; its effect on the two sensitive ladies who had come out, with the best will in the world, to find what India meant, was little short of disintegrating. It is the central fact of the book, this gloomy expedition arranged with so much solicitude and affection by Dr Aziz to give his guests pleasure. A lesser novelist than Mr Forster could have shown everything going wrong, could have emphasized the tragic waste of Aziz's hospitality and kind intentions, could have blamed Fate. But no one else could have given the affair its peculiar horror, could have so dissociated it from the common course of experience and imagination, could have left it at once so vague and so clear. Unlike many catastrophes in fiction, it seems unavoidable whichever way we look at it; we cannot belittle it by saying that the characters should have behaved more sensibly, the sun need not have been so hot or the scales weighted against happiness. And not only by the accident of the caves does Mr Forster illustrate the incalculable disastrous fluctuations of human personality, but he subtly works in the black magic of India, crudely presented to us in a hundred penny-dreadfuls about the stolen eyes of idols and death-bearing charms.

A Passage to India is a disturbing, uncomfortable book. Its surface is so delicately and finely wrought that it pricks us at a thousand points. There is no emotional repose or security about it; it is for ever puncturing our complacence, it is a bed of thorns. The humour, irony and satire that awake the attention and delight the mind on every page all leave their sting. We cannot escape to the past or the future, because Mr Forster's method does not encourage the growth of those accretions in the mind; he pins us down to the present moment, the discontent and pain of which cannot be allayed by reference to what has been or to what will be. The action of the book is not fused by a continuous impulse; it is a series of intense isolated moments. To overstate the case very much, the characters seem with each fresh sensation to begin their lives again. And that perhaps is why no general aspect or outline of Mr Forster's book is so satisfactory as its details.

40
Bo-oum or Ou-Boum?

JOHN MIDDLETON MURRY

It was only to be expected that Mr E. M. Forster's novel when it did come, after a silence of fourteen years, would be a remarkable one. What might further have been expected was that it would in itself contain an explanation of that abnormal interlude. *A Passage to India* does this: it tells us that the miracle is not that Mr Forster should have taken fourteen years to write it, but that he should have written it at all. For evidently the best part of those fourteen years was occupied not in writing this very fine novel, but in wondering whether there was indeed anything on earth, or in the heavens above, or in the waters under the earth, worth writing about. And even then, in that long space of years, Mr Forster did not *decide* that there was. No, the balance faintly inclined, the pointer dribbled over towards 'To be,' and the silence was interrupted.

I scarcely think it will be interrupted again. The planning of Mr Forster's next novel should carry him well on to the unfamiliar side of the grave. It will take him, I imagine, a good deal more than fourteen years to find the word which will evoke a different echo from the primeval cave of Marabar: and I fancy (such is my faith in his intellectual honesty) that he will not speak again without the assurance of a different reply.

But what is the echo of the cave of Marabar? This is what it is absolutely:

> The echo in a Marabar cave ... is entirely devoid of distinction. Whatever is said, the same monotonous voice replies, and quivers up and down the walls till it is absorbed in the roof. *Boum* is the sound as far as the human alphabet can express it, or *bou-oum*, or *ou-boum*,—utterly dull. Hope, politeness, the blowing of a nose, the squeak of a boot, all produce *boum*. Even the striking of a match starts a little worm coiling, which is too small to complete a circle, but is eternally watchful. And if several people talk at once, an overlapping howling noise begins, echoes generate echoes, and the cave is stuffed with a snake composed of small snakes, which writhe independently.

SOURCE *Adelphi*, July 1924, pp. 150–3.

And this is what it was to an elderly woman who was gifted (or cursed), like her creator, with 'the twilight of the double vision':

> The echo began in some indescribable way to undermine her hold on life. Coming at a moment when she chanced to be fatigued, it had managed to murmur, 'Pathos, piety, courage—they exist, but are identical, and so is filth. Everything exists, nothing has value.' If one had spoken vileness in the place, or quoted lofty poetry, the comment would have been the same—*ou-boum.*

A cave of Marabar is the symbol of the universe for Mr Forster: no wonder then that he should have waited so long before inviting an echo from it. He might almost as well have waited an eternity. 'It is a good book'—*bou-oum*; 'it is a bad book'—*ou-boum*; 'it is a good bad book'—*bou-oum*; 'it is a bad good book'—*ou-boum.*

To be or not to be? was once the question. But now, *Ou-boum* or *bou-oum*? Of these one is as good as the other. And yet, I wonder, is that indeed the only echo which reaches Mr Forster's metaphysical ear? Is *ou-boum* or *bou-oum* really the rich and rippling recompense for the dropping of this novel into the everlasting void? If it is, then Mr Forster is a hero: but if it is not . . .

I am speaking not of the outward fiction, which is brilliant and dramatic and absorbing, but of the inward significance of *A Passage to India.* That is the same (though expressed in how different a dialect!) as the significance of Mr Joyce's savage and hyperborean *Ulysses.* The outward fiction politely declares: 'I am revealing a strange and unknown continent—India—as it has never been revealed before.' That is true. But the inward significance whispers: 'I am obeying the word: Command that these stones be made bread.' And that not even Mr Forster can do.

One after the other they go, the talents of our age, dropping into the void. *Ou-boum* or *bou-oum*? The echo of *A Passage to India* is one of the greater ones: so many of the others are no more than 'the little worms coiling, too small to complete a circle.' Mr Forster's echo completes a circle utterly. And that is a great achievement. But what then? When the subtle, delicate, wistful voice of Mr Forster evokes the same response as the vulgar braying of ******? Is it enough to have given companions he would despise a symbol they will not understand? Can it be that one so skilful should have lost his way because he has forgotten a simple but difficult truth: that the head cannot really find room for that which the heart rejects, or both will wither and grow old? Can it be that, like his own Mrs Moore, Mr Forster

> has come to that state when the horror of the universe and its smallness are both visible at the same time—the twilight of the double vision in which so many elderly people are involved. If this world is not to our taste, well, at all events there is Heaven, Hell, Annihilation—one or other of those large things, that huge scenic background of stars, fires, blue or black air. All heroic endeavour, and all that is known as art, assumes that there is such a background, just as all practical endeavour, when the world is to our taste, assumes that the world is all. But in the twilight of the double vision, a spiritual

> muddledom is set up for which no high-sounding words can be found; we can neither act nor refrain from action, we can neither ignore nor respect Infinity.

Whether or not this is Mr Forster's condition, in that last half-sentence is contained the genesis and the import of *A Passage to India* . . .

41
Review

J. B. PRIESTLEY

Mr E. M. Forster has had a very different fate from that of any other member of that group of promising, brilliant young novelists, the 'coming men' of, say, nineteen-hundred-and-ten to-twelve. Many of his colleagues, instead of writing themselves 'in,' have by this time succeeded in writing themselves out. Mr Forster, after the publication of his very successful *Howards End,* apparently stopped writing fiction, and this new story of Anglo-Indian life is the first novel he has produced for at least twelve years. His return should be regarded by every intelligent reader of fiction as an event. He has brought back his own exquisite sanity into the English novel, and his curious sensitiveness, honesty and, perhaps above all, his civilising quality (for surely he is the most civilised writer we have), make some of our more recent discoveries among novelists look very cheap. Once more we are given a real novel, an honest thing in three dimensions, and not an amusing literary gesture, a bag of coloured tricks, seven shillings worth of careless and dishonest autobiography served up with sixpenny worth of creative effort. Everything is present, ideas, character, action, atmosphere—a genuine civilised narrative. While I enjoyed every moment of this book, however, I cannot help feeling sorry that Mr Forster did not choose to mirror contemporary English society in that astonishingly just and sensitive mind of his. Anglo-India is caught here, I imagine, as it has never been caught before, and its sharp divisions, its crushing institutionalism and officialism, its racial and herd thought and emotion, provide an excellent background for Mr Forster's somewhat elusive philosophy of personal relationships. But it is too much of a 'special case,' and unless we too happen to be Anglo-Indians, Mr Forster's little thrusts are too apt to give us the pleasant task of applauding the discovery of weaknesses outside ourselves instead of the less pleasant but more salutary and exciting business of acknowledging our own weaknesses. But how cunningly the

SOURCE *London Mercury,* July 1924, pp. 319–20.

scene is presented, and with what extraordinary justice. Two ladies arrive from England, one, Mrs Moore, the old mother of the district magistrate, the other, Miss Quested, his prospective wife and their presence in Chandrapore, their desire to know 'the real India,' and their distrust of the official Anglo-Indian attitude have the same effect as a stone flung into a pool. Mr Forster has distributed his interest, so that this is nobody's story, or rather it is everybody's. Person after person; Mrs Moore, old, weary of the needless complications, the fussiness of life, looking for an hour or so of quiet with the huge staring universe; Miss Quested, so curiously barren like all her kind, who laboriously desire to do right without really spending themselves; young Heaslop, the conscientious Indian civilian, only frustrated by the knowledge of his own rectitude; Aziz, the Europeanised Oriental, drifting, emotional, and only contemptible when glimpsed against a background that is not his; and so on and so forth; person after person is brought before us in the shifting and re-shifting of the action, and everyone is treated as real persons should be treated—with a certain detached sympathy that is the very height of human justice. So too, group after group, Anglo-Indians, Mohammedans, Brahmans, are similarly caught. And what a wealth of ideas and impressions the narrative holds, from such flicks of the whip as these:

> They (the Anglo-Indians) had started speaking of 'women and children'—that phrase that exempts the male from sanity when it has been repeated a few times. Each felt that all he loved best in the world was at stake, demanded revenge, and was filled with a not unpleasing glow, in which the chilly and half-known features of Miss Quested vanished, and were replaced by all that is sweetest and warmest in the private life, 'But it's the women and children,' they repeated, and the Collector knew he ought to stop them intoxicating themselves, but he hadn't the heart.

to such characteristic passages of dialogue and subtle impression as this:

> 'But it has made me remember that we must all die: all these personal relations we try to live by are temporary. I used to feel death selected people, it is a notion one gets from novels, because some of the characters are usually left talking at the end. Now "death spares no one" begins to be real.'
>
> 'Don't let it become too real, or you'll die yourself. That is the objection to "meditating upon death". We are subdued to what we work in. I have felt the same temptation, and had to sheer off. I want to go on living a bit.'
>
> 'So do I.'
>
> A friendliness, as of dwarfs shaking hands, was in the air. Both man and woman were at the height of their powers—sensible, honest, even subtle. They spoke the same language, and held the same opinions, and the variety of age and sex did not divide them. Yet they were dissatisfied. When they agreed, 'I want to go on living a bit,' or, 'I don't believe in God,' the words were followed by a curious back-wash as though the universe had displaced itself to fill up a tiny void, or as though they had seen their own gestures from an immense height—dwarfs talking, shaking hands and assuring each other that they stood on the same footing of insight. They did not think they were

> wrong, because as soon as honest people think they are wrong instability sets up. Not for them was an infinite goal behind the stars, and they never sought it. But wistfulness descended on them now, as on other occasions; the shadow of the shadow of a dream fell over their clean-cut interests, and objects never seen again seemed messages from another world.

It is some time since I read *Howards End,* and it has not been possible for me to read it again for the purpose of comparison, a matter of some interest after such a long silence on the part of an author. Writing, then, after such a long interval, I can only suggest that a certain curious evocative power, a certain unusual and very characteristic pregnancy of style, which was at its height in the earlier work, has not been here entirely recaptured. On the other hand, this is the more rounded, complete and satisfying narrative, if only because it never for a moment ceases to be entirely convincing, whereas in *Howards End,* the two most important incidents in the narrative, the seduction of one sister and the marriage of the other, never failed to leave me frankly incredulous. No, Mr Forster has not returned to disappoint us. Unlike his Anglo-Indian males, he is one of those fortunate few who are able to allow nothing to 'exempt them from sanity,' and now that he has come back, as a novelist, to a world that is even more insane and even more in need of his clear-sighted exquisite charity, than the world he stopped writing about so many years ago, now that he has returned we should celebrate the event. In that neurotic's home and that dreary smoking-room which together represent contemporary fiction, a window has been opened and once more we can catch a glimpse of the mountains and the stars.

42
Interpreters of Their Age

REBECCCA WEST

It is always entertaining to speculate as to who of the younger writers are going to step into the places of the acknowledged great men when they go; and there has been a book published recently which hints at one who next will strike this generation as mirroring the changing spirit of the age with this impressiveness, and what that change will be. That book is Mr E. M. Forster's *A Passage to India.* I am a little frightened lest readers on the American side of the Atlantic fail to appreciate it, for it is primarily a very conscientious study of a certain problem of the British Empire. It is a political document of the first importance; and since it will be filed in our archives and not yours that may seem against it. But note that it is full of passages of universal beauty, of universal interest, that one simply cannot compare with anything save the mystical poetry of Vaughan the Silurist. There is, for instance, the description of the caves of Marabar:

> They are dark caves. Even when they open towards the sun, very little light penetrates down the entrance tunnel into the circular chambers. There is little to see, and no eye to see it, until the visitor arrives for his five minutes, and strikes a match. Immediately another flame rises in the depths of the rock and moves towards the surface like an imprisoned spirit; the walls of the circular chamber have been most marvellously polished. The two flames approach and strive to unite, but cannot, because one of them breathes air, the other stone. A mirror inlaid with lovely colours divides the lovers, delicate stars of pink and grey interpose, exquisite nebulae, shadings fainter than the tail of a comet or the mid-day moon, all the evanescent life of the granite, only here visible. Fists and fingers thrust above the advancing soil—here at last is the skin of its body, finer than any covering acquired by the animals, smoother than windless water, more voluptuous than love. The radiance increases, the flames touch one another, kiss, expire. The cave is dark again, like all the caves. . . .

That is only the first verse of a poem about the caves which in the end

SOURCE *Saturday Review of Literature* (New York), 16 August 1924, p. 42.

creates a symbol of that willingness to imagine an eternity that is not motherly, an infinity which is not kind, an absolute that is not comforting, which makes certain forms of Indian mysticism terrifying to the Western mind.

Beautiful that writing, perfectly beautiful in a strange way that occasionally recalls *Kubla Khan*; and an entirely adequate symbol. Mr Forster possesses the secret of all poets, which is intensity of perception. Thinking of Eastern mysticism, he sees all aspects of it, and the essence of each. Thinking of the caves, he sees all of them, the faintest scratch on the polished wall of the least visited of them, and he remembers the most tedious whisper of the blind guide concerning them. Being in possession of all the facts he can synthesize them, make them serve the interests of the truth at which he has arrived after this fullest possible consideration of the evidence. Thus does he do with every conceivable aspect of Indian life, culminating in the superb trial scene, where the account of the pitiful contentions of the Anglo-Indians and the Indians is given its right values by the description of the man who pulled the punkah. He is seen at the beginning . . .

> Almost naked, and splendidly formed, he sat on a raised platform near the back, in the middle of the central gangway . . . He had the strength and beauty that sometimes come to flower in Indians of low birth. When that strange race nears the dust and is condemned as untouchable, then nature remembers the physical perfection that she accomplished elsewhere, and throws out a god—not many, but one here and there, to prove to society how little its categories impress her. . . .

He is seen at the end . . .

> Before long no one remained on the scene of the fantasy but the beautiful naked god. Unaware that anything unusual had occurred he continued to pull the cord of his punkah, to gaze at the empty dais and the overturned special chairs, and rhythmically to agitate the clouds of descending dust.

Apt symbol he is for the pointing of the just view of the contending parties, which is also a merciful view. He was beautiful because he was in the dust and nature plays such tricks, and he was in harmony with the dust and with nature. The litigants had lost their beauty, because they were trying to rise above the dust, to bring a higher order into nature. He can use the punkah-wallah so well because he has observed him with this intensity of perception which is the result—like his choice of this complex and disputatious subject—of an enormous, an insatiable will to understand.

It is perhaps in Mr Forster's possession of that quality that he is mirroring the change in his age. Was there ever, indeed, a period of the world since time began when humanity so simply, so purely, so exclusively, wished to understand? Even the Greeks complicated their desire for comprehension by discussing the connection between knowledge and virtue, and later ages made no bones about wanting it as a basis for the most effective action. But now we wish to understand, apparently for the sake of understanding alone. The books that men read concerning the late war are not celebrations of its valors nor denunciations of its cruelty, but analyses of its causes. To take this novel itself as an example, the average Englishman was used to regard India with the pride of the possessor; it was desirable for his national prosperity that he should; but now he would rather understand it, and he is reading *A Passage to India* with avidity. It may be that this desire for understanding may result in an age of impotence. That has been the belief of the men of action in all ages. Few armies have not held that it was the duty of a good soldier to die mentally in the service of his country. Yet we are safe in assuming that this age also is going to be glorious, for its celebration by its appropriate artist has the authentic sacramental quality.

Aspects of the Novel
(1927)

43
The Art of Fiction

VIRGINIA WOOLF

That fiction is a lady and a lady who has somehow got herself into trouble is a thought that must often have struck her admirers. Many gallant gentlemen have ridden to her rescue, chief among them Sir Walter Raleigh and Mr Percy Lubbock. But both were a little ceremonious in their approach; both, one felt, had a great deal of knowledge of her, but not much intimacy with her. Now comes Mr Forster, who disclaims knowledge but cannot deny that he knows the lady well. If he lacks something of the others' authority, he enjoys the privileges which are allowed the lover. He knocks at the bedroom door and is admitted when the lady is in slippers and dressing gown. Drawing up their chairs to the fire they talk easily, wittily, subtly, like old friends who have no illusions, although in fact the bedroom is a lecture-room, and the place the highly austere city of Cambridge.

This informal attitude on Mr Forster's part is, of course, deliberate. He is not a scholar; he refuses to be a pseudo-scholar. There remains a point of view which the lecturer can adopt usefully if modestly. He can, as Mr Forster puts it, 'visualize the English novelists, not as floating down that stream which bears all its sons away unless they are careful, but as seated together in a room, a circular room—a sort of British Museum reading-room—all writing their novels simultaneously.' So simultaneous are they, indeed, that they persist in writing out of their turn. Richardson insists that he is contemporary with Henry James. Wells will write a passage which might be written by Dickens. Being a novelist himself, Mr Forster is not annoyed at this discovery. He knows from experience what a muddled and illogical machine the brain of a writer is. He knows how little they think about methods; how completely they forget their grandfathers; how absorbed they tend to become in some vision of their own. Thus though the scholars have all his respect, his sympathies are with the untidy and harassed

SOURCE *Nation and Athenaeum*, 12 November 1927, pp. 247–8.

people who are scribbling away at their books. And looking down on them not from any great height, but, as he says, over their shoulders, he makes out, as he passes, that certain shapes and ideas tend to recur in their minds whatever their period. Since story-telling began, stories have always been made out of much the same elements; and these, which he calls The Story, People, Plot, Fantasy, Prophecy, Pattern, and Rhythm, he now proceeds to examine.

Many are the judgments that we would willingly argue, many are the points over which we would willingly linger, as Mr Forster passes lightly on his way. That Scott is a story-teller and nothing more; that a story is the lowest of literary organisms; that the novelist's unnatural preoccupation with love is largely a reflection of his own state of mind while he composes—every page has a hint or a suggestion which makes us stop to think or wish to contradict. Never raising his voice above the speaking level, Mr Forster has the art of saying things which sink airily enough into the mind to stay there and unfurl like those Japanese flowers which open up in the depths of the water. But greatly though these sayings intrigue us we want to call a halt at some definite stopping place; we want to make Mr Forster stand and deliver. For possibly, if fiction is, as we suggest, in difficulties, it may be because nobody grasps her firmly and defines her severely. She has had no rules drawn up for her, very little thinking done on her behalf. And though rules may be wrong, and must be broken, they have this advantage—they confer dignity and order upon their subject; they admit her to a place in civilized society; they prove that she is worthy of consideration. But this part of his duty, if it is his duty, Mr Forster expressly disowns. He is not going to theorise about fiction except incidentally; he doubts even whether she is to be approached by a critic, and if so, with what critical equipment. All we can do is to edge him into a position which is definite enough for us to see where he stands. And perhaps the best way to do this is to quote, much summarized, his estimates of three great figures—Meredith, Hardy, and Henry James. Meredith is an exploded philosopher. His vision of nature is 'fluffy and lush.' When he gets serious and noble, he becomes a bully. 'And his novels; most of the social values are faked. The tailors are not tailors, the cricket matches are not cricket.' Hardy is a far greater writer. But he is not so successful as a novelist because his characters are

> required to contribute too much to the plot; except in their rustic humours, their vitality has been impoverished, they have gone thin and dry—he has emphasized causality more strongly than his medium permits.

Henry James pursued the narrow path of æsthetic duty and was successful. But at what a sacrifice?

> Most of human life has to disappear before he can do us a novel. Maimed creatures can alone breathe in his novels. His characters are few in number and constructed on stingy lines.

Now if we look at these judgments and place beside them certain admissions and omissions, we shall see that, if we cannot pin Mr Forster to a creed, we can commit him to a point of view. There is something—we hesitate to be more precise—which he calls 'life.' It is to this that he brings the books of Meredith, Hardy, or James for comparison. Always their failure is some failure in relation to life. It is the humane as opposed to the æsthetic view of fiction. It maintains that the novel is 'sogged with humanity'; that 'human beings have their great chance in the novel'; a triumph won at the expense of life is, in fact, a defeat. Thus we arrive at the notably harsh judgment of Henry James. For Henry James brought into the novel something besides human beings. He created patterns which, though beautiful in themselves, are hostile to humanity. And for his neglect of life, says Mr Forster, he will perish.

But at this point the pertinacious pupil may demand, 'What is this "Life" that keeps on cropping up so mysteriously and so complacently in books about fiction? Why is it absent in a pattern and present in a tea party? Why is the pleasure that we get from the pattern in the Golden Bowl less valuable than the emotion which Trollope gives us when he describes a lady drinking tea in a parsonage? Surely the definition of life is too arbitrary and requires to be expanded.' To all of this Mr Forster would reply, presumably, that he lays down no laws; the novel somehow seems to him too soft a substance to be carved like the other arts; he is merely telling us what moves him and what leaves him cold. Indeed, there is no other criterion. So then we are back in the old bog; nobody knows anything about the laws of fiction; or what its relation is to life; or to what effects it can lend itself. We can only trust our instincts. If instinct leads one reader to call Scott a story-teller, another to call him a master of romance; if one reader is moved by art, another by life, each is right, and each can pile a card-house of theory on top of his opinion as high as he can go. But the assumption that fiction is more intimately and humbly attached to the service of human beings than the other arts leads to a further position which Mr Forster's book again illustrates. It is unnecessary to dwell upon her æsthetic functions because they are so feeble that they can safely be ignored. Thus, though it is impossible to imagine a book on painting in which not a word should be said about the medium in which a painter works, a wise and brilliant book, like Mr Forster's, can be written about fiction without saying more than a sentence or two about the medium in which a novelist works. Almost nothing is said about words. One might suppose, unless one had read them, that a sentence means the same thing and is used for the same purposes by Sterne and by Wells. One might conclude that 'Tristram Shandy' gains nothing from the language in which it is written. So with the other æsthetic qualities. Pattern, as we have seen, is recognized, but severely censured for her tendency to obscure the human features. Beauty occurs, but she is suspect. She makes one furtive appearance—'beauty at which a novelist should never aim, though he fails if he does not achieve it'—and the possibility that she may emerge again as rhythm is briefly discussed in a few interesting pages at the end. But for the rest, fiction is treated as a parasite which draws its sustenance from life, and must, in gratitude, resemble life or perish. In poetry, in drama, words may excite and stimulate and deepen without this allegiance; but in fiction they must, first and foremost, hold themselves at the service of the teapot and the pug dog, and to be found wanting is to be found lacking.

Strange though this unæsthetic attitude would be in the critic of any other art, it does not surprise us in the critic of fiction. For one thing, the problem is extremely difficult. A book fades like a mist, like a dream. How are we to take a stick and point to that tone, that relation, in the vanishing pages, as Mr Roger Fry points with a wand at a line or a colour in the picture displayed before him? Moreover, a novel in particular has roused a thousand ordinary human feelings in its progress. To drag in art in such a connection seems priggish and cold-hearted. It may well compromise the critic as a man of feeling and domestic ties. And so, while the painter, the musician, and the poet come in for their share of criticism, the novelist goes unscathed. His character will be discussed; his morality, it may be his genealogy, will be examined; but his writing will go scot free. There is not a critic alive now who will say that a novel is a work of art and that as such he will judge it.

And perhaps, as Mr Forster insinuates, the critics are right. In England, at any rate, the novel is not a work of art. There are none to be stood beside *War and Peace, The Brothers Karamazov,* or *A la Recherche du Temps Perdu.* But while we accept the fact, we cannot suppress one last conjecture. In France and Russia they take fiction seriously. Flaubert spends a month seeking a phrase to describe a cabbage. Tolstoy writes *War and Peace* seven times over. Something of their pre-eminence may be due to the pains they take, something to the severity with which they are judged. If the English critic were less domestic, less assiduous to protect the rights of what it pleases him to call life, the novelist might be bolder too. He might cut adrift from the eternal tea table and the plausible and preposterous formulas which are supposed to represent the whole of our human adventure. But then the story might wobble; the plot might crumble; ruin might seize upon the characters. The novel in short might become a work of art.

Such are the dreams that Mr Forster leads us to cherish. For his is a book to encourage dreaming. None more suggestive has been written about the poor lady whom, with perhaps mistaken chivalry, we still persist in calling the art of fiction.

44
Extract from 'Three English Critics'

EDMUND WILSON

E. M. Forster's *Aspects of the Novel* is an extraordinarily entertaining series of lectures delivered at Cambridge (England). Mr Forster is interesting because he is a novelist writing on his art and because—what doesn't always follow in these cases—he has thoroughly read its literature. I should agree with Ford Madox Ford, in a recent review, that there is about the informal tone of these papers far too much of the facetiousness of Punch: Forster's irrepressible kittenishness is certainly the worst feature of his book. But I disagree with Ford in his contention that Forster underestimates the importance of 'form' in the novel. Ford himself is a novelist who seems to understand only one kind of form, the form of Henry James and Flaubert. But it seems to me that Forster's value as a critic lies precisely in the fact that he is a sophisticated novelist who appreciates all kinds of novels. James, for example, could not read Dostoyevsky, and considered that Dostoyevsky had no 'form'; yet, in his own way, Dostoyevsky has form, and has, in any case, something else which compensates us amply for the lack of James's kind of form. Perhaps the most interesting chapter in Forster deals with what he calls the 'prophetic novelists'—a group in which he includes Dostoyevsky, D. H. Lawrence, Emily Brontë and Herman Melville. On other subjects, he is less satisfactory. After an admirable analysis of Henry James's *Ambassadors*, in which he has made the moral of the story quite clear, he goes on to deny that James's novels were intended to have any moral; and of *Ulysses* he says that it is 'a dogged attempt to cover the universe with mud ... a simplification of the human character in the interests of Hell.' Now the world represented by Joyce in *Ulysses* is certainly very badly drained, both within and without; but how can it be said to simplify human character in

SOURCE *New Republic*, 22 February 1928, pp. 21–2.

the interests of Hell? Does it make humanity seem any more ignoble than, say, the novels of Arnold Bennett, who has the same opinion of *Ulysses* as Forster? Haven't Joyce's characters, as a matter of fact, in spite of all the demons by which their minds are visited, a good deal of moral dignity? We feel in Forster a curious limitation which we do not at first expect of him: he appears to be an exceptionally intelligent man, yet, beyond a certain point, his intelligence does not seem to function. He is willing half or three-quarters to understand the writer with whom he is dealing, but beyond that he is content to confront him with an insensitive and complacent British countenance.

45
Forster and the Novel

I. A. RICHARDS

To be provocative, if it is *thought* that is provoked, is merely a duty or a decency in a critic. What can be accepted with undisturbed placidity is probably not worth much when received. The provocations of Mr Forster's Clark Lectures, now published in book form, are not mitigated by the charming, unobtrusive, almost feline modesty with which they are given. The soft blow to our cherished preconception comes with such coy disarming grace that for a while we feel doubly disabled. The reply only occurs to us in some connection so far removed that it hardly seems a reply at all. For example, Mr Forster's defamation of 'the story.'

> It runs like a backbone—or may I say a tape-worm, for its beginning and end are arbitrary ... It can only have one merit: that of making the audience want to know what happens next ... It is the lowest and simplest of literary organisms.

Only much later when we sense something missing in Mr Forster's handling of 'pattern' do we see where his unkindness to 'the story' has landed him. For the story, the mere narrative of the succession of events, can, as the Book of Job witnesses, be given a pattern and then it obtains both a wide and a delicate power upon us. Our interest, our desire to hear further, may be noble as well as ignoble; and if Mr Forster were to say that its nobility always derives from its superstructure, from the other aspects, he could be faced with the dilemma:—either a story is inseparable from the character of the events which make it up, or it is something not worth mentioning even as an object for witty abuse.

Or consider Mr Forster's dealings with what he calls 'prophecy.' It is

> an accent in the novelist's voice ... His theme is the universe, or something universal, but he is not necessarily going to say anything about the universe; he proposes to sing.

SOURCE *Cambridge Review*, March 1928, 304–05.

This quality is illustrated by four writers, Dostoevsky, Melville, D. H. Lawrence and Emily Brontë; Mr Forster can find no others. The claims of Hardy and Conrad are set aside. 'Hardy's novels are surveys; they do not give out sounds' a judgment that applies perhaps to any one of Hardy's novels taken as a whole but not to the separate pulses that make them up, though it must be admitted that their sounds have a desolate ring. So too with Conrad, 'He has seen too much to see beyond cause and effect.' To have a philosophy—even a poetic and emotional philosophy like Hardy's and Conrad's—leads to reflections on life and things. A prophet does not 'reflect.' But Dostoevsky and Melville also reflected, and we have to separate their reflections from their 'prophecy'. Mr Forster himself in an admirable passage makes this separation for D. H. Lawrence. What then does his distinction between 'prophecy' and what is not 'prophecy' come down to? I cannot help thinking that it is a question, not of the depth of implications, the way in which characters or scenes 'reach back'; but of the very thing Mr Forster sets as the limit of his subject, the prophet's message. That prophecy 'gives us the sensation of a song or a sound' will not do as a criterion itself. Too many other writers, in addition to Mr Forster's chosen, give it, and his own four 'sing' in such different ways. If degree of significance be the test, Tolstoy, Arnold Bennett (though this is a thing too often difficult to believe), George Moore, as at the end of *Esther Waters* and in at least one place in *The Brook Kerith*, James Joyce in patches, Flaubert, Voltaire and at least as many more would have to join Mr Forster's quartet. The implications are as infinite, though it is true that these authors only become 'prophets' at rare moments and 'prophecy' is not what we think of as the constant quality of their work. If Mr Forster excludes them I believe it is because the 'messages', the implications conveyed, are less congenial, not because the work is essentially of a different order.

Mr Forster's strength as a critic is the more shown the nearer he comes to the actual text of his authors. His amazing knack of collocation wins him his best points at once. To set Samuel Richardson beside Henry James, Dickens beside Wells, and Sterne beside Virginia Woolf was a stroke of genius, and later on George Eliot and Dostoevesky in his hands generate a mutual blaze of illumination. He grows less certain and less satisfying when he stands back from his novelists to toy with definitions, to contrast the life of time with the life of value, to indulge fantasies about people in life and people in books. At such passages a reader in a controversial mood may become irritable, he may find himself scoring points which seem hardly worth making. For the theoretical apparatus of *Aspects of the Novel* was never intended for this kind of discussion. And while trying to hunt a little further some of the hares Mr Forster has started, with even a doubt whether they are hares at all and not rather the herrings of fantasy, we run the risk of forgetting that those were simply some of the pleasantest lectures ever given in Cambridge. And in again deploring (it is the theme of all his work) Man's inability to be at the same time impressive and truthful, Mr Forster has brought the real difficulty of all this kind of criticism to light. The job of unpicking the hard unnecessary knots in our received ideas cannot be made into a graceful performance. Choosing to delight our minds rather than to disentangle them he has not made us any the less his debtors.

46
Novelists at a Round Table

WILBUR CROSS

Mr E. M. Forster, a fellow of King's College, Cambridge, is the author of *A Passage to India*, one of the outstanding novels written since the Great War. Last year he delivered at his university a series of lectures on English fiction with some comment, by way of comparison, on European fiction in general. These lectures he has now collected under the title of *Aspects of the Novel*. It is a brilliant book written in a gay colloquial style, giving from the most modern point of view a survey of fiction from Defoe to Joyce, who in *Ulysses* attempted 'a simplification of the human character in the interests of Hell.' The historical manner is eschewed on the ground that 'art stands still,' having no periods nor development. Art is art always.

Though probably not quite serious, Mr Forster makes out a plausible case for his contention in an amusing chapter, where, casting aside sequence of time, he exhibits in pairs novelists of different periods and shows by quotations from them that the style and outlook of each pair are so nearly alike as to be indistinguishable. It is as if they were all seated at a round table and writing together. Thus James and Richardson in a wire-drawn style complain of the little satisfaction that life can give. Wells and Dickens describe a funeral in much the same phrasing. And Virginia Woolf and Sterne flutter similarly around some trivial thing—the one taking a spot on the wall, the other a squeaking door-hinge. The procedure is so clever that one overlooks the fallacy involved in the assumption that the later writer of a pair had no direct acquaintance with the books of his predecessor. Still, too much has been made by literary historians of the influence of one novelist upon another, and it is a good corrective to have attention called to similarities in temperament as an explanation of resemblances between them.

Mr Forster has many witty observations on the elements that enter into novels as written by different eminent hands. The story as such he regards

SOURCE *Yale Review*, July 1928, pp. 792–4.

as 'the lowest and simplest of literary organisms,' reminding him, as in Scott's romances, of 'a tapeworm, for its beginning and end are arbitrary.' And yet, he adds, there can be no novel without a story hidden away somewhere in the plot or the pattern, which, however, have their dangers. Did not Meredith and Hardy, for instance, sacrifice their people more or less to plot? And did not James squeeze all life out of his men and women so that they might fit into his pattern? For a novel where everything is mostly satisfactory on its particular scale, one must look away, it is held, from English fiction to Proust, Tolstoi, and Dostoevsky, however unpatriotic such a view may appear. This is a rather hard saying. English and Continental fiction in this cosmopolitan age, when one novelist quickly learns from another, differ, I should say, not so much in art as in the social environment out of which the characters rise. To this fact may be ascribed the failure to transplant the French or Russian novel into England or the United States.

In a notable passage Mr Forster shows how the characters in a novel may resemble the men and women whom we think we know but are never the same, for they are projections of the author's imagination, which, going beyond the evidence of word and act, claims to fathom the inner consciousness so as to create in the mind of the reader an illusion of complete knowledge. Art thus improves upon ordinary perception and insight, giving us people, we say, more real than our most intimate friends. This is one of Mr Forster's admirable statements as he lets his mind play in and out of many novels on to a sound generalization.

The Eternal Moment and Other Stories (1928)

47
Review

ANONYMOUS

There is a slight suggestion of warning to be found in the note that precedes Mr E. M. Forster's little volume, *The Eternal Moment and Other Stories*. They were written, we are told, 'at various dates previous to 1914, and represent, with those in the Celestial Omnibus volume, all that the writer is likely to attempt in a particular line'. That announcement has, indeed, an effect of closing a phase of development; and any judgement of the various items must take account of the fact that for more than fourteen years Mr Forster has had no further impulse to express himself in this form or, what is still more important, in this mood.

For it is the mood rather than the method that deserves attention in this collection. Mr Forster, the artist, reached a high level of achievement early in his career, and has maintained it ever since. He found a mode that satisfied him; and his own pronouncement, made in his lectures on 'Aspects of the Novel', that 'the novelist who betrays too much interest in his own method can never be more than interesting', ranks him with those who regard with impatience the late Charles Doughty's boast of valuing his style far more than his matter. But Mr Forster, the philosopher, must be judged for our present purpose solely as a pilgrim in a certain stage of his journey—a familiar stage, that of *Howards End*, with the slightly pathetic cry of that book's keynote, 'Only connect', still faintly audible. In his first, and terrible, picture of humanity become the slaves of one vast machine that controlled the comfort of the whole earth, the individual is presented as almost finally isolated. He communicates with the rest of the world by telephone and television. The son who calls to his mother from the antipodes, expressing his desire to see her again in the flesh, is a freak in that society, representative of a type that the 'Central Committee' does not wish to perpetuate. And when the machine stops, this slightly didactic little fancy closes with a frank moral.

SOURCE *Times Literary Supplement*, 5 April 1928, p. 256.

> They wept for humanity, those two, not for themselves ... Ere silence was completed their hearts were opened, and they knew what had been important on the earth. Man, the flower of all flesh, the noblest of all creatures visible ... beautiful naked man was dying, strangled in the garments that he had woven ... Truly the garment had seemed heavenly at first, shot with the colours of culture, sewn with the threads of self-denial. And heavenly it had been so long as it was a garment and no more, so long as man could shed it at will and live by the essence that is his soul, and the essence, equally divine, that is his body.

Here the cry is clearly audible; in the other five items that make up the collection it sounds less easily recognizable as the motive of the fugue. Sir Michael, the Civil servant, who begot three children, died and went to a hell that he tried hard to persuade himself was truly heaven until a spirit crossed the river and taught him desire; Mr Andrews, who truly went to a heaven after the manner of Captain Stormfield's and left it dissatisfied to enter again into the 'world soul'; Miss Haddon, the schoolmistress whose futile scheme of co-ordination was upset by a spirit intrusion that taught her pupils to co-ordinate 'through the central sources of Melody and Victory'—all these fail to 'connect' in the wider sense that Mr Forster seeks, or perhaps sought, to expound. In the two remaining stories the aid of the spirit-world is not invoked, or if invoked in the case of the Italian fisherman who heard the Song of the Siren, has left us to infer its message. Lastly, *The Eternal Moment* keeps very near to earth in its account of the revisiting of Vorta in Italian Switzerland by Miss Raby, who had written a successful novel on the place in her youth, thereby making Vorta's fortune as well as her own; returned to it after twenty years; and found the young guide who had once in a mad moment of passion proclaimed his love for her transformed into a stout, complacent *concierge*.

Because it was Mr Forster who wrote these six stories they are all interesting, have each of them some effect of penetrating below the appearance, of seeking, if now and again a trifle impatiently, the true essence of life. But the phase, the mood, seems to be of dissatisfaction. It is as if Mr Forster were at that time almost painfully aware of the fatuity of existence and sought something too uneasily to explain it.

48
Review

C. M.

On page 27 Mr E. M. Forster gives a convenient standard for suggesting, if not estimating, the merits and the defects of the six stories, all written before 1914, reprinted from various periodicals, in this collection. Escaped from 'the machine' that rules the world, the hero of the first story says: 'Man is the measure. That was my first lesson. Man's feet are the measure for distance, his hands are the measure for ownership, his body is the measure for all that is lovable and desirable and strong'. So we might add that man's nature is the measure of all that is profitable in fiction. By this standard the title story, which is placed last in the volume, comes first in esteem, because everything in it is relative to the behaviour of men and women, without mechanical or supernatural interference. It might be rash to describe the people in it as 'ordinary', though Miss Raby, the heroine, is extraordinary only by being more practical than is common. On her way out to an Alpine resort in the company of Colonel Leyland, with Elizabeth, her maid, for propriety, Miss Raby recalls that twenty years before a young man had made a declaration of love to her in the place they are approaching. He was a porter, not even a certificated guide, 'a male person who was hired to carry the luggage, which he dropped'. At the time she did what a young lady should, screamed and ran; but she now recognises two things: that the incident had been one of the great moments, and the most enduring, of her life, and that the novel, inspired by it, which had made her reputation, had also vulgarised the place where it occurred. The young man is now the concierge of the hotel, fat, prosaic, and obsequious. Not because she is in love with him, but from the sheer necessity for her of getting at reality, Miss Raby reminds him of their previous encounter—and his scared behaviour and the embarrassment of the listening Colonel will be comic or tragic to the reader according to the point of view. For us Miss Raby is the belated discoverer of what really counts in life, compared with which external circumstances are the dream; to her companions she is an old maid, slightly 'touched'. Her unflinching quest for

SOURCE *The Manchester Guardian*, 20 April 1928, p. 7.

reality brings the Colonel—who has mild expectations—and the quaking concierge to the same level.

The other stories are less well adapted to the human scale, though they all deal in one way or another with the contrast between the reality which is human and the dream—or the nightmare—which is mechanical. All are good in idea, but most of them fail, comparatively, in execution, being, or seeming, calculated rather than conceived. 'The Machine Stops' fails to convince us that a machine so inefficient ever began—much less obtained mastery of the world—since it is still at the stage of telephone receivers and pneumatic posts. The result is that we cannot get very excited about anybody who contrives to escape from the machine—even though it is into the death which is life, under the 'untainted sky'. Next to 'The Eternal Moment' we should place 'Mr Andrews', who went to heaven on a loving thought—and came out again when he found that heaven fulfilled his expectations but not his hopes. But the chief interest of these stories is as showing the inventive stage, intelligent but crude and stiff in adjustment, of a writer who has passed on to creation. In writing them—and he says that he is not likely to attempt others in their particular line—Mr Forster was learning his first lesson, that man is the measure. His peculiar gift is an acute sense of idiosyncrasy in human character combined with a firm belief in a spiritual background, in a power which sustains, feeds, as it were, both the good and bad qualities in his people. All these stories were written before 1914, and it is remarkable how little they seem to 'date'. No doubt if he were to write it to-day the story called 'The Machine Stops' would be given a rather different form by Mr Forster; but in its deep and wise attack on the growing fear of personal relationship, of intimate human contact, it has a poignant meaning for a world which has rushed more and more into the refuge of the machine, and abandoned the search for meaning to wallow in the shallow comforts of ingenuity. The human appetite for device, for invention, the human admiration for the merely cunning were never more in evidence than now; and in his superbly uncomfortable parable, Mr Forster exposes the logical end of these evasions from life. The title story, in a different way, is occupied with the same theme. Miss Raby, the novelist, revisiting the village in Italia Irredenta, the village her novel made famous ten years before, discovers the old simple life, the exquisite verities overwhelmed by international conventions, covered by the designs of convenience. In a way the best story is perhaps 'The Story of the Siren', published some years ago by the Hogarth Press. Here Mr Forster gives us once more his vision of beauty, beauty misunderstood and slain by men unready to take risks, nervous of the depths, however clear and silver-reflecting, where the siren lives but cannot sing. The book is a treasure of lovely things, low-toned no doubt, and only not despairing because of the author's evident belief in the validity, if not in the temporal triumph, of splendid and eternal things.

49

In Six Fantasias, E. M. Forster Freshens Stale Conceptions and Credits his Readers with Sense

THOMAS BEER

In 1912 a redheaded youngish priest told me in the smoker of a way train between Thief River Falls and Duluth that eminent authors were of two kinds—those who trusted to the reader for a little sense and those who didn't. 'The former,' he said, 'are artists and the latter are famous.' I repeat the epigram without wholly believing in it. One must make some exceptions in favor of artists, such as Thomas Hardy, who just happen to be garrulous and artists who have a mania for the didactic. But as to the rest of the gang, the sentence stands. Often and often, while being insulted by the late Marcel Proust and a lot of eminent school teachers in the same mode, I have wanted to send that priest some converts or a barrel of apples. Perhaps he was a symptom of the weak, but spreading, revolt against the 'make you see—above all, make you see' dogma. I have repeated his heresy, and now propose an application.

Take the first tale of the six included in Mr Forster's present book at hand. Mr Forster has long shown an incalculable talent for arranging utterly stale topics and wringing something new out of them. You begin 'The Machine Stops' with a shudder. Holy St Dunstan! Here is another yarn of the mechanical future! Vashti, in the year Something Or Other, is sitting in a subterranean chamber, surrounded with appliances, talking to her son in his mechanized room on the other side of the globe. It sounds pretty tough. Recollections of Wells, Ugahne, Bellamy and the others pile at you.

SOURCE *New York Evening Post*, 12 May 1928, Literary Review, p. 8.

Vashti goes to her son by air. Her son, of course, has rebelled against the Machine. He has crawled up on the surface of the earth, and has been dragged down by the feelers of the Machine. Nothing new so far, but you are by this time caught. Mr Forster has taken you with him. He has elaborated not at all, but he has established two mentalities before you and you follow them.

Well, the great Machine that tends those hairless, tepid and sluggish people of the year Something Or Other gets out of gear and the committees in charge have forgotten how to mend it. Discomforts begin in the underground cities. The radio music rasps, the lights are impaired and the beds refuse to function. Then the Machine stops. Up on earth's crust a race of outcasts, bred in real air and real rain, will go on with man's game, but the society of the larval, subterranean world is damned. Vashti and her son are lost in the welter as an airplane crashes down through layers of the artificial hive.

It is hardly new, is it? No, but Mr Forster's art does things to it. Where Mr Wells would have dilated, he contracts his scales. Where Mr Wells would not have tried to resist a comic effect, the newer man passes by. Scorning color—and often inept when he uses it—Mr Forster manages a gray, monotonous dryness in his dealing with the Machine's children. Almost immobile in their cells, afraid of physical contact, they pass their time trying to manufacture ideas. But the human wanting and all the adventure of intercourse have gone out of mankind. Vashti resents her journey to see her son. She passes over Asia with distaste. The Himalayas give her no 'ideas.' Ideas, finally, that are suggested by earth, by love and fear are too gross for the exalted philosophy of the Machine's adherents. This is the new thing that Mr Forster finds to tell us, and his uninsistent forwarding of the notion—his simple use of the word 'idea' half a dozen times raises an effect of the ghastly. He has dug out the appearance of logic which is everything in fantasy of the type, and his real distinction of mind covers what is actually stale with the freshness of a very positive talent.

For, except 'Coordination,' not one tale of the six is at all novel. 'The Point Of It' could be claimed as a free variation on one of Kipling's themes. 'Mr Andrews' has been on the counter ever since 1849 at least. 'The Story of the Siren,' in some shape or other, is written yearly by a clever boy in prep school and was once delightfully put through by Mr Gouverneur Morris as a sophomore at New Haven. Even 'The Eternal Moment' has had its predecessors. But what of it? Let us briefly explore Mr Forster's arms of offense.

To begin with, he really knows what not to do in the way of suggestion. In 'The Story of a Siren', a young man dives into the sea on the Italian coast without crossing himself and sees the Siren.

> We pulled him into the boat, and he was so large that he seemed to fill it, and

> so wet that we could not dress him. I have never seen a man so wet . . . The doctor came and took money, and the priest came and spattered him with holy water. But it was no good. He was too big—like a piece of the sea. He kissed the thumb bones of San Biagio and they never dried till evening.

That is all the mystery created, but unless you like to be insulted, what more do you want?

Or, from 'The Eternal Moment,' you can have,

> A landslip, in that valley, never hurried. Under the green coat of turf, water would collect, just as an abscess is formed under the skin. There would be a lump on the sloping meadow, then the lump would break and discharge a slowly moving stream of mud and stones. Then the whole area seemed to be corrupted: on every side grass cracked and doubled into fantastic creases, the trees grew awry, the barns and cottages collapsed, all the beauty turned gradually to indistinguishable pulp, which slid downwards until it was washed away by some stream.

Censoring out the word 'fantastic' as an impediment, the effect could scarcely be much improved. It is not aimed at the heart, but at the head. Thus, with an air of not bothering much about anything, Mr Forster lifts himself out of the pack of current writers and is to be forgiven some occasional heavy sentiments and a little good old English moralizing.

Or is a dislike of the insincere, and flabby and the swollen a displeasing load of morality? In 'The Point Of It,' Sir Michael finds himself in Hell, a sunken monster embedded in a sandy plain.

> . . . he knew one of the sins here punished was appreciation; he was suffering for all that praise that he had given to the bad and mediocre on earth; when he had praised out of idleness, or to please people, or to encourage people.

I can conceive that Mr Forster's lack of concessiveness, his occasional employment of the sort of imagery lamented as 'brutal' and his intolerance of explanation do him a deal of harm in roundabout ways.

But he cannot be called soft, and many of us are grateful that he does not swell out of his dry, precise narrative with the fashionable paddings. He has been platitudinous and occasionally dull as a Channel fog. Not one tale in *The Eternal Moment* is likely to be hailed as 'great.' But I have not seen a more amusing collection of short stories in some years, and I am not aware of an English writer who can evoke the awkwardness of living more deftly or with so much speed.

50
Review

EDWIN MUIR

'These stories,' Mr Forster informs us, 'were written at various dates previous to 1914, and represent, with those in the Celestial Omnibus volume, all that the writer is likely to attempt in a particular line.' There is nothing for it but to accept this fact; Mr Forster is the only judge of the matter; but the reader cannot but regret that any imagination so just and so original should cease to express itself in the form where its justice and originality are most incontestably evinced. When, *apropos* such novels as *A Passage to India*, critics speak of Mr Forster's genius, one has a feeling of doubt; talent, a talent so accomplished as to attain exquisiteness, one may allow the book; but there is something missing, and that, one imagines, is precisely genius. But if genius be the power to do what nobody else can, it cannot be denied to certain stories in this volume. The best are the deliberately symbolical, the stories about Heaven and Hell, and the supernatural in general. Of these, 'The Point of It' and 'The Story of the Siren' are perhaps the most remarkable. The first is the tale of an amiable, sympathetic, cultured man before and after death. He is received into Hell.

> He had seen good in everything, and this is itself a sign of decay. Whatever occurred he had been appreciative, tolerant, pliant . . . He had mistaken self-criticism for self discipline, he had muffled in himself and others the keen, heroic edge. Yet the luxury of repentance was denied him. The fault was his, but the fate humanity's, for everyone grows hard or soft as he grows old.

This passage is rather too flatly elucidatory, it may be complained; the best thing in the story, and indeed in the book, is the evocation of Hell, a Hell which breathes the atmosphere of humanity's hidden frustrations and shames, and is effective because it is psychologically profound. 'The Story of the Siren' is about an Italian sailor who sees the Siren and afterwards has no desire for action, and no interest in human affairs. He finds a woman who like him has seen the Siren, but when their child is about to be born,

SOURCE *Nation and Athenaeum*, 12 May 1928, p. 184.

she is killed by a superstitious priest. The man's brother tells the story:

> Never in my life will there be both a man and woman from whom that child can be born, who will fetch up the Siren from the sea, and destroy silence, and save the world.

That is all the tale says, but there is such a wealth of suggested meaning throughout, conveyed so certainly and yet with such an absence of direct insistence, that it stands out from all the others. It is pure imagination.

Except for these two stories, however, and 'Mr Andrews', a charming trifle, the volume is rather disappointing. 'The Eternal Moment,' though witty and profound in flashes, is unconvincing psychologically. 'The Machine Stops,' which takes up a third of the whole book, and stands at the beginning, is also unconvincing. When Mr Forster is writing of Heaven and Hell he may let his imagination range freely, so long as it is in pursuit of symbolical truth. But in 'The Machine Stops' he is writing of the future; and that future, as it is ours, must be conceivable in terms of the world we know. Mr Forster's picture of the future is quite inconceivable, however. In its last stages, he tells us, humanity will live in cells under the ground, shut off from the outer air, the surface of the earth, the sea, the sky, and one another; and everything will be done for them by pressing a button. But we immediately want to know why they should live under the ground, and as we cannot imagine why, the story becomes unreal. Perhaps Mr Forster's imagination is rather clogged here with sociological notions.

51
Border-Line Fiction

MORTON DAUWEN ZABEL

His brief foreword tells us, regrettably, that Mr Forster will add no more short narratives to the twelve which this new volume and a former collection, *The Celestial Omnibus*, contain. Yet even those readers who find in his exquisite art a saving grace amid all the confusions and shortcomings of current fiction will reflect upon this statement with satisfaction and respect. It is another indication of that cautious, sensitive artistry which has made the author of *Howards End* and *A Passage to India* a singular, independent figure among contemporary novelists, a writer whose first merit is his abstention from print unless he has something of sound, fearless merit to present. All of these stories antedate 1914, so it may seem to be the Forster of an earlier period, rather than the one who came into general favor with his later novel of 1924, that we are reading here. But no adjustment is necessary on the part of the reader. Mr Forster had the fortune to find in his very first essay in narrative a style and viewpoint essentially his own, to which he has adhered consistently ever since. When students some day undertake to write critical studies of his works they will be confronted with the difficulty of detecting growths and changes where none exist; thus far five novels, two collections of tales and two volumes of essays have testified to a unity of attitude and style which he possesses in joint ownership with only a few kindred spirits in English literature today—Mr De la Mare, Mr Housman and Mr Beerbohm.

The supernatural is never very far away from the characters of the Forster novels, no matter if it visit them on the meadows of Wiltshire, the hillsides above Florence or in the Marabar caves in India. It is in his shorter narratives, however, that the shapes of fantasy and strangeness become most concretely embodied, even to the extent of surrounding the scenes and persons of ordinary life with powers beyond ordinary comprehension and grasp. In the longer novels this strife between the forces of stodgy

SOURCE *Commonweal*, 20 June 1928, p. 190.

material complacency and the diviner forces of imagination goes on between clumsy mortals—between Mr Wilcox and Helen Schlegel, Agnes Pembroke and Stephen Wonham, Mr Vyse and George Emerson, the Herritons and the immortal Gino, and Mrs Moore and the official encampment at Chandrapore. But in the stories of a briefer kind, the partisans of fantasy and melody actually call to their aid companions from the shadows and mists. In 'The Story of a Panic', Eustace escaped in this manner from the blunt cruelty of his family and friends, and in 'The Celestial Omnibus', the little boy triumphed through Shelley's and Sir Thomas Browne's kindly intervention.

The present volume handles similar conflicts. In 'Coördination', Miss Haddon finds her release from the drudgery and ugliness of her schoolmistress life through the collaboration of Napoleon and Beethoven; in 'The Point of It', Micky first feels the keen edge of truth after he withdraws from the easy life which has never once tested his metal, while in 'The Story of the Siren', one contact with mystery startles an entire Sicilian community. To the delicate elusive material of such stories Mr Forster has brought again his enviable understatement, and his salient poetic insight. In 'The Machine Stops' we have one of those terrible allegories of the mechanical world of the future which at first sight reminds us of the first tales of Wells or, better still, of the later plays of the brothers Capek or Ernst Toller. Yet with the picture of doom there presented, the first enthusiasm of Wells has little connection; hero and heroine, before the final explosion of the world, 'weep for humanity . . . strangled in the garments that he had woven.' From this picture of horror we pass in relief to the more familiar atmosphere of the final story, 'The Eternal Moment', where we encounter the English tourist as we have so often encountered him before, scattering misunderstanding and riding roughshod over beauties to whose doom the unfortunate Miss Raby has unwittingly contributed. Without this tale the volume would be incomplete in representing almost every salient aspect of Mr Forster's art; with it, we have a treasurable survey of one of the most remarkable talents of contemporary literature.

52
Review

ANONYMOUS

The way in which one's tastes and opinions differ from and sometimes coincide with what seem the prevalent tastes and opinions of one's fellow man may be a source of depression or complacency—preferably complacency for it is a happier frame of mind. Mr Forster's *Howards End* aroused our enthusiasm many years ago, when others seemed to know nothing about it; his *A Passage to India* made him famous and did not interest us at all; there was a small and curiously interesting volume called *Pharos and Pharillon* published shortly before which was spoken of and then dropped; and here is a collection of short stories, fantasies like the previous collection called *The Celestial Omnibus*, to remind one that Mr Forster has become a personage in English letters, established and peculiar. He remarks in a preface that he is not likely to do any more like these, for the War has driven fantasy underground.

But fantasy in Mr Forster's hands has gravity and intention. All the stories have a similar underlying moral, something to the effect that the eternal moments, the only ones that count, are always moments of fierce strain or intense desire, moments of ecstasy or pain. It is not the point that the road to hell is easy. The point is that easy roads lead to hell by virtue of their easiness. The grub becomes a lunar moth by desperately bursting loose. Salvation is seizing the chance of not remaining a grub. The story called 'The Machine Stops' represents a society mechanically perfect and contented, and the only salvation was for the machinery to break down and drive men back to a world of doubts and pains and visions. 'The Point of It' is perhaps the most artistically finished piece of work, the story and the allegory come around the turn and meet so accurately. 'Mr Andrews' and a Turk arrive at the gates of heaven together and are admitted, but, the only happiness they experienced was the moment at the gate when each hoped that the other would be let in. We are not sure what 'The Story of a Siren'

SOURCE *Saturday Review of Literature*, 13 October 1928, p. 250.

means. To meet a siren is an experience that revolutionizes one's whole nature. One should grasp one's eternal moments, but where the eternal moment consists in meeting a siren the value of it seems debatable.

Mr Forster's definition of salvation is not the only possible one, but there is force in it.

Goldsworthy Lowes Dickinson
(1934)

53
Review

DAVID GARNETT

Looking at the photograph on the cover of E. M. Forster's biography of *Goldsworthy Lowes Dickinson* (Arnold, 10*s.* 6*d.*), which shows him in his seventieth year wearing the Chinese Mandarin's cap which he used to put on at dinner, I asked myself of whom, besides its subject, it reminded me. In someone else I had met, not those features, but exactly that expression. Then I remembered: it was an old Nanny. Half-crippled by rheumatism and age, stoical, unselfish and uncomplaining, she watched the babies play and quarrel without illusions, without sentimentality and without austerity. The resemblance was far more than the expression of old age (Dickinson looked older than his years), it was due to things which he and Nanny shared in common: a complete lack of fuss, a personal reserve which seemed to have a faint flavour of ironing day and soap and water. But, above all, an indulgent humanity: Dickinson I saw, brought to the whole of mankind the love and understanding which the old nurse felt for children between certain ages belonging to one particular family. And perhaps it was that which called out in almost everyone who knew him that deep devotion which is felt for the rare people whose faintly astringent love can be permanently relied on.

Dickinson left a mass of autobiographical material to be published at the discretion of his literary executor and from this Mr Forster has constructed a book which is absolutely delightful yet which leaves out too much; it might well have been longer and have contained more records of his friendships and of his talk. I have hardly ever enjoyed listening to two peoples' conversation more than to that of Dickinson and C. P. Sanger. No intelligence was so lightning quick as Sanger's and his wit and scepticism stirred Dickinson to humorous and uneasy profundity. The life of a man whom one has known oneself has a personal interest which makes it impossible to judge quite objectively, but I shall be astonished if those who

SOURCE *New Statesman and Nation*, 21 April 1934, p. 600.

did not know Dickinson do not read it with almost the same interest as his friends. For Mr Forster while patching together a mosaic of the Recollections has, by adding to it, created a living portrait. It is not a question of style or literary skill, that we may take for granted, the unique merit of this book depends on what there was in common between subject and biographer, particularly on their sense of humour.

There is one aspect of Dickinson's life which was a surprise to me and it is hard to say whether very young men or their parents ought to find it more consoling, that is the number of false starts in life into which he was led by his idealism. He was very innocent and grew up slowly. Thus as an undergraduate he joined the volunteers and occupied himself in trying to reform his companions, on one occasion inviting an atheist who had been drunk to join the Church of England Temperance Society.

> the atheist was headachy and polite, 'but he declined the siren's voice.'

The discovery of Shelley's poetry helped to free him and turned him from crude missionary work to an interest in politics, but

> If Shelley rose like a morning star, Plato was heralded by the dubious light of Esoteric Buddhism ... he approached Plato not as a writer of dialogues, or as a depictor of Athenian society, or a logician, or politician or a publicist, but as an adept who was in possession of absolute truth, which he had concealed in his writings, probably in his myths.

The result was that his first work of learning was a dissertation in which the doctrines of Plato and Plotinus are compared and harmonised. He then joined a Socialist experiment on the land which had been started by Mr Harold Cox, then a Socialist, on a piece of barren heath in Surrey. He learned to plough, but found milking a cow was beyond him. The experiment collapsed, Harold Cox went to teach mathematics in India and Dickinson records:

> I have met him since and he still retains the personal charm he always had. But over the farm experiment a great ox sat upon our tongues.

This experience was followed by the delivery of a course of lectures on Carlyle, Emerson, Browning and Tennyson in provincial centres which seems to have been almost as ill-fated as Coleridge's. Dickinson explains his failure:

> I had no notion how to get into touch with ordinary people and no desire to do so, for I thought I was the bearer of a message which transcended all actual life.
>
> The message was sometimes inaudible, [adds Forster.] And according to one of his friends he would turn his back on his audience when he became interested and toddle away over the platform on his heels, patting himself meanwhile with both his hands behind.

Failure as a lecturer led to a startling reaction: he decided to become a doctor, a most fortunate decision, for though his career as a medical student lasted only a year, it led to his forming a friendship which endured until his death since:

> Roger Fry was also doing medicine though with neater fingers and would sometimes extricate him from the frog or worm with which he was involved.

Then luckily, his dissertation on Plotinus won him a fellowship, after which he made no more false starts.

Though Dickinson and Forster had many qualities in common, it was not so with their tastes:

> Shelley's influence . . . dominated Dickinson to the day of his death . . . and the same applies to two other arrivals from the world of books, Plato and Goethe.

And his biographer confesses that one of his limitations in discussing Dickinson is that these three writers have little appeal for him. When they travelled together to the Orient with R. C. Trevelyan, Forster stayed in India, which inspired in him a sympathy of which we know the fruits, while Dickinson's comment was:

> And *why* can't the races meet? Simply because the Indians *bore* the English. *That* is the simple adamantine fact.

'I disagree . . . Perhaps he was overtired,' says Forster, refusing to admit the adamantine fact which is so painfully true to many of us. In China he found his land of heart's desire. Trevelyan left him in Canton and hurried back to take part in the Lake Hunt and while he was racing up the Fell side, Dickinson was presenting a copy of *The Letters of John Chinaman* to the 76th Duke descended from Confucius. He was beloved by the Chinese but the country in which he was most appreciated was America and since he might have had an enormous influence it is a pity he could not have lived there more. My own first memory of Dickinson is linked with that of a strange American whom he was to have brought to the Old Vicarage, Grantchester, but who arrived alone. After waiting over an hour we sat down to lunch in the garden and the American remarked in a voice as desiccated as a beetle's:

> I see, Mr Brooke, that you do not utilise the formality of spoken Grace. No words seem sufficiently informal yet some expression of worship is necessary. The beautiful solution we use in my home is to take hold of each other's hands beneath the table. Shall we do so now?

It was a stretch for me to reach Rupert's hand and when I found it we exchanged vicious pinches with decorum. After the meal was over, Dickinson appeared streaked with black mud and shivering. He had been tempted to bathe, had plunged naked into the river, but the sound of feminine voices had induced him to take shelter in a reed bed where he sank up to his waist in mud while a boatload of townspeople had picnicked on the opposite bank. His teeth chattered as he described his adventure, which appealed strongly to his sense of the ridiculous, yet at the same time he was anxious lest his American, to whom he was mysteriously attached, had been having an awkward lunch. It was then I saw his charm:

> Charm in most men and women is a decoration. It genuinely belongs to them as a good complexion may but it lies on the surface and can vanish. Charm in Dickinson was structural.

54
Lowes Dickinson

HUGH KINGSMILL

At the close of this biography of Lowes Dickinson, Mr E. M. Forster writes: 'The truest words about him were said by his former bedmaker at Cambridge, Mrs Newman: "He was the best man who ever lived."' If Lowes Dickinson was indeed the best man who has ever lived, Mr Forster must be the worst of all biographers, for of the sublime qualities implied in Mrs Newman's praise Mr Forster has given us no hint at all. He has, however, drawn a pleasant portrait of a sincere and thoughtful man, whose interest for those who did not know him personally lies in the fact that he was an almost perfect example of the academic millenialist.

Dickinson, as one would expect, hated his time at a public school.

> I curse the time as I look back on it [he wrote in his Recollections.] It seems to me all evil and no good ... Despised, and as I think rightly, yet by people who were themselves despicable ... physically unfit, mentally undeveloped—was ever a sadder drearier more hopeless entry upon life?

He felt that the other boys belonged to a different world from his, and he adds:

> I have never lost this feeling. Indeed in my old age I feel it as never before. Men become to me simply unintelligible.

Commenting on Dickinson's unhappiness at Charterhouse, Mr Forster suggests that the difference between his boyhood and his manhood was that as a boy he could not escape from the horrors of existence, and that as a man he would not escape from them. Put less romantically, the difference between Dickinson's situation as a boy and as a man was that at school he could not choose his companions or his experiences, and that as a Fellow of King's and a congenital bachelor he could observe the perils of life at a comfortable distance, as one observes through a telescope on a hotel terrace a party climbing Mont Blanc. Nevertheless, he was not quite at ease

SOURCE *English Review*, June 1934, pp. 746–9.

on the terrace. Much as he had disliked reality close at hand in a public school, he made several attempts to immerse himself in life before settling down at King's. He worked on a co-operative farm, he lectured in the provinces, and he studied medicine with the intention of becoming a doctor. Back at Cambridge once more, he resigned himself with relief to his destiny, and for some years left the world to shift for itself as best it might. His hatred of school had not sprung from any aversion to the young of his own sex. At Cambridge, where he could select his friends, he was, if not happy, yet more poignantly aware of the happiness which eluded him than anywhere else.

> Still their forms appear in the golden mists of dawn [he writes of his youthful friends,] and almost I catch their voices through talk of younger generations, heard under the same chapel walls and the same chestnut groves, on the same great lawns, under the same stars reflected in the same sluggish yet lovely stream that will hear perhaps for centuries yet the same voices at the same budding time of youth; unless—who knows? they fall silent even before the eternal silence closes upon me.

The concluding words reveal his fear of life, of the incalculable menacing world, which, always terrifying, had, since the war become a nightmare of horrible possibilities. Even Cambridge was not safe, even King's might be stormed by the English disciples of Lenin and retaken by the English disciples of Mussolini. The war had unnerved him, for that Europe, and especially England, should fall into what Mr Forster calls the Devil's trap, Lowes Dickinson never conceived possible, although during the Boxer riots he had felt, in Mr Forster's words, 'the first shudderings of personal horror.' His attitude to the war seems indeed to have been very like the attitude of Claudius to the corpse of Polonius: 'It had been so with us had we been there'—a sudden pained realization that violent men are not guided by either taste or tact in the selection of their victims. During the first fortnight of the war, under the impulse of this realization, he sketched out the idea of the League of Nations, and during the next few years wrote and lectured on behalf of this body, which he hoped would create a better-behaved Europe. It is no doubt to these efforts that Mr Forster refers when he says that Lowes Dickinson, as a man, refused to escape from the horrors of existence. But, unless one takes the perhaps arguable position that the League of Nations is itself one of the horrors of existence, these efforts of Lowes Dickinson can more reasonably be interpreted as the attempt of a man who was frightened of life to construct a cage into which the terrifying monster might be driven. His visits to Geneva, after the League had been formed, showed him that his efforts to safeguard the oasis of King's had merely resulted in creating another oasis, at Geneva, in which pleasant spot he could always find some of his old King's friends meditating on the relative advantages of Geneva and The Hague as retreats from an undisciplined world.

Shelley and Goethe, Mr Forster tells us, were two of Dickinson's chief inspirers. What he learnt from Goethe is not apparent. To a young German, who told Goethe he was thinking of going to America, Goethe replied 'Your America is here and now.' A vague panacea like the League would not have appealed to Goethe. Dickinson's love for Shelley is more comprehensible, for the America of that distracted poet was here and there, not here and now. Dickinson doubtless loved him, too, for his recklessness, and envied the spirit with which he fell single-handed upon life. For Shelley was a Don Quixote, and Dickinson was only a don.

55
Review

KINGSLEY MARTIN

I well remember my excitement when, as an undergraduate at Cambridge after the war, I discovered Lowes Dickinson's books—*The Modern Symposium, Letters from John Chinaman, From King to King, The Meaning of Good, Justice and Liberty,* and the *Greek View of Life.* Here was a philosopher who opened new doors into the world of ideas, one who treated them with respect whenever they were sincere, and could laugh them off the stage when they were pretentious or dogmatic. I learned that he was a don at King's, that he taught politics by the Socratic method, and that I might, if I were good and lucky, become a member of his seminar. I wrote to him for advice. His reply was: 'Come to tea on *Thirsday.*' I was surprised, for that was my first introduction to his remarkable typewriter, that original instrument that invented so many new words, put semi-colons in the middle of the orthodox ones, and printed the capital letters half-way between the lines. (Mr Forster's biography includes a facsimile of one of Goldie's letters—I say 'Goldie's' because the nickname became universal, being used, as Mr Forster relates, by undergraduates whose own names Goldie himself did not know.)

I went, of course, and we had tea in Goldie's room overlooking the Backs, with the Chinese scrolls on the walls and the Roger Fry over the mantelpiece. His charm was extraordinary—like Mr Forster, I cannot avoid the word—and he seemed to want me to talk. I needed little encouragement, and it was only after I had left him that I realised with a hot shudder that it was I who had been holding forth almost all the time. It was a comfort when I met him a year later—he was away from Cambridge 1920–1—to find that he had completely forgotten me and that I could begin again. He always had a bad memory for folly. But he would notice any bit of sense that came out of you and make it seem important. With him stupid people were apt to find themselves unexpectedly wise, and superior people to behave

SOURCE *Political Quarterly,* July 1934, pp. 447–52.

with simplicity and sincerity. He was always interested in the content rather than the form; he never suffered from the vice of those Cambridge philosophers who imagine that they have refuted an idea when they have exposed the formal errors which disguise its expression.

It was this sensitivity to the real and valuable in ideas of every kind that particularly distinguished Lowes Dickinson as a writer and thinker. He did not sit down, as an ordinarily honest critic does, and say to himself: 'Well, I do not agree with this fellow, but I'll do my best to be fair to him.' If the point of view was sincere and worth while at all, Goldie did more than that. He absorbed himself in it, until for the time at least he shared it and could defend it better than its sponsor. Thus, in the *Modern Symposium* a sensitive reader will find himself agreeing with each of the speakers in turn—with the exception, perhaps, of Remenham (Mr Gladstone) and the Scientist, both of whom speak with pretence and dogmatism. Similarly, if you agree with Goldie's conclusions in *Justice and Liberty*, or the *Meaning of Good*, you will do so because you have been persuaded, after the fullest and fairest appreciation of the rival arguments, that the truth has emerged from the dialogue. The Platonic dialogue and symposium forms were exactly suited to his genius. He minded much more about the truth than about your agreement. The result was that he never employed popular arts and let slip his moment of dawning fame after the publication of *John Chinaman*. Popularity can only be won at the expense of endless repetition. He preferred to move on to other inquiries. It was the war that disturbed this detachment.

To one who trusted so unwisely in human reason, 1914 was a devastating shock and Lowes Dickinson faced the fact that, if thought and the pursuit of truth are to continue in the world at all, to discover new facets of truth and to discuss them with a small body of students is not enough. Hence he forced himself to go to committees, to draft memoranda, and to write more popular books. He was one of the very small group of men who may be considered the real founders of the League of Nations, and one of the first and most effective popularisers of its fundamental concepts. Today few people can realise the courage needed for this shy don to emerge into the Press, to write *The Choice Before Us*, the *European Anarchy*, *War: Its Cause and Cure*, and, finally, with years of the most determined and accurate research, to present the full political background of the war in *The International Anarchy*. It is still far the best book on the subject; fair, accurate, learned, comprehensive and convincing. From the young mystic, who won his Fellowship with a quite uncritical exposition of Plotinus—Mr Forster quotes his laughing remark that he was an 'Indian' from the ages of 20–25—to the very unmystical author of the post-war years, was a long pilgrimage, marked throughout by the struggle of the poet and artist, who is forced by a social conscience to leave the natural haunts of his genius for the irksome frontier in which thought must be translated into the compromises of political action. Writing of his *Modern Symposium*, Lowes Dickinson says:

> But still it does not solve the problem, which is perhaps insoluble, of making the bridge between speculation and art and the side of life which is called practical politics. For practical politics involves fighting, and the object of such a book as this, as it was Plato's object long ago, is to raise the mind above the fighting attitude. There lies here obscurely the great problem of the relation of ideas to passion and interests which I do not seem able clearly to formulate. It seems impossible to go into active life of any kind without being ready to kill, to lie and to cheat.

I can hear Goldie saying this, just as I once heard him say, in a mood of half-humorous bitterness, that the clearest thing in the world was that man was not a reasoning animal. The Ariel side of him, as Mr Forster puts it, was constantly baulked by the necessity of releasing Caliban and converting Antonio. But while he outgrew religion and mysticism, he never became so immersed in practical life that Ariel altogether disappeared. He is there in Goldie's poetry, and in occasional passages in all his books. Goldie is always among the first of modern English stylists, and when Ariel speaks he joins the immortals. At the end, having said and done what he could about the problem of war, Goldie returned, during his last few years, to his main function—the more detached and philosophic interpretation of social ideas. And in so doing he found a new opportunity of influence and, to his surprise, of popularity. His extraordinary capacity for sympathetic exposition made him a unique broadcaster, and thousands of people who had never heard of him, or perhaps of Plato either, listened to and appreciated his wireless talks. Goldie conscientiously ploughing through vast volumes of German documents was an unhappy man; the *International Anarchy* finished, he was again creative, gay and able to play his part in public life without illusions, but with less strain and with increasing detachment.

Mr Forster has not, I think, done all that might be done in appreciating Lowes Dickinson as a political thinker. The elusive task of tracing the development of his views, and relating this to events, has still to be done, and more needs saying about the philosophic roots and political significance of his writing. The task is certainly elusive, for Goldie has left no clear record in his writings to explain his evolution from the Henry Georgite who worked on a communal farm with the then Fabian Harold Cox, to the conservative who defended the House of Lords in the *Development of Parliament in the Nineteenth Century* (1890), and joined the Volunteers in the Boer War, to the pre-war Liberal and the post-war Socialist whose analysis of the economic structure of society was published in the *Political Quarterly*. (Incidentally, Lowes Dickinson was a member of the Editorial Board of the *Political Quarterly*, a fact worth recording here, since it has escaped mention in Mr Forster's book.) I must add that the very careful bibliography of Lowes Dickinson's writings contributed by Mr R. E. Balfour, and printed at the end of the book, will be of the greatest service to any student who wants to fill up the gaps in Mr Forster's book. On the personal side the biography could scarcely be bettered. Mr Forster has succeeded best of all in the early chapters, which describe Lowes Dickinson's home, and the muddle engendered by a Puritan upbringing and the conflicting moral code of a public school; and which take us on from the misery of school to the glorious release of Cambridge (due so much to Oscar Browning), and to the comedy of his false starts as a young man who thought he ought to be an Extension lecturer, a social reformer or a doctor. (What would have happened to Lowes Dickinson if he had not been made a fellow of Kings?) To people who had not the luck to have seen Goldie's eyebrows lift in ironic merriment, I think Mr Forster's book will convey, as well as print can, the delight of his personality, the unique quality of his friendship, and the nature of his influence on generations of students. Most difficult of all to convey is his gaiety. My most persistent memory of Goldie at breakfast in his rooms, or walking to Grantchester or staying in the country, is that we were always discussing the world's calamities amidst constant laughter. And that laughter is not easily communicable, for Goldie's humour was not the repeatable jesting kind, but that rarer species which is expressed in a turn of phrase and finds its food in the ironic twists of circumstance. Mr Forster quotes Goldie's own comment on himself as a young man. Smitten with a very pressing passion to reform the morals of his fellow men, he

> invited an atheist who had been drunk to join the Church of England Temperance Society. The atheist was headachy and polite, but he declined the siren's voice.

During the last few years of his life Lowes Dickinson had found a new happiness and new creativeness, and Mr Forster rightly says that his last books were among his best. But on the personal side there is comfort in the fact that he died before the Nazi revolution and the collapse at Geneva. I have heard him say that the two people who knew most about life were Goethe and Mozart; music meant far more to him than the other arts and Germany meant more to him, I think, than any other foreign country except Greece and China. To one whose whole active life was devoted to the service of reason, and to the development of individual personality, the present revolt against reason, the belief in violence and the magnification of the state as an end in itself, would have been blows only less crushing than 1914 itself. In the *Magic Flute*, that exquisite fantasy in which the bitterness of the war—it was published in 1919—is imperfectly transmuted, but which in its conclusion, perhaps, most clearly sums up his philosophy, he tells of the struggle of man after the ideal and of reason against the blind forces of instinct and passion. In the Hall of Sarastro Tamino says:

> 'You have not shown me Plato.'
>
> 'No,' replied Aureole, 'and with reason. For though he came here and was,

> by all repute, the most gifted of our members, yet he fell back in the end under the dominion of the Queen of Night.'
>
> 'How so?'
>
> 'He came to prefer religion to reason, authority to liberty, and the state to the individual. And these are the three great heresies which no one holding can remain of our Order.'

It will be seen that Goldie's own evolution was the opposite of Plato's. While his Master in the dark days of Greek civilisation lost faith in humanity, and fell back upon religion and authority, Goldie grew out of the rather superior conservatism of his training and the mystical limbo of his young manhood and became, with every setback, a more valiant member of that select company which fights with faith but without comfort for liberty, individuality and reason.

56
Lowes Dickinson

W. H. AUDEN

To write the biography of a teacher is not easy; for a teacher, like an actor, leaves little behind him; his life lacks the compulsive thrill of that of the man of action, the nervous excitement to know what happened next, and also the works of the artist, the tangible relics to be reverently examined and compared; what remains are other lives, and a life of Shakespeare by Hamlet would probably not be a good one.

> They don't mind dying much in China, do they? shouted Liebling to the Chinaman, hoping to introduce a story he had heard about how one could buy a substitute to be accepted for one. 'Always dying' said the Larmah 'millions by starvation flood plague at this moment so thick on the ground.' That explains why they believe in metamorphosis don't you think said the clever student confidentially to the Larmah. 'May be it's true for all I know' said the Larmah shaking his hands towards the two remaining sausages reposing on their cold beds of mincemeat, and just for a moment Liebling was quite certain that in the whole world there was only this funny old man sitting in front of two cold sausages saying I don't know my dear boy, and feeding the starving.

Liebling describes perfectly the feeling that any great teacher inspires, but he could not for that very reason have written Lowes Dickinson's biography.

It requires a kind of love which is impossible to define but is easy to recognize when found, and nowhere, I think, is it more obvious and pervading than in this book of Mr E. M. Forster's.

Of course Mr Forster has many qualifications, the novelist's, skill in presentation *e.g.*, his arrangement of the letters, verbal sensibility—

> But these amenities lay at the edge of his life. Its centre was covered with rubbish and worry. And at its opposite edge lay an imbecile boy whom he sometimes kicked in order to ingratiate himself with his school-fellows;

SOURCE *Scrutiny*, December 1934, pp. 303–06.

sense of humour—

> Nor was he ever insensitive to the joys of Jingoism; there are some letters to R. C. Trevelyan during the Diamond Jubilee of 1897 which make painful reading for his steadier admirers; he explains how wonderful it is to see the Empire marching past, and he contemplates bicycling down to Spithead to see the Naval Review. He never reached Spithead. It was too far;

and the necessary detachment—he did not share Dickinson's tastes for Plato, Shelley and Goethe; and further he has a thorough dislike and distrust for all professional influences:

> One hesitates to call him 'a popular don,' for the words suggest some cheery empty creature.

But none of these explain his success. Perhaps the secret which he shares with Dickinson and which made them friends is a sense of the mystery of life, a hatred of all tabus and systems which would enforce a proscribed pattern, and a belief that what matters is that each should discover his unique treasure.

For that is the lasting impression which this biography makes: that Lowes Dickinson, every bit as much as Napoleon, was a man of destiny; he discovered his life and lived it; and what other success is there? Those who do not earn their living with their bodies should not fail to read this book; it will teach them to avoid their besetting sin, jealousy of the other world.

We do not know enough about either heredity or psychology to know exactly which conditions produce the intelligent and the sensitive: if the causes lie probably in the parental relations, if most intellectuals are psychically bound to their mothers, they are not thereby explained.

The effect on Lowes Dickinson of his mother's death, as described by himself (p. 33), the enhanced feeling for Cambridge, the release from dogmatic religion, is intensely interesting and illuminating, but Mr Forster wisely abstains from comment.

Whether intellectual curiosity, the wish to understand experience rather than be lived by it, is first caused by emotional frustration, or inability to feel and act as impulse directs, or whether the curiosity causes the isolation, the two are generally found together, and found early in life, and further the combination of intelligence and sensibility with physical grace and skill is rare, *e.g.* Dickinson's typing.

Lowes Dickinson's problem is the problem of everyone who finds himself committed before his choice to a life of understanding.

For such who seems to himself to stand and to be stood outside the world of action and passion with all its powers and awards, there are two temptations, either to take fright and retire into a private world of phantasy, religious or bookish, or denying his gift to adore uncritically blood and action, an invalid poet hoping with an ode to buy the society of an inarticulate boxer.

Except for the unsuccessful bicycle-ride to Spithead, Lowes Dickinson was never guilty of this treason of the clerks; his danger was the first rather than the second. The interest and example of his life to an outsider lies in his steady progress from himself to others, from a few to many, his persistent testing of ideas by things. It did not come easily to him; he made all kinds of false starts. Buddhism, Hegel, Medicine, an attempt to combine sensibility and action which was unsuited to him, but once he discovered political history he never looked back. More capable of intimate friendship than most, he came to write

> I cannot understand how I thought that this personal passion in transitory individuals could be the key to the universe.

The young extension lecturer who

> had no notion how to get into touch with ordinary people, and no desire to do so, for I thought I was the bearer of a message which transcended all actual life

became the Lowes Dickinson of the broadcast talk; the shy young don, the inspirer and the confidant of perky undergraduates.

People and civilizations are saved by a change of heart; whether physical violence, loathsome as it is, is necessary to secure it, or whether if we are concerned enough, it can be brought about by 'mental fight' alone, we cannot answer, but at a time when intellectual is a term of abuse fit only for the Jews, it is particularly important that those capable of waging the latter should not lose patience: to such Lowes Dickinson and also, I think, E. M. Forster, are examples permanent and alert.

Abinger Harvest
(1936)

57
Review

ELIZABETH BOWEN

In an age when novelists hum like factories, keeping up to date with themselves, Mr E. M. Forster's output has been, in bulk, small. The novels which, with their 'new standard of truth,' create an absolute world are five, only, in number. It is over thirty years now since the first: *Where Angels Fear to Tread* was short, and contained in embryo all the other books. The authority with which the novels are written, the power they have to expand inside the mind account, perhaps, for the patience with which his silences are received—he has never been mistrusted and never declined. An artist does not rank somewhere between entertainer and tradesman for nothing; he is expected to ring up the curtain again promptly, punctually to deliver the goods. Silence is undue, and makes the public suspicious. But a quality in all Mr Forster's work makes peremptoriness of this kind impossible. The books are so clearly more than efforts of his intelligence; when they do come they have so clearly imposed themselves that it is impossible to demand them when they do not come.

Actually, he has not been so silent. Two collections of stories, *Pharos and Pharillon*, *Anonymity*, *Aspects of the Novel*, the Lowes Dickinson biography have been landmarks down the last twenty years. And the eighty or so 'articles, essays, reviews, poems, &c.,' reprinted in *Abinger Harvest* have been appearing since 1904. If they were nothing more—and they are much more—they would be notes on his so-called silences: the absorption and rapture of travel, the exploration of books. That he has been prevailed upon to assemble and republish them is a matter for gratitude.

Too often, collections are to be dreaded. They are the severest test a writer can face. Tricks of mind, prejudices, an overworking of privilege, an iota too much of accomplishment in the writing stick out in the short essay, the *tour de force*: cumulatively, the effect may be desolating, show up unsuspected weakness in other work. Too many collections are scrapheaps

SOURCE *Spectator*, 20 March 1936, p. 521.

from well-known workshops—shavings, filings no doubt of excellent wood or metal, but the dismal topicality of decades ago sits on them like dust, or a journalistic smartness tarnishes them. Too few writers are right in throwing nothing away. Mr Forster is one great exception: *Abinger Harvest* comes with harvest richness and timeliness.

The essays have been assembled in four groups—The Present, Books, The Past, The East—and the scenario, which is beautiful, of the Abinger Pageant stands alone at the end. The order is vital and should, I feel, be followed—though it is tempting to keep darting backwards and forwards, attracted by titles or opening paragraphs. The collector's desire to be read in this order is more than a whim; it gives the book a form, unity and intention rare in its kind. The dates, startlingly various, of the essays play no part in their arrangement, and should not: there has never been any question of Mr Forster's *development*; there never seems to have been any early work. The age factor with him must have stayed outside and arbitrary; his maturity is innate. That so many of the essays should be so short, too short, seems less a fault in them than in circumstance. (Many appeared in weeklies.) This tantalising briefness, whatever its first object, is the one trying element in the book—the Greek beauty-box, the physician Cardan, the Doll Souse, The Emperor Babur, the rational Indian wedding, Cnidus in the rain, the Jodhpur dragon, the Scallies pass for moments into the light and disappear too soon. But, for all one's own regrets and disruptions, the book has its own, an extraordinary continuousness. Perhaps because Mr Forster has changed so little, perhaps because his mind does not flick on and off—it must impregnate not only his writing but all his conscious moments; its abeyances, even, must have their colour. What is remarkable, in these essays as in the novels, is his power of having access to the whole of himself, to what he has called 'the lower personality': the obscure, the involuntary, the general that is in us all the stuff of dreams and art, the source of perception, the arbiter of memory. Few intellects so active are less isolated from the whole of the being. Mr Forster does not make a doctrine of spontaneity; 'intuition,' he even says, 'makes dancing dervishes of us.' He must have come to terms with his intuition: happen to him what may, he remains, or appears to remain, at once the most active and the governing factor in his own experience. If the perfectly adjusted person does not suffer, Mr Forster is not the perfectly adjusted person: the perfectly adjusted writer I feel he is. With him, intellect not so much controls susceptibility as balances it; many of us have not the wits to feel. Given this highly sensitive equanimity, the effect of this quick succession of essays is, his not so much pitching upon a series of subjects as momentarily enclosing and then releasing them, added to.

To criticism he brings the make-up of the artist. He perceives in another man's work what he himself knows—which accords with his theory of the deep down, giant part of us being general. In his own novels the sense of conscious life's being built up over a somewhat august vault of horror, that rings under the foot, that exhales coldly through cracks, is constantly palpable. Of *The Waste Land* he says: 'the horror is so intense that the poet has an inhibition and cannot state it openly.' And, later in the same essay: 'In respect of the horror that they find in life men may be divided into three classes' ... He finds the romantic in Ibsen, in Proust the adventurer. If he is hard on a writer it is in the manner of one accustomed to being hard on himself; he has none of the critic's godlike non-participation. He detects the finest fatal crack in the bowl. He sees Conrad's 'central obscurity.' 'The secret casket of his genius contains a vapour rather than a jewel.' Love for Jane Austen steels him against Miss Austen, who forgot the nobility of Anne, the wise wit of Elizabeth, when she wrote letters. In some of the critical essays his own image more nearly appears than elsewhere; they are the least, in his own sense, anonymous of his work.

The prose throughout *Abinger Harvest* is the prose of the novels; not a word he uses ever obstructs the mind—prose which makes objects appear brighter than themselves, as in very clear morning light, instead of darkening behind a mesh of words. Like Flaubert's, though so unlike, here is a style made perfect by being subject to purpose, and beautiful with vitality. Its Rhythm is so inherent in its content that one cannot detect it without analysis. The least frigid of writing, it is the most impersonal; he is enemy to all those lovable little tricks. 'Literature,' he says elsewhere, 'tries to be unsigned,' and as far as manner goes he approaches anonymity. But in prose the point of view is inevitable; every sentence must bear, however lightly, the stamp of the mind, its governing quality. Behind his irony, his impersonality, his gentleness, Mr Forster is passionately civilised. The novels are manifestos, these essays ring with a note that is startling because it is rare. Passion will out, however much, however wisely irony may temper it. Beliefs that root in the nature cannot be silenced: his give him an unmistakable touch on a page. That he has written little that could be wrongly attributed is not as he would wish, but too few people are like him.

58
Mr Forster Tidies Up

CHRISTOPHER ISHERWOOD

The literary sweepings of our important writers are usually a sad and exhausting affair; but Mr Forster is unique, anything from his pen—and alas! we get too little—is in the nature of an event, and whatever he produces, whether a novel or a book-review, has a rare and exquisite finish.

Abinger Harvest contains about eighty articles, essays, sketches and reviews, together with two poems, a pageant and a speech. The material is divided into four parts—'The Present', 'Books', 'The Past', 'The East'. The first is mainly serious and satiric: it comments on passing events, discusses the English Character, pokes fun at the Dolls' House and Mrs Grundy, dislikes some politicians, pays tribute to Roger Fry, defends Liberty in England. The 'Books' are by Forrest Reid, Ibsen, Eliot, Proust, Virginia Woolf, Firbank, Howard Sturgis, Sinclair Lewis, Conrad, Colonel Lawrence and Jane Austen. 'The Past' harbours some strange figures, known and unknown: we encounter Cardan here—and must pause for a quotation:

> The supernatural powers were assiduous in their comments on his life, but they were singularly ill-informed, and rarely told him the truth. They never prophesied what happened, and they prophesied what never happened. He is to die at the age of forty-one, and frames his life accordingly. He lives till seventy-six, thus finding himself with thirty-five unexpected years. He goes for a walk, and a crow seizes on to his clothes and tears a hole in them. Nothing happens. He dreams of a large red hen. He fears it will speak to him. It does speak to him. He cannot remember what it says and nothing happens.

—and Gemistus Pletho, visit Cnidus and Battersea Rise, watch Gibbon drilling soldiers and Voltaire beheading snails, glimpse Keats in the middle distance, discover Coleridge under an alias and in danger of the confluent smallpox. 'The East', as was to be expected, is mainly about India, but Egypt and Asia Minor come in as well, with Wilfrid Blunt and two departmental studies in the author's best manner, of a titled antique-snatcher and of two

SOURCE *Listener*, 25 March 1936, p. 603.

warring experts on the behaviour of the River Nile. Finally, by way of an epilogue, we have the scenario of a pageant produced in 1934 at the village of Abinger, where Mr Forster lives.

These items practically cover the century, for the earliest is dated 1903. They are as various in mood and manner as the products of a single writer could well be. Presumably, they are reprinted here with little or no revision: some of the opinions expressed are, indeed, contradictory. Then why isn't *Abinger Harvest* just 'sweepings', a brilliant, fascinating mess? What power is it that pulls these papers together, gives them an essential sequence, transforms them into a book?

Mr Forster, who once wrote a pamphlet on *Anonymity*, is himself among the most anonymous of living authors. Incapable of the nobler forms of self-advertisement, he is the very last person one can imagine sitting down to tell the world the story of his life. Only piecemeal can we get anything out of him; but the pieces, which we have waited thirty years to collect, do at last fit together. That is why *Abinger Harvest* is a book and not a mess: it is really all about Mr Forster himself: it is his own involuntary autobiography.

The author's personal appearances are few but suggestive. We see him saying goodbye, after a Continental holiday, to an Indian friend. The Indian is plunged into despair. Mr Forster points out that they will be meeting again in the course of a few weeks. The Indian is not to be consoled. Later, they do meet.

> I began by scolding my friend. I told him that he had been wrong to feel and display so much emotion upon so slight an occasion; that it was inappropriate. The word 'inappropriate' roused him to fury. 'What?' he cried. 'Do you measure out your emotions as if they were potatoes?' I did not like the simile of the potatoes, but after a moment's reflection I said, 'Yes, I do; and what's more, I think I ought to'.

The Indian is deeply shocked.

> 'If those are your opinions, they part us forever,' he cried, and left the room. Returning immediately, he added: 'No—but your whole attitude towards emotion is wrong . . . I happened to feel deeply. I showed it. It doesn't matter whether I ought to have felt deeply or not'.

Mr Forster is impressed by these remarks but cannot agree with them. Emotion is valuable and must be conserved:

> If I poured it out on small occasions I was afraid of having none left for the great ones, and of being bankrupt at the crises of life. Note the word 'bankrupt'. I spoke as a member of a prudent middle-class nation, always anxious to meet my liabilities. But my friend spoke as an Oriental, and the Oriental has behind him a tradition, not of middle-class prudence, but of kingly munificence and splendour.

There is much of Mr Forster the novelist in this anecdote—the capacity for self-orientation ('I know that I am I'): the faculty, which arises out of it, of seeing and appreciating other people objectively, in the round: the pinch of irony which slyly tips the scales. Other reminiscences, equally pleasing, build up, with a few rapid strokes, the thumb-nail self-portrait which is half a caricature. We see Mr Forster at lunch with Howard Sturgis, the author of *Belchamber*, dropping a frightful brick over some embroidery: 'Simultaneously I received the impression that my novels contained me rather than I them. He was very kind and courteous, but we did not meet again'. In India, Mr Forster visits the ruins of Ujjain, attends an 'advanced' Mohammedan wedding, is not ashamed to acquire a taste for chewing *Pan*. We see him in Egypt, too, at Alexandria, during the war, at a concert-party for the troops, and at Cairo, where he sprained his ankle (a somewhat mysterious accident, this) while waiting for a tram. The sprained ankle led to convalescence in the garden of a friend: it was here that he was able to disintoxicate his system for a few happy days from the poisons of the War Press by reading Huysmans' *A Rebours* and Mr T. S. Eliot's *Prufrock*:

> Here was a protest, and a feeble one, and the more congenial for being feeble. For what, in that world of gigantic horror, was tolerable except the slighter gestures of dissent? He who measured himself against the war, who drew himself to his full height, as it were, and said to Armadillo-Armageddon 'Avaunt!' collapsed at once into a pinch of dust. But he who could turn aside to complain of ladies and drawing-rooms preserved a tiny drop of our self-respect, he carried on the human heritage.

Speaking of Huysmans, he exclaims:

> Oh, the relief of a world which lived for its sensations and ignored the will—the world of des Esseintes! Was it decadent? Yes, and thank God. Yes, here again was a human being who had time to feel and experiment with his feelings, to taste and smell and arrange books and fabricate flowers, and be selfish and himself. The waves of edifying bilge rolled off me, the newspapers ebbed; Professor Cramb, that profound philosopher, and Raemaekers, that inspired artist, floated out into an oblivion which, thank God, has since become permanent, and something resembling reality took their place.

This is admirably expressed, refreshingly sane; but it is not the voice of the first President of the Council for Civil Liberties. In a between-war world of increasingly complex issues, Mr Forster, like many another writer of intelligence and honour, has come to feel that 'the slighter gestures of dissent' are not enough. His more æsthetic admirers may be startled and even pained by the savage, uncompromising irony of 'A Voter's Dilemma' and of the dialogue between the two Gallipoli graves, written at the time of the Chanak crisis. These earlier essays in indignation are not, perhaps, Mr Forster's most elegant productions; but it does one good to read them. Since then, he has mastered the technique of the polemic more completely. Here he is, speaking to the International Writers' Congress, at Paris, last year:

> As for my politics, you will have guessed that I am not a Fascist—Fascism

> does evil that evil may come. And you may have guessed that I am not a Communist, though perhaps I might be one if I was a younger and a braver man, for in Communism I can see hope. It does many things which I think evil, but I know that it intends good. I am actually what my age and my upbringing have made me—a bourgeois who adheres to the British Constitution, adheres to it rather than supports it, and the fact that this isn't dignified doesn't worry me. I do care about the past. I do care about the preservation and the extension of freedom. And I have come to this congress mainly to listen to what is being done and suffered in other lands.

There is Mr Forster as one most likes to think of him; as one admires and respects him most. *Abinger Harvest* does not entirely contain him—no book could; but it has captured something essential. It is like a gramophone record which we shall want to listen to again and again.

59
Review

R. A. SCOTT-JAMES

Since his early creative period of novel writing just before the war Mr Forster has not been a very prolific writer. His books have appeared infrequently, and in recent years he has dropped fiction. Yet the eighty or so articles, essays and reviews selected for this volume from his occasional writings of the last twenty-two years serve to show the continuity of his intellectual interests. If he does not write very much, none the less students of contemporary literature have not ceased to be conscious of him as a living force. He does not waste words, and with him a few words go a long way. He may not rush into print (though surprisingly he may) when the news is hot, but has his say on the things that interest him when they have fallen into their proper place.

He is the sort of person who could not conceivably under normal circumstances be hurried. I say 'under normal circumstances,' because I can imagine occasions when his perceptions might hasten a crisis, and then perhaps he might be acting before most people had realized that anything had happened. His manner of life demands leisure—the leisure to take things in, to see all round them, and be intensely aware of them—to this, busy-body activity would be destructive. He speaks in one of these essays of 'a country (of the mind) where the will is not everything, and the braying patriots of the moment made no sound.' In another, where he is writing about the English character, he says that 'the English instinct is to do what can be done first, and to postpone the feeling as long as possible.' From which one may gather that, deep as is his affection for England, he is certainly not typically English; and one remembers that that 'Orient' which he has experienced in India, in Egypt and elsewhere (and is not to be confused with the Flowery-mysterious Orient of Loti, still less with the 'East is East' of Kipling) has its peculiar attractions for him. Doing quickly is one form of activity; feeling when it is accompanied by perception is another;

SOURCE *London Mercury*, April 1936, pp. 635–6.

activity of the latter kind becomes of the greatest value when the imagination actively relates impressions and shows us our world sanely and clearly in perspective.

To perceive things clearly—that is Mr Forster's power—to see them with a kind of artistic precision, in a fine light, without exaggeration yet without fear of the occasional superlative; unconventionally, without cleverness just as much as without banality, intimately, and in a fearless personal way; for there is no other way in which the direct impact of life at first hand can be recorded. The language must correspond. It is direct, easy, free from affectation, and choice. It lends itself readily to being a vehicle for sentiment, of which Mr Forster is not the least afraid; there are moments when he reminds us of Charles Lamb; but his humour, his ironic sense, and his intellect make it unthinkable that he should ever be sentimental, as Lamb often was.

The range of interest covered by these essays is extraordinarily wide. He writes about the middle-class characteristics of English culture; about liberty; about India. He discusses authors and literature in general. He carries himself back to past events, as when he writes about Gemistus Pletho. He gives us reflections engendered by incidents in his travels. And he successfully enters the region of pure fantasy, as when he writes of Mickey Mouse or addresses the portraits in the Royal Academy; but there is more than fantasy in the conversation between two Graves in Gallipoli. 'Why,' asks the Second Grave, 'do the eminent men speak of "our" graves, as if they were themselves dead? It is we, not they, who lie on Achi Baba.'

On such a subject as Ibsen it is well that we should read Mr Forster, for we have heard too much from the Ibsenites about everything in his later plays except the persistence in them of the romanticism of his earlier period. In his appreciative study of the qualities of Mr Forrest Reid there occurs a description of the magical valley of the Lagan near Belfast. It seems to me to be the valley itself, as I remember it from long ago, with its river and no less lovely canal. In writing of Joseph Conrad he is rather severe. I could give an example of Conrad's gruffness similar to that given by Mr Forster; and also of the generosity and charm with which he made amends when he discovered that he had been in error. Jane Austen's novels Mr Forster admires so much that he is disappointed with her letters. When I read the collection of letters of which he is writing I was not in the least disappointed; they seemed to me to be exactly what I should have expected. Did Mr Forster expect too much, or I too little? Perhaps he was bound to be disappointed with the real Jane Austen, admiring her novels, as he does, this side [of] idolatry.

His book should be read slowly, if the reader would get from it all that is to be had. It belongs to that order of high literature where thought and feeling correspond, where all that is expressed has passed through the fine mechanism of sensibility, having the self-consistency of what is consistent with himself. He writes only when he is sure that he has something to say. The time should soon come when he will address himself to a major creative work—let us hope a novel—with this generation as his subject.

60
Review

Q. D. LEAVIS

Apart from the Clarke Lectures, reprinted as *Aspects of the Novel*, and the memoir of Lowes Dickinson, this is the only book Mr Forster's eager public has been given since *A Passage to India*, and it is a disappointing book. It is composed of reprinted essays, reviews, articles, etc., divided into sections: one is of literary criticism, another about the East, another on aspects of contemporary England, and one of essays mostly in the popular historical manner (née Strachey) on figures of the Past. The publishers tells us 'the range of outlook is even wider' here than in Mr Forster's previous work, but even his greatest admirers will hardly find anything more than a casual re-statement of Mr Forster's outlook, split up as it were under a spectroscope. *Abinger Harvest* ought to be an occasion for some critic to make a revaluation of the novels too. However, we must be content here with summarizing what this volume alone shows.

It is a mixture of autobiography and criticism. What it chiefly does is to furnish a key to Mr Forster's peculiar poise, that poise which constitutes the individuality of his novels and from which his characteristic irony springs. Under the spectroscope it is seen to be a balance between a critical and a charming stance. He is gifted with impulses in both directions, and, hovering as he necessarily does between the serious and the playful, this makes him unduly concerned to be whimsical. He is often here merely playful and then he tends to become a bore (*e.g.* last half of the group of sketches called 'Our Divisions'), or personal in the worst sense. His weakness, felt in the novels as an uneasy wobble in some of the ironic effects, is here revealed as a frequent inability to decide which he wants to be—critical or charming. You get the impression that he is positively unable to resist following out a whimsical train of thought, whatever the business in hand. 'My Wood' is an instance of turning this habit to profit by the use of a serious overtone, but it stands almost alone on this level. Generally his

SOURCE *Scrutiny*, June 1936, pp. 100–05.

poise in these essays is unstable, he seems, as so rarely in the novels, to be uncertain what he intends to convey or where he means to alight (hence perhaps his liking for Ronald Firbank, who will remain a tiresome fribble to most of us). 'A Flood in the Office' shows a characteristic surrender to the easier current; it starts from a dispute between two eminent engineers about the irrigation of Egypt and continues, at a tangent, about Father Nile. Mr Forster sees from the corner of his eye the real significance of the dispute—the eternal antipathy between the disinterested intelligent man and stupidity allied with vested interests—but it is not the spectacle of integrity struggling to make its voice heard that arrests his imagination: it is the whimsical fancies suggested by 'the unique mass of water.' Of course it makes a more amusing essay this way. The objection is that the consistently whimsical outlook has the effect of making any other appear priggish—exactly as *Punch* does, which Mr Forster very feelingly denounces on other grounds. And you do get the impression that Mr Forster is disinclined to risk being thought too serious, he takes so much care to elicit the 'How amusing' response.

The literary criticism carries us a step further in our analysis. The intuitions are good, there are striking flashes of discernment (some of the critical stuff, such as the essay on Sinclair Lewis, is better than anything in *Aspects of the Novel*), but he doesn't seem to know how to consolidate. As in that book, it is amateur criticism; there is some kind of mental habit that prohibits discipline and sustained effort. The amiably whimsical-personal approach is not made to seem justified as a profitable mode of literary criticism: essays like that on T. S. Eliot are so inadequate that it is surprising that Mr Forster should have thought them worth reprinting. The brief note on Conrad makes the radical criticism of this novelist who has been written and lectured about with so little profit:

> This isn't an æsthetic criticism, nor a moral one. Just a suggestion that our difficulties with Mr Conrad may proceed in part from difficulties of his own. What is so elusive about him is that he is always promising to make some general philosophic statement about the universe and then refraining with a gruff disclaimer ... These essays [*Notes on Life and Letters*] do suggest that he is misty in the middle as well as at the edges, that the secret casket of his genius contains a vapour rather than a jewel ...

And again on Ibsen, how acute, how just:

> Although not a teacher he has the air of being one, there is something in his method that implies a message, though the message really rested on passing irritabilities, and not on any permanent view of conduct or the universe ... Moral ugliness trespasses into the æsthetic ... Poetry might perhaps be achieved if Ibsen's indignation was of the straight-hitting sort, like Dante's. But for all its sincerity there is something automatic about it, he reminds us too often of father at the breakfast table after a bad night, sensitive to the defects of society as revealed by a chance glance at the newspaper, and apt to blame all parties for them indiscriminately. Now it is the position of

> women that upsets father, now the lies people tell, now their inability to lie, now the drains, now the newspaper itself, which he crumples up, but his helpers and servers have to retrieve it, for bad as are all political parties he must really see who got in at Rosmerholm.

Yet you feel he is not wholly aware of the force of his criticisms, for he always proceeds to shy away from the point he has made so convincingly and go back on himself—generally out of benevolence.

You go on to conclude that Mr Forster is not so adequate a critic as he might be—as he ought to be, judging by his natural endowments. His blind spots are particularly instructive; they seem to be created by a social environment whose influence would repay investigation. There is the section of essays on The Past. They have none of Lytton Strachey's hateful quantities—the cheap irony, the vulgar prose effects, the assumption of superiority to his historical puppets—but it is significant that he should be sufficiently an admirer of Strachey's to try his hand at this genre, and sad that he should have been encouraged to think the attempts worth republishing. [But no doubt many will find them delicious.] In these circumstances his personal touch deserts him.

> Presently the old mistress [Hannah More] will ring a bell, Louisa will fail to answer it, there will be horror, disillusionment, flight, the Industrial Revolution, Tolstoy, Walt Whitman, Mr and Mrs Sidney Webb.

This, along with *The Common Reader* 2nd Series from which it might have come, shows the unfortunate meeting-ground of three writers. It is distressing to see so distinguished a writer sinking to this. From this volume posterity will do some deducing about Mr Forster's background: he feels amiably towards the submerged layers below him ('Me, Them and You,' and there other indications of a desire, creditable rather than effective, to gear in with the great world); and is critical of those aspects of his economic class which his circle have agreed to consider targets (*e.g.*, '"It is different for me"'), but his most successful achievements here are in a very small way (*e.g.*, 'The Doll Souse' and 'The Scallies'). There isn't much appearance of sharply-felt first-hand criticism. Everything points to an uncritical taking-over of group-values. For instance, he boldly confesses to being one of the highbrow minority who can 'make fun' of Wembley, while the next essay displays him revelling in the deliciousness of Mickey Mouse and Co.; anyone who has observed a highbrow film audience relaxing from the effort required to appreciate Russian or surrealist films and preparing to really enjoy themselves when the Walt Disney turn follows must feel this a worthier subject for an ironical pen. A satirist, to command our respect, ought to be aware of his blinkers as well as of his tether. Thus it seems at least somewhat arbitrary to assume that the British Empire is ridiculous whereas Mr Clive Bell isn't; posterity's Bloomsbury (not very long hence) may judge otherwise.

Where suitable subjects occur, when his critical abilities are able to function on important topics that are also congenial, Mr Forster produces his best work. The best section in this volume is that on The East, and the best essay in it on 'The Mind of the Native Indian State.' This is not merely whimsical, merely charmingly witty, but witty to a serious purpose; it is responsible:

> The Princes have studied our wonderful British Constitution at the Chiefs' Colleges, and some of them have visited England and seen the Houses of Parliament. But they are personal rulers themselves, often possessing powers of life and death, and they find it difficult to realize that the King Emperor, their overlord, is not equally powerful. If they can exalt and depress their own subjects at will, regard the State revenue as their private property, promulgate a constitution one day and ignore it the next, surely the monarch of Westminster can do as much or more. This belief colours all their intercourse with the Government of India. They want to get through or behind it to King George and lay their troubles at his feet, because he is a king and a mighty one, and will understand. In the past some of them nourished private schemes, but to-day their loyalty to the Crown is sincere and passionate, and they welcomed the Prince of Wales, although his measured constitutionalisms puzzled and chilled them. Why did he not take his liegemen aside and ask, in his father's name, for the head of Ghandi upon a charger? It could have been managed so easily. The intelligent Princes would not argue thus, but all would have the feeling, and so would the reader if he derived extensive powers under a feudal system and then discovered that it was not working properly in its upper reaches. 'His Majesty the King-Emperor has great difficulties in these days': so much they grasp, but they regard the difficulties as abnormal and expect that a turn of the wheel will shake them off. However cleverly they may discuss democratic Europe or revolutionary Russia with a visitor, they do not in their heart of hearts regard anything but Royalty as permanent, or the movements against it as more than domestic mutinies. They cannot understand, because they cannot experience, the modern world.

It concludes with a sample of Mr Forster's personal brand of wisdom—a deprecating refusal to be easily wise. The same note is struck elsewhere, as in the capital little sketches 'Advance, India' and 'The Suppliant,' which might both have come from *A Passage to India.* It is sustained in the most impressive thing in the book, the courageous and useful address, delivered last year to the International Congress of Writers at Paris, on 'Liberty in England,' which contains passages that every civilized person will be grateful to Mr Forster for. [This recalls Mr Forster's valuable report of that congress in *The New Statesman and Nation,* July 6th, 1935.] Along with this goes 'A Note on the Way,' which is personal in the best sense. You conclude that Mr Forster's courage—and courage is readily felt to be an important part of this writer's make-up—is not associated with his irony so much as with his delicate emotional machinery. Certainly it is something in the nature of courage which provides the mainspring: courage to assert the virtue of the finer feelings. Compared with the other major novelists of this century Mr Forster exhibits a lack both of personal vigour and of that intellectual strength which impresses as the best source of vitality; you can't imagine him making the kind of personal judgments that Lawrence made nor has his irony anything in common with the refreshing sardonic quality of Lawrence's. Nor has he shown a capacity for such an ironical achievement as *Cakes and Ale*, which, side by side with a sardonic criticism of the writer's environment, exhibits positive values convincingly incarnated. Niceness has its drawbacks apparently, in letters if not in life; Mr Forster in *Abinger Harvest* shows himself to be the nicest kind of person, but so nice as to be somewhat tame perhaps—or else what accounts for the disappointment the book leaves? Though his public work (*e.g.*, formerly as president of the Society for Cultural Relations with Soviet Russia and till recently as president of the National Council for Civil Liberties) is a reminder that it is not necessarily his most ponderable side that is presented to the reader.

61
Gestures of Dissent

JOHN CROWE RANSOM

Abinger Harvest is one of the notable literary miscellanies of our time. It cannot often be said that the critical intelligence of a writer never wanders, and yet that his writing is always effortless and charming. Mr Forster is a humanist; I do not mean, of course, that this has anything to do with what is called Neo-Humanism. He is a man of sensibility, and also a wit. He has the narrative gift. In fact, he has every perfect gift that the great writer needs except one: he was not born into the right age.

His fame rests, I think, on his novels, *A Passage to India* and *A Room with a View.* The first is a classic for its understanding of the Indian and Anglo-Indian mind, beside which the mind of the English rulers is both simple and harsh. The second is English, a *jeu d'esprit* in which love is wiser than families, or whole battalions, of trained snobs. But I remark that both are comedies, and that the comic attitude is now just about untenable by thoughtful writers whether upon India or upon Western society. That Mr Forster does not write more comedies, when his mastery of the type is so obvious, is a credit to his time sense, and should fill his admirers with a sense of calamity.

The papers here have a wide range. There are historical and biographical excursions, whose scholarship is not tainted by pedantry. Mr Forster could have had a brilliant career in history. There are occasional pieces about trifling things, and the penetrating 'Notes on the English Character.' These do not engage his whole mind. Most important are the essays in literary criticism. And what a critic Mr Forster would be if he had the will to be it! Informal as these papers are, we have had nothing within the like compass superior to his impressions of Ibsen, T. S. Eliot, Proust, Virginia Woolf, T. E. Lawrence, and Wilfred Blunt.

If he had the will. Certainly Mr Forster has a will, but it is one which he hardly has the heart to exercise in our desperate days. It is not a form of the

SOURCE *Yale Review*, 26, September 1936, pp. 181–3.

political or economic will. Nor is it the will of an artist who would hold a mirror up to the world in order to contemplate and render the tragic effects. But these so occupy the foreground as to inhibit him from rendering much of anything.

Very significant is the turn his mind takes upon reading T. S. Eliot's earlier poems. (The poetry, not the criticism; Eliot's theory is always affirmative, it is the poetry which is skeptical and revealing.) Mr Forster was in war service when he came upon the lament of Mr Prufrock:

> *I should have been a pair of ragged claws,*
> *Scuttling across the floors of silent seas.*

He remarks:

> Here was a protest, and a feeble one, and the more congenial for being feeble. For what, in that world of gigantic horror, was tolerable except the slighter gestures of dissent? He who measured himself against the war, who drew himself to his full height, as it were, and said to Armadillo-Armageddon, 'Avaunt!' collapsed at once into a pinch of dust. But he who could turn aside to complain of ladies and drawing-rooms preserved a tiny drop of our self-respect, he carried on the human heritage.

I have the idea that the limitation Mr Forster has placed upon the volume of his work represents one of the important losses of the war, and of that destruction of society which seems still to follow it.

Two Cheers for Democracy
(1951)

62
A Private Voice

V. S. PRITCHETT

Mr E. M. Forster is the least moderate of men, but, in the last forty years, what extremists our elders have been; how we know them, as we know all extremists, by what they have left out. Shaw, Wells, D. H. Lawrence, T. S. Eliot—I say nothing of the violent names in arts other than literature: in the sciences or in politics—they certainly correspond with our violent world, reflect its belief in will, rage and assertion; they are full of faith, driving us forward or back—to something. We can only guess about such things but I have the suspicion that even among the faithful, Faith pure and simple, is out. At any rate, Mr Forster's extremism, which is of the opposite kind, seems a more powerful survival. He does not, he has told us, 'believe in Belief'; we ought to have as little as we decently can; we had better rely on weakness rather than strength; private life comes before the cause; keep the planners off the individual; a spell of inertia, apathy and uninventiveness is desirable; freedom and variety are indispensable and democracy deserves 'two cheers' because it allows them; but there is no call for enthusiasm here: 'Two cheers are quite enough; only Love, the Beloved Republic deserves three.' And Mr Forster sits on his deck chair, cut off by the tide, looking sternly at it but without surprise. He points out that things are likely to get worse for Liberals like himself, but a shocked, rebuking look comes into his eye as he declines the ropes, lifebuoys and rescues we hysterically offer him from the shore. He replies in a voice that we can only call tellingly inadequate, unmoved, personal, relaxed and nonco-operative.

> Faith to my mind, is a stiffening process, a sort of mental starch, which ought to be applied as sparingly as possible. I dislike the stuff. I do not believe in it for its own sake. Herein I probably differ from most people who believe in Belief, and are only sorry they cannot swallow even more than they do. My law-givers are Erasmus and Montaigne, not Moses and St Paul.

The passage I have quoted comes from a volume of collected articles,

SOURCE *New Statesman and Nation*, 3 November 1951, pp. 496, 498.

reviews, broadcasts and lectures which go back to before the war. They are all touched by that dislike of the will and the intellect which, as Mr Trilling noted in his brilliant little book on Forster, has been discernible in European literature since the time of Matthew Arnold. There is a coolness, a hardness, sufficiency and maturity in Forster's throw-away lines which indicate not the sad æsthete, but the man who is extreme because he thinks the time has come for redressing the balance. He has the worldliness of the saint. Society, society, society; it is the unceasing theme in the nineteenth century, since the French revolution. Is society really what the private man is or ought to be interested in now?

> I believe ... in an aristocracy of the sensitive, the considerate and the plucky. Its members are to be found in all nations and classes, and all through the ages, and there is a secret understanding between them when they meet. They represent the true human tradition, the only permanent victory of our queer race over cruelty and chaos.... On they go, an invincible army, but not a victorious one.

Uplift? No, he knows love does not work in public life. If tolerance is going to be necessary in the post-war world—he is talking in a war-time broadcast—tolerance means more than live and let live; a comfortless virtue, it means 'putting up' with people. The thing we notice about these broadcasts is their freshness, their freedom from what can in any sense be called an official view, a party line, and the sense—so rare in public utterances—that we are listening to a person. For it is the measure of Mr Forster's integrity that he speaks privately in public, and nowadays there is nothing so arresting, indeed so hard to come by, as a private voice. It can be preserved only by continuous refusals. The streak of personal inadequacy is carefully, cunningly put in; the astutely dated slang plays its part in the masked battery of weakness. Swanky, a cert, a mess: there is nothing breezy in words like these; they are put in to deflate, not to raise the wind. They are put in for the sake of shabbiness. Shabbiness, in our official time, may be a deadly weapon. Even the jokes are flat, by calculation: that one about the Scotsman who wanted less chastity and more delicacy, is there no recall that civilisation exists where a flat story may point an angry moral. To be austerely at a disadvantage, to appear arrestingly feeble may be a strength in an age of power. There is a comic piece about an official dinner in Pretoria where the author had the chicken broth poured over him by a nervous servant. Mr Forster's natural self laughed hysterically. He dressed up in a fancy costume for the rest of the day, and for days afterwards the African dust unfailingly picked out the fantastic, undignified, unofficial stains on a cheap suit. An odd story; like episodes in one or two of Mr Forster's novels, it briskly argues for loss of dignity, for the authority of anti-climax.

Then there is the brilliant piece on *Mrs Miniver* which was first published in this journal. It began with just that touch of subtle English social rudeness which may be seen in Jane Austen or *Alice in Wonderland* (as Mr Edmund Wilson once pointed out) and then went on to wreck the national tea party in the classical British way: Mrs Miniver might be all right but she was not out of the top drawer. Neither, Mr Forster added artlessly, after the poor lady was made to look foolish, was he; nor, he went on, were we, her readers and his. It was one of Mr Forster's deadliest themes, for in Mrs Miniver one of his own characters had appeared, a descendant of the Schlegels or the rescuing lady in *Where Angels Fear to Tread*, and she had upon her that brave uneasiness which is evoked by the word 'relative,' that defensiveness or shame of human connection, which is the cross our middle class, rather gladly, bears. (Its strength, too.) Like Jane Austen, Mr Forster has been sharp and unfailing in detecting that all his people were relatives: they had the blood relationship of class. Here is the vinegar that gives his comedy its bite.

If Mr Forster puts *Mrs Miniver* in her place with social precision, he has the same quick brief decisive manner with ideas. His politeness is of the iron kind that proceeds by inquiry. Do you? Can we say? There will be no mess, no muddle, no 'good mixing.' There will be the choice of unsatisfactory answers:

> The State believes in education. But does art educate? 'Sometimes, but not always' is the answer, an unsatisfactory one. The State believes in recreation. But does art amuse? 'Sometimes, but not always' is the answer again. The State does not believe in experiments in the development of human sensitiveness in directions away from the average citizen. The artist does, and consequently he and the State—who will soon be his sole employer—must disagree ... There is a danger and indeed a probability that art will disappear.

Or, what about criticism? Has it any first-class *raison d'être* in the arts? Is there a point at which criticism and art meet? No, it can have no first-class *raison d'être*. It is educative, it encourages precision, but it teaches the artist next to nothing. It belongs to the world of culture which has no close relationship with the artist himself:

> The only activity which can establish such a *raison d'être* is love. However cautiously, with whatever reservations, after whatsoever purifications we must come back to love. That alone rises to the co-operation with the artist which is the sole reason for our æsthetic pilgrimage.

And why this pilgrimage?

> The work of art is the only material object in the universe which may possess internal harmony. It achieves something which has often been promised by society, but always delusively. Ancient Athens made a mess, but the *Antigone* stands up. Renaissance Rome made a mess—but the Sistine ceiling got painted. James I made a mess—but there was *Macbeth*. Louis XIV—but there was *Phèdre*. Art for art's sake. I should just think so and more so than ever at the present time—*c'est le meilleur témoignage que nous puissions donner de notre dignité*.

And when we talk about art among ourselves—

> Our job is to enjoy ourselves and not to lose heart, and to spread culture not because we love our fellow men, but because certain things seem to us unique and priceless, and as it were push us out into the world on their service. It is a Gospel, and not altogether a benign one.

All this is the wisdom of the contemplative man, the non-participant, who belongs to the secret society of hermits who make their signals—a favourite metaphor of Mr Forster's—in the night. When he applies himself to specific books and writers, our expectations are disappointed. His Gibbon, his Butler, his Tolstoy are pleasing enough; these essays have the virtue, which he seeks, of unselfing him and bringing him into the skin of his subject. But afterwards all one can say is 'Yes, I had better read Gibbon or Tolstoy or Butler. They sound unique.' Whereas one wants more than that from our most distinguished living novelist. Tolstoy was possibly unjust about Maupassant, but he *added* to the subject. What he added may have been wrong, but it was the uniqueness of Tolstoy. Do we really need to be taught to contemplate? Don't we have to be taught, even clumsily, to add? Mr Forster is writing here very well, but deliberately and on principle (it seems) below his powers, humbling himself to our level.

It is an irony, one begins to think, that Wells who did not believe in art, and Forster (the anti-Wells of *The Machine Stops*) who *does* believe in it, should be alike in their extremism: both abandoned art in order to teach. One begins to ask if the pursuit of the good life is not, like the pursuit of the World State and so on, inimical to the creative act. The work of art is the sole exemplar of an internal order? Yes—but does the artist know this? Is he not drowning in chaos, in confused participation? A bucket, we are told, is let down into the unconscious and then the work of art arises; but what sends the bucket down, what winds it up again? Surely, the artist's will. And when we have said the word Will, then everything Mr Forster is opposed to comes rushing in. The bad heart, to begin with; the bad hearts of Dickens, of Swift, of Proust, of all the great artists, in short. There is no personal choice about being committed to the world; it is not in our hands at all; it is done for us by others, that is the tragedy or the comedy of the human condition. Of course, Mr Forster knows this. The great extremists always know what they are leaving out. The Idea of Will and Greatness had reached the point where, in his opinion, the returns for the individual and for the value of living, had hopelessly diminished. Somewhere in this book he tartly warns us man has tried everything except exhaustion. If we are not careful, if we do not redress the balance, that may come next.

63
Four Cheers for Mr Forster

JOCELYNE BROOKE

I wanted to begin this review by saying, quite firmly, that Mr Forster is the 'greatest living English writer'—but somehow the words stuck to my pen-nib, and refused to write themselves without the ironic qualification of inverted commas. A great writer—the phrase seems too pompous, suggesting beards and collected works. 'Important' then? Ye-es—but again the word will not quite do; one infers something 'difficult' and *avant-garde.* Fumbling for the word I wanted, I happened to look again at the short essay on Gide included in this volume. Gide, says Mr Forster, 'had not a great mind. But he had a free mind, and free minds are as rare as great.' A free mind—that, I think, strikes the right note. Greatness, says Mr Forster in the same essay, 'is a nineteenth century perquisite, a Goethean job'; Gide is no bearded, thunderous prophet, but a liberator. 'He has taught thousands of people to mistrust façades, to call the bluff, to be brave without bounce and inconsistent without frivolity. He is the humanist of our age—not of other ages, but of this one.'

This description could be applied, it seems to me, without modification to Mr Forster himself; like Gide, he is one of the great liberators, and as a novelist he has had influence primarily in the moral sphere. 'Only connect' is his message—only connect the monk and the beast in man, and you shall be saved. His weakness—if it is a weakness—has been a certain inability to commit himself. Like Professor Godbole in *A Passage to India,* he prefers to leave the question open. What *did* happen in the cave? What is Mr Forster really getting at? What are his novels *about*? The 'undeveloped heart'—that is one of his themes, and an important one, but it is not all-important. Should we love one another? Yes, most certainly, for God is Love—or rather (as the

SOURCE *Spectator,* 9 November 1951, p. 609.

Indian draughtsman wrote it in the temple at Mau) 'God si Love.' Once again the element of doubt creeps in. Is 'God si Love' the final message of India—and (one might add) is it Mr Forster's final message too?

No, I do not think so; Mr Forster once remarked (in *Aspects of the Novel*) that, while one is reading *War and Peace*, 'great chords begin to sound, and we cannot say exactly what struck them.' One could say the same, I think, of *A Passage to India* or *Howards End*; for the 'meaning' of a Forster novel impinges with something of the mysterious effect of music—chamber-music, perhaps as opposed to the full orchestra of Tolstoy. In other words Forster is an artist, and, if his influence has been, as I have said, chiefly a moral one, it is none the less a triumph of art.

Two Cheers for Democracy contains all Mr Forster's published (and a few unpublished) pieces written since *Abinger Harvest*. It falls roughly into two sections: *The Second Darkness*, essays and broadcasts in war-time and since the war; and *What I Believe* (the title of an essay published in 1939 and reprinted here), comprising sections on *Art in General*, *The Arts in Action*, and *Places*. The second part includes the important address on *The Raison d'Être of Criticism in the Arts*, and the delightful lecture on Skelton delivered at Aldeburgh, besides much criticism of novels, poetry and plays, and some short pieces about music. Few writers appear at their best in such collections, but Mr Forster is an exception to this as to most other rules; one can say of this book that it is greater than the sum of its parts, for Mr Forster's 'occasional' writing never descends to mere journalism, and these essays, though immensely readable and entertaining, are no less serious, by intention, than the novels.

All the old qualities are here: the deceptive casualness of exposition, the wit (e.g. *Not Listening to Music*), the occasional malice (he is downright rude to Mrs Miniver). The oblique, sinuous sentences worm their way into one's mind, apparently so off-hand, yet carrying a weight of meaning which seems disproportionate to their spare and elegant scaffolding: Mr Forster is always taking one off one's guard; a subtle, profound phrase darts suddenly from the page like the flicker of a snake's tongue, so quickly that one almost misses it. Wit, wisdom, subtlety—yes, they are all here; but one does notice, I think, a firmer tone. If one wants culture, one may have to fight for it; perhaps one cannot always remain aloof from the battle. 'It is impossible to be fair-minded when one has faith,' says Mr Forster, and he is prepared to strike a blow for what he deprecatingly calls 'this cultural stuff.' Faith, he says, makes one unkind, and 'I am pleased when culture scores a neat hit.' Culture, alas, does not score many hits nowadays, and when hits are attempted, they are too often apt to rebound upon the hitter. This book is no atom-bomb to pulverise, in one big bang, the citadel of Philistia; its effect, one hopes, will be more like that of the ivy, whose slow prehensile rootlets, creeping year after year through the jerry-built foundations, may bring down the house at last.

64
In Defense of Values

JOSEPH WOOD KRUTCH

The publishers call this collection of essays Mr Forster's 'first full-length book in fifteen years.' Such stretchings of a point are not always justified, but this one is. To be sure, the volume is a collection and a very miscellaneous one at that, for the subjects as well as the forms vary all the way from broadcast talks during the late war through personal essays to pure literary criticism. But it is unified more than such collections usually are by the fact that the author is possessed of a very unified personality and by the fact that this personality is very much present no matter what he happens to be talking about. Both his temperament and his opinions are, as he would be the first to admit, what are commonly called old-fashioned. He is a defender of values often overlooked and sometimes rejected by moderns; and though he by no means either washes his hands or surrenders to despair he certainly looks toward the future with a good deal of misgiving. Obviously he sometimes wonders if he is not what his opponents complacently call a characteristic phenomenon of a dying culture.

The book's title, which may at first sight seem trivial and which Mr Forster says was first suggested as a joke, is actually extremely apt. One's attitude toward democracy is today a touchstone, and two, rather than three, cheers precisely defines what Mr Forster is. He is almost as far from Eliot as he is from Hitler or Stalin. Yet at his most unhappy he can say:

> Democracy is not a Beloved Republic really, and never will be. But it is less hateful than other contemporary forms of government, and to that extent it deserves support.

Or, two hundred pages further on, speaking of the shift from agriculture to industrialism:

> It has meant the destruction of feudalism and relationships based on land, it

SOURCE *Saturday Review of Literature*, 1 December 1951, pp. 25–6.

> has meant the transference of power from the aristocrat to the bureaucrat and the manager and the technician. Perhaps it will mean democracy but it has not meant it yet and personally I hate it.

The nearest Mr Forster comes to any summings-up are in two essays, one called 'The Last Parade,' in which he gives an impressionistic account of the Paris Exposition of 1937, where for the last time the modern world demonstrated playfully the toys with which it was about to destroy itself; the other called more formally 'What I Believe', dated two years later. But wherever one turns one finds some facet of the unified attitude, and one realizes that Mr Forster has no all-sufficient faith in Democracy for the same general reason that he has none in any of the other magic formulae such as Economic Law, Proper Conditioning, Psychological Adjustment, or for that matter Christianity. He is not a Utopian; he does not believe that all our problems will ever be solved; and while he admits that tolerance, good temper, and sympathy—in which he does believe—probably require faith as a 'stiffening' even if 'the process coarsens them,' nevertheless, 'I dislike the stuff.'

Inevitably Mr Forster is concerned with the arts—with literature as a professional, with music and painting as an amateur. There are essays on Tolstoy and Proust, on Virginia Woolf and, what is surprisingly enough the best of the lot, on John Skelton. But here again there is unity, not merely because he has definable and defensible literary tastes, but also because literature is one of the provinces in that realm of human activity where, far less dubiously than in politics or economics or even physical science, unmistakable and enduring achievements have been celebrated. Yet it is perversely just those achievements which democracy as well as every other form of organized power discounts, discourages, and destroys. Not too much has been gained if we escape from the condescension of the aristocratic patron only to fall into the hands of those who insist that art must be, even if not doctrinally correct and demonstrably useful, then at least 'democratic,' which is taken to mean 'universally accessible.' And though here again Mr Forster's conclusions are scattered through half a dozen different essays—and the better for so being—it would not be too difficult to synthesize a body of doctrine.

In the next to the last paragraph of the very last essay occurs the sentence, 'The sense of a world that asked to be noticed rather than explained was again upon me.' Perhaps nothing else could sum up better his convictions concerning the point at which art begins, no matter now far on from there it may go and no matter to what extent all sorts of other things may become involved in it. There is nothing wrong, he says elsewhere, with 'art for art's sake', though there is a great deal wrong with the assumption that nothing except art is important; and probably that little problem has never been more neatly disposed of. If the artist or even the mere lover of the arts is sometimes inclined to give up the whole matter of artistic education and to conclude that since most people care nothing about it there is no reason why he should attempt to make them, he cannot really follow that inclination because the higher pleasures are a kind of religion and the impulse to pass them on is irresistible. Yet, as Mr Forster says elsewhere, 'a writer's duty often exceeds any duty he owes to society' and if he finds 'the ideals of his age' hateful 'he often ought to lead a forlorn retreat.' Still again:

> Our chief duty is to enjoy ourselves and not to lose heart, and to spread culture not because we love our fellow men, but because certain things seem to us unique and priceless, and, as it were, push us out into the world on their service.

Not everyone, certainly not every 'liberal,' will find such ideas congenial. But at least even such should be willing to admit that Mr Forster has a rare combination of virtues: detachment enough to see clearly; involvement enough to understand what the issue is. He may be the proprietor of an ivory tower, but he is not shut up in it. Towers can also be used to look out from.

65
Review

MICHAEL OAKESHOTT

There is, of course, the puzzle why a writer, who is usually rather finicky than otherwise about what he publishes, should have allowed himself to be persuaded into collecting together a volume of (for the most part) scraps and snippets, brief reviews of books, obituary notices, broadcasts of the moment, lectures of the occasion. But it would be unwise to delay over it: most readers before they reach the end of the book will have come to the conclusion that it was worthwhile—not because everything included is worth its place on its own merit, but because the pieces re-enforce one another in a manner which might escape notice had they not been collected together.

They re-enforce one another not, however, as parts of an argument, but as manifestations of a temperament, a disposition: these pieces are essentially the responses of a disposition to various occasions—personal, geographical, political and literary. It is a well-knit disposition; and it is a pre-eminently 'civilized' disposition. Consequently, the pieces may be read for the excitement of observing the disposition at work: its integration is such that, given a theme, the reader can before long anticipate what is going to be said (though not the felicity with which it is said) and remark the trueness to form which every performance exhibits. Or they may be read with admiration for the quality of the disposition—civilized without being over-civilized, detached without being olympian, flexible but not flabby, sympathetic but not sentimental.

As a civilized man, Mr Forster is disposed to suspect most of the things which make the largest stir in the world: 'Faith', violence, great men, great power, great hopes or fears, great causes and projects, great victories or failures—great anything. These are dangerous where they are not actually disastrous, if they do not destroy the quiet exercise of individual taste and preference, they hinder its enjoyment or retard its growth. What he values

SOURCE *Cambridge Journal*, April 1952, pp. 436–8.

supremely is 'personal relations', the contact of the individual man with his fellows and with the things of the world. But from 'greatness' Mr Forster would not have us turn to 'littleness'; his disposition is not given to extremes or absolutes of any kind: he is always on his guard against making too much even of what he values most. And above all it is a mistake to think that the world is or ever could be expressly organized in a manner likely to encourage the pursuit of personal relations. There have been times when the world (or parts of it) was better organized from this point of view than it is at present (indeed its present condition is peculiarly hostile to this kind of activity) but it is not to be supposed that perfection in this respect could ever come about. This kind of activity can only be enjoyed in the imprecisions of any social and political organization. Life, from this point of view, is not a campaign, but a skirmish, a game of tip-and-run in which we may hope to win a point here and there, but never hope to defeat finally the forces of worldliness. Mr Forster's disposition is, therefore, optimistic without being progressive; he is a rebel without being a reformer. This disposition belongs to him pre-eminently as an artist (for an artist can hope for nothing more than to be allowed to live and work in the imprecisions of the social order); but it belongs to him also as a man. Indeed, it would appear that since what is finally good in human life is the enjoyment of these 'personal relations', and since the artist is specially dedicated to that enjoyment, he is, in this respect, the representative civilized man.

Now, Mr Forster's arguments in support of this view of things are few and not very remarkable: if he begins an argument, he never pursues it very far; and in arguing he writes at a peculiar half-way level, neither on the surface nor in the depths, but floating in a lucid middle region where there are no difficulties—the simple problems have been solved already, and the more difficult never appear. But if the argument in Mr Forster's pages is not remarkable, what is remarkable is the manner in which this view of things is consistently reflected in the direction of his attention and in the style of his writing. Everything here—books, pictures, music, men, women, places and politics—is presented at the level of a 'personal relationship,' a reflection in the mirror of this disposition. The objects of the world are here seen only in their relation to Mr Forster himself, and in this manner he exemplifies his point of view rather than argues or expounds it. The persons who hold his attention are, for the most part, his blood relations and his friends, and they are studied as relations and friends, not as independent existences. And the point of view, the doctrine, flows over into the style: his suspicion of 'greatness' appears in his faculty for understatement, his suspicion of power appears in the studied absence of force with which he presses his judgments. This gives to Mr Forster's writing the appearance of half-heartedness and of turning away just when the intellectual difficulties begin. But everything is so much of a piece—doctrine and style so closely knit—that the critic who is disposed to convict Mr Forster of half-heartedness finds himself outmanœuvred: here is a doctrine of personal relations uncovered in a series of personal relations, here is understatement not as a device or as an ornament, but as a principle, here is a cultivated (not a casual) lukewarmness; and what could be more appropriate? And yet it won't quite do. It is difficult to put one's finger on the principle of the defect, but here and there oddities appear above the surface which indicate that something is amiss.

The figures from the past who hold Mr Forster's admiration are Erasmus, Montaigne and Gibbon: Erasmus for his tolerance, Gibbon for his aristocratic detachment, Montaigne for his scepticism. But to set Mr Forster's disposition beside that of Montaigne is revealing. The one is no more concerned than the other to argue his case or to convince the reader by mere logic, but in place of the robust self-confidence of the Master, the disciple displays a certain finicky self-centredness; the large, loose sympathy of the one is partnered in the other by a more intense sympathy but one of a narrower range; the serene humility of the one appears in the other as an unquiet humility, unquiet because it is touched with superiority. The genuine ground is there in Mr Forster's disposition, but it has been overlaid by something circumstantial: here is a Montaigne unfortunately at home in Bloomsbury. There is, also, something erratic in some of Mr Forster's judgments: his over-estimation of Lytton Strachey's achievement, of T.E. Lawrence and of Voltaire spring from the purely personal point of observation which he occupies.

Mr Forster knows that there is a problem here, he discusses it in one of these essays, 'Anonymity: An Enquiry', but he never gets to the bottom of it and his doctrine conflicts with his disposition. Since everything is known in a personal relation, the activity falls short of contemplation and therefore falls short of being either art or philosophy. And again, although there is nobody writing who is freer than Mr Forster from the illusion of the abstract, he is unable to prevent the abstract noun from creeping in—'civilization', 'culture', 'tolerance', 'Germany', 'democracy', 'the individual': the substantialist fallacy which the use of those words promotes is never quite avoided; manners of activity are turned into 'things' just when we hope that the force of Mr Forster's disposition (which is all in the other direction) will rescue him. And once more, there is ambivalence in what Mr Forster has to say about the artist and 'society'. With admirable insight he propounds the doctrine of co-operation through independence and even conflict, but he ends up by wishing to have it the other way as well. He complains that the artist is hardly done-by, and accounts for the present difficulties of the artist by attributing a 'sudden' hardening and centralization to society, forgetting that the 'diffuse society' in which the artist finds himself most at home is altogether abnormal and that in any case its occasional appearance does not touch the principle of the matter. Here, as elsewhere, Mr Forster has a sharp eye to recognize and identify his enemies, but he does not fully understand them. And on more than one occasion he hints at a golden age in the past: it is 'Hitler's Germany' which ruined what promised to be a 'golden moment', or it is 'the mentality of 1918' the loss of which brings down the 'second darkness'. Anyone who is going to discuss these matters must have a longer perspective than Mr Forster's disposition allows him.

The defect, then, such as it is, of Mr Forster's point of view is that it remains the creature of a disposition while unavoidably suggesting that it is something more. It is an admirable disposition whose activity uncovers much that lies hidden from more pretentious observers: there is more insight in these essays into the character of the 'democratic' manner of politics than in most of the more formal examinations. Mr Forster at least perceives that 'democracy' and pelagianism, so frequently identified, are, in fact, hostile to one another. But it remains a perception; it never achieves the status of a conclusion. The most argumentative of the pieces, 'What I Believe', is the most thorough exposition of the temperament which informs all these essays, but, because it remains at the difficult middle level of argument, the reader will turn from it to the essay on 'Mrs Miniver' for a less ambiguous exhibition of his skill and insight. For here the fact that nothing is pursued very far, that nothing is finished, is not a defect but belongs to the character of the piece. Mr Forster's touch has great delicacy and he can handle both with care and severity; but to grasp and to hold does not belong to him. His genius, therefore, lies in 'personal relations', where to grasp and to hold is to destroy. But when it comes to argument a different principle must prevail. To complain that his scepticism, remaining mild, never becomes a burning scepticism would be to mistake the defect; what is lacking is a profound scepticism.

The Hill of Devi
(1953)

66
Review

WILLIAM PLOMER

At the beginning of April, 1921, E.M. Forster sat on a chair and 'reflected with pleasure that there was not another European within a radius of twenty miles.' How many English novelists of his generation, or of a younger generation, have ever been able to say the same? Would it not have been better for them, and for us, if there had been more of them? Whatever the answers to those questions, India provided Mr Forster with what he calls 'the great opportunity of my life.' *The Longest Journey* could be considered his most surprising book; *Howards End* may or may not be the best known and most widely read of his novels; but *A Passage to India* may conceivably be seen, when the uncertainties of contemporary assessment have fallen away, to be his most significant book. If there is any other imaginative work of twentieth-century literature in English which is in the least to be compared with it as a foreshadowing of the now wholly altered relationship of Europe and Asia, or as an illumination of the eve of the change, it would be interesting to know its name.

The chair on which Mr Forster sat so fruitfully reflecting was in a palace in the State of Dewas Senior, the less unimportant of a pair of small States in the middle of India which have since come to an end. It was not the first time he had been there. The first visit, a brief one, was in 1912–1913, in company with Lowes Dickinson. The second was from April to November, 1921, when he held the post of private secretary to the ruler of the State, whom he had from the first admired and soon came to love. When *A Passage to India* was reprinted in the Everyman series in 1942 the dedication had been enlarged to include the name of 'His Highness Sir Tukoji Rao Puar III, K.C.S.I., Maharajah of Dewas State Senior, whom I knew as Bapu Sahib.' By that time Bapu Sahib was dead. On first acquaintance in 1912 he had seemed 'a most charming and able young man'; in retrospect he is described as 'certainly a genius and possibly a saint'; and the measure of Mr

SOURCE *New Statesman and Nation*, 17 October 1953, pp. 457–8.

Forster's special regard for him is in the statement:

> Quite often I did not understand him—he was too incalculable—but it was possible with him to reach a platform where calculations were unnecessary. It would not be possible with an Englishman.

Bapu Sahib, much harder for the reader to understand in spite of elucidation, is one of the two principal figures in Mr Forster's new book; the other is Mr Forster himself.

Parrot voices down the years, even among the intelligentsia, have been heard protesting that he has not written enough, or often enough. Sometimes the parrots, if discussion has ensued, have shown themselves not to have read anything like all the works of this author and not to have apprehended very well the ones they have read. But even the dullest of them had an inkling that while other fictionists might be more copious, Mr Forster had a quite uncommon claim to attention, because when he did write he spoke with what seemed unique conviction in a voice unlike anybody else's. To survey his writings as a whole, including the occasional essays and pamphlets and book-reviews, is to see each, even when below his best, as part of the whole utterance of a man with a forceful, complex, and altogether fresh comment to make about human beings. His knowledge of the way they do behave is inseparable from his concern about the way they might behave. It is as a critical commentator, as philosopher or moralist, not as a yarn-spinner, that he makes at the same time so entertaining and so formidable and consistent an effect.

The Hill of Devi is immensely entertaining and effective. Amounting, as its author says, to a 'record of a vanished civilisation,' it consists mostly of letters written by himself from Dewas in 1921, with a few from the earlier visit to India. They describe Bapu Sahib and his Court, the everyday happenings, the ceremonies and pleasures, the deeper aspirations and surface absurdities, the private and public harmonies and crises, notably those involving Indians with Anglo-Indians. All is reported vividly and with a play of feelings, with gaiety, indignation, anxiety, tenderness, sadness—but especially gaiety. And an interspersed commentary puts everything in perspective—or at least in Mr Forster's perspective, for it was hardly his plan in this book to balance the merits of the British Raj, or the virtues and achievements of many of its upholders in his own or earlier times against the strains of the situation in India as he knew it.

Mr Forster has himself written *What I Believe,* and Rose Macaulay, in her book about him, had already made lists of things he believed in—including personal relationships, individuality, affection, liberty, and democracy—and of those he disbelieved in—including nationalism, empire, militarism, Christianity, dictatorship, big business, and schoolmasters. It is plain that his opinions must have been widely regarded as evidence of sentimentality, weakness, or mischief-making, and they may continue to be strong irritants in some spheres. It is much to be hoped so. To have a head as well as a heart, and to be capable of letting the heart prompt if not rule the head, does not always make for the incubation of temperate views or for a demonstrative support of accepted notions: it is more likely to lead to the formulation of vital and sometimes uncomforting truths. Nor does the liberal rationalism of Cambridge and Bloomsbury—which has its blind spots and its own conventionalities—always act as an emollient. 'Nothing enrages Anglo-India more,' he wrote in *A Passage to India*, 'than the lantern of reason if it is exhibited for one moment after its extinction is decreed': for 'Anglo-India' it would be possible to substitute, with equal truth and at any time, far greater herds in other stamping-grounds. The gentleness, the wit, the skill, the charm of Mr Forster's writing are famous: what is sometimes overlooked is its determinedly revolutionary nature. The playfulness of the letters in *The Hill of Devi* is delicious—but they are depth-charges. They are part of Mr Forster's life-long indication of a way of living our lives very different from any that is ever likely to be officially taught or approved anywhere.

'I have had twenty-five years' experience of this country,' said the 'thin, biting voice' of the Collector in *A Passage to India*, and during those twenty-five years I have never known anything but disaster result when English people and Indians attempt to be intimate socially.' Some of us, who have had the luck to find ourselves for any length of time in places where there was 'not another European within a radius of twenty miles,' whether in Asia or Africa or elsewhere, and who have been able to 'reflect with pleasure' upon such a situation, have heard and pondered similar pronouncements. Without saying 'I told you so,' without pretending—at least too openly—to superior wisdom, we can at least remember having had some foresight of what the fear of intimacy might lead to, and having murmured some sort of warning. Affection, Mr Forster remarks, was the only force to which Bapu Sahib responded, and, in the last of his letters of 1921, he observes that although good manners may not avert a political upheaval, they can minimise it. Intimacy and affection apart, in the rise of civil disobedience he saw a 'paying for the insolence of Englishmen *and* Englishwomen out here in the past.' So others have seen elsewhere—for instance, in the rise of Mau Mau—something generated by that lack of proper consideration on the part of a governing race towards the governed which amounts to an absence of good manners. Without them there can be no confidence and little hope, and nothing even approaching affection or intimacy.

Confidence, affection, intimacy: these were just what developed at Dewas between Bapu Sahib and Mr Forster. But the post of private secretary to Bapu Sahib involved him in responsibilities for which he did not feel himself fitted by temperament or training. In the end he had to tell His Highness so, and furthermore to point out that he had not been required to do the sort of things he was fitted to do. Fancy expecting Mr Forster to fiddle with electric light and motor-cars and irrigation, as if all Englishmen must be mechanically minded!

> Pipes have been laid on (for example) all down the flower border, and connected with an empty water tank ... It is connected—in its turn—with an almost empty well, and if there was any water in the well it would be raised into the tank by an electric pump of insufficient power to raise the water. You are not at the end of the chain yet, for the electric pump is connected with the Electric House, which is only on at night when all its energies are required for the Palace lighting. So there we are, and there are the flowers dying.

As it happened, more than the flowers were dying: a civilisation was dying. Not just inefficiency but a blend of 'idleness, incompetence and extravagance' was leading to bankruptcy for the State and exile for its ruler. Mr Forster saw the muddle quite as clearly as any official could have done, indeed saw it more clearly than most officials might have done, because he always saw that there was 'something precious' among the rubbish. Not having more than temporary and incidental responsibilities in his post he was without the anxieties of a career official, and could laugh, or seem to laugh, at nearly everything, at least in his letters home. He meant them to be amusing. They were and are, and it looks as if some day many Forster letters, collected and edited and printed, are going to make a full and brilliant complement to his printed work. It is a safe bet that they will prove more durable, as they are certainly more truthful and diverting than—no, comparisons are uncalled for.

One of the show-pieces of this new book is an account of a religious festival and its fantastic 'rites in which a European can seldom have shared.' It shows Mr Forster doing his best to understand religious emotion and to make allowances for it, like somebody in a Max Beerbohm drawing. When his biography comes to be written, it will be illuminating if his anti- religious feelings can be traced to their various sources, some of which are obvious. The account of the festival prompts a re-reading of certain chapters in *A Passage to India.* About the composition of that book Mr Forster now prints a note, with the interesting information that he might not have completed it without the encouragement of Leonard Woolf.

67
A Private Secretary for the Maharajah

NEWTON ARVIN

Probably not many of E. M. Forster's readers are aware that he was once, for a few months, private secretary to the Maharajah of a small Indian state, that he was elevated for his services to the rank of a minor noble, and that, on his departure, he was invested with the highest honor but one that the little state could confer, the Tukoji Rao III Gold Medal. Yet this is the case, and *The Hill of Devi* is the record of that experience.

It was in 1921 that Mr Forster's short and certainly unexpected career as an administrator was played out. On an earlier trip to India in 1912–13 he paid a visit to the State of Dewas Senior in Central India, and though this visit was a matter of only a few days, it had been long enough for him to form a lively impression of the somewhat comic-opera quality of Dewas as he himself puts it, making the familiar Gilbert and Sullivan allusion and a much more serious impression of the reigning Prince, the complex and puzzling but genuinely likeable and admirable Bapu Sahib, whose official title was Sir Tukoji Rao III.

Bapu Sahib had, on his side, formed a pleasant impression of Mr Forster, and when, in 1921, the office of private secretary fell vacant, Mr Forster was appealed to come out to India and occupy it. As it happened, he had already begun *A Passage to India* and perhaps the desire to go on with the book in more or less the setting it represents was one of the motives that led him to agree. At any rate, out he did go, and from April to October he made as it appears a manful effort to carry out the duties his curious office entailed—the supervision of the gardens, the tennis courts, the motors, the Guest House and the Electric House. He himself came to feel that he was accomplishing nothing and that the general muddle, incompetence and

SOURCE *The New York Times Book Review*, 25 October 1953, pp. 3, 49.

inefficiency had proved too much for him, all this, however, did no injury to his relations with the warm-hearted Bapu Sahib, and when they parted on Mr Forster's leaving Dewas, it was as the most genuine of friends.

The Hill of Devi is composed mainly of letters Mr Forster wrote both in 1912–13 and in 1921 to people in England, though these letters are supplemented by explanatory or amplifying passages written for the sake of the book itself. The result, without being or claiming to be a work of massive importance, and without throwing any specially new light on Mr Forster's literary powers, has at least much of the interest, much of the novelistic liveliness and intellectual acuteness that one would expect of any work of Mr Forster's, however secondary.

Many readers, quite naturally, will read it partly with *A Passage to India* in mind, though, in fact, there is no very close *superficial* relation between the two books. The novel was finished after Mr Forster returned to England, and was published in 1924, but neither Dewas Senior as a scene nor Bapu Sahib as a personage is to be encountered in its pages—understandably, since the work was conceived and perhaps even thought out with some fullness before the episode of 1921.

Intangibly, nevertheless, one is reminded of certain *strains* in the novel as one reads *The Hill of Devi* and there are at least two passages in the latter work that, so far as this reader's memory serves, do 'point forward' quite tangibly to *A Passage to India.* There is a story about a near accident to a motor-car occasioned by an unidentified animal dashing out of a ravine and charging it, which suggested a supernormal interpretation to the strangely endowed Bapu Sahib, and which reappears in the episode of the automobile accident in the eighth chapter of *A Passage.* On a larger scale, the evocation of the Birth Festival of Krishna, in the last chapters of the novel, clearly derives from Mr Forster's exhaustive and, to him, exhausting impressions of the Gokul Ashtami Festival as it was celebrated at Dewas in August of 1921.

There are one or two other festivals in these letters, and a great deal that is partly amusing and partly depressing by way of evoking the confusion, the utter lack of privacy, the noisiness, the incompletion or ruinousness, the 'rubble and mortar' of everything, that characterized life in Dewas Senior. But in the end the deepest interest the book has, and its imaginative center, is the really affecting treatment of the character and career of Bapu Sahib himself.

The career was a tragic one, in a pretty strict sense of the word 'tragic'. Bapu Sahib died in Pondicherry, sixteen years after his son and heir had fled from Dewas with fantastic charges against his father of attempted poisoning, seven years after the little state had gone bankrupt, and four years after he himself, having quarrelled violently with the Government of India, had virtually fled from his domains and holed himself in French India, where, of course, he could not be molested.

There was a sense in which this catastrophe was, as such catastrophes always are, the product of Bapu Sahib's limitations as a person his touchy pride, his suspiciousness, his failure in what we call 'realism,' and so forth but the preponderant and final impression we get of him is not that of his shortcomings but of his virtues—his humor, his resourcefulness, his spontaneous affectionateness and expansive generosity, his extraordinary insights and deep religious feelings. There is a strong suggestion of greatness in the portrait Mr Forster does of him. Bapu Sahib, he says, 'was certainly a genius and possibly a saint and he had to be a king.'

68
Genius and Saint

V. S. PRITCHETT

Mr E. M. Forster gave two cheers for democracy, and it looks as though he would now go to two and a half for the defunct Indian state of Dewas Senior, which he describes in *The Hill of Devi* (Harcourt, Brace). Devi—the Goddess's Residence—is the sacred mountain that stands above the capital city. At the summit is the cave of Chamunda, inhabited by a barbarous vermilion object whose peculiar religious power presides over the town below and the book. Mr Forster was in Dewas in 1912 and 1913 and again in 1921, the first time as a guest of the ruler, the second time as his private secretary. From this Gilbertian monarchy, Mr Forster sent home letters to his mother, his aunts, and one or two friends; these letters he has since recovered. Linked by commentary and by a portrait of the ruler, they make an ingenious and deceptively negligent impression of life at the court of an Indian prince whose little kingdom was going to pieces. Mr Forster's genius has always been for the casual touch, the seemingly amateur and personal view. He has been the sternest opponent of professional attitudes. The velvet glove of the softy encloses the iron hand of independent liberal principle. Who else is so adroit in his timing or so simply imparts the strict, proselytizing ethic of the right to personal fuss? There are many good photographs of the court in the book, though none of Dewas, and one astonishing picture of a lady got up in the extravagance of the Edwardian mode. This fancy-dress article turns out to be Mr Forster himself, in the regalia he was obliged to wear in Dewas. A visiting British governor was so shocked by this Schiaparelli touch that he coldly ignored the ritual of squirting scent on Mr Forster's handkerchief at a formal reception. The 'insult' did not pass without major political repercussions in Delhi, matters of deep principle being involved. (Could one squirt a European in Indian dress?) I need hardly say that Mr Forster won. The moral of *Howards End*

SOURCE *New Yorker*, 30 January 1954, pp. 85–9.

is borne out by life; the Schlegels of this world beat the Wilcoxes every time. Hurrah for the anti-team spirit!

In Mr Forster's time, Dewas was a family affair, divided into the Senior and Junior branches. Two rajahs, cousins, governed independently, each with his own palace and shrines in the same small capital, each with his own army, brass band, and waterworks; their only common property was the national flagstaff, the upper half belonging to one ruler and the lower to the other. Their domain was divided not by towns or sections but field by field and street by street. The conditions of life and the customs of the people belonged to the Fourteenth century, but at court they were confounded by the grotesque invasion of the Twentieth, for the young ruler of Dewas Senior liked to be modern. Modernity meant motorcars that always broke down and elaborate water systems not connected with the water supply, electricity whose equipment was never properly installed (throughout the book there are cries of 'More trouble with the electric light!'), grand pianos whose keys had stuck and whose frames had been split by the heat and in which squirrels hid, pictures like 'Love Me, Love My Dog' and appalling oleographs on the walls. A new suite of drawing-room chairs lay disembowelled in the palace, for the court preferred to sit on the floor, and the bathroom cupboard was full of teapots. When apprised of all this by the worried new secretary, the ruler was delighted. He at once dictated long telegrams to Bombay and other places. He loved sending telegrams.

The problem of the ruler's character is the subject of many of Mr Forster's letters. What kind of man was he? Hard to say. He was twenty-four, and one of those tiny, diamond-bright, and delicate Hindus who are affectionate, mischievous, and proud. He had a serious religious temperament of the questing and mystical kind. He was deeply susceptible to women. He was 'a genius, and possibly a saint, and he had to be a king.' The last was his tragedy. States are run on money, and he was erratic with it; he collected tribute in silver coin and paid out only when pressed. He was hampered by the intrigues of his powerful female relatives, especially the terrifying dowager, his aunt. She fatally offended his wife's family, which was damaging to his marriage. And after a few years of picturesque muddle his state went bankrupt; the British deposed him and he died, snubbed by the Viceroy and in angry exile. His only political memorial was a scathing obituary in the London *Times.* About this judgment, Mr Forster is indignant. The ruler believed, like Mr Forster, in the heart. The author adds, 'I think he was fond of me, though one can never be sure of saints.' One can also never be sure of kings.

Mr Forster could not ever find out what his function in Dewas was. If it was mending the electric light or tinkering with the water supply, he was lost. If it was writing, he tried—this was in 1921—to go on with *A Passage to India,* which had been in suspense for years, but to write was impossible, for there was not only the daily struggle with the electricity and the water, there were intrigues at the court, state visits, perpetual noise, feasts, processions, and a royal childbirth, when the royal band played almost continually for a week, sometimes in the mother's chamber, 'to cheer her up' while the child was being born. The hot season was ferocious, the monsoon deafening. How Mr Forster wished that he had the practical gifts of his predecessor, the Colonel Wilson he temporarily replaced, a planner of the old school and a rumbustious, natural handyman, who had nevertheless introduced the water system without noticing there was no water. Ill and in England, the Colonel, already suspecting that Mr Forster was after his job and opening his correspondence from his lady friends, was showing signs of temper amounting to persecution mania. Mr Forster gave up and devoted himself wholly to his affection for the ruler.

The ruler's tastes were now sensual, now ascetically religious. God, he thought, had become separated from man unintentionally because He had been so distracted by the incessant demands of creation. One might modestly hope that He would one day turn His head and remember. In the meantime, the ruler saw omens and was piously purified after train journeys. When a jungle animal dashed out at his car one evening, he was disturbed. He surmised that this was the soul of a man whom he had knocked down and killed in an accident some years before, that the soul had now assumed animal form and was taking its revenge. For relaxation, the ruler and the court gave themselves up to practical jokes, and the author of *Howards End* found himself passing childish evenings in knocking people's turbans off and tickling their ankles while indulging in fits of giggles.

The playfulness in Dewas was continuous. The tiny ruler bounced up and down with delight in the cushions of his throne whenever a state function was over. There were large elements of mischief and horseplay in the sacred ceremonies, even in the eight-day feast of Gokul Ashtami, in honor of the rebirth of Krishna. The bad taste was worrying to the English member of the household. The only beauty in the religious observances was in the faces of the worshippers. Even the ruler's role at this feast was strange. There was his ritual vigil before the sacred Feather Bed. There was the dance at the altar, recalling the ritual dances of Seville and the dancing of David, when the ruler jigged up and down twanging a stringed instrument. At the end of two hours, he reached the point of ecstasy or trance and started composing poetry, which was taken down by a clerk. How to reconcile the fatuous with the evident exaltation? Very puzzling to the future Fellow of King's College, Cambridge, who was dressed up in petticoats and had his face smeared with red and black powders. And there was more to come. When, in the course of this celebration, the doll called Krishna, which had a face like 'an ill-tempered pea,' was 'born,' a model of the village in which it was born was thrown into a lake, colored smoke was discharged, and the ruler performed a fertility ritual that involved churning imaginary milk with a stick. Real butter was also dabbed on the forehead of a noble, who had to try to lick it.

Very deep meaning in all this, said His Highness, though few know it, and Mr Forster modestly adds:

> I had a little butter, too.

And after that:

> We went under a huge black vessel, rather handsome, that was hung up in the aisle and we banged it with our painted sticks, and the vessel broke and a mass of grain soaked in milk fell down on our heads. We fed each other with it. This was the last of the games and the mess was now awful and the swarms of flies came in.

Since a great deal of the interest of *The Hill of Devi* lies in the fact that it is the raw material from which *A Passage to India* was written, we naturally turn to the corresponding scenes in that novel. There the problem of bad taste is solved by stressing the symbolism. Here is some correlative scripture:

> All laughed exultantly at discovering that the divine sense of humour coincided with their own. 'God is love!' There is fun in heaven! God can play practical jokes upon Himself, draw chairs away from beneath His own posteriors, set His own turbans on fire, and steal His own petticoats when He bathes. By sacrificing good taste this worship achieved what Christianity has shirked: the inclusion of merriment.

The rice becomes 'the divine mess,' the flies come in and 'claim their share of God's bounty.' It may all be true, but one is never quite happy about the symbolism in Mr Forster's novels. I prefer the direct statement of *The Hill of Devi* in this particular episode.

What did the ruler himself believe? It was impossible to tell. One could only know that the Unseen was close to him, but what was the Unseen? The ruler was mercurial, his moods visibly moving, like the changes of light and shadow over his face, his delicate hands, and his feet. The evanescence of these continual movements could suggest mystery when perhaps there was no more than the radiance of change. Did he simply have what we call temperament? Mr Forster, with his lifelong interest in symbolism and allegory, will not leave it at that prosaic and rational level. The ruler, he says, believed in the heart, but if we are to believe in the virtue of that susceptibility, we must also believe in the follies, the hatreds, and the repugnancies of the heart. There were, in any case, certain Wilcoxian figures, fancy-dress ghosts from some Indian *Howards End*, to be reckoned with. There was the Maharajah of Chhatarpur, for example, who wrote to Rider Haggard and asked him to send out a secretary exactly resembling the Olaf of one of that writer's novels. Another and vulgar potentate got the dowager drunk on brandy:

> 'Not good of His Highness, not right of him. It's his joke,' she sighed . . .

> 'Now, my dear Morgan, now [said the ruler to Mr Forster], you begin to realize some of my problems.'

Then there is the mystery of the collapse of the ruler's marriage. Hopeless to get at the truth here. The affair had begun inauspiciously. The groom and his father-in-law met in the state procession on the wedding day, the band playing 'Oft in Danger, Oft in Woe':

> Elephants with silver howdahs and trappings of gold, two of them dragging a sort of railway saloon into which the Dewas ladies were pushed; the bridegroom perched on high on the roof of the saloon—it was fenced with a golden rail to prevent him falling off. Slowly they advanced and swiftly the ladies quarrelled. His aunt was always jealous and awkward and tried to separate him from his mother, whom she accused of having 'unlucky feet'—i.e., the evil eye; a bitter feud sprang up in his sumptuous camp which he had to pacify.

By a lucky and familiar stroke of incompetence, the bomb that was to be thrown at the couple did not arrive in time, but the dowager was really more formidable than any bomb. Whether her intrigues wrecked the marriage, whether the ruler seduced one of his wife's maids (he denied this accusation), we cannot tell. The fact is that behind the attempt to rule by the heart—or, at any rate, to live by it—there was Intrigue. Intrigue was the heart's seamy side. Mr Forster noted that the face and mind of his affectionate friend changed when that word was mentioned; it became cunning and cruel. The diamondlike saint and genius who was in contact with Krishna in his ecstasies was in touch also with forces darker and more intricate than any his English secretary could imagine. Mr Forster does no more than forgivingly suggest that the ruler might have been more ascetic as the years went on. As for the dowager, she seemed a likable woman of the worldly kind, having 'that slight air of despair that suits an Indian lady.' In view of her reputation as a poisoner, Mr Forster says, taking tea with her was like banqueting with Catherine de'Medici. But *was* she a poisoner? More mystery, and in mystery the ruler loved to live. Clearly he was entranced by it; it was not unlike the uncertainties, the elaborate quests of his religion. (Perhaps his religion was a sort of spying on God.)

In the meantime, the India outside this charmed and idiotic kingdom had become turbulent. The Indian revolutionaries had no use for this rotting state; the British, who were efficient administrators, could no longer afford to tolerate its scandalously bad administration. Reforms were proposed; the ruler was bewildered but hoped to put trouble off by 'proclaiming a new constitution,' which meant merely that he would make a pretty speech. The British became insistent. Lord Reading, the Viceroy, who had ruthlessly climbed into eminence up the ladder of the law, was no man to deal with rare human beings. (He and the whole Delhi set were indignant when *A Passage to India* came out.) The ruler's pride was offended, but the Viceroy refused to see him. Sending off more long telegrams, refusing all the compromises those who loved him had recommended, the ruler went into exile. Living by the heart had failed, and that, Mr Forster says, is the kind of thing that goes down in history. The ruler was indeed a rare spirit, but rare spirits do odd things; his flight turned out to have been carefully prepared, for he went off to the French territory of Pondicherry with an immense amount of royal treasure. Even the howdahs of his elephants had been stripped of their silver.

The Hill of Devi is a gracious piece of collage done by a writer who has brought the art of leaving out to a high point of perfection. Casually he will utter the worldly aphorism 'It is poor work at the best of times, spending money on rich men,' and will take his usual stand for the importance of weakness, for the value of the unofficial face, the unofficial manner, the personal look from which integrity has removed all the egotism, vanity, and offense. A less vain writer does not exist. Does the book throw any light on the controversy about Mr Forster's understanding of the Indian scene? He certainly went very deep in Dewas. Being a man of principle, he was eager to argue the supreme value of personal relationships from a 'bad' case. But just as he did not know or did not experience the sensual side of the ruler's character and was cut off by intellect and temperament from the sensual life of the Hindus, so also one feels that his sympathy and insights are those of the disengaged. People are committed by their passions. The vulgar British whom Mr Forster satirized in *A Passage to India* were unjustly treated by him; they, too, had their allegory and symbols, and were men committed where he was not. In that book, he was like Nurse, who ruthlessly punishes the bad boys, but, like Nurse, he had his favorites. It is odd to have been in India without understanding excess. The intellectual humanism of Cambridge was separated by centuries from the trances and sensualities of Dewas. It is odd, too, to have been worried chiefly by the aesthetic anomalies. Mr Forster understands being but he does not understand action, because passion and will direct it, because guilt and remorse will be its outcome, because they commit. But he redressed a balance, and *The Hill of Devi* shows an original mind in the making. It was Mr Forster who was the genius, if not the saint.

69
Forster's India

STEVEN MARCUS

The Hill of Devi is E. M. Forster's account—composed mainly of letters written to people in England—of his two trips to the Indian state of Dewas Senior; the first, in 1912–13, ended quickly; the second was longer and took place in 1921 when Forster was employed as Private Secretary to the ruler, His Highness Sir Tukoji Rao III, K.C.I.E., the Maharajah of Dewas Senior. The book is chiefly occupied with descriptions of the daily life of the Court of the Maharajah, the way the little, anomalous state was ruled and misruled, bankrupted and finally ruined; it also follows the rapid degeneration in the fortunes of the Maharajah himself, concluding with his flight from his Palace to Pondicherry, where he exiled himself and died.

Dewas Senior was 'an amazing little state, which can have no parallel, except in a Gilbert and Sullivan opera.' The royal family was Rajput and Maratha, split in the middle of the eighteenth century into Senior and Junior halves, ruling tiny, neighboring states. A queer and apparently motiveless rivalry sprang up between the sections of the dynasty, and the atmosphere of the Court of Dewas Senior was heavy with spies and emissaries from the adjacent court, with spies from other more powerful states, with British Political Agents, Agents to the Governor General, rumored and impending visits from the Viceroy and the Prince of Wales, and all the familiar and cruelly farcical apparatus, rigmarole and stage machinery of colonial government—a story often told, but one always worth listening to again. Dewas Senior was in the middle of rebuilding and abortively Westernizing itself (the Maharajah had read Aristotle's *Politics* with his English tutor), and had, like so much else in Colonial India, got bogged down through lack of energy and money; it was a chaos and a shambles when Forster arrived, and was even worse when he left.

> The New Palace ... is still building, and the parts of it that were built ten years ago are already falling down. You would weep at the destruction,

SOURCE *Partisan Review*, January–February 1954, pp. 115–19.

> expense, and hideousness, and I do almost. We live amongst rubble and mortar, and excavation whence six men carry a basket of earth, no larger than a cat's, twenty yards once in five minutes ... two pianos (one a grand), a harmonium, and a dulciphone, all new and all unplayable, their notes sticking and their frames cracked by the dryness ... dozens of warped towel-horses are stabled there or a new suite of drawing-room chairs with their insides gushing out. I open a cupboard near the bath and find it full of teapots, I ask for a bookcase and it bows when it sees me and lies rattling on the floor. I don't know what to do about it all, and scarcely what to feel. It's no good trying to make something different out of it, for it is as profoundly Indian as an Indian temple.

The life of the Court proceeded through this mess, or perhaps it is more precise to say that the life of the Court *was* this mess: confusion and vulgarity and broken-downness were the conditions under which it thrived as well as perished. For although Gilbert and Sullivan might have written an opera describing this state, the original version surely was in German, a burlesque in three acts by Hegel, called *The Philosophy of History*. It is amazing how cogent Hegel's analysis of the spiritual life of India still seems, how thoroughly a book like *The Hill of Devi* ratifies its speculations. Almost everything Forster describes offers the reader a view of the Spirit still entangled with nature not at one with it, but not yet separated into self-consciousness either. And the struggle of the Spirit to find itself, to become sensible of its existence in the material and social reality that encompasses and, in the denseness of India, almost strangles it, generates the two dominant modes of consciousness in Indian life—the alternate obliviousness to and worship of that overwhelming material reality. In a typical Indian complex of ideas, spirit seems to be both absent and immanent everywhere at the same time; for the Indian there seems to be no sense of the contradiction, or at least the unruliness, present in this notion, which at once disquiets the Westerner.

> The unseen was always close to him, even when he was joking or intriguing. Red paint on a stone could evoke it ... It was difficult to be sure what he did believe (outside the great mystic moments) or what he thought right or wrong.

In this garbled world oleographs of Krishna and the Archbishop of Canterbury can hang next to each other on the wall, and men and cows can sleep, undisturbed, in the same room. Forster, making decorations for the religious festival Gokul Ashtami, the celebration of the birth of Krishna—the same ritual described in *A Passage to India*—took some abandoned 'glass battery cases' and filled them with water and live fish, 'into which some humanitarian idiot dropped handfuls of flour so that the fish should not starve. You couldn't have seen a whale.' Not an idea or an object is allowed to remain for a moment in an unassimilated state, but is at once caught up in the swirling disorganization of the Court. (One wonders just how long the beautiful geometrical patterns of Le Corbusier's new city in India will stand as they are, how soon it will be before they begin to burgeon with festoons and votive images, and to succumb to the static heterogeneity of Indian culture.)

Into this scene comes—as he has always done—the Englishman; but in *The Hill of Devi* he is not a conqueror or a merchant, a missionary or an educator. From Sir Walter Raleigh to Sir Evelyn Baring the destiny of a considerable part of the English upper classes has been involved with subjugated peoples, and the attitudes Englishmen have developed toward them are almost as various as those they admit to in the relations of the classes at home. But Forster is no T. E. Lawrence, toying with his personality and acting the great white Sheikh, nor a Mary Kingsley, with Bible and black bombazine umbrella, stalking through the jungles, imperturbable in her convictions and her love. Forster has sundered all relations with the gunboats and the cotton mills; he has deliberately renounced the shibboleth of the Colonial, the *Civis Romanus sum*, that dreadful apostrophe by whose authority the battleships were sent into the harbors of Piraeus and Canton, polo fields laid out in every outpost, and Englishmen universally compelled to dress for dinner in the tropics. Forster casts a jaundiced eye on everything English and everything the English have done. He squats with the Indians until his legs cramp:

> The courtiers saw that I was in pain, and told the servants to move the tray that I might stretch, but I refused, nor would I touch the entire English dinner that was handed round during the meal.

He is happy that he is alone with them, contemplating 'with pleasure that there was not another European within a radius of twenty miles.' On the other hand he is no Bishop Colenso, converted by the natives he came to convert:

> ... it is difficult to make vivid what seems so fatuous. there is no dignity, no taste, no form, and though I am dressed as a Hindu I shall never become one. I don't think one ought to be irritated with idolatry because one can see from the faces of the people that it touches something very deep in their hearts. But it is natural that missionaries, who think these ceremonies wrong as well as inartistic, should lose their tempers.

Forster always tries to maintain those trying attitudes of disinterested intelligence and enlightened sympathy, the only things he knows that he can trust: unlike the colonial English he has no faith in the white man's mission, or God's either, for that matter. His principal motive for being there at all is intellectual curiosity, that quality whose absence from the English middle-class mind was so deplored by Matthew Arnold. Forster has faith only in the occasional intelligence of human nature, and he keeps going, in the face of the greed, inefficiency and stupidity which surround him, by believing that if one looks hard enough he will find people who are interesting and worth loving.

In Bapu Sahib, the Maharajah of Dewas Senior, he found that person, 'Affection, all through his chequered life, was the only force to which Bapu Sahib responded.' 'He was certainly a genius and possibly a saint, and he had to be a king.' The Maharajah was a deeply religious Hindu; he spoke and wrote excellent English (Forster speaks no Indian tongue), and in several ways resembled Aziz in *A Passage to India*—a man who unsuccessfully tried to straddle two cultures. Surrounded by spies and courtiers, pampered and bullied by the Colonial Administration, alternately intimate and remote, he was just the character who, in his incalculability, has always fascinated Forster. And yet his personality never comes through in the book. It is the one thing Forster does not conceive successfully—one has merely Forster's word that the mystery surrounding the being of the Maharajah is there, but one never gets the full sense of that mystery, and whether it really touches something universal and imponderable in all human affairs. And, one suspects, Forster overrates the Maharajah's genius as well, for those sayings and writings of his that Forster includes in this book are not nearly so impressive as he supposes them to be. This is the same kind of failure that has been noted about *A Passage to India* in relation to the Marabar Caves and Mrs Moore—the mystery is more an assertion by the author than an actual presence; if the reader feels the mystery, it is by submitting to Forster's belief in it rather than by experiencing it directly in the fabric of the novel. What is clear in *The Hill of Devi*, however, is the deep bond of affection that was forged between Forster and the Maharajah; all the silliness which cost the latter a kingdom could not damage it. But the content of that relation is never realized.

It is not easy to suggest why this should be once again the weakness in Forster's writing. No doubt there is a hiatus between the ability to describe accurately the conditions of life and spirit in Dewas Senior and the more demanding skill required to present its most complex personality—a hiatus that might be bridged by the evocation, say, of Hegel rather than Gilbert and Sullivan, although not necessarily so. I don't mean to imply that Forster doesn't, in general, apprehend his subject with his usual acuteness, but there is clearly a reticence on his part to do more than hint at what this personality is like. Perhaps this relaxing of his critical faculties in relation to the Maharajah is the result of love and friendship—perhaps it is something more, a refusal to consider personality in abstract terms, a fear of defiling an affectionate memory by relating it to ideas. Whatever it may be, the character of the Maharajah, and what it was like to be in close relation to such a remarkably talented Indian, is the weakest thing in the book, while the description of the State of Dewas Senior, and its effect on an intelligent Englishman, is the strongest. *The Hill of Devi* is an excellent account of what it was to be an Englishman and a liberal in a decrepit Anglo-India, and that leaves it an excellent travel book, one of the best I know.

Marianne Thornton
(1956)

70
Review

RONALD BRYDEN

Henry Thornton, the Evangelical banker and M.P. for Southwark, died in 1815, leaving three sons and six daughters, the eldest named Marianne, the second youngest Laura. Laura Thornton married a Welsh clergyman, the Rev. Charles Forster, and had a son, Edward, who in turn married and produced, in 1879, a son who was christened Edward Morgan. Eight years later, Marianne Thornton died at the age of ninety, bequeathing to this great-nephew of hers a legacy which enabled him to go to Cambridge, travel to Italy and India, and become the finest English novelist, so far, of this century. This book is E. M. Forster's memorial to his benefactress: a work of piety and affection, and also of extraordinary fascination and art.

A good deal of its fascination is historical. Mr Forster sub-titles it 'a domestic biography'; but the domestic life of the Thorntons at Battersea Rise, their vast old house on Clapham Common, was led only just behind some of the more stirring scenes of the early nineteenth century. Henry Thornton was a leading member of the 'Clapham Sect', and his house became a meeting place for its elders—the Venns, Grants, Macaulays and Stephens. Hannah More and Wilberforce were intimate friends, with whom he worked closely in the cause of Abolition and popular education. The Thornton children used to visit the More sisters down in Somerset, where they lived with two old servants and a couple of cats named Non-Resistance and Passive Obedience, and be regaled with country fare and tales of Hannah's early friendships with Burke, Dr Johnson and Horace Walpole. Marianne became, after her father's death, the Sect's chief correspondent with Hannah, bed-ridden now, and had to describe for her the triumphant May Meeting of 1824, when Tom Macaulay burst to fame with a blazing speech against slavery. Wilberforce, so oddly child-like himself, often played with them in Battersea Rise garden; there, after one painful afternoon trying, with a parliamentary deputation, to persuade a half-drunken Queen

SOURCE *Cambridge Review*, 12 May 1956, p. 536.

Caroline to renounce her coronation for an allowance from George IV, he came to solace his spirit among the flowers, and was overheard murmuring praises to a tranquil, splendid moss-rose, ending 'And Oh how unlike the Queen's countenance!'

Other windows open more generally on the past. Marianne visits Waterloo with her guardians in 1817, and boys offer her bones, buttons and hair for sale. She attends a meeting of Edward Irving's apocalyptic 'church', and compares the shouts of its spirit-taken witnesses, shuddering, to the unforgettable screams of a cousin operated on at Battersea Rise some years earlier, for cancer perhaps, without anaesthetics. And the central incident of her life opens a particularly curious window upon a dead world of conscience. The Thornton clan were broken, exiled from the family home they loved almost better than bridegrooms, by the decision of Marianne's brother, Henry Thornton the younger, to marry his deceased wife's sister. To us, the old prohibition is a footnote to *Culture and Anarchy*, a joke in *Major Barbara*. To them, it is tragedy and ruin. Wounding letters fly. Angry sisters, vicious with the shame, shut their doors forever on their brother and the wanton sister-in-law. Defiant, the outcast pair flee abroad to perform the incestuous rite. Battersea Rise stands empty, dishonoured. Only Marianne, homeless after fifty years at her brother's side, bewildered between love and revulsion, struggles to save something from the wreck: a suspicious truce, a melancholy amity.

But inevitably, the light Mr Forster sheds on his family and the past cannot interest us as much as the light he allows them to shed on him. In form, the book is a proper Victorian memoir, told mainly by the letters and diaries of the subject: but in format, it is a companion to *The Hill of Devi*, and like that volume, lets biography shade into autobiography. Unobtrusively, Mr Forster is always at the reader's elbow, pointing and appraising, delighted by Marianne's kindly practicality where it is a question of family or baby-schools, depressed by her heavy little jibes at Jews and governesses, her Victorian fascination with deathbeds. And he reveals himself not only in judging her. He places her, finally, in family mythology: the family mythology in which he himself grew up, a precocious and didactic small boy. Battersea Rise was its lost Eden, the sin of his great-uncle Henry and poor Emily Dealtry its Fall. Marianne becomes the Moses who guides the tribe through the wilderness, the custodian of the family covenant and laws. We leave her as the small boy saw her: the last great trunk proclaiming where the fallen oak-circle of the older Thorntons stood, asserting their order with a majesty his rebellious young mother and aunts, Darwinians and bluestockings, may resent, but never deny. We are allowed to see the tradition from which he escaped, by which he is still held.

The mythology gives the book its structure, as subtle as any of the novels. Gradually we realise that it entails a theme, as profound as any of theirs. We stumble on it with Mr Forster's comment upon one of the foolish cruelties which rose out of the family smash. Marianne had invited Henry's children to stay with her during their father's and their aunt's honeymoon. Their coming was agreed, a day and hour promised. At the last minute, vindictive with jealousy and fear, the step-mother changes her mind without writing. The hours pass, they do not arrive.

> Anyone who has waited in vain for a beloved person will understand what she felt. A wound has been inflicted which no subsequent reunion quite heals. The insecurity against which we all struggle has taken charge of us for a moment—for the moment which is eternity. The moment passes, and perhaps the beloved face is seen after all and the form embraced, but the watcher has become aware of the grave.

We recognise that insecurity. The universe of the novels is built upon it. It is the formless, terrifying inanity which Ansell detected at the heart of Agnes Pembroke's character, in *The Longest Journey*: the hollowness Margaret Schlegel knew to reside at the heart of Napoleons and Pierpont Morgans, the men without identity who cannot say 'I', but only 'Want this, want that'. It is the Thing which confronts Adela Quested and Mrs Moore in the booming blackness of the Marabar Caves, reducing heroism to filth, friends to unpredictable enemies. Against it, men struggle to build order: to bridge its abysses with love and trust, to combat its meaningless chaos with art and understanding. Our weapon is connection—'Only connect...'—and Marianne, for all her limitations, knows how to wield it, turning love and memory to the task of holding together her family. She emerges as a heroine of the war against panic and emptiness, to stand besides Mrs Wilcox and Mrs Moore.

The last letters fall into place like stones of an arch. Suddenly and graciously, she writes asking her ostracised sister-in-law for some milk from Battersea Rise. To her five-year-old nephew she relates how at this age, almost a century before, she was taken by her father to the opening of Parliament, and heard mad old George III address the crowd as 'My Lords and Peacocks.' Her longest bridges are completed, the huge wastes of time she has come through forced into pattern and significance. Mr Forster, who has built so enduringly upon the foundation his great-aunt gave him, has repaid her in this book with the currency she taught her descendants to value—bricks against oblivion.

71
The Great Aunt of Mr Forster

LIONEL TRILLING

E. M. Forster has written the biography of his great-aunt. It sounds odd as one says it; it rings with the enchanted precision of a French exercise. *Voici la vie de ma grand'tante, dit le grand écrivain anglais.* Marianne Thornton was the sister of Mr Forster's paternal grandmother. In what way was she notable above other women? So far as deeds go, she is likely to be remembered for only one, an act of public beneficence. When she died, at the age of ninety, she left her grandnephew £8,000, and this, as he says, made possible his career as a writer. It is with the recording of this legacy that Mr Forster brings his book about Marianne Thornton to a close, as if it were the crown of her life, as indeed it is.

Gautier said of his friend Flaubert that part of his creative endowment was the comfortable income which he had inherited from his father. Americans, always a little hoity-toity about money, and inclined to suppose that cash and 'spiritual values,' especially art, are ever at war with each other, might be led to think that Gautier was speaking ironically. Nothing could have been further from his intention. He had, poor man, experienced all too much financial exigency, he knew all too well what effect the lack of money has upon the management of a talent, to be anything but simple in his remark. He knew that to a writer money means peace and the opportunity to take thought. There are, no doubt, writers who do not need or want peace and the opportunity to take thought, but Mr Forster is not one of these. And although his life of his great-aunt is, for several reasons, very heavily charged with irony, there is only the simplest piety of gratitude as he speaks of her bequest to him.

> This £8,000 has been the financial salvation of my life. Thanks to it, I was

SOURCE *Griffin*, Summer 1956, pp. 4–12.

> able to go to Cambridge—impossible otherwise, for I failed to win scholarships. After Cambridge I was able to travel for a couple of years, and travelling inclined me to write. After my first visit to India and after the First World War the value of the £8,000 began to diminish, and later on it practically vanished. But by then my writings had begun to sell, and I have been able to live on them instead. Whether—in so stormy an age as ours—this is a reputable sequence I do not know. Still less do I know how the sequence and all sequences will end, with the storms increasing. But I am thankful so far, and thankful to Marianne Thornton; for she and no one else made my career as a writer possible, and her love, in a most tangible sense, followed me beyond the grave.

One is sorry that the £8,000 has vanished, not only for Mr Forster's sake but for the sake of the money itself—it was such good *old* money, and it had a good deal of tradition attached to it. It got its start early in the eighteenth century in the Russian trade and then went into banking. It was more or less the kind of money that W.B. Yeats liked to think he was connected with when he wasn't keeping in mind his presumed relationship with the Duke of Ormonde—money and blood are always very close to each other, and Yeats took pleasure in saying that his blood came from the loins of men who made their money in one way and not in another, from the loins of 'merchants,' not of 'hucksters.' In the heyday of such feelings Dickens meditated on the mystery of a brewer's natural social superiority to a baker. The answer, of course, is that in these things largeness is all—had there been wax-paper to permit loaves to attain a national rather than a local distribution, a baker would have had as much chance of a peerage as a brewer. Then there was the matter of personal service: to *wait upon* a customer in a shop was degrading almost beyond redemption by prosperity, and in 1882 Marianne Thornton was in despair and called in the family lawyers because the widow of a favorite nephew undertook to marry a Mr Aylworth; he was a well-to-do man, and a good man, and an excellent musician, but he kept a Shop.

The Thorntons had been in finance for nearly a century before Marianne was born. They had been an ecclesiastical family until the end of the seventeenth century, at which time they shifted their talents from the Church to the City and made money for generations. Robert Thornton, great-grandfather of Marianne, was a director of the Bank of England and it was he who, in 1735, settled the family on what was to become its native heath, Clapham. His son John duplicated his father's career, but added certain intellectual and religious features. He was a friend of William Cowper, and of Cowper's Rev. John Newton, and he established the family in the Evangelicism which became one of its chief characteristics. Marianne's father, Henry, was John's younger son. He too was a banker.

But he was a good deal more than that, and had he been my great-grandfather, I think I should have been more open in my admiration than Mr Forster is. For example, I should have done as much by him as the

Dictionary of National Biography does in perpetuating John Stuart Mill's handsome compliment to his *Enquiry into the Nature and Effects of the Paper Credit of Great Britain.* Mill said that it was the clearest exposition known to him in English of the subject with which it deals. I think, too, that I should have been rather more solemn about his work in Parliament, not only his efforts to abolish the slave trade, made in alliance with his cousin and close friend, William Wilberforce, but also his intelligent stand on the French Revolution, on Parliamentary Reform, and on Catholic Emancipation. 'Cold, intellectual, public-spirited, fastidious, and full of integrity, Henry stands, and his hand rests upon a parliamentary bill'—it is thus that Mr Forster describes Hoppner's striking portrait of Henry Thornton. I find rather more in the face and posture than that, more possibility of inner and intense experience than Mr Forster is willing to admit; and I can't help feeling that in this sentence about a man of intelligence and integrity, whose mode of thought was political, the parliamentary bill ought not stand in the position of ironical anti-climax which it is made to occupy. But he is not my great-grandfather, and Mr Forster must do as he pleases with his own.

Henry, who died at fifty, brought the Thorntons to their high point as a family, if only because he built Battersea Rise, the house that became the center of all the family emotion. Mr Forster, as we know, is a great one for houses; and in this book he speaks of the Hertfordshire home of his boyhood and of its connection—wych-elm and all—with Howards End; we know too of his feeling for the lost Abinger. But Battersea Rise, although he saw it only once as a small boy and remembers it scarcely at all, is for him, by reason of the family adoration of it, the prototype of all consecrated houses. To the Thornton children, he says, 'it was a perfect playground and in after years a sacred shrine.'

> It satisfied in them that longing for a particular place, a home, which is common amongst our upper and middle classes, and some of them transmitted that longing to their descendants, who have lived on into an age where it cannot be gratified. There will never be another Battersea Rise, and the modest imitations of it which lasted into the present century and became more and more difficult to staff have also disappeared.

Battersea Rise stood on Clapham Common. Clapham, of course, proposes the Clapham Sect; and it is rare indeed to come across a reference to this group which is not sniffishly superior. I recall the first mention of Clapham and its sect I ever heard—a professor of mine, a New York dandy of an older day, told us that Robert Browning's father had been a member of the Clapham Sect, and the dandiacal shrug of despair with which he imparted this information led me to see dull houses on a respectable street, and tea, and catarrh, and cotton gloves, and conversation rather more literate but not more enlightened than that of Mr Stiggins of the Brick Lane Branch of the United Grand Junction Ebenezer Temperance Association (this is the elder Mr Weller's Mr Stiggins). And later, when I read Matthew Arnold's remarks about the British middle class, 'drugged with business' and intoxicated by the religious emotions of Dissent, it was the Clapham Sectarians who came to my mind as examples, even though I knew that as Evangelicals they were not Dissenters.

Nothing, of course, could have been further from the truth. The life of the great Clapham families—the Wilberforces, the Macaulays, the Stephenses—was anything but dull and narrow. And Battersea Rise was nothing if not expansive. The recollection of it tells us how people once found it possible to think of themselves, how they could express their ideas of themselves in their manner of life—in, most especially, those great houses that, from century to century, from Jonson to Yeats, have captured the high fancy of the English poets. Henry Thornton was, to be sure, a wealthy man; but he was also a man of strict life, and he exemplified the quality that Mr Forster says the Thorntons shared with two other nineteenth century families, the Darwins and the Wedgwoods, the quality of remaining stubbornly 'provincial and non-aristocratic.' Battersea Rise was not an aristocrat's home, and Henry Thornton would not have wanted it to be; he was contemptuous of his brother Robert's social aspirations and much annoyed by the breakfast party which Robert gave for Queen Charlotte and her daughters, and he regretted that his father had allowed his sister to marry Lord Leven. But Henry Thornton's house represented an idea of dignity and freedom which, as Mr Forster implies, scarcely anybody in England now would venture to express in a house, nor in America either.

The original house was a compact brick structure of the age of Queen Anne. When Henry Thornton bought it in 1792, Clapham, although only four or five miles from London, had but recently become safe, and the country was still unspoiled. The grounds were extensive and the gardens elaborate; and as late as 1887 cows were still maintained. Thornton threw out large wings on either side of the original house. 'The heart of the house,' says Mr Forster, 'was a fine oval library,' which had been designed by Thornton's political chief, William Pitt. There were thirty-four bedrooms.

It was a house intended for a family, and the large family (nine children) flourished in it, and, of course, never got over it. In my father's house are many mansions: the nearest approach to heaven, the poets are always suggesting, is a really large and handsome house. They like to think of it as well run and very orderly. Battersea Rise had, of course, its appropriate complement of gardens, pleasances, fruit trees, horses (ponies for the very young), and servants of crusty eccentricity and absolute permanence, ministering angels of an inferior but self-respecting grade. The tone and the principles of the Thornton family were responsive to the best suggestions to their sacred house; among the principles was the hope and expectation of an actual heaven. The parents were good people. To be sure, they believed that they *should* be good, and this is an idea that alienates us from those who hold it and suggests to us that they have no true sensibility. But actually the Thorntons did have sensibility; they were not only good but kind and gracious, and not only to their friends but to their children and their servants.

> Such was the atmosphere, such the household, into which Marianne Thornton was born: affections, comfort, piety, integrity, intelligence, public activity, private benevolence

—and Mr Forster closes his list with what

> transcend[ed] them all, an unshaken belief in a future life where the members of the household would meet again and would recognize each other and be happy eternally.

Eventually Battersea Rise was but a pious memory to the children, and for some of them a bitter memory. The father died in 1815, the mother ten months later. This did not bring the life at Battersea Rise to an end; in the spacious manner of an older day, the young people who had been named as the children's guardians, Sir Robert and Lady Inglis, moved into the great house and the family lived on together. For two of the sisters, Isabella and Marianne, the life together survived the first marriage of the eldest brother, Henry, who had fallen heir to Battersea Rise; and Marianne lived on with Henry after Isabella's late marriage and Henry's widowerhood. But for Marianne the Battersea Rise life did not withstand the second marriage of Henry, for he chose as his second wife his Deceased Wife's Sister. It is hard for us now to understand the feelings that raged around the issue of whether or not a man should be allowed to marry the sister of his dead wife; by the Marriage Act of 1835, and on obscure doctrinal grounds, that inoffensive and often helpful relative had been placed within the prohibited degrees, and marriage with her carried not only canonical but also civil disabilities. The issue was felt by some to be one of morality, by others to be one of taste, by many to be one of loyalty to the church; and the liberals made it a political issue. The younger Henry Thornton fought for the passage of the parliamentary bill which would make his marriage legal, but the Deceased Wife's Sister Bill was not passed until 1907 and he had to go abroad to marry. The scandal itself was bad enough, but in addition this particular Deceased Wife's Sister was disliked; Emily Thornton was thought an inferior woman and a scheming one. Marianne removed to her own establishment and there was the inevitable family quarrel over furniture. She lived on Clapham Common, a half mile from Battersea Rise and within sound of its dinner bell, but her tie with the great house was at an end.

It was not until she was dying that she again opened communication with the house. The incident must be given in Mr Forster's words.

> A week before she died she wrote an extraordinary letter to Emily Thornton. She asked for some milk. No biographer could have foretold such a request, no novelist before Proust could have invented it. After thirty-five years' alienation she asks for some milk.

The Deceased Wife's Sister, now a widow, replied graciously; milk from the cows of Battersea Rise was sent and letters of an affectionate sort were exchanged.

She was fifty-nine when she left Battersea Rise. There seems never to have been any question of her marrying. She was, Mr Forster says, a good-looking girl; her letters speak of her intelligence, vivacity, and wit. But we have no record of any suitors—'not one hint of an affair, not the shadow of a name.' And Mr Forster speculates that she remained a spinster because she was in love with Battersea Rise, or because she was devoted to her brother Henry, or to her father's friend Wilberforce. (He was, by all present accounts of him, a most engaging man; it seems to have been his two sons who gave the name its unhappy aura, one of them, the Bishop of Oxford, being called, it is well known, Soapy Sam, the other, it is less well known, Dull Robert.) Mr Forster does not suggest that her father was a possible barrier to matrimony. Yet Marianne's relation to her father was exactly of the sort that often makes it difficult for a girl to marry. Cold the elder Henry Thornton may have been, but not to his eldest child. She was a timid little girl—phobic, as we should now say—and he valued courage beyond any other quality; yet she remembers long afterwards how he never laughed at her fears or scolded her for them, but soothed and indulged her. He took her very seriously; he wrote her charming and loving verses, and he also taught her to examine her life and to mend it—Mr Forster finds him more attractive in the former activity than in the latter; perhaps so, but certainly the two in conjunction must have been enormously engaging to an intelligent child. He taught her to understand public affairs and to discuss them with him; so that the devil would not find employment for idle hands, he engaged her as 'a sort of secretary' as soon as she could write legibly. Add that he was a handsome man, of perfect integrity, heroic in his notions of work, and magnanimous in all his acts. It would have been hard for her to look upon his like again.

She never sought to distinguish herself in the world. She had a continuing active interest in the education of the lower classes, derived from her old close friend Hannah More, and she wrote school readers which reflect the tart realism which was characteristic of her. But she had no thought of making public use of her ready pen and her powers of witty and robust observation. She did not even seek her social life in the world of professional intellect; James Knowles, who, as the founder of the Metaphysical Society and of *The Nineteenth Century*, knew everybody worth knowing, was her close friend, but she never entered his circle; the Macaulays were old Claphamites, but the Tom who figures in her letters is a childhood friend with whom she exchanges opinions and witticisms but never Thomas Babington Macaulay, let alone Lord Macaulay. She did not become literary, she became an aunt. She became the most impressive aunt in history after Jane Austen. Of no other aunt except Jane Austen—with whom she does indeed have certain literary affinities which she displays in her voluminous letters—could it have been said, as Mr Forster says of Marianne Thornton, that a *cult* grew up around her.

> . . . She never married and so she never altered. She represented continuity Childless herself, she became the family life that does not die with death.

Among her nephews and nieces she had a series of favorites; of these the last was Mr Forster, to whom, in her devoted infatuation, she gave the nickname The Important One; by this dreadful appellation she undertook to arouse in Mr Forster's young and early-widowed mother a due sense that her son must take priority over any plans she might have for her own life. There was a good deal of the Betsey Trotwood in her, and quite as much of the early Betsey Trotwood as of the later. She could be charmingly generous—and she could suffocate with attention, advice, and good sense. She really liked young people and knew how to please them, she had great tact in pleasing the young. But as she aged she pressed too hard, and interfered, and seemed insupportable. It is a common fate of the gifted and generous-minded old.

Mr Forster calls his memoir of his great-aunt 'a domestic biography,' by which he would seem to suggest the homely modesty of his subject. But we must not be misled. The continuity that Marianne Thornton represented is indeed the 'family life that does not die with death,' but in this instance the family life stands for a good deal more than itself. It stands for a massive cultural tradition—the continuity of modern English culture is a family continuity.

In the first chapter of his biography of Leslie Stephen Mr Noel Annan documented in considerable detail the English phenomenon that has often been noted in a general way, the extent to which the leading members of the intellectual professions are related to each other by ties of blood or marriage. A relatively few families of the upper middle class—some having a heritage of intellectual achievement that dates as far back as the seventeenth century, others coming to the intellectual life in the nineteenth century—proliferated, and intermarried, and continued in the intellectual life until now it may be said that the culture of England is in their hands. Mr Annan has returned to this subject again and in even more detail in a fascinating essay called 'The Intellectual Aristocracy' which he contributes to *Studies in Social History*, a collection prepared in tribute to G.M. Trevelyan, who, by his own family connection, handsomely illustrates Mr Annan's point.

It is not possible here to suggest either the complexity or the stubborn consistency of the familial reticulation which has been in the making for several generations. Every learned profession—and some artistic professions, but the class established itself first in the universities and the emphasis is still largely on science and scholarship—is involved in it, is largely staffed by the descendants of the Macaulays, the Darwins, the Huxleys, the Arnolds, the Conybeares, and other families of similar kind. To an American, the phenomenon must inevitably seem faintly comic and entirely astonishing—for there have been very few American families that have established an intellectual line.

To some Americans the thought will inevitably occur that something more, or less, than intellect has been at work to make this 'caucus of power or influence,' as Mr Annan calls it. But this is not the case. What we have, rather, is hereditary talent which takes pleasure in exercising itself and is encouraged by being given the opportunity to do so. Mr Annan insists that it has not been unduly exclusive, that it is hospitable to properly qualified recruits. An Englishman and not an American must pass upon the accuracy of this judgment, just as an Englishman and not an American must look for the shortcomings of the class as a whole.

In the development of this class Evangelicism played an obvious part. Mr Annan puts it thus:

> There was the sense of dedication, of living with purpose, or working under the eye, if not of the great Taskmaster, of their own conscience—that organ which Evangelicism magnified so greatly. There was the sense of mission to improve the shining hour and the profession to which they had been called. There was the sense of accounting for the talents with which Providence had endowed them. There was also the duty to hold themselves apart from a world given over to vanities which men of integrity rejected because they were content to labour in the vineyard where things of eternal significance grew—in the field of scholarship where results were solid not transient.

To this Mr Annan adds the influence of the pride of class, the sense at once of separateness from the aristocracy and of established individual worth, which is always a great help to an intellectual worker.

This, then, was the cultural-familial continuity that Marianne Thornton represented and that Mr Forster tacitly celebrates in his 'domestic biography.'

72
Review

REX WARNER

Mr Forster has performed a work of piety and understanding in commemorating the long life history of his great aunt. Marianne Thornton was born in 1797 and died in 1887 when Mr Forster himself was eight years old. He can remember her vividly as she was during the comparatively short period of time in which he knew her personally, and he has succeeded, with the aid of family documents and reminiscences, in recreating her character from her childhood in days that seem so distant until the time of her still vigorous old age.

The book is not only a tender, penetrating and sympathetic exploration of a family relationship, but also a most interesting historical document. It has ceased now, I think, to be fashionable to underrate the Victorians, who, in any case, have usually been their own best critics. Certainly it is unfair to blame them for a smug stability simply because we happen to know that the volcano on which they lived was about to erupt. We often mistake for smugness something that was merely formal and sincere; and, in our own age of instability, are tempted to envy or deplore what we are unable to achieve ourselves. Moreover there is an important sense in which we tend to expect more from life—more security, more pleasure, more satisfaction—than ever did these wealthy, religious and high-minded exemplars of the Victorian middle-class. Here, for instance, is a quotation from Marianne Thornton's father, who is writing to propose marriage to his future wife:

> I will tell you fairly, and thus early, that my own views of this life and the happiness of it, even in the best situations, are very moderate, and it is in the pleasing certainty of your being one that will help my everlasting interests, and one whom I may hope to meet in a better world, that I look on you with the most complacency.

This is a sentence which, as Mr Forster says, 'can be best understood by

SOURCE *London Magazine*, November 1956, pp. 79, 81.

readers who tolerate an outmoded approach to love'. It is nevertheless sincere. Nor is it just to use the word 'hypocrisy' of the Thorntons, Wilberforces and others who, while agitating with the greatest fervour against slavery abroad, were either indifferent to or approved of what amounted to industrial slavery in their own country. Mr Forster well writes:

> The really bad people, it seems to me, are those who do no good anywhere and help no one either at home or abroad. There are plenty of them about, and when they are clever as well as selfish they often manage to slip through their lives unnoticed, and so escape the censure of historians.

Mr Forster is the kind of historian who is not in the first place concerned with the awarding of praise or blame. He is always affectionate, shrewd, understanding, and often amused. Is he, perhaps, in this study a trifle too meticulous? Certainly the material is all interesting, but sometimes I felt that there was too much of it, and that the pruning of some details might have strengthened the general effect. Though 'strengthen' is not the word to use, since the effect is not intended to be monumental. The effect is much more like life. There are isolated and clearly remembered scenes, long nagging episodes, curious details which either in themselves or in the language are dream-like, half familiar and half remote; there are settings, among which stands in particular the reality or the memory of a great house; there are characters seen with varied degrees of clarity, and perhaps some of the dimmer of these might have been allowed to lapse into oblivion.

The central character is firmly and beautifully presented. 'No weakness, no contempt.' In her paper of wishes for the arrangement of her funeral, Marianne Thornton wrote that she would like to be buried 'under the large spreading tree at which I used to look on Sunday when waiting for the First Service to end that I might go in for the Holy Communion afterwards.' I hope that some such an English Elysium exists and that in a more ample air Marianne Thornton is now reading the words of a great-nephew who writes that 'she and no one else made my career as a writer possible'. She would be, as we all are, glad of this, and she would welcome and applaud his incursion into the world of the dead as Anchises did that of Aeneas.

73
Thornton's End

L. COMPTON

Philanthropy, money-making, piety, public affairs. These were the preoccupations that brought together the Clapham Sect, that curious group of nineteenth-century middle-class English families which derived its name, not from any person or doctrine, but from the district a few miles northeast [*sic*: south] of London where they happened to have settled. One does not wonder that the alliance carried the moral weight it did in public matters. When one sets the Wilberforces and Macaulays beside Hannah More and the Thorntons they make a formidable phalanx. From handing out free bibles its members went on to their own individual political and literary triumphs; from the Sect's 'May Meetings' which Marianne Thornton describes with sympathetic hilarity came an event with even more important consequences for America than England: the abolition of slavery in the colonies in 1833.

Of all these families, the one which has remained most dim in the eye of history has been the Thorntons. Rich, capable, and earnest—solid auxiliary troops in the Sect's endeavors, they scaled no peaks on their own, literary or social. Indeed the one moment when a Thornton did hold the public spotlight proved all but disastrous. Henry Thornton, son of the banker who founded the dynasty at Battersea Rise and his successor in the family business, defied the gods by making a national issue of a domestic scandal: the result was ignominious failure and temporary banishment from England. Deprived of its leading member, the family seemed headed for well-heeled obscurity under a competent but undistinguished regency of aunts and cousins. All the cleverer, one concludes, of Marianne, the sister whom fate had rather brusquely elevated to the top of the pyramid, to discern in an obscure grandnephew, hardly more than a baby, its ultimate justification. Fate, by keeping E.M. Forster in reserve, had, so to speak, held the last card up its sleeve. Forster was not yet in his teens when his great-

SOURCE *Chicago Review*, 10.3, Autumn–Winter 1956, pp. 83–6.

aunt died, but the relationship between the boy of nine and the woman of ninety was nevertheless a real and effective one, and it is he who has now undertaken to write the family history.

How do the Thorntons fare on being brought to judgment by their most distinguished living representative? Surprisingly well, on the whole. Recalling *The Way of All Flesh,* that biographical bomb designed by Samuel Butler to blow the Victorian family to smithereens, one might have been inclined to brace his feet for an explosion, particularly on noting the identity of the ingredients that make up the Pontifex-Butlers and the Thorntons: inherited wealth and Evangelical starchiness. Here is Forster on the touchiest moment of the family history—the ostracism of Henry after he had shocked convention by marrying his sister-in-law and had failed, through pressing the Marriage Act of 1850, to get such unions legitimized.

> To the moralist so much discomfort [Henry had been forced to leave Battersea Rise, settle in France, and sever his banking connections] will seem appropriate. To the amoralist it will offer yet another example of the cruelty and stupidity of the English law in matters of sex.

(Forster is presumably thinking of the present debate in England on the subject of homosexuality.) But the situation was redeemed, to the extent that it could be, by Marianne. Disapproving deeply of the marriage, and besieged by fulminating clerics (even so normally cool a writer as Matthew Arnold saw the Marriage Act as an invitation to 'Solomonic' license), she refused to adopt an attitude of outrage, and when years later the offending couple came back to England amicable relations were re-established. It is she who comes out best in the crisis, and Forster's choice of her as the family heroine is motivated by more than the fact that her life covers the longest span of years and provides the richest remains in the form of letters and journals.

This is obviously not the world of the Pontifexes. What accounts for the differences? For one thing, there was no parental bullying or will-shaking—the family atmosphere seems to have been remarkably easy and affectionate, and the incessant emphasis on the afterlife, which, carried to the extremes that it undoubtedly was, might have been merely ludicrous, yielded instead an unexpected virtue—humorous detachment. The Thorntons were all, even the renegade Henry, Sunday's children—'bonny, blithe, and good, and gay'—but their gaiety had no naïveté about it; it was shrewd and witty, as befitted a family of bankers. And there is something almost Jewish about their family life. Neither doctrine nor liturgy obsessed them, the part of religion that meant most to them was, significantly, family prayers. It was no doubt this peculiar orientation that kept the Claphamites within the established church with so few tensions. 'Sect' is quite the wrong word if it suggests religious bickering, the right one if it suggests something tribal.

It was, in fact, the most admirable sort of tribe, one with an admirable sense of its own identity, but with no undue contempt for outsiders. If the combination of self-sufficiency and otherworldliness made them, by modern standards, almost incomprehensively blind to the plight of the industrial worker, it also made them indifferent to the aristocracy, thus promoting a lack of self-consciousness rare in Victorian middle-class circles. They could also on occasion be divinely superior to the public schools and universities. Here is Hannah More on the subject of Oxford and Cambridge:

> I pray God to preserve Henry from the contagious atmosphere of Cambridge. He carries with him Christian principles and lack of practised evil, he had a high call. He must never forget that he is the oldest son of *Henry Thornton*. Much will be expected from him, his example must give the tone to young men who have not the advantage of such parents I am much changed with respect to the two universities. I had used greatly to prefer Cambridge, but this summer I have had so much intercourse with men of talents and piety from Oxford that I believe not only that the general discipline there is much stricter but in two or three colleges religion is in more esteem.

If such an attitude is not to be unbearably priggish, it had better be mixed with a large dose of sophistication, and in Marianne's case it fortunately was. Marianne, in contrast to Hannah, adored the French, saw them at many points as superior to the English and thoroughly enjoyed it when, in the course of her continental travels, chance threw her among social groups remote from her own.

Forster himself speaks of certain aspects of the family life of the Thorntons as approximating a kind of 'cult,' and I think a case may be made that some of these have influenced his novels. There is, for instance, the obscure sense of the presence of some tutelary deity, the Mrs Wilcox or Mrs Moore whose uncanny power for good extends beyond the grave. Marianne—it was, after all, a brilliant stroke of intuition on her part to arrange for the legacy that made it possible for Forster to travel and write—is an obvious prototype. Another is Battersea Rise. The huge house in Clapham became, for three and almost four generations of Thorntons, a Platonic ideal of the middle-class home, a sort of temple or shrine; and other Thornton houses, like the one Forster occupied in Hertfordshire as a child, seem to have partaken of its arcana. Forster tells us that he used the latter as a model for *Howards End*. This house, he writes,

> has given me a slant upon society and history. It is a middle-class slant, atavistic, derived from the Thorntons, and it has been corrected by contact with friends who have never had a home in the Thornton sense, and do not want one.

The distinction is interesting: it suggests the contrast between the Schlegel sisters and the uncommitted Fielding of *A Passage to India*, between the spirit of Jane Austen and a slightly pessimistic Whitman, between agoraphobe and agoraphile.

There are, of course, some clear breaks with Thornton tradition. The coolness with which Forster announces the deaths of important characters in his novels is a different approach from that of Marianne, who filled a dozen, two dozen—in one case sixty—pages of her journal with accounts of various deathbeds. But the cool tone should not deceive us; the meaning of death is one of the central themes of Forster's novels, and the most significant moments in these books are likely to appear to the superficial eye as the most trivial. This is part of the calculated technique of indirection which Forster describes in *Aspects of the Novel*: the intense spiritual loyalty to the dead which he speaks of as a Thornton characteristic has merely been transposed to another key.

There is nothing of Strachey's superior knowingness here. The impulse that led the twenties to cock a snook at the Victorians is not much in evidence these days. Forster's attitude is one of acceptance, but it is a hard-won and critically sophisticated acceptance of his ancestors. Mr Leavis helped rectify the earlier mistake in *The Great Tradition*: his exasperation with an era that tended to regard morality as a hilarious and slightly perverse game invented by one's grandparents is partially justified—such an attitude is amusing but not really helpful. However, it does no good to pretend that no chasm yawns between the nineteenth and twentieth centuries and no attempt to cross the gap by levitation. D.H. Lawrence hated Jane Austen, and for reasons that are quite intelligible. Forster is wiser than either Leavis or Lawrence. His bridge to the past is only apparently fragile. In a sense more Virgilian than Wordsworthian, he has undertaken to link age to age 'by natural piety.' This loyal and intelligent biography is Forster's personal pilgrimage to the Elysian fields.

Maurice
(1971)

74
Open Windows

C. P. SNOW

It was known for many years that E. M. Forster had written an explicitly homosexual novel. At one time, everyone in certain literary circles seemed to have read it in manuscript. One used to hear the question whispering round: ought he to publish it? He didn't, in his own lifetime. The book, it now appears from Mr P. N. Furbank's introduction, was largely written in 1913–14, that is after *Howards End* (1910) and before the final novel, *A Passage to India* (1924). Now, in 1971, Forster's literary executors have decided to let it free. In my view, they hadn't any choice.

I will give the reasons later. They are not the merits of the work itself. Although it exhibits some of Forster's good qualities, it makes even more clear his major weaknesses.

The novel is very short, and the story simple. Maurice is a good-looking athletic youth, without distinguished intelligence or insight. He comes from what Forster calls a 'suburban' family, but the usage has changed. Maurice is more than comfortably off, belongs to the moneyed upper middle-class, goes to a public school and Cambridge, where he has social contacts with young men recognisably in the Lytton Strachey circle. All through his school-days Maurice has been vaguely disturbed about his sexual make-up. At Cambridge, in his own college, he meets another young man, Clive, who has from the age of 15 been certain about his own sexual make-up. Clive is a 'county gentleman,' high-principled, clever: he recognises at once that he is in love with Maurice, who after various false starts, tentatives, quarrels decides that he returns the love. In fact, after walking through the court in distress one night, he climbs through Clive's window and gets into bed with him. Although Clive isn't in doubt about his homosexuality or Maurice's, he imposes the rule that the relation must be kept chaste: and this Maurice cheerfully and happily accepts.

The relation continues in this sublimated Edward Carpenter-like fiction

SOURCE *The Financial Times*, 7 October 1971, p. 28.

(the book was begun under the influence of Carpenter) for several years: and then, almost overnight, Clive realises that his tastes have been transmogrified. He is now exclusively heterosexual. This happens in his mind without the physical intervention of a woman. Maurice can't believe it. But in time, after much grief, he has to believe it, for Clive gets married and sets up as a respectable landowner (and prospective Tory M.P.) on his ancestral estate. There Maurice visits him, still hankering after a return of love. He is totally abandoned. He even visits a hypnotist, to see if he too can become heterosexual. But on Clive's land is employed a young gamekeeper. He catches sight of Maurice and falls in love with him.

Once more, in the most casual of meetings, Maurice realises that something unexplained has happened to himself. One night, staying in Clive's house, he calls out of his bedroom window yearningly into the dark. Once more some window climbing, this time by Alec the gamekeeper. He duly gets into bed.

The book ends with Maurice explaining to Clive that he and Alec propose to live together like 'outlaws.' Clive is horrified. We are left to assume that he won't meet Maurice again but that Maurice and Alec are going to enjoy a fully sexual and satisfactory life.

About a piece of advice by Maurice's grandfather, Forster remarks that 'it was sincere, it came from a living heart.' Almost exactly the same could be said about this novel. It is sincere, desperately so. First, and least significant, it is an expression of sexual guilt. Most of this guilt Clive and Maurice (not the gamekeeper, who is represented as an example of working class pagan innocence, that curious creation of the bourgeois early twentieth-century mind) would believe to be caused by the social and legal climate in which they were living. But compare Proust. There is a weight of sexual guilt in *Sodome et Gomorrhe* although Proust's characters and Proust himself were living in an appreciably more tolerant society, and one where Charlus and Morel at least weren't in danger in any kind of legal prosecution. Of course, the Wolfenden Report did good: it would have banished fears from these decent and honourable people of 50 years before; but it wouldn't have removed everything.

However, that isn't the main point of the book. It is a novel with a purpose, and the purpose is to proclaim that homosexual love, in its fullest sense, can be happy and enduring. Hence the ecstatic ending. It rings artistically quite wrong, as a wish-fulfilment: and yet anyone who reads it will hope, without any knowledge of the biography, that for the writer the wish ultimately came true.

In literary terms, though, the purpose—as with most explicit purposes in art—cripples the novel. It brings out, and exaggerates, all Forster's lack of feeling for people different from those he mixed with. The Wilcoxes in *Howards End* are pretty fair cardboard: here we have the same dismissal, only more contemptuous—'throughout life he had been the ordinary business man.' Except in the writer's mind, what in God's name is the ordinary businessman? It is only very spasmodically in *Maurice* that the characters exist in their own freedom. Maurice himself is well done, and it wasn't easy for a very clever and subtle man to create convincingly a dull one: but, aside from his sexual predicament, the rest of his life is shadowy. So—and again this is an exaggeration of a common Forster weakness—is the grip on the physical world. This applies to illness as much as to sex: Edwardian medicine wasn't so highly developed as our own, but writers like Bennett dealt far less vaguely with physical sickness than Forster does. There is even—shades of Dean Farrar, who is not far away from other passages in the novel—a reference to *brainfever.*

As for the ordinary avocations which these young men must have had, and the games which Maurice is reported as enjoying, Forster is as remote as a rather miffish observer from Japan, and frequently gets the most commonplace idioms wrong. His ear lets him down with a dull thud. The cricket match at Clive's country house is the most absurd and incomprehensible since Dingley Dell. None of this would matter so much if he weren't writing about supposedly hearty young men. There it shows, more nakedly than in his other novels, the blinkering of his interest and vision.

In that case, should the book have been published at all? As I said before, his executors really had no choice. If the writer of Forster's reputation leaves unpublished manuscripts, they are going to be produced some time or other, and it might as well be now as later. Forster himself seems to have attached—understandably enough—great value to the book, and probably wanted it published. If he didn't, he was experienced enough to have destroyed it.

Will it affect his reputation? Very little I fancy. With committed Forsterians, and there are plenty, not at all. With those like myself, who have always had doubts, those doubts won't be strengthened, because this book merely underlines what has been felt for a long time: that there is a weakening ambiguity in his novels which is not the result of art but a kind of equivocation. For instance, 'personal relations' often didn't mean what persons outside his private world took them to mean. Reticences are usually not damaging to high art, but evasions sometimes can be.

Anyway, many of us passionately devoted or more qualified, have made up our minds. The interesting question remains, how this book will affect readers under say 30. To a good many, even among the most intelligent and imaginative, I suspect it will seem utterly distant, possibly without meaning. They ought to realise, though, that in a sense, not so much literally as historical, this book was true, not of many people, but of a section of a small class, for a short period. They may have been unlucky in their temperaments and sexually diffident: but it did happen, and just for once, we can say that things are somewhat better now.

75
A Man's Man

COLIN WILSON

E. M. Forster's career is one of the mysteries of modern literature. In the five years between 1905 and 1910, he produced four important novels, including *Howards End.* Then there was a silence for fourteen years, followed by *A Passage to India.* After which, he dried up for good, although he lived for almost another half-century. The only parallel case that comes to mind is Sibelius; but at least his output *during* his productive years was tremendous. Forster seemed to have the capacity, but to have preferred not to use it.

Most of Forster's friends knew he had written a homosexual novel, and many of them had read it. I never met Forster, but I was told about *Maurice*—by one of his friends—several years ago. Unlike Lytton Strachey—whom he portrays in *Maurice*—Forster believed in being extremely discreet about his homosexuality. Strachey's Cambridge circle thought him altogether too discreet and colourless—Strachey described him as 'a mediocre man,' the kind to whom waiters are naturally rude. All this certainly explains the non-publication of *Maurice* in Forster's lifetime. What I had not expected was that *Maurice* should prove to be the key to the whole of Forster's work, and the vital clue to his artistic tragedy.

Those early novels—*Where Angels Fear to Tread, The Longest Journey, Room with a View*—are brilliant, but oddly frustrating. Forster seems to see himself as a kind of English Ibsen. He loathes and detests the middle classes, with their snobbery and prejudice; he also hates clergymen, schoolteachers, and authority in general. Like D. H. Lawrence, he feels that all this needs to be blown up. Without ever losing his temper—as Lawrence and Aldous Huxley are inclined to—he impales them like butterflies. But obviously, he needs a standard of happiness and vitality to oppose to all this deadness—and this is where he comes unstuck. He is never quite sure what to oppose to middle-class deadness. In *Where Angels Fear to Tread* there is a magnificent Italian

SOURCE *Spectator,* 9 October 1971, p. 512–13.

youth Gino, who adores his baby son. But he is rather stupid, and in the main scene of the book, he tortures a man by twisting his broken arm. This sneaking admiration for violence appears in several of the early novels.

And neither violence nor sensuality seem all that much preferable to the things Forster hates—money, corruption, 'withered hearts.' Of course, there's also honesty and decency; but in Forster, these also tend to become rather negative virtues, symbolised by nice but frustrated spinsters who long to go to bed with the magnificent Italians, but never do. In *Howards End* the ambiguity becomes maddening. At first you think he's contrasting the decent and cultured Schlegels with the stupid, narrow middle-class Wilcoxes, but by the end of the novel it's all been qualified so much you don't know where you are.

The answer now sticks out a mile, and I'm ashamed that I didn't spot it earlier. Forster certainly wasn't sparing with the clues—all that admiration for Greece and Italy and healthy male bodies. In the story 'Albergo Empedocle,' the young Englishman Harold remarks about his past incarnation as a Greek: 'I loved very differently . . . Yes, I also loved better too.'

It was not simply a matter of being homosexual, like Strachey, Keynes and the rest. He was a Platonic homosexual, obsessed by the notion of friendship, the feeling that two men can be closer together—spiritually—than a man and woman can ever be. There was also the amusing complication that, as a shy, subtle, withdrawn man, he had a sexual preference for stupid and extroverted males. (This later developed into a preference for policemen, says my informant—a taste he shared with Hugh Walpole and James Agate.) *Howards End* is all about women—there is not an interesting male in the book. Forster dried up for four years. Then he decided he would try to unstop the creative springs with the novel he had always wanted to write.

Maurice is a very fine novel, if much simpler in structure than *Howards End* or *A Passage to India.* The hero is, inevitably, a healthy, cheerful, rather stupid young chap. With his intellectual inferiority complex, he becomes fascinated by a clever young man called Clive Durham; when Clive confesses to being in love with him, Maurice is shocked, then slowly realises that he is a homosexual, and always has been. ('At the bottom of their hearts, [girls] disliked him entirely, but they were too confused mentally to know this.') A love affair follows, although Forster implies they never actually have sex; they confine their activities to kisses and stroking one another's hair. Then, abruptly, Clive turns 'normal.' (I found this the one unconvincing touch in the novel; I suppose it does happen, but I have never come across a case.) Maurice, left high and dry, goes through a long period of misery, and even tries to get 'cured' by a psychiatrist. Then, staying at Clive's house (after Clive's marriage), he ends up in bed with the gamekeeper (this was years before *Lady Chatterley*, as Forster points out). The gamekeeper originally intends to blackmail him, but they end by falling in love and going off together—to live happily ever after, Forster implies. I found this ending unsatisfactory; not because I am not homosexual, but because I feel that Forster has allowed himself to be blinded by sentimentality. He is always bright enough to see that a marriage between a sensitive man and a stupid woman won't work; but he is too involved in his own wish-fulfillment fantasy to see that the relation between Maurice and Alec Scudder could not last for long.

Maurice was finished in 1914, and Forster felt much better. He launched into another novel, *Arctic Summer,* which would again concern the relationship between two men—one 'intellectual,' the other a simple soldier. But he now knew what he was writing about; he really wanted to get them into bed together, but he wasn't allowed to—at least, if he hoped to publish the novel. So it was abandoned after a few chapters. And the problem remained, and haunted *A Passage to India.* The relation between Fielding and Aziz in that novel ought to be homosexual; but this was out of the question. The whole story—as everyone knows—turns on the delusion of a frustrated virgin that Aziz has tried to rape her. It all peters out, leaving you oddly up in the air. Inevitably, because the frustrated virgin theme needed the counterpoint of a fulfilled homosexual relation theme.

And Forster knew it. So he stopped writing novels. The really brave alternative would have been to publish *Maurice* (which would have been quite feasible after *The Well of Loneliness*), and possibly jeopardise his job as a don. It would probably have allowed him to develop into a great writer. As it was, his work was virtually superseded by Lawrence, who treated all Forster's themes, but treated them better because he could be frank about sex.

No one has the right to blame Forster for the choice he made. But one can't help wishing that he'd been a little less cautious and discreet . . . .

76
Forster's Love Story

PHILIP TOYNBEE

It was no secret among his friends that E. M. Forster had once written a homosexual novel, which was not published until after his death. Now that the whole topic is so much, and so properly, in the open there is no conceivable point in trying to conceal that Forster was himself a homosexual and for many years a fully practising one.

But nor should this ever allow us to forget that in the Edwardian years—the years of all Forster's previously published novels except *A Passage to India*—male homosexuality was an unmentionable subject except in the most sophisticated circles, and homosexuals—I take this from *Maurice*—were commonly described as 'Unspeakables.' The Wilde case was still reverberating and English homosexuals were living in greater fear, shame and distress than they had done even in the middle years of the nineteenth century.

If one adds that Forster came from a thoroughly conventional middle-class home and attended a profoundly Philistine public school, the anguish that he suffered must have been very acute. It is little wonder that Cambridge came to him as an almost miraculous revelation: he made several homosexual friends there and quickly learned that his condition was neither rare nor universally regarded as shameful. How natural, then that this very intelligent and sensitive young man should have wished to express his true feelings, by some means or other, and that he should have felt a crusading zeal in doing so. *Maurice* is a *roman à thèse* with a vengeance; a defiant declaration that 'the love which dares not speak its name' *ought* to dare to speak both frankly and proudly.

Though Forster first wrote *Maurice* in 1914 he continued to revise it until 1970: he showed it to several friends at different times and received at least enough encouragement to persuade him that the book might be publishable after his death. Yet he was also full of doubt, and by the end of his life

SOURCE *The Observer*, 10 October 1971, p. 32.

he suspected that the book was both 'dated' and 'a fake.' His final comment, inscribed on the cover of the 1960 typescript, was 'Publishable—but worth it?'

I fear that Forster's literary executors have given the wrong answer to that question.

In all Forster's writings, except his masterpiece, *A Passage to India*, there was a disturbing element of Victorian fine writing, whimsicality and high-minded gush. But this flaw was controlled and counter-balanced by a splendid litheness, even toughness of mind: above all by a pervasive humour which was by no means always good-humoured. The reason why *Maurice* should never have been published is that this depressing work isolates and concentrates the worst of Forster's faults, and is almost totally devoid of his great virtues.

Maurice tells the story of a young, upper-middle-class Englishman growing to manhood at the turn of the century, through prep school, public school, university, and the City. The point is heavily made that Maurice Hall is a very ordinary, rather Philistine boy and man—after Cambridge he takes over his dead father's partnership in a firm of London stockbrokers—whose single peculiarity lies in the fact that he happens to have been born a homosexual. After a long platonic affair with a Cambridge friend and a brief, dazzled infatuation with a Woolwich cadet, he falls in love with a gamekeeper (pre-Mellors vintage) and enjoys a complete physical relationship for the first time.

As in so many of Forster's other books the point comes when the hero is put dramatically to the test. Will this conventional young stockbroker choose 'life', 'the heart,' 'real' reality; or will he choose the fake, conventional and heartless values of suburb and city? (It required a novelist of Thomas Mann's stature to do equal justice to both sides in this traditional romantic argument.) Anyway, unlike several of Forster's other heroes, this one makes the right choice, and the book ends with Maurice and Alec vaguely making off into 'the Greenwood,' there to live happily ever after as lovers and manual workers.

I shall forbear to quote: it must be enough to say that *Maurice* is novelettish, ill-written, humourless and deeply embarrassing. And with the wisdom of hindsight I think I can see why it was almost inevitable that this should be so. To begin with, much of the worst in the other novels came from the general thesis that Forster was constantly propounding. It is the thesis which Lionel Trilling has described as an assault on 'the under-developed heart'; a defence of all naturally loving, innocent and fearless human beings against the prevailing deadness and cruelty of that society which Forster epigrammatised as 'the world of telegrams and anger.' Yet I think this novelist's real talent was for seeing, understanding and describing, rather than for making a moral point. In *A Passage to India*, in *Howards End* to a lesser extent, he made a true novelist's attempt to show the tensions and conflicts of human reality, without drawing any explicit lessons from his demonstration. In *Maurice*, where the lesson is all-important, everything else is perfunctory to the point of painful incompetence.

But there is something else here as well. However much Forster may have fretted at the taboos of his time it is the case that every good writer needs his own system of prohibitions and restraints—and it sometimes seems hardly to matter whether these are imposed from within or from without. The notion of total self-expression, an opening of the floodgates to their fullest extent, is a modern absurdity which has led to some of the worst writing ever seen in print.

It now seems that one of the special restraints which Forster needed was precisely that he should *not* express his homosexual feelings directly: that they should be sublimated, transmuted and confined within the banks of that millrace which proved, in so many of his books, to be such an effective driving-force.

A further question, of course, is whether there really is such a thing as a specifically homosexual sensibility, or vision, or mode of apprehension. In the course of the present novel Forster suggests that a homosexual has two distinct approaches to, for example, a drawing of a young man by Michelangelo, whereas the heterosexual has only one. (Correspondingly the heterosexual has the advantage of two approaches to, let's say, one of Renoir's *jeunes filles en fleur.*) But this is surely too simple, for we all, mercifully, have enough sexual ambiguity to enable us to *lend* a bit of our minority impulse whenever the occasion demands it.

Certainly I can detect nothing particularly homosexual about *Maurice* except that it happens to be about homosexuals. There is plenty of 'hellenic' talk, several rather febrile descriptions of male beauty and one lively passage of anti-female disgust. But all the high sentiments—both of love and of passion—could just as easily have been inspired by the most heterosexual of romances. As, indeed, dozens of contemporary romancers were demonstrating at the time when *Maurice* was first written.

77
Books versus Biceps

ANGUS WILSON

Few writers of distinction have been as ill-served by his critics as E. M. Forster. Professor Trilling's book on Forster's novels is his only undiscerning work. Professor Wilfred Stone's banally entitled *The Cave and the Mountain* has most of the faults unfairly ascribed by Dr and Mrs Leavis to their latest bugbear, 'American criticism'. In another field, I am very conscious that my own interview with Forster published in *Encounter* was highly unsatisfactory. There is a great deal in Forster's work and there was much in his personality to bring out the inept, the pompous and the insecure in near-strangers.

The critical failure in his lifetime and the inevitable reaction that follows a writer's death together make the line of Forster's reputation especially wobbly, the relative 'placing' of the merits of his books more than normally in dispute. I, for example, feel increasingly certain that *A Passage to India* is a good, almost a very good, book, and that taken as a whole, *Howards End* is a bad book; but many critics whom I respect would refute these valuations. Given the current re-estimation of his literary standing, I confess that, while I respect Mr Oliver Stallybrass's loving and exact editing of unpublished works like the present volume of short stories, I wonder whether the decision of Forster's trustees to issue such works is not an unfortunate continuation of his critical bad luck, dogging him even beyond the grave.

None of the stores in *The Life to Come* reflects Forster's own judgment of his work, for there does not appear to be any evidence as there is in the case of *Maurice*, that he especially valued any of them, even those that he might have published if their content had not been overtly homosexual. Some are very ephemeral indeed, including his contribution to a long piece of 1930s book-making described very aptly by the editor in (unconsciously?) period language as 'a post-prandial *folie à quatre*.' This and other very magazine-

SOURCE *The Observer*, 8 October 1972, p. 39.

type stories (not by any means always the most light in intention) do seem to me unfortunate. Forster would not have published or re-published them; they can surely only weaken the total effect of the collection; the time is certainly not yet, if ever, for the complete works including laundry lists.

But here, perhaps, one is being pompous again. Does it matter so much if some adequate but inferior work is published? One of the comic homosexual pieces is 'What Does It Matter? A Morality.' The objection to fuss here is specifically to moral fuss about 'poking' (I use Forster's word), whether heterosexual or homosexual. The good sense characteristically comes from a young peasant, a soldier. I am myself not so certain that this natural ease in sexual matters among the sons of the soil is not an Edwardian homosexual myth. But again, that doesn't really matter, for the moral attack on Victorian repression is a good one from whatever source it comes.

But the trouble with this 'don't fuss' argument, whether applied narrowly to sexual intercourse or more widely to a system of moral and aesthetic values, is that it applies only a part of the time. Sometimes 'poking' *is* just poking and no more. Sometimes it involves a lot more of the human personality. And it isn't very easy always to tell when or how. I am sure that Mr P. N. Furbank's statement to the editor about the homosexual stories, namely that Forster saw the comic 'dirty postcard' ones as quite separate from the serious 'other love' ones, is quite correct. But, of course, it doesn't work out that way. Because of the inevitable intermingling of aesthetic and moral values, some of the farces have the most serious overtones and some of the solemnities are nearest to unintended farce especially in their melodrama.

As even in Forster's best work, the subtlety and ambiguity are shot through with over-simplified oppositions. On the evil side, the culturally earnest predatory middle-class financées, the octopus-like Maters, the businessmen who bring money into sex or love, the invalidish, life-evading bookworms, above all the Christian missionaries corrupting pagan nature with their false spiritualised 'love.' And, set against them, the good amoral Asian natives or half-castes, the handsome ox-like young public schoolmen with their single moments of vision destroyed by the women around them, the working-class pickups puzzled in their sexual straightforwardness by the suggestion of payment for the easy 'poke' (a rare tribe they, I suspect).

There's some truth in it all, of course, in the need to subvert the long century of Victorian over-earnestness and hypocrisy and sniggering. But it's too simple by far for the subtlety of Forster's art at its best. Only one story, 'Ansell' (lovers of *The Longest Journey* will note the name), really transcends this and poses the problem of brawn versus brains, books versus biceps with wit and skill and sufficient ambiguity to be Forster at his best. But many of the others are good fun.

78
Old and Gay

J. I. M. STEWART

This volume opens with five early stories of only minor interest. In 'Ansell' a young man arrives at a cousin's country house with a box full of books and notes which will enable him to write a fellowship dissertation on the Greek optative. But the box falls into a river; its contents are carried away and lost; as a result the budding scholar is lured by Ansell (formerly the garden boy, now almost the gamekeeper) into shooting, pony-riding, bathing, and similar rural pursuits. This story is as innocent as *Bevis*. In 'Albergo Empedocle' we are with the English in Italy. A girl called Mildred is engaged to a young man called Harold, and when Harold thinks 'how marvellously cold would be the pale blue pools along the rocks' Mildred endeavours to 'recall him to higher pleasures by reading out of her Baedeker.' Upon such familiar matter the familiar preternatural breaks in. Harold (who is quite unimaginative) discovers in a dream that he has been here before—a citizen of Acragas, in fact, in classical time. Mildred, who is dead silly, at first goes along with this, but later agrees with everybody else that Harold is mad. And Harold (with characteristic Forsterian over-kill) is committed to an asylum. This, too, is an innocent tale, although Mr Oliver Stallybrass (who is playing himself in very promisingly as editor of the *Abinger* Forster in some twenty volumes) helpfully tells us that the 'two fallen columns' between which Harold drops to sleep 'are clearly the legs of a gigantic male figure, one of a series of *Atlantes*,' which may be inspected at Girgenti today.

Skipping an ineffective ghost story and two inconsiderable anecdotes, we thus arrive at the much heralded 'sexy' or 'indecent' part of the collection. (These are Forster's terms.) There are eight tales: four facetious and four serious. With one exception, they date from after *A Passage to India*, and are thus by a very mature writer. Indeed, if 'The Torque' was close to 1958 it represents a more than Yeatsian determination to be old and gay. Marcian,

SOURCE *Spectator*, 21 October 1972, pp. 629–30.

a young provincial Roman of the early Christian era, is raped—during a kind of rugger scrum and more or less in mistake for his tiresomely pious sister Perpetua—by a Goth called Euric. The experience does him good. He has a marvellous dream in which he retaliates upon his ravisher in kind; and when Perpetua and the local basilica are happily destroyed by a thunderbolt he takes energetic and joyous charge of the family affairs, arranges a comfortable and amusing old age for his parents, and in due time takes the virginities of his adoring younger sisters. He never sees Euric again, but gives the name to his favourite mare, whose stable he shares on dark nights. This is quite a funny extravaganza, and so is 'What Does It Matter?'—a Ruritanian fable teaching that we ought not to make heavy weather of out-of-the-way sexual behaviour.

Less agreeable is 'The Obelisk', in which a bored lower-middle class couple on holiday meet two sailors by whom they are respectively and simultaneously seduced, each unbeknown to the other. The husband and wife are given a competent wash of authentic Forster comedy, but the sailors are pasteboard—which may be why the blurb likens this rather squalid story to 'one of those comic picture-postcards that so delighted George Orwell.' Finally, here, there is 'The Classical Annex,' in which an early Forster theme—the irruption of ancient myth or magic into a stuffy modern world—is given a 'sexy' twist. Just as in 'Other Kingdom' Miss Beaumont is metamorphosed into a beech-tree, so the son of the curator of the municipal museum at Bigglesworth is turned to stone while mysteriously in the embrace of a worthless late-Roman statue of an athlete. In after years the resulting group is known as The Wrestling Lesson.

'The Classical Annex' is a perfunctory and uninteresting affair, and it was written long after Forster had, it seems, begun to suspect that his 'indecent writings' clogged him artistically, were written not to express himself but to excite himself, were thus positively dangerous to his career as a novelist, and had therefore better be shoved in the fire. But he does not, so far as the present editorial record goes, appear to have expressed such doubts about the 'serious' homosexual stories. If he had faith in these latter he was, I think, right. None of the four is any more of an unqualified success than *Maurice* is. But all are moving and impressive attempts at an enlarged artistic integrity; at standing up, in fact, to be counted.

Unlike *Maurice*, all four end in tragedy. In 'Arthur Snatchfold' a cold bisexual hedonist seduces and thrusts money upon a young milkman; his 'clever manoeuvres for a little fun' result in the lad's being sent to jail while he himself—thanks to the lad's loyalty—goes undetected; he is very far from being left without a sense of guilt. In each of the other three stories delight has a more violent end. 'The Life to Come' tells of a young missionary who succumbs to mistaken notions of the injunction 'Come to Christ' on the part of a handsome native chief; upon this a long nightmare of hypocrisy succeeds: the story ends with murder and suicide in the moment of something like a renewed embrace. 'The Other Boat' has an almost identical conclusion; its setting is a double cabin on a P & O liner; the two men are a Turton- or Burton-like Englishman and a Eurasian youth rendered rather in the idiom of Dr Aziz in *A Passage to India.* 'Dr Woolacott' is the strangest of these stories—confused, incoherent, uncertainly dream-like, and with too much of the old magical trimmings. But Forster described it as having been written, along with 'The Life to Come,' more from my heart than anything else that I have been able to turn out,' and T. E. Lawrence was to describe it as the most powerful thing he had ever read. Very powerful it certainly is.

All these stories exhibit, as does *Maurice,* Forster's having the greatest difficulty in realising the figure of the spontaneous young lover who emerges out of the greenwood. It is significant that, with the exception of the milkman (who is only lightly sketched) these lovers come from a racially remote or socially nebulous world. Mr Stallybrass quotes from a memorandum of 1935: 'I want to love a strong young man of the lower classes and be loved by him and even hurt by him.' But in Forster's fiction at least, this young man remains a shade.

79
Hazards of an Honest Life

SAMUEL HYNES

'I am quite sure I am not a great novelist,' Forster once remarked in an interview. 'Because I have only got down on to paper really three types of people: the person I think I am, the people who irritate me, and the people I like. 'There is a charming, Forsterian modesty in that judgment, but we had better take it seriously; Forster was a penetrating critic, and he knew the value of what he had done. His remark describes what less-than-great fiction is like, but it also describes the personal, limited sources out of which it rises. Forster knew that he was not a great novelist, and he knew why—because he was locked in himself.

One of the personal sources of art is the artist's sexual nature and experience, and in Forster's case that was homosexual, though apparently both knowledge and experience came late. The 'Terminal Note' to *Maurice* dates the turning point in his sexual awareness as September 1913, when he was 34, and had written all but one of the novels that he published during his lifetime. Immediately after that date he wrote *Maurice*, an explicitly homosexual novel that remained in manuscript until after his death, and following that, *A Passage to India*, where the homosexual themes are muted, but evident. Then, as he put it, he dried up. He felt no decline in his powers, and he still wanted to write, but he no longer wanted to write what he called 'respectable novels.'

Instead he wrote, and went on writing, what he called his 'indecent writings'—short stories about homosexual acts and desires. He kept these stories secret; to have published them would, he thought, have brought him scandal and notoriety. One can't help thinking that it might also have made him a hero, that publication would have been a brave gesture in defense of the freedom to love; but Forster was not made for heroism. Like the elderly character in one of his stories, faced with a similar choice, 'he did not want greatness. He was not up to it.' And so he went on writing his sexual

SOURCE *The Washington Post Book World*, 3 June 1973, p. 3.

fantasies, sharing some with sympathetic friends like T. E. Lawrence and Lytton Strachey, destroying others, but keeping the secret of his sexual nature from the world.

In a time of *Last Exits* and *Last Tangos*, Forster's defensive reticence must seem extreme. But then, he wasn't of our time. He was born nearly a century ago, came of age while Victoria still reigned, and wrote all but one of his novels before the First World War. Those novels strike us as mild enough now, but even their restrained improprieties were shocking once: Edmund Gosse thought *Howards End* 'sensational and dirty and affected' because it contained a high-born maiden who has a baby; what would he have made of 'The Life to Come,' in which a missionary makes love to a native chief? How, in his own lifetime, could Forster have published the person he thought he was? Yet, being the honest man he was, how could he deny what he was? The only possible course was the one he chose—to go on writing, but to be silent in public, and to accept the consequences of silence. 'I should have been a more famous writer if I had written or rather published more,' he wrote in his diary just before his death; 'but sex has prevented the latter.' Obviously he regretted that this should be true, but he accepted it, as he accepted the other hazards of an honest life.

The 'indecent writings' of a man like Forster are bound to be interesting. From them we can learn a good deal about social attitudes toward sexual deviance in his time. More important, perhaps, we can learn something about the relation between Forster's sexual nature and his creative imagination (and perhaps, by extension, something about this complex relationship in general). We can see, looking back from these stories to Forster's major novels, that the conflicts are the same: on the one hand Society, 'the people who irritate me,' the insensitive and cruel social demand for conformity, and on the other hand the Individual, 'the person I think I am,' desiring freedom, but weak, confined and guilty. There is only one Forster theme, really: he simply told it over and over, in different terms.

Yet, having said that the stories are interesting, I must add that as stories they are not very good—and this applies not only to the overtly homosexual stories but to the half-dozen other pieces in the volume, the gathered cast-offs of Forster's early career. They are worth reading, because the inferior work of any major artist is worth attending to, but none has any great literary merit. Some notices of this book have obscured this simple truth, in the process of canonizing Forster as a sort of secular saint of Liberalism. I've never met a saint, and I never met Forster, but I see no reason to believe that he was more saintly than other men, and even if he was, what to do with his work? Surely what we owe him, by his own example, is honesty. What could be more un-Forsterian than to praise bad writing in the name of affection? And this is, by his standards, bad. But never mind, there is enough good Forster to feed our affections for a long while; and even what is less than good is worth having, as a part of the one story of his work.